Infant Development

Charles W. Snow

East Carolina University

PRENTICE HALL
Englewood Cliffs, NJ 07632

Library of Congress Cataloging-in-Publication Data

Snow, Charles W.,
    Infant development / Charles W. Snow.
        p.   cm.
    Bibliography: p.
    Includes index.
    ISBN 0-13-463613-9
    1. Infants--Development.   I. Title.
    [DNLM: 1. Child Development.   2. Growth--in infancy & childhood.
    3. Infant.   WS 103 S6741]
    RJ134.S66 1989
    612'.654--dc19
    DNLM/DLC
    for Library of Congress   88-25439
                                                              CIP

Editorial/production supervision and
  interior design: Jan Stephan
Cover design: 20/20 Services, Inc.
Cover photo: Gary S. Chapman/The Image Bank
Manufacturing buyer: Ray Keating

 ©1989 by Prentice-Hall, Inc.
A Paramount Communications Company
Englewood Cliffs, New Jersey 07632

Printed in the United States of America

10   9   8   7   6

ISBN   0-13-463613-9

Prentice-Hall International (UK) Limited, *London*
Prentice-Hall of Australia Pty. Limited, *Sydney*
Prentice-Hall Canada Inc., *Toronto*
Prentice-Hall Hispanoamericana, S.A., *Mexico*
Prentice-Hall of India Private Limited, *New Delhi*
Prentice-Hall of Japan, Inc., *Tokyo*
Simon & Schuster Asia Pte. Ltd., *Singapore*
Editora Prentice-Hall do Brasil, Ltda., *Rio de Janeiro*

Dedicated
To my wife, Dora, and our daughters, Carla and Kristin,
and
To infants and parents everywhere.

Contents

2   THE BIRTH PROCESS   34

Preface

This book presents a comprehensive overview of growth and development during the first three years of life. It is designed primarily as an introductory text for courses in infant development, infant care, and early intervention. The increasing number of courses on infancy that are being introduced in institutions of higher education throughout the United States is a reflection of the interest and attention currently devoted to infants by the scientific community and the general public. Anyone interested in learning about infants should find *Infant Development* informative and helpful.

Through the years, numerous disciplines have contributed to our knowledge and understanding of infant development. Consequently, this book has been written from an interdisciplinary perspective. Information from child development and family relations, psychology, pediatrics, nursing, nutrition, biology, and other disciplines has been incorporated into the various chapters. The quotations from classical and contemporary literature that introduce each chapter are included to add interest as well as to express a major theme.

Comprehensive information on each topic of importance in infant development is included. With the exception of two chapters on the prenatal and the newborn periods, the material is organized topically, with a chapter on each developmental area. One of the unique features of this text is the extended coverage of nutrition, health, and safety. A chapter is also devoted to infant caregiving and education in the context of contemporary family situations and lifestyles.

A concerted effort has been made to achieve a balance between theory, research, and practical information. The important theories that attempt to explain when, how, and why infants develop in certain ways are presented as recurrent themes throughout the book. Contemporary and classic research studies are used to document and illustrate prevailing scientific opinions. Controversial issues as well as gaps in our understanding of infants are presented. Suggestions for enhancing infant growth and development are incorporated in the various chapters.

Several features are used in the book to facilitate student understanding and learning. An introduction presented at the beginning of each chapter summarizes the basic topics that are covered. Important terms are highlighted and carefully defined as they occur in the text, and again in the glossary for easy reference. Real-life examples are used to illustrate difficult concepts. Photographs, drawings, and tables are sprinkled throughout the book to enhance the discussion. Each chapter ends with a summary of the main points.

ACKNOWLEDGMENTS

I want to express appreciation for the help I received from many people in the preparation of this book. The librarians in the Health Science and Joyner Libraries at East Carolina University (ECU) were extremely helpful in the process of identifying and obtaining essential materials. Dr. Thomas Irons, Associate Professor of Pediatrics in the ECU School of Medicine, reviewed the chapter on Health and Safety and offered numerous helpful comments. Dr. Kathryn Kolasa, Professor, Department of Family Medicine in the ECU School of Medicine, provided valuable suggestions for the chapter on nutrition. The comments of the anonymous reviewers secured by the Prentice Hall editorial staff contributed to improvements in the final organization and content of the book.

Jan King, Peggy Nobles, and Martha Postma, graduate students in the Department of Child Development and Family Relations at ECU, were extremely helpful in the preparation of various drafts of the manuscript. My wife, Dora, deserves special credit, not only for her suggestions on grammar and style but for her patience and understanding during my extensive involvement with this project.

Finally, I am especially grateful to Susan Finnemore, Psychology Editor, Jan Stephan, Production Editor, and other members of the Prentice Hall editorial staff for their patience and guidance in making this book a reality.

CWS

Introduction

All the world's a stage,
And all the men and women merely players.
They have their exits and entrances,
and one man in his time plays many parts,
his act being seven stages.
At first the infant, mewling and puking in the nurse's arms.

–Shakespeare

The term *infant* is derived from a Latin word meaning "without speech." If we use the literal definition, infancy covers the period between birth and 12 to 18 months, when the baby begins to talk. However, current definitions of infancy tend to cover a broader age range, encompassing the newborn and toddler stages. In this book, infancy includes the age span from birth to 3 years of age. Since the first act in life's drama actually begins before birth, the prenatal period is also included as an important part of our discussion.

SOME BASIC QUESTIONS

This book is designed to acquaint you with the important concepts, characteristics, stages, and underlying processes of infant development. The basic questions we consider throughout the book are:

1. How do infants grow and develop? What are the characteristic abilities and needs of infants at various stages in their development from conception to the third year of life?
2. Why do infants grow, develop, and behave in the ways they do? What important variables or factors influence development from conception through infancy?
3. What child-rearing practices facilitate the development of healthy, competent infants?

This introductory chapter alerts you to some additional issues, recurring themes, and perspectives that are important to the study of infant development.

IMPORTANCE OF INFANCY

How far back in time can you remember? Try this exercise. Close your eyes, relax, and turn your thoughts to the earliest experiences of your life. If you are like most people, you remember very little, if anything, that happened to you during the first two or three years of your life. Can infancy be a very important period of development, then, if we have little or no recollection of what happened to us then?

There is widespread agreement that infancy is a very important phase of the human life cycle. However, the extent to which infancy represents a **critical period** is the subject of a continuing debate. A critical period is the period of time when an individual is most open, or susceptible, to lasting environmental influences. We know that various organs of the body can be irreversibly damaged by exposure to environmental hazards or by deficits at delicate formation stages during the prenatal period. Whether there are comparable critical periods in psychological development is less certain.

Sigmund Freud (1940) was one of the first psychologists to view experiences during the infancy years as having lifelong effects. He believed that all personality neuroses are acquired during the first six years of life (Rutter, 1987). Freud believed that the first two years were the most important within that time period. A famous study by René Spitz (1945) of infants who were reared in an orphanage is sometimes used to support the critical period hypothesis. The infants he studied had few toys and lay in their cribs most of the time with little human contact. As a result of this deprivation of normal "mothering," the infants failed to grow and became severely depressed and withdrawn. The infants had little resistance to disease, and many of them died. Spitz believed that the severe deprivation resulted in psychological damage that was practically irreversible. However, critics point out that Spitz failed to determine whether or not the infants were normal before they were institutionalized.

On the other hand, considerable evidence against the critical periods hypothesis has been cited. For example, Kagan and Klein (1981) observed infants in an isolated Guatemalan village who spent the first year of life in a windowless hut with little attention from caregivers. The infants were found to be silent, apathetic, and retarded. In spite of their early retardation, however, these infants grew up to be active, happy, and intellectually competent 11-year-olds. Rutter (1985) reviewed research studies on children from severely deprived backgrounds who were subsequently placed in much better environments. He concluded that "the effects of early bad experiences can be 'neutralized' to a substantial extent by good experiences in later life . . . (p. 360). The evidence runs counter to the view that early experiences irrevocably change personality development" (p. 364).

The view of infancy as a fixed and absolute critical period of psychological development has been, in the minds of many people, replaced with the "sensitive periods" concept (Rutter, 1985). According to this position, infants are in many ways more sensitive or vulnerable to their environment than older children. As the first stage of life, infancy provides the foundation for later development. In some cases the effects may be long-lasting but not necessarily irreversible. The extent to which psychological handicaps or benefits from infancy persist depends upon a complex chain of events linking the first stage of life to the last (Rutter, 1987).

HISTORICAL PERSPECTIVES

Today infants are regarded as the most precious of all creatures. Whether or not this has always been true is a matter of debate by historians. In this section we take a brief look at two contrasting views about how infants have been treated in the past. It is important to look at the past before we can understand contemporary attitudes and practices in infant care.

Negative Views

According to many historians (e.g., de Mause, 1974), before the seventeenth century infants and young children were considered to be inferior creatures and were placed at the very bottom of the social scale (Pollock, 1983). Parents were perceived as largely indifferent to the needs of their offspring. Until the early 1800s, infants were often subjected to very cruel treatment. For example, from ancient times until the fourth century **infanticide** was practiced in many cultures. Newborn infants who were sickly, deformed, or otherwise viewed as a burden to their parents were killed, usually by exposure or starvation.

During the fourth century, the practice of infanticide was largely replaced with the practice of abandonment (de Mause, 1974). Whenever possible, problem infants were given away to be reared by substitute families or religious orders. As recently as the 1800s, many young mothers in Europe and America left their babies on the steps of a church or a mansion in the hope that they would be adopted (Langer, 1975). In addition, many wealthy parents turned their infants over to "wet nurses" for the first two years of life as a means of avoiding close contact. Love and affection generally were not considered important for infant development (Kagan, Kearsley, & Zelazo, 1978). Discipline was harsh, and beating of children was common.

By the end of the 1800s, the concept of infancy as a separate and important stage in life had started to evolve. Infants were given a central role in the family, and their rights were protected by the state (Pollock, 1983). Parents gradually became more physically and emotionally involved with their infants. By the early 1900s we entered a new age of concern about the development and care of infants. Pediatrics was established as a separate field of medicine. The infant death rate declined as sanitation and medical practices improved. In the United States, public-spirited citizens worked to improve the living conditions of infants and their families (Barclay, 1985). De Mause (1974) refers to current views of infancy as reflecting a "helping mode" era.

A Contrasting View

The poor treatment of infants discussed above has been widely acknowledged, but some historians (Pollock, 1983; Hanawalt, 1977) disagree with claims that the mistreatment of infants has been widespread. Pollock (1983) believes that, apart from social changes and technological advances, child-rearing practices have not changed dramatically through the centuries. According to this view, infanticide, abandonment, and other forms of cruelty to infants were practiced in the past, but not by the majority of parents. Nearly all children were wanted, and most parents were not cold and indifferent to their children's welfare. Changes have occurred in specific practices, such as feeding, and changes in parental attitudes have been observed. However, for the most part, infant care has remained remarkably consistent through the years (Pollock, 1983).

STUDYING INFANTS

Although the answers to many questions about infant growth and development are tentative and incomplete, we now have more and better information than ever. During the past twenty years, our knowledge of infant development has increased dramatically. The numerous books, magazine articles, and scientific publications on infant development currently available reflect the information explosion. The rapidly growing amount of infancy research is, in part, the result of the development of some innovative methods of studying infants.

Techniques

The first known efforts to study and record the behavior of infants were found in several "baby diaries," the first of which was published by German philosopher Dietrich Tiedemann in 1787 (Tiedemann, 1787/1927). A baby diary is a day-to-day record of an infant's behavior by an adult observer, usually a parent-scientist. Diary records published by Charles Darwin (1877) and William Preyer (1888) were a little more systematic than Tiedemann's records and have received wider recognition. The information reported in baby diaries is considered to have limited value because the information may not be very objective. In addition, observations of a single subject cannot be generalized to other infants.

Jean Piaget (1951) combined the naturalistic observation method used in the baby diary with informal experiments performed on his own three infants (Miller, 1987). For example, Piaget gave an infant an object to manipulate or a problem to solve and then systematically recorded the infant's response. Piaget's conclusions about infant development based upon such observations have been widely accepted, but only because they have been verified by other researchers using more sophisticated procedures.

Contemporary researchers have searched for more objective and reliable methods. However, the scientific study of infants has been extremely difficult for a variety of reasons. For one thing, securing the baby's cooperation is a problem. The baby may be too sleepy, fussy, distractable, or active to concentrate on the experimental situation. Even when an infant is cooperative, how do researchers find out what the infant is thinking or feeling before language begins? In the absence of infant language ability, researchers have had to find other ways to assess the infant's experience of the world.

Infant responses such as looking, sucking, facial expressions, body movements, respiration rate, heart rate, and brain waves are typically used in experimental studies. Sophisticated videotape equipment, computerized scanners, and other high-tech equipment are now available to monitor, record, and analyze the responses of infants. Through the years, researchers have been ingenious in designing more and better ways to measure responses they can then use to make inferences about what is going on inside the baby's mind (Miller, 1987). Two of the most frequently used methods are visual preferences and habituation-dishabituation. You will find examples of additional infancy research procedures throughout this book.

Visual Preference Technique. Robert Fantz (1958), a modern-day pioneer in infancy research, developed an innovative technique to study, visual perception. In this study, an infant is placed in a special apparatus equipped with a peephole and a "looking chamber." Two pictures are hung in the looking chamber within the infant's field of vision. The pictures are separated so that the infant has to turn his or her head slightly to look from one to the other. The lighting conditions are such that an image of the stimulus is reflected in the infant's eye. The observer looks through the peephole and records what the infant is viewing and the amount of looking time the infant devotes to each picture or its parts. Using this procedure, researchers can determine what infants spend the most amount of time watching and whether they can discriminate between various stimuli.

Other researchers (e.g., Hainline & Lemerise, 1982) have added high-tech electronic equipment to Fantz's original procedure (see Figure I-1). Pro-

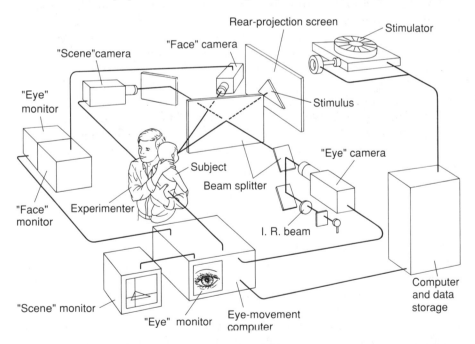

FIGURE I-1   A System for Recording the Eye Movements of Infants.
Source: L. Hainline and E. Lemerise (1982). Infants' scanning of geometric forms varying in size. *Journal of Experimental Child Psychology, 33*, p. 241. Copyright 1982 by Academic Press. Reprinted by permission.

jectors, video cameras, monitors, and computerized data-recording equipment are now used to record the infant's smallest eye movements and detailed visual images. With this equipment, researchers can make more accurate observations and study more complex visual behaviors, such as infant scanning patterns and form perception.

Habituation-Dishabituation. You probably have had the experience of going into a store where background music is playing. You notice the music at first, but within a few minutes you are no longer listening to it. This progressive decline of response to a repeated stimulus is referred to as **habituation**. If a catchy tune comes on, you find yourself listening to the music again. If the music stops, you become aware of its absence. The recovery of interest in and response to a changing stimulus is called **dishabituation**.

To determine when an infant has habituated or dishabituated to a given stimulus, investigators measure changes in the infant's heart rate, breathing, visual activity, startle reflex, and other reactions. When an infant pays less attention to a picture, after seeing it a few times in succession, the infant is demonstrating the capacity to remember the picture. If the infant indicates renewed interest when a new picture is shown researchers infer that the infant can detect the difference between the two pictures (Trotter, 1987). Habituation-dishabituation has been used to study a variety of infant abilities, including learning, memory, visual, taste, and sound discrimination.

UNDERLYING ISSUES AND RECURRENT THEMES

The study of infancy involves struggling with several basic issues and problems. Throughout this book you will be confronted with divergent views about when, how, and why infants behave in certain ways. This means that you will need to decide which points of view or which answers make the most sense to you. You will also find that several themes reappear from time to time. These recurrent themes are as basic to human development as the underlying melody, or motif, is to a musical composition. This section is designed to introduce some of the themes you will encounter in the study of infant development.

Norms and Individual Differences

Throughout this book we consider typical patterns of growth and development, which are referred to as *norms*. The normal age ranges for major milestones, such as the first spoken word and the social smile, are discussed. However, within these average growth and developmental trends there is plenty of room for individual differences. Consequently, you should always keep in mind that no two babies are exactly alike. Human infants differ in appearance and behavior within and between racial and ethnic groups. Even identical twins differ in significant ways. Although there is an average rate and sequence of development, no infant should be thought of simply as an "average" child.

Interrelations Among Developmental Areas

In this book, infant growth and development are described in seven major domains or areas: physical, motor, cognitive, language, personality, social, and emotional. These areas are closely interrelated. When an infant makes progress in one area, there is usually a chain effect whereby development occurs in other areas as well.

Numerous illustrations of how development in one area relates to that of another area can be given. For example, the development of the ability to move around and explore the environment is accompanied by marked improvement in sensory perception. When an infant advances to a higher stage of cognitive functioning, for instance, a new milestone of language development has been reached. Changes in social and emotional development, such as smiling and stranger anxiety, are apparently related to changes in the cognitive domain.

Directions of Development

Two basic laws or principles of developmental direction are evident in the growth and development of all infants. According to the **cephalocaudal principle**, development proceeds from head to foot. The head and upper extremities develop and become functional earlier than the trunk and lower extremities of the body. In accordance with the **proximodistal principle**, development proceeds from the center of the body toward the outer extremities. For example, the arms and legs develop and become useful before the fingers and toes.

The Competent Infant

Human infants are born into the world more helpless than the young of any other species. Human infancy lasts a relatively long time. However, even at birth infants possess remarkable abilities. We used to believe that infants were blind at birth. We now know that the newborn not only can see, but is capable of other sophisticated sensory functions. What you will see emerging in this study of infancy is not so much a picture of an infant "mewling and puking" as an infant with an impressive amount of ability in various areas of development.

Robert White (1959) used the term **competence motivation** to describe the infant's tendency to explore and master challenges within the environment. Infants thrive on such challenges as putting a peg in a hole, finding a lost object, or saying a new word. Infants are also tough and resilient. They have a tendency to "grow toward health" (Kagan, 1979, p. 21). This means that infants are capable of overcoming a lot of adversity.

Reciprocal Interactions

Another theme in the study of infants is the reciprocal (mutual) nature of adult-infant interactions. The socialization of infants is not a one-way process. From the beginning, infants are interactive partners in the child-rearing process. Infants influence their caregivers in numerous ways, even as caregivers influence them. For example, parents respond differently to a male baby than to a female baby. A baby who is calm and easygoing receives different treatment than a baby who fusses a lot and is difficult to manage. Therefore, to a significant extent, infants play an active role in creating their own environment.

The Nature-Nurture Controversy

One question that is central in the study of infant development is "Which is most important, heredity or environment?" Obviously, certain physical features such as hair and eye color are clearly controlled by heredity. When it comes to human behavior, though, philosophers and scientists for centuries have debated the relative importance of nature and nurture in human development. The nature side of the debate is represented by the **maturationists** and **nativists**. Maturationists believe that the key to growth and development is found in the genetic foundations. Physical growth, motor development, and other abilities proceed according to a genetic timetable. Nativists believe that infants come equipped with innate ideas, feelings, and personality traits. For example, they believe that infants are genetically endowed with the ability to understand the rules of grammar.

On the other hand, the "nurture" point of view is advocated by the **empiricists**, who believe that the course of infant development is shaped by experience. This position is based on the proposal that John Locke (1961) made in 1691 that the infant mind is a "blank slate." Infants are thus viewed as passive creatures, molded by external environmental forces.

The contemporary view of infant development recognizes that both heredity and environment are important and act together in complex ways to shape development. This point of view is referred to as the **interactionist** position. This view recognizes that both heredity and environment contribute to the infant's development. Biological and hereditary factors set the limits on development, while environmental factors determine the extent to which the limits will be stretched. However, the two sets of factors interact and combine in ways that make infant development more than simply the sum of the two parts.

THEORETICAL PERSPECTIVES

Much of the literature on infant development is written in the form of theories. Developmental theories are assumptions, hypotheses, or best guesses about how and why babies develop and behave in certain ways. Theories serve as systems or frameworks for viewing infant development and conducting research. Most theories represent a particular view of such issues as human nature, the nature-versus-nurture debate, the importance of early experiences, the ways in which individuals learn, and the stages of development. Theories vary widely in scope, complexity, scientific support, and popularity.

Some of the most important and controversial theories of development are presented in this text. Most of these theories can be divided into four general categories:

1. *Behavioral* theories emphasize the importance of the environment and experience in shaping the human infant. B. F. Skinner (1972) is the most well known representative of behaviorism.

2. *Nativistic* or *maturational* theories, which stress the importance of innate characteristics, are represented by Arnold Gesell (1945) and Noam Chomsky (1975).

3. *Psychoanalytic* or *psychosocial* theories stress the importance of early experiences and the role of emotions in shaping human personality and behavior. Sigmund Freud (1917) and Erik Erikson (1963) are the major proponents of these points of view.

4. *Cognitive developmental* theories emphasize the interaction between genetic inheritance and environmental factors. Understanding the development of cognitive processes is the key to human behavior. Jean Piaget (1929) is the chief representative of this theory.

More specific information about these and other theories is provided at the points where they relate to specific features of infant development.

SUMMARY

1. This book covers infant growth and development from conception to the beginning of the third year of life. Important characteristics, concepts, and underlying processes of infant development are examined, and suggestions for child-rearing are made.

2. As the first stage of life, infancy is considered a very important period. The extent to which infancy is a critical period in human development continues to be the subject of scientific debate.

3. Until the late 1800s, many unwanted infants were murdered or abandoned by their parents. Many others died from disease or abuse. During the 1900s medical care, attitudes, and child-rearing practices have gradually improved. The current "helping" mode reflects an increased concern for the physical and psychological development of infants.

4. Techniques for conducting research with infants have improved dramatically since the first "baby diaries" were recorded. The use of high-tech

equipment and sophisticated research procedures now make it possible to assess a variety of infant responses.

5. Some of the underlying issues and recurring themes of infant development discussed in this book are the importance of individual differences, interrelationships among different areas of development, the concept of the competent infant, ways in which infants and adults influence each other, and the nature-nurture controversy.

6. Theories of infant development discussed in this book include behavioral, maturational-nativistic, psychoanalytic-psychosocial, and cognitive-developmental.

1

Prenatal Development

Where did you come from baby dear?
Out of the everywhere into here.
–George MacDonald

Zygote, blastocyst, embryo, fetus. These are among the terms used to label the developing human infant at various stages of prenatal development. None of these words, however, adequately conveys the profound complexity of the drama of life before birth. For centuries, scientists have attempted to understand the process of how life begins in the hidden world of the mother's womb. Although much of the mystery remains to be solved, the intricate details of prenatal development have been meticulously catalogued through the analysis of specimens of medical and spontaneous abortions.

This chapter provides a chronological summary of the major developments during the various stages of the prenatal period. In addition, factors that affect the health and well-being of the human infant before birth, as well as after birth, are discussed.

CONCEPTION AND FERTILIZATION

Prenatal development begins the moment one of the father's sperm cells (spermatozoa) unites with the mother's egg cell (ovum). Around the fourteenth day after the onset of menstrual bleeding, an egg cell is released from one of the mother's ovaries into the fallopian tube (see Figure 1-1). Occasionally two or more ova are released simultaneously and, if fertilized, result in a multiple pregnancy. An ovum is about the size of the point of a needle.

Approximately 300 to 500 million sperm are deposited in the vagina close to the mouth of the uterus (cervix) during intercourse (Pansky, 1982). Spermatozoa are much smaller than ova and cannot be seen without the aid of a microscope. Unlike ova, sperm have the capacity to move on their own by lashing their tails back and forth. Sperm swim through the cervix into the uterus and up the fallopian tubes to meet the ovum. They usually remain alive for about 24 hours, but some sperm may be capable of fertilization for up to three days.

If an ovum is not fertilized in 12 to 24 hours after ovulation, it dies (Moore, 1983). Only 300 to 500 sperm reach the usual fertilization site in the widest part of the fallopian tube (Pansky, 1982). Although many of the spermatozoa may contact the ovum at the same time, only one reaches the nucleus and accomplishes fertilization. In the very rare case in which more than one sperm fertilize an ovum, the embryo aborts, or the baby dies shortly after birth (Carr, 1971).

Germinal Stage

Once the ovum has been fertilized, a series of rapid changes takes place. The nuclei of the two parent cells merge, and the hereditary material from each is arranged into a blueprint for a new life. Within 36 hours, the fertilized ovum (zygote) divides into two cells. As the zygote moves slowly through the fallopian tube on the way to the uterus, cell division continues. The series of rapid cell divisions results in a progressively larger number of increasingly smaller cells (Gasser, 1975).

By the third day, the mass of cells approaching the uterus is composed of sixteen cells and resembles a mulberry in shape. At this point, the cell mass is called a **morula.** When the morula enters the uterus about one day later, the cells, numbering about 58, cluster around a central cavity and become known as a **blastocyst.** Inside the blastocyst a small group of microscopic cells clusters to one side and begins to form the embryo along with the supporting membranes.

Implantation

For two or three days, the blastocyst floats freely in the uterus. It is about the same size as the original ovum, but its content has been dramatically altered. Around the sixth day, the blastocyst attaches itself to the lining of the uterus. By this time the blastocyst has grown an outer layer of cells called **tryphoblasts**, which bury into the uterine lining by secreting enzymes that break down the cells at the implantation site. After implantation is completed, around the tenth day after fertilization, enzymatic digestion stops as abruptly as it began. The implantation is usually healed over in a scarlike cyst by the thirteenth or fourteenth day. Occasionally, implantation is accompanied by bleeding that can be mistaken for menstruation.

Implantation Sites

In most cases, implantation occurs in the upper half of the uterus (see Figure 1-1). If the blastocyst becomes implanted in the extreme lower part, there is a risk of bleeding after the fourth month of pregnancy. This condition is called **placental previa** and endangers both the mother and the baby (Dryden, 1978). Implantation close to the opening of the uterus (cervix) is called a **cervical pregnancy.** This situation rarely occurs but usually leads to spontaneous abortion (Moore, 1983).

Not all fertilized ova become attached to the uterus. Scientists estimate that about one-third to one-half of all zygotes fail to implant and are flushed out of the uterus with the onset of menstruation (Pansky, 1982). Occasionally the zygote becomes lodged in the fallopian tube or makes its way to the abdominal cavity, the ovary, or the pelvic area. Implantation outside the uterus is called an **ectopic pregnancy.**

Ordinarily ectopic pregnancies lead to the death of the embryo during the second month. In some cases the health of the mother is threatened because of excessive bleeding. In instances too rare to calculate, an ectopic pregnancy may continue long enough to result in the birth of a live baby. One such exceptional case was reported in Burlington, North Carolina, where a 32-

year-old woman gave birth to a normal 6-pound, 4-ounce baby boy. The baby had developed in the mother's abdomen and was removed surgically. No one knew the woman had an ectopic pregnancy until the time of delivery (*News and Observer*, 1979).

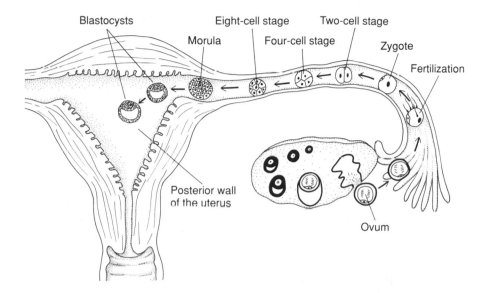

FIGURE 1-1 Ovulation, Fertilization, and Development through Implantation.
Source: K.L. Moore (1983). *The Developing Human: Basic Embryology and Birth Defects* (2d ed.). Philadelphia: W. B. Saunders Co., p. 32. Adapted by permission.

NOTE: The ovum is released from the ovary and passes into the uterine (fallopian) tube, where it is met and fertilized by a sperm. The zygote divides repeatedly as it passes down the uterine tube and becomes a morula. The morula enters the uterus, develops a cavity, and becomes a blastocyst. The blastocyst usually implants itself into the lining of the posterior wall of the uterus.

EMBRYONIC PERIOD

The word *embryo* is based on the Greek word *embryon* meaning "a swelling." The term signifies the growth (swelling) of cells inside the fertilized ovum, as well as the beginning of all major internal and external structures of the body. The embryonic period covers the time from seven to eight days after conception until the end of the eighth week (Moore, 1977).

The Germ Layers

By the time the process of implantation is complete, the inner cell, a mass clustered to one side of the blastocyst, has formed a tiny disc that will develop into the embryo. At the end of the second week, the embryonic structure consists of two layers of cells called the *ectoderm* and the *endoderm*. The ectoderm is thicker and will later form the nervous system, the skin, hair, nails, and parts of the eyes and ears. The endoderm will develop into the digestive tract, respiratory system, liver, and various glands. A third layer of cells sandwiched between the ectoderm and endoderm begins to develop around the beginning of the third week. This middle layer of cells, the mesoderm, forms the circulatory and urinary systems, skeleton, muscles, and connecting tissues.

Supporting Membranes

Approximately three weeks after fertilization, the outer layer of cells surrounding the embryo is called the **chorion**. This membrane, which resembles a round sponge, encloses the embryo and its supporting tissues. One side of the chorion is attached to the lining of the uterus and, combined with the maternal tissues, develops into the **placenta.**

The placenta provides the link between the mother and the embryo where exchanges of nutrients, waste products, oxygen, hormones, and antibodies take place. Unfortunately, viruses and other harmful substances can also cross over from the mother to the embryo. The placenta continues to develop throughout pregnancy. At three weeks it covers about 20 percent of the uterus. By five months, half of the uterus is covered. At full term the placenta is about 6 to 8 inches in diameter, 1 inch thick, and weighs approximately one-sixth as much as the baby (Rugh & Shettles, 1971).

The early embryo is attached to the placenta by a mushroom-shaped connecting stalk, the forerunner of the umbilical cord. The umbilical cord serves as the lifeline that allows the developing infant to float freely within the chorion, somewhat like an astronaut in outer space. The cord contains two arteries and a vein. The arteries carry blood containing waste products to the placenta, while the vein carries nutrients, oxygen, and other substances to the embryo. At full term, the cord is typically one-half to three-quarters of an inch thick and approximately 20 to 24 inches long (50-55 centimeters) (Jirasek, 1983).

Amnion.   When the embryonic disc is formed, a small space, called the amniotic cavity, is formed on one side of the inner cell mass. A larger cavity, known as the primary yolk sac, is formed on the other side. The embryo stretches between the amniotic cavity and the primary yolk sac. As the embryo develops, the amniotic cavity enlarges. Eventually the yolk sac disappears and the amniotic cavity totally encloses the embryo within the walls of a thin, tough transparent membrane called the **amnion.** The cavity is filled with a salty liquid called amniotic fluid. The amniotic sac, often called the bag of waters, serves as a shock absorber, allows freedom of movement, and helps control the temperature of the developing infant.

Yolk Sac.   As the amniotic sac expands, the primary yolk sac decreases in size and forms a much smaller, secondary yolk sac. The human yolk sac, unlike that of bird eggs, contains no nutrients. However, it is apparently instrumental in the transfer of nutrients to the embryo before the placental connection is made with the mother. The yolk sac also serves as a source of blood cells until the liver begins to function around the fifth week (Moore, 1977).

Embryo at 4 Weeks

At the end of the first month of development, the embryo and its supporting membranes are about the size of a pea. The embryo has a head that, because of the rapid growth of the brain, makes up about one-third of the length of the body. The three primary parts of the brain are already present. On the opposite end, the embryo has a pointed tail that curls up in a C-shape, almost touching the top of the bulbous head as it bends downward. The tail is only temporary and will eventually form the coccyx—the end of the spine. A string of budlike structures, called **somites**, have formed along the outer arch of the embryo. The somites serve as the foundation of the skeleton. The arm buds develop slightly ahead of the leg buds. The limb buds are now visible as small swellings on the embryo's surface. At this stage, the embryo looks more like a shrimp or a tadpole than a human.

The U-shaped heart tube starts its first fluttering beats around the twenty-third day after fertilization (Dryden, 1978). Like the head, the heart is large in proportion to the other organs and resembles a light bulb protruding from the center of the C-shaped structure. Even though it is relatively incomplete at this stage, the heart is strong enough to circulate blood produced by the embryo through a primitive system of veins and arteries, the umbilical cord, and the placenta.

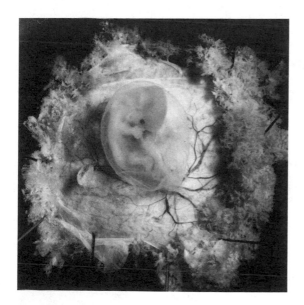

Seven-week-old embryo.

Embryo at 8 weeks

During the second month of life the various parts of the embryo continue developing at a fantastic rate, changing almost daily. Rapid brain growth causes the head to grow to almost one-half of the total body length. The brain is developing in both size and complexity, but it has not assumed control of the body at this stage. The embryo is still top-heavy but is no longer C-shaped. The internal organs have continued to develop, and all the major systems are present. Some have even assumed their permanent functions. The embryo develops three successive sets of kidneys during the fourth and fifth weeks. The third set begins secreting urine by the eighth week and remains as the permanent kidneys. The urine is secreted into the amniotic fluid (Moore, 1983).

The basic form of the skeleton is completed by eight weeks. However, the embryonic skeleton consists mostly of cartilage, a rubbery material found, among other places, in the end of an adult's nose. Deciduous (temporary) teeth have begun to form beneath the gums. The primitive beginnings of some of the permanent teeth form as early as the twelfth prenatal week.

At the end of eight weeks (fifty-six days), the appearance of the embryo is unmistakably human. It measures about 1½ inches long from head to buttocks and weighs about one-third of an ounce. The embryo resembles a tiny doll with a large head, carefully formed arms and legs, and a protruding abdomen. The face is characterized by slitlike eyes and small ear lobes (Rugh & Shettles, 1971). The embryo is now called a fetus—a "young one." The name change signifies the completion of human form and the appearance of the first bone cells in the skeleton. A new act in the drama of life before birth begins.

FETAL STAGE

Third Month (Weeks 9–12)

The weeks in the third month are sometimes referred to as the "period of initial activity," because the fetus begins to move (Pansky, 1982). The fetus can kick, turn its head, curl its toes, squint, frown, move its lips, and make a fist (Rugh & Shettles, 1971). As yet, none of these movements is felt by the mother. By 12 weeks of age, the fetus is approximately 3 inches long and weighs about half an ounce (Moore, 1977). The uterus has grown to the point where the mother's pregnancy begins to "show."

The eyes, which began as two shallow grooves on each side of the 22-day-old embryo's forebrain, have undergone further development. By the third month, the various parts of the eyeball have formed, including the cornea, lens, and retina. The optic nerves, which began to develop at 4 weeks, now link the eyes directly to the brain. The eyelids develop as two layers of skin that completely cover each eyeball and are sealed shut around the tenth week. They remain closed until about the twenty-sixth week.

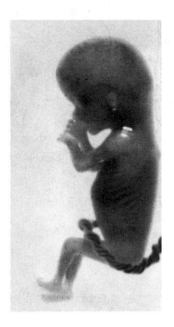

Fetus at three months.

The third month has also been called the "period of sexual emergence" (Rugh & Shettles, 1971). The sex of an infant is determined at conception by the sperm that fertilizes the ovum. However, all human embryos go through a primitive stage of development when their genital systems are not distinguishable as male or female. Internally, sex differentiation begins toward the end of the second month. External sex organs begin to appear early in the fetal period but are similar in males and females until the ninth week. Their mature form is clearly observable and distinguishable in the twelfth week (Pansky, 1982).

Fourth Month (Weeks 13–16)

The fourth month is a period of rapid fetal growth (Pansky, 1982). The length of the fetus doubles from 3 to 6 inches, while the weight increases from half an ounce to 4 ounces. The legs grow longer as the head becomes proportionately smaller. The hands and feet are well formed. Bone cells grow rapidly during this stage. The fetal heart is beating at 120 to 160 beats a minute and circulating blood throughout the body (Rugh & Shettles, 1971). Heartbeats can be heard through a nonamplified stethoscope at about 16 weeks. The fetus becomes sensitive to light at this time and will turn away from bright light shown on the mother's abdomen (Bernhardt, 1987).

Fifth Month (Weeks 17–20)

The mother reaches the halfway point of her pregnancy at the nineteenth week. She begins to feel the movements of the fetus around this time, which are referred to as **quickening**. By this time, the skin of the fetus is covered with a waxy, cheeselike substance called **vernix caseosa**. The vernix ("varnish") forms from secretions of the sebaceous (oil) glands which then mix with flakes of dead skin. The covering protects the fetus's skin from chapping and cracking during the long immersion in the amniotic fluid. By 20 weeks the fetus is also covered with tiny, downlike hairs called **lanugo**. The eyebrows and scalp hair appear by the end of this month. The lanugo usually falls out during the seventh month, but some of it may still be present at birth.

Scientists estimate that all the billions of brain cells (neurons) the fetus will develop are present early in the fifth prenatal month (Hubel, 1979). The neurons grow in size and form trillions of connections with each other. In addition, a fatty substance called myelin must form around each neuron before the nervous system reaches maturity. This process begins around 20 weeks and accelerates until around 32 weeks, when it slows down.

Sixth Month (Weeks 21–25)

A picture of the 6-month-old fetus reveals a thin layer of pinkish red transparent skin. With little fat underneath, the blood vessels are clearly visible. Although still top-heavy, the proportions of the body are now more similar to those of the newborn infant. At the end of six months the fetus weighs about 1½ pounds and measures 10 to 12 inches from the top of the head to the rump. The fetus sleeps and wakes at regular intervals (not necessarily the

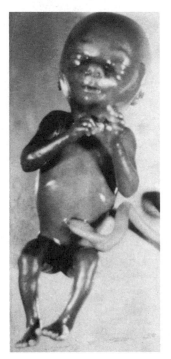

Seven-month-old fetus.

same as the mother's!) and has a favorite resting position. The fetus may suck its thumb and engage in other reflexive activities such as swallowing and grasping.

Seventh Month (Weeks 26–29)

The lower parts of the brain are mature enough to function at this time. The lungs have developed the capacity to breathe, even though they are not completely mature. In addition, a layer of fat is deposited beneath the skin as the weight is doubled, to about 3 pounds. Height reaches about 16 inches from head to foot. The fetus has reached the "age of viability." This means that the baby has a reasonable chance of surviving with specialized care if it is born at this time.

Eighth Month (Weeks 30–34)

During the last few weeks before birth, the fetus rapidly puts on protective fat in preparation for life in the outside world. Its living quarters become crowded as the fetus grows to 4 or 5 pounds and measures 18 inches. Now (or possibly earlier) the fetus apparently can hear the mother's heartbeat and other internal noises or muffled sounds from the outside world (Nilsson et al., 1977).

Ninth Month (Weeks 35–Birth)

This month represents the "finishing period," the final act in the drama of intrauterine life. The baby does not change much in appearance except to add weight and height. Most importantly, the fetus acquires antibodies from the mother that provide temporary protection against some communicable diseases such as measles, mumps, whooping cough, and polio. As the placenta ages and becomes less efficient, the fetus's growth rate slows down. The end of the prenatal period and the beginning of the birth process are near.

INFLUENCES ON DEVELOPMENT

Each year approximately 7 percent of the babies in the United States are born with serious defects (Goldman, 1984). Birth defects are sometimes called **congenital** (meaning "present at birth") **malformations**. Congenital malformations are caused by genetic factors or environmental influences. Frequently it is difficult to separate genetic from environmental conditions, and most malformations probably come from a complex combination of both factors (Moore, 1983).

Genetic Influences

Genetic factors play a significant role in human development throughout the life span. At the moment of conception, an infant receives the genetic code that is a blueprint or set of instructions for cell division and the development of individual features. The genetic code, which is unique for each individual, is carried by genes and chromosomes. Each parent contributes hereditary material to the infant by means of the reproductive or germ cells (sperm and ova) created in the testes of the father and the ovaries of the mother.

The human body contains two types of cells: somatic (body cells) and sex (reproductive cells). Growth cells for the formation and replacement of body tissue are formed through the process of **mitosis**. During mitosis, body cells divide and make exact copies of themselves. Each body cell contains twenty-three matching pairs (total = 46) of chromosomes. The process by which reproductive cells are formed is called **meiosis**, or reduction division. During meiosis, each chromosome pair separates and goes to a separate cell. Consequently, the sperm or ova produced by meiosis contain only a total of twenty-three single chromosomes. The process is directed by the genetic code that originates in the fertilized ovum. When the sperm and ovum unite at the time of fertilization, a total of forty-six chromosomes is once again attained.

The chromosomes consist of smaller units of heredity called genes. Each chromosome contains thousands of genes. The genes determine the infant's individual hereditary characteristics such as eye, hair, and skin color, as well as internal organ systems. Because of the complex laws of genetics, an individual may inherit a specific characteristic, such as blue eyes, even when one parent or both parents have a different characteristic, such as brown eyes.

Some human characteristics are determined by a single pair of genes, one from the father and one from the mother, whereas other traits are controlled by multiple gene pairs. Some genes are dominant, and others are recessive. When a dominant gene is paired with a recessive gene, the hereditary trait carried by the dominant gene is always present in the individual. A hereditary trait carried by a recessive gene prevails only when it is paired with a recessive gene of the same type. For example, the genes containing the code for blue eyes are recessive. A blue-eyed baby receives one "blue-eyed" gene from each parent. This recessive trait is possible even if both parents have brown eyes, because the genes from their blue-eyed ancestors are passed on to their offspring.

Genetic Disorders.   The complexity of the information contained in the human genetic program is enormous. Scientists estimate that a human zygote contains 100 billion bits of information, which is equivalent to 10 million printed pages. Considering the complexity of the genetic code, it is amazing that the large majority of infants are born without defects (Goldman, 1984).

Defects in the genes or chromosomes result in the birth of a child with a genetic disorder. Some of the genetic problems are relatively mild and non-handicapping, whereas others make normal development virtually impossible. Many genetic flaws are obvious at birth, but some are "time bombs" that cause problems only later in life. Genetic disorders usually are classified into three types: (1) chromosomal abnormalities, (2) single gene disorders, and (3) multi-factorial inheritance.

CHROMOSOMAL ABNORMALITIES.   Handicaps may be caused by the inheritance of more or less than the normal forty-six chromosomes. The most well-known and common handicapping condition caused by a chromosomal problem is Down's syndrome (also called mongolism or Trisomy 21). An infant born with Down's syndrome receives an extra chromosome (No. 21), making a total of forty-seven instead of the normal forty-six chromosomes. Down's syndrome occurs in approximately 1 out of every 500 to 600 births (Fuhrmann & Vogel, 1983). Children with this condition have facial features that give an oriental appearance, small hands with stubby fingers, a large protruding tongue, and thin straight hair. They usually do not grow to normal height. The disorder results in severe to moderate mental retardation.

Other major chromosomal abnormalities are sometimes found in the sex chromosomes (No. 23). The most frequent sex chromosome abnormality is Klinefelter's syndrome, which occurs when a male child is born with two X chromosomes and one Y chromosome. Klinefelter's syndrome may not be noticeable until after puberty, when the male begins to develop feminine breasts, small testes, and a very sparse beard and pubic hair. The disorder frequently results in mental retardation.

A comparable sex chromosome disorder that affects females is called Turner's syndrome. This condition occurs when the infant is born with only one sex (X) chromosome, resulting in a total of forty-five chromosomes. Victims of Turner's syndrome suffer growth retardation, have webbed necks, and ovaries that do not function. Most females who have this disorder develop normal intelligence, but mental retardation is a possibility.

Additional problems sometimes result from defects in the structure or shape of the chromosomes. Breaks in the chromosomal structure may occur, resulting in the loss of a portion of a chromosome (Moore, 1983). Cri du chat syndrome is a disorder caused by a missing section of chromosome No. 5. The cry of the infant affected by this problem resembles the meowing of a cat. These infants suffer from severe mental retardation as well as other handicaps.

SINGLE GENE DISORDERS.   Many genetic disorders result from a single gene or a pair of genes contributed by one or both parents, following the laws of genetic transmission. These abnormalities may be classified according to a dominant, recessive, or sex-linked pattern of inheritance.

Hundreds of disorders resulting from dominant genes have been identified, including dwarfism (achondroplasia); some forms of glaucoma; Huntington's chorea (a progressive degeneration of the nervous system); and polydactyly (extra fingers and toes). If one parent has such a disorder, each offspring has a 50 percent chance of being affected by the same problem. Dominantly inherited disorders are usually handicapping but are relatively mild in comparison to recessive disorders.

Both parents must carry the defective recessive gene before the off-spring can be affected. There is a 25 percent chance in such pregnancies that the infant will have the recessive trait. Phenylketonuria (PKU) is one of the major recessive genetic disorders. The infant with PKU cannot produce an enzyme necessary for the digestion of an amino acid (phenylalanine) found in milk and many other foods. The unmetabolized phenylalanine accumulates in the infant's body and, over time, causes severe brain damage. Infants born in the United States are routinely tested for PKU. The ones who are affected (approximately 260 in the United States each year) are placed on a special diet to eliminate the offending substance. When brain development is almost complete, around 10 to 12 years of age, the child can go on a regular diet.

Other recessively linked disorders that result in severe, life-threatening problems include

Cystic fibrosis—a disease that affects the mucous, sweat, tear, and salivary glands, causing congestion in the breathing passages.

Sickle-cell anemia—a blood disease that produces malformed red blood cells and weakens resistance to infection and other symptoms; this disease primarily affects black people.

Tay-Sachs disease—a fatal disease that causes the nervous system to degenerate; this condition primarily affects infants of eastern European Jewish ancestors.

These diseases are almost always fatal, but many infants live for several years.

SEX-LINKED DISORDERS.   A variety of hereditary disorders are caused by defective genes carried on the sex chromosomes. Most of these are recessive genes attached to the X chromosomes. Color blindness, hemophilia (deficiency in blood clotting), gargoylism (dwarfing and body deformities), and some forms of muscular dystrophy are examples of defects caused by sex-linked genes. More male than female infants are affected by such genetic abnormalities. Since males have only one X chromosome, it automatically has freedom to express any defect inherited from the mother. Females are less likely to inherit sex-linked diseases because they have two X chromosomes.

MULTIFACTORIAL DISORDERS.   Characteristics that result from the combined effect of several genetic and environmental factors are called multifactorial inheritance. Among normal infants, most differences such as intelligence and body size are caused by several factors. Spina bifida (exposed spinal cord), anencephaly (incomplete brain and skull), hydrocephaly (enlarged head with excessive fluid), cleft lip and palate, and congenital heart disease are examples of multifactorial birth defects.

Environmental Factors

Although the human embryo is well protected in the amniotic sac, a variety of toxic substances can cross the placental barrier and cause malformations or other problems. Drugs, viruses, radiation, and other agents that cause major birth defects are called **teratogens**. The root word for teratogens means, literally, "formation of monsters." Scientists have made remarkable progress in recent years in identifying products and other environmental conditions that are associated with birth defects.

Drugs and Medications. The adverse effects of a variety of drugs and medicines have been documented in numerous research studies over a period of thirty years (Hill & Kleinberg, 1984a). Maternal use of prescription, non-prescription, and illegal drugs may affect the embryo in both dramatic and subtle ways. The most clearly observable effects are physical deformities, retarded growth, central nervous system disorders, and internal organ dys-functions. A tragic example was seen in the use of the tranquilizer Thalidomide. Scientists discovered in the 1960s that a single dose of this drug taken between 21 and 35 days after conception often produced babies with severely malformed or missing limbs. More subtle effects of drugs used during pregnancy include learning disabilities and behavioral problems such as irri-tability or hyperactivity.

Most infants born in the United States are exposed to an average of three to five pharmacological substances between conception and birth. About 80 percent of prescription and nonprescription medications are not officially approved for use during pregnancy. The drugs that may possibly produce birth defects or other problems are numerous. The list includes heroin, LSD, cocaine, drugs given to treat epilepsy, diabetes, and infection, as well as tran-quilizers, hormones, and barbiturates (Hill & Kleinberg, 1984a).

There is growing concern about widely used medicines such as aspirin, antihistamines, diuretics, and antacids. Researchers have found an association between the mother's use of aspirin during pregnancy and the tendency of premature infants to bleed inside the brain. Studies have also found that chronic users of aspirin have an increased rate of infant mortality, low-birth-weight infants, prolonged pregnancies, and hemorrhaging before and after childbirth (Turner & Collins, 1975; Collins & Turner, 1975). The aspirin substitute acetaminophen appears to be less risky for use during pregnancy (Hill & Kleinberg, 1984b). Unfortunately, there is not enough evidence for researchers to form definite conclusions about the safety of aspirin substitutes and most nonprescription medicines.

ALCOHOL.   Babies of alcoholic mothers may be born with **fetal alcohol syndrome**. These infants suffer many of the following problems: growth retardation, facial malformations, inadequate brain growth leading to mental retardation, heart defects, motor development delay, skeletal defects, hyperac-tivity, and other problems (Abel, 1983). The effects of alcohol may be most severe during the second and third trimesters of pregnancy (Stechler & Halton, 1982). Estimates of the incidence of fetal alcohol syndrome range from 1 in 600 to 1 in 1,500 births (Bachman, 1983). Women who are not

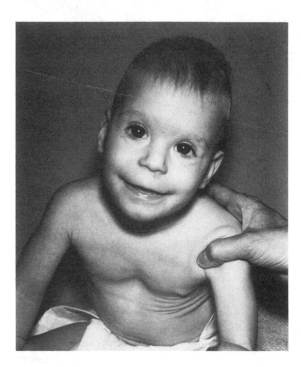

Infant with fetal alcohol syndrome. Notice the thin upper lip and wide, flat nose.

alcoholics, but who drink regularly, have an increased chance of having a spontaneous abortion or a low-birth-weight infant.

Researchers have tried to determine whether there is a safe amount of alcohol that can be consumed during pregnancy. No one has yet been able to determine exactly how much alcohol is necessary to produce fetal alcohol syndrome or other developmental problems. Research evidence indicates that the consumption of one to three alcoholic drinks each day places the fetus at risk for growth retardation (Mills et al., 1984; Niebyl, 1982). There is no evidence from research to indicate that consuming less than one alcoholic drink daily affects birth weight (Stein & Kline, 1983). However, to be totally safe, mothers are advised to avoid consuming alcohol in any amount during pregnancy.

TOBACCO.   When the mother smokes, the fetus smokes. Nicotine and carbon monoxide inhaled while smoking result in a decrease in the supply of oxygen available to the developing baby (Quigley et al., 1979). A massive amount of research evidence exists to document the adverse effects of tobacco smoke on fetal development. The potential problems associated with smoking during pregnancy include

spontaneous abortion (Kullander & Kaellen, 1971)

reduced body weight, length, and head circumference (Miller, Hassanein, & Hensleigh, 1976) increased perinatal mortality rates, including sudden infant death syndrome (Abel, 1983)

preterm birth (Niebyl, 1982)

cleft lip and cleft palate (Abel, 1983)

congenital heart disease (Himmelberger, Brown, & Cohen, 1978)

behavior disorders and learning difficulties (Abel, 1983)

The impact of smoking on the unborn infant may be minimized if the mother quits smoking early in the pregnancy (Gallahue, 1982). However, no period can really be considered safe for smoking during pregnancy.

MARIJUANA.   In contrast to the large amount of research data on alcohol and tobacco, there is very little information about the effects of marijuana on unborn infants. Heavy use of marijuana (six or more times per week) has been statistically associated with preterm births and decreased height at 8 months of age (Barr et al., 1984). However, babies with birth defects and low-birthweight babies do not appear to occur more often among marijuana users (Linn et al., 1983). Until additional information is available, marijuana use during pregnancy should be avoided.

CAFFEINE.   There appears to be little doubt that high doses of caffeine (equivalent to twelve to twenty-four cups of coffee per day) produce birth defects in rats (Hill & Kleinberg, 1984a). A few human studies have associated high caffeine consumption with fetal death, birth defects, and prematurity (Lechat et al., 1980). However, other studies have reported no such adverse effects (Brooten & Jordan, 1983; Linn et al., 1982). To be completely safe, until further evidence is available, expectant mothers should eliminate caffeine from their diets.

Radiation.   Exposure to low doses of radiation during prenatal X-rays may cause childhood tumors, leukemia, and other forms of cancer. A study of twins conducted at the National Cancer Institute (Harvey et al., 1985) found that children who are exposed to X-rays before birth face about two and one-half times the usual risk of cancer. Doctors once routinely X-rayed women patients if a multiple pregnancy was suspected, but this practice has been replaced by other diagnostic procedures.

Maternal Nutrition.   Good nutrition during pregnancy is essential for a successful pregnancy and a healthy baby. Severe malnutrition may cause stillbirth, preterm birth, low birth weight, mental deficiency, and infant death during the first year of life (Annis, 1978). Apparently malnutrition is most harmful during the last three months of pregnancy. This is the period when most of the weight gain and rapid growth of the brain cells occurs (Stein et al., 1974).

Maternal weight gain is considered to be one of the best overall indicators of a healthy pregnancy. Prenatal and infant mortality rates are lowest when maternal weight gains are between 24 and 27 pounds. On the average, weight gains in this range contribute to ideal infant birth weight as well as desirable maternal weight after pregnancy (Gormican, Valentine, & Satter, 1980). However, women who are overweight at the start of pregnancy probably need to gain only around 16 pounds, whereas underweight women may need to gain as much as 30 pounds during pregnancy (Naeye, 1979; Satter, 1983).

Many women report changes in food preferences and eating habits during pregnancy. In addition to pickles and ice cream, some expectant mothers develop a compulsion for eating nonfood substances. This phenomenon is called **pica**. Clay, charcoal, laundry starch, soot, ashes, and coffee grounds are some of the items that may be consumed. Pica should be discouraged because some of the substances may be poisonous to the mother or fetus. Nonfood items replace nutritional foods in the diet and may lead to malnutrition, iron-deficiency anemia, or obesity.

Maternal Age.   The years between 20 and 35 appear to be the "golden age of pregnancy" (Rugh & Shettles, 1971). Teen-age mothers (especially those under 17) experience more complications during the birth process and give birth to more low-birthweight babies, preterm babies, and babies with birth defects than mothers in any other age group. The death rate for babies born to teen-agers is twice as high as that of older mothers (Alan Guttmacher Institute, 1981). However, it is difficult to separate the effects of age alone from the effects of poverty, since teen-agers are more likely than older mothers to be poor before and during pregnancy.

At the other end of the age continuum, fetal and infant mortality rates, genetic abnormalities, and congenital malformations increase as the mother gets older (Naeye, 1983). The risk of having a child with Down's syndrome increases dramatically after a woman reaches age 35. At age 35 the risk is 1 in 365, but at age 45 the chances increase to 1 in 32 (Hook & Lindsjo, 1978).

Age of the Father.   For many years the age of the father was not considered to be as much of a problem as the age of the mother for the outcome of pregnancy. However, researchers are now looking at this factor with a little more concern. For example, Down's syndrome rates double when the father is 55 years old (Stene et al., 1977; Matsungaga et al., 1978). Rare genetic disorders such as achondroplasia, Apert syndrome (facial and limb deformities), and Marfan syndrome (height, vision, and heart abnormalities) are more common among the offspring of fathers over 35 years of age (Evans & Hall, 1976). Congenital deafness and heart disorders may also be linked to the age of the father (Day, 1967).

The father's age may not be as important as the age of the sperm. Apparently sperm go through an aging process in which they become defective over the passage of time. Spermatozoa age in the male reproductive tract after long periods of sexual rest (Vander Vliet & Hafez, 1974). A prolonged interval between insemination and fertilization of the ovum may also cause a sperm to age beyond its optimum quality (Salisbury & Hart, 1970). Aging also occurs in sperm stored for artificial insemination. Spontaneous abortion (Guerrero & Rojas, 1975) and chromosomal abnormalities (Tesh & Glover, 1969) have been linked to aging sperm.

Maternal Emotions. Strong emotional stress, such as fear, anxiety, or anger may result in chemical and endocrine changes in the mother's blood. There is a possibility that the chemicals will enter the developing infant's bloodstream or will direct blood flow away from the placenta. High levels of stress for an extended period of time during pregnancy may increase the chances of giving birth to a baby with such problems as low-birthweight, hyperactivity, cleft palate, and digestive disorders (Stechler & Halton, 1982).

Statements about the effects of maternal emotional states on prenatal development must be made with caution. Folklore about pregnancy and childbirth tends to perpetuate the belief that a mother may "mark" her unborn child through a traumatic experience or strong emotional desires. For example, a mother may believe that her child was born with webbed toes because she was frightened by a frog during pregnancy. There is no scientific evidence to support such beliefs, and connections between birth defects and such maternal experiences are coincidental.

Maternal Health. Physicians monitor the health of the expectant mother very carefully. Illnesses and communicable diseases of the mother during pregnancy may also influence the well-being of the embryo or fetus. For example, if the mother is diabetic, her pregnancy may end abruptly with a miscarriage, or the baby may gain excessive weight or be born with a congenital defect. Iron-deficiency anemia and high blood pressure also are conditions that threaten the developing infant. A small percentage of expectant mothers develop toxemia (preeclampsia). This condition causes swelling and fluid retention, excessive weight gain, and high blood pressure. Severe cases can threaten the life of the mother and baby. Viral infections, such as German measles or herpes, during the first twenty-six weeks of pregnancy, may cause the baby to be born blind, deaf, retarded, or with other problems (Batshaw & Perret, 1981).

RH Factor. Approximately 1 out of every 200 pregnancies is affected by an incompatibility of blood types between mother and fetus. Human blood is either Rh-positive or Rh-negative. The blood type is controlled by the genes. When the mother has Rh-negative blood and the developing baby has Rh-positive blood, an adverse reaction may occur.

The mother's blood and the baby's blood are separated by the placenta. However, during the prenatal period, and especially during the birth process, some of the baby's blood usually leaks into the mother's system. The Rh-negative mother is allergic to the biochemical substances of the Rh-positive blood and produces antibodies to fight off the foreign invaders. Normally, the antibodies do not build up in sufficient quantities to cause a problem during a woman's first pregnancy. However, if the woman has another pregnancy in which the baby is Rh-positive, serious complications may arise. The antibodies from the previous pregnancy destroy the red blood cells of the fetus.

The effects of Rh incompatibility range from mild anemia to deafness, brain damage, cerebral palsy, and death. Fortunately, an injection of Rh immune globulin can be given to the Rh-negative mother soon after an Rh-positive baby is born. The injection prevents the formation of antibodies so that the next Rh-incompatible pregnancy does not have serious complications.

PRENATAL TESTING

The first thirty-eight weeks of human life spent inside the womb are potentially more dangerous than the first thirty-eight years lived in the outside world (Bachman, 1983). Consequently, scientists are continuing to develop sophisticated techniques and equipment for monitoring the fetus and its intrauterine environment. Detection of congenital abnormalities or other critical problems before birth provides parents and their physicians information on which to select from the following alternatives: (1) selective abortion, (2) treatment after term, (3) preterm induced delivery for early treatment, (4) delivery by Caesarean section, (5) possible surgical or medical treatment before birth (Hill & Breckle, 1983).

Ultrasound

Since its introduction in the early 1960s, ultrasound has become the most commonly used technique for prenatal assessment (Hill & Breckle, 1983).

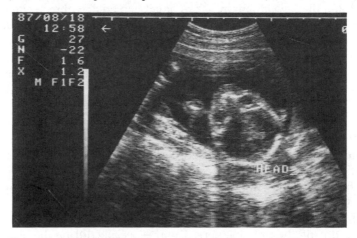

Sonogram of five-month-old fetus.

High-frequency sound waves are bounced off the fetus to form a live video image called a sonogram. In normal pregnancies, obstetricians use ultrasound to establish the age of the fetus (at about 4 to 5 weeks), evaluate fetal growth, and determine the baby's sex (week 16) if a sex-linked disorder is suspected. Ultrasound can be used to locate and examine the condition of the placenta, check for congenital abnormalities, estimate the amount of amniotic fluid, and diagnose a multiple pregnancy (Powledge, 1983).

Ultrasound is more versatile than either X-rays or techniques that invade the uterus, and is considered to be much safer. Short-term studies of children exposed to ultrasound before birth have revealed no obvious harmful effects. Any long-range problems or subtle effects on tissue and behavior are yet to be determined (Stratmeyer & Christman, 1982).

Amniocentesis

In cases for which ultrasound does not provide adequate information about the condition of the fetus, an **amniocentesis** test may be used. Guided by a live sonogram, a skilled physician inserts a hollow needle through the woman's abdominal wall into the amniotic sac. A small amount of fluid containing cells and other substances from the fetus is withdrawn for laboratory analysis. Laboratory analysis detects the presence of numerous genetic diseases, including chromosomal errors, biochemical disorders, and defects in the nervous system.

Unfortunately, amniocentesis cannot be used until sufficient fluid is available for the test, around 16 to 20 weeks. The procedure is rather expensive and involves a three- to four-week waiting period to obtain the test results. Another disadvantage of amniocentesis is the risk of injury to the fetus, spontaneous abortion, or infection. Statistics indicate that amniocentesis performed in the second quarter of pregnancy increases the risk of spontaneous abortion almost 50 percent (Kaiser, 1982). The chances of fetal injury are uncertain, but estimates indicate that there may be 4 to 6 fetal injuries out of each 200 testing procedures. However, the risk factor is usually considered small in comparison to the benefits of the procedure.

Blood and Urine Tests

Maternal blood or urine samples are sometimes analyzed for concentrations of an estrogen substance called estriol. Steadily increasing amounts of estriol are associated with a healthy pregnancy, whereas a decrease in the chemical may indicate a dangerous change in the welfare of the fetus. This test is especially useful in monitoring the pregnancy of a mother who has diabetes or hypertension or an overdue delivery. The mother's blood may also be tested for the presence of a chemical—AfP—that is a sign of a brain defect in the fetus. Blood and urine tests are not extremely accurate and are used mainly in combination with other tests (Franz, 1983).

Chorionic Villus Sampling

Physicians sometimes use a procedure called **chorionic villus sampling** (CVS) to diagnose genetic diseases early in the first trimester of pregnancy before amniocentesis can be safely performed. The ninth and tenth gestational weeks are considered to be the most suitable time for this procedure, although it is sometimes performed a little earlier (Brambati & Oldrini, 1986). A live sonogram is used to guide a surgical tool through the birth canal to the fetal chorion. A sample of the chorionic tissue, which presumably contains the same genetic material as the fetus, is obtained. The tissue is analyzed to determine whether suspected chromosomal, metabolic, or blood disorders are present. The risks of this procedure to the fetus or the mother are generally considered to be minimal. However, since CVS is relatively new, additional evidence is needed to fully evaluate the safety and accuracy of this diagnostic approach (Brambati & Oldrini, 1986).

Fetoscopy

With the use of an instrument called a **fetoscope** and special lighting equipment, doctors can look at the fetus inside the womb. The fetoscope is attached to a hollow needle and inserted into the amniotic cavity as in the amniotic procedure. The fetus can then be visually inspected for physical abnormalities such as cleft palate or defective limbs. Samples of fetal blood and cells from the fetal membranes can also be obtained. The same procedure is occasionally used to conduct corrective surgery on the fetus before birth. Fetoscopy is not used until after the sixteenth week of pregnancy.

GENETIC COUNSELING

A genetic counselor can help prospective parents assess their chances of having a child with a genetic disease. Prospective parents should seek genetic counseling if any of the following conditions apply: (1) either one has a blood relative with a genetic disorder, (2) they have had three or more miscarriages, (3) they already have a child with a genetic disorder or with abnormal physical or behavioral development, (4) the female is over 35 years of age, (5) they are members of an ethnic group with specific genetic disorders such as Tay-Sachs disease or sickle-cell anemia, and (6) either one has a history of drug use, exposure to industrial chemicals, or other possible teratogens (Bachman, 1983).

SUMMARY

1. Fertilization of the mother's ovum by the father's sperm cell takes place in the fallopian tube. The prenatal period, which begins with fertilization, is divided into three stages: germinal, embryonic, and fetal.

2. During the germinal stage, the fertilized ovum, called a zygote, changes into a morula (16 cells), and a blastocyst (58 cells). The blastocyst begins to implant itself in the lining of the uterus around day 6. Occasionally an ectopic pregnancy occurs when the blastocyst is implanted outside the uterus.

3. The embryonic period begins with the formation of the embryonic disc around the eighth day and continues until the eighth week of pregnancy. The growth that takes place during this period is rapid and dramatic. The size and appearance of the embryo change almost daily. The chorion, placenta, amnion, and umbilical cord develop early as supporting membranes for the embryo. By the end of this period the beginnings of all limbs and internal organs and the skeleton have been established. The heart is pumping blood; the kidneys and other organs are beginning to function.

4. The fetal stage begins at the ninth week and continues until the baby is born. The name change from embryo to fetus signifies the completion of the human form and the appearance of the first bone cells in the cartilage of the skeleton. The body structures and organ systems develop further. The sex of the fetus is distinguishable. By midpregnancy, the fetus begins to move and is covered with lanugo and vernix caseosa. The complete set of neuronal cells are present in the brain. The process of myelination of the nerve cells has also begun. During the last two months of pregnancy, the fetus gains weight rapidly, increases in length, and practices many of the functions that are necessary for life in the world outside the womb.

5. Both genetic and environmental factors influence growth and development during the prenatal period. The genes and chromosomes are responsible for such characteristics as sex and eye color. Defective genes and chromosomes result in many handicapping conditions, including Down's syndrome, phenylketonuria, and cystic fibrosis.

6. Numerous drugs, viruses, and other environmental factors have been associated with birth defects and developmental problems. The list of substances pregnant women should avoid includes a variety of drugs and medications, alcohol, tobacco, marijuana, large quantities of caffeine, and exposure to radiation. Inadequate nutrition during pregnancy also may cause problems such as low birth weight and mental deficiency. Maternal age, paternal age, maternal stress, and blood incompatibility are additional risk factors.

7. Techniques that are used to monitor the condition of the baby and to detect developmental problems include ultrasound, amniocentesis, blood and urine tests, chorionic villus sampling, and fetoscopy. Information obtained from tests performed before pregnancy and during the early stages of prenatal development can be used to provide genetic counseling to the parents.

2

The Birth Process

'Issues from the hand of God, the simple soul'
To a flat world of changing lights and noise, . . .
Moving between the legs of tables and of chairs,
Rising or falling, grasping at kisses and toys, . . .
Eager to be reassured, taking pleasure
In the fragrant briliance of the Christmas tree, . . .
Pray for us now and at the hour of our birth.

−T. S. Eliot

Childbirth is a relatively brief period of transition between prenatal development and life in the outside world. Montagu (1964) refers to birth as a bridge between two stages of life. The birth process is marked by a series of dramatic events affecting all the participants. For the fetus, the tranquility of the mother's womb is abruptly interrupted, for better or worse, by powerful forces projecting the fetus through the birth canal. For the parents, particularly the mother, the months of waiting are coming to an end, but only after a few more exciting and stressful hours. For the physicians, nurses, or other birth attendants, decisions must be made about when and how to assist mother and baby in the process.

This chapter explores the physiology of labor, how labor begins, and what happens during each of the three stages of childbirth. The various types of delivery, the use of medication, contemporary methods of prepared childbirth, and the participation of the father in the birth process, are discussed. In addition, we take a look at alternatives available for labor, delivery, and care of the baby after birth.

PHYSIOLOGY OF LABOR

The process of childbirth is commonly referred to as labor because the mother works to give birth. Normally she exerts a considerable amount of energy in pushing the baby out of the uterus. However, the process is more complex than the term *labor* implies. Labor is affected by the interplay of various physiological conditions, including hormonal substances, contractions of the uterus, dilation of the cervix, and the position of the fetus. In addition, psychological factors such as the mother's anxiety level and pain threshold play important roles.

Onset of Labor

Approximately 95 percent of all babies are born within two weeks of their expected delivery date. The date of birth can be estimated but not accurately predicted. Actually, scientists do not clearly understand what causes labor to begin. The answer to this mystery is obviously very important for predicting and controlling labor as well as for preventing premature births.

Researchers have tried for years to identify the factors that lead to the onset of labor. In addition to finding the mechanism controlling labor, scientists are also faced with the task of identifying whether the mother, the fetus, or both are responsible for its initiation. The most recent investigations have focused on the identification of hormones and other chemical substances that may, either singly, or in combination, trigger the birth process. Oxytocin, cortisol, progesterone, and estrogen are some of the hormones that have been associated with the beginning and maintenance of labor contractions.

Research studies on prostaglandin activity appear to offer the most promising clue to the mystery of human labor. Prostaglandins are members of a group of substances known as fatty acids, which are found in most body tissues and fluids. Scientists have identified at least fourteen prostaglandins that influence a variety of bodily functions, such as muscle contractions, blood pressure, reproduction, and secretion of stomach acid.

Prostaglandins (PGs) have been found to be effective in inducing labor and in ripening of the cervix at any stage of pregnancy. Chemical substances that interfere with the absorption of PGs in the body inhibit labor (Gravett, 1984; Pritchard, MacDonald & Gant, 1985). The evidence is still too fragmentary to determine whether the PGs responsible for labor originate in tissues of the fetus or the mother. Some scientists (Gravett, 1984; Liggins, 1979) believe that the chorion and the amnion play a major role in the release of the prostaglandins that initiate labor. Others (Pritchard et al., 1985) speculate that the fetus sends a biochemical message to its mother, perhaps through the urine, to increase the formation or absorption of PGs in sufficient amounts for labor to begin.

Induced Labor

In some cases, labor is started by artificial methods such as injections of prostaglandins, oxoytocin, or rupture of the fetal membranes (amniotomy). The reasons for inducing labor are many and varied. Labor is usually induced as a response to a prolonged pregnancy or complications such as maternal diabetes, bleeding, excessive amniotic fluid, RH incompatibility, toxemia (infection), failure of labor to begin within 24 hours after rupture of fetal membranes, or intrauterine fetal death.

Induced labor may also be done because the patient lives a long distance from the hospital or simply for the convenience of the parents, the doctor, or both. Many people oppose routine induction of labor because it is more unpredictable, complicated, painful, and stressful for both mother and baby (Hawkins & Higgins, 1981).

Contractions

The onset of labor is signaled by regular contractions of the uterus. A labor contraction is the tightening and shortening of the muscles in the uterus. The mother has no control over the contractions. When labor begins, the

Placenta

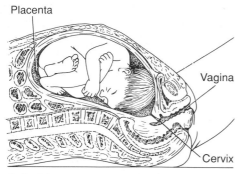

Vagina

Cervix

A. Prelabor. The cervix is thick and closed.

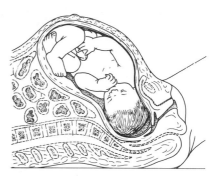

B. Early labor. Contractions, dilation, effacement and head engagement.

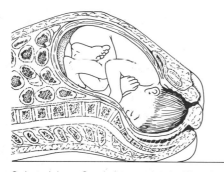

C. Late labor. Cervix is completely dilated; head is in the birth canal.

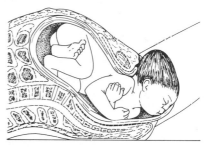

D. Delivery. Baby's head begins to emerge.

FIGURE 2-1 Labor and Delivery.

contractions are usually 10 to 30 minutes apart and last for 30 to 45 seconds. At the end of labor, the contractions are closer together and last from 60 to 90 seconds.

Contractions usually begin at the top of the uterus and move downward, reaching a peak and then becoming weaker. Occasionally the progress of labor is impaired by reverse contractions, which begin in the lower part of the uterus and move upward, or uncoordinated contractions in different parts of the uterus. The contractions become stronger, last longer, and get closer together as labor progresses. During the process, the baby's head is pushed into the lower part of the uterus. As labor progresses, the upper part of the uterus becomes thicker and smaller, while the lower portion stretches thinner and larger. The uterus is slowly pulled upward, as if a turtleneck sweater is being pulled over the baby's head (Oxorn, 1980).

Braxton Hicks Contractions (False Labor)

Throughout pregnancy the muscles of the uterus occasionally contract in what is referred to as Braxton Hicks contractions. These contractions are usually not strong enough to be felt by the mother until approximately the last month of pregnancy. Braxton Hicks contractions are sometimes referred to as "false labor" because the mother may believe that labor has begun. These contractions are irregular and short. In contrast, however, true labor contractions occur at regular intervals, while gradually increasing in strength and frequency (Oxorn, 1980).

Dilation and Effacement

The **cervix** is the lower part, or mouth, of the uterus that protrudes into the vagina (see Figure 2-1). During most of the pregnancy the cervix is about 1 inch (2.5 centimeters) long, with an opening about the width of the end of an unsharpened pencil (Oxorn, 1980). During pregnancy the opening is closed with a mucous plug to protect the fetus.

Toward the end of the prenatal period, physical and chemical changes in the uterus soften or "ripen" the cervix in preparation for the birth process. During labor, the cervix becomes shorter and thinner through the process of **effacement**. Before the baby can leave the uterus, the cervix must open to its widest capacity, which is about 4 inches (10 centimeters), or about the size of five fingers on an average hand. This process is called **dilation** (also *dilatation*). Usually effacement and dilation occur simultaneously.

This woman is having a labor contraction. The father provides assistance and support.

STAGES OF LABOR
Preliminary Signs

Toward the end of pregnancy there are a number of signs that labor is approaching. Approximately two to four weeks before labor begins, the head of the fetus usually moves or "drops" downward into the pelvic cavity. This is called "lightening," since there is less pressure on the mother's diaphragm, allowing her to breathe more freely. Other warning signs include a pink vaginal discharge or a bloody "show" caused by the loss of the mucous plug from the cervical opening. Diarrhea, stomach upset, increased Braxton Hicks contractions, low back pain, and 2-to-5-pound loss of weight are other pre-labor symptoms.

In some cases, the amniotic sac breaks before a labor begins. There may be a sudden gush of water or a slow leak, depending on the size of the break in the membranes. In most cases (85 percent), labor begins within 24 hours after the amniotic sac breaks. The major problem the mother faces is the risk of infection. Some physicians induce labor within 3 to 12 hours, but others recommend waiting at least 24 hours for spontaneous labor to begin (Conway et al., 1984).

Position of the Fetus

The process of labor is dramatically affected by the position of the fetus and the body part that first enters the birth canal. Approximately 96 percent of all babies are born in the head-first (vertex or cephalic) position as shown in Figure 2-2 (Hamilton, 1984). Ideally, the smallest part of the baby's head is directed down the birth canal first, with the face turned toward the spinal column. However, the presenting part may be the face or the brow, with the head turned, in relation to the spinal column, at one of a variety of angles.

In approximately 3 to 4 percent of pregnancies, the fetus is in a **breech** position when labor begins (Hamilton, 1984). In a breech delivery, the baby is born with the buttocks, feet, or knees first, A variety of breech presentations are possible (Fig. 2-2). The **frank** breech is the most common, in which both feet are extended straight up beside the ears, and the buttocks enter the birth canal first. In a **full** or **complete** breech, the buttocks are born first, while the knees are drawn against the stomach and the feet extended downward. Breech births also occur in which the feet (footling) or knees (kneeling) are born first.

Breech births are more difficult and may take longer than normal births. The contractions are not as efficient in pushing the baby out because the largest part of the baby, the head, follows the smallest parts, the buttocks and feet. In a few deliveries (less than 1 percent) (Hamilton, 1984), the fetus is turned crosswise in the uterus in a transverse presentation (Fig. 2-2). The shoulder blade is typically positioned in the birth canal. In a transverse presentation, the baby must either be turned or be surgically removed through a Caesarean section.

1. Vertex presentation

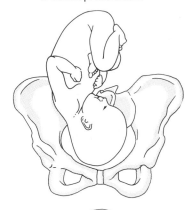

2. Transverse lie

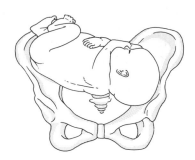

3. Breech

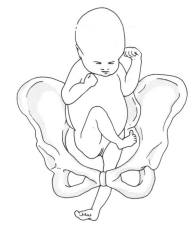

A. Complete breech

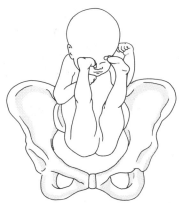

B. Frank breech

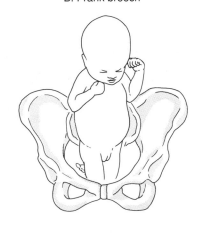

C. Footling breech

D. Kneeling breech

FIGURE 2-2   Possible Positions of Fetus During Labor.
Source: H. Oxorn, *Oxorn-Foote Human Labor and Birth,* 4th ed., Appleton-Century-Crofts, New York, 1980. Adapted by permission.

Dilation of the Cervix

The first stage of labor begins with the first true contractions of the uterus and ends when the cervix is completely effaced and dilated. The first stage of the birth process is the longest. In many cases, the father stays with the mother throughout labor and delivery to provide emotional support and assistance.

The dilation stage typically lasts from 6 to 18 hours for women delivering their first baby (primaparas), and 2 to 6 hours for the second and subsequent deliveries (mutiparas). The time, however, varies widely with individuals. This first stage is divided into three phases: latent, active, and transition.

Latent phase. Contractions during the latent phase are usually mild in intensity. They occur from 15 to 20 minutes apart and last about 30 seconds. A calm and relaxed attitude by the mother tends to speed up dilation and decreases the amount of time needed to complete this phase. Under normal conditions, mothers are advised to walk around rather than lie down. The latent phase may last 8 hours or more for primaparas but is usually shorter (5 hours or less) for women having a second or third baby.

Active phase. The mother enters the active phase when the cervix is fully effaced and dilated—about 1½ inches (4 centimeters). The time between contractions decreases to about 2 to 5 minutes. The contractions last longer (45 to 60 seconds) and increase in intensity. Some women with uncomplicated labor wait until this phase to enter the hospital (Parfitt, 1977). The spontaneous rupture of the membranes most often occurs sometime during the active phases (Pritchard et al., 1985). The time needed to complete the active phase is usually 4 hours for primaparas and 2 hours for multiparas (Moore, 1977).

Transition. The transition phase covers the last inch of dilation (3–4 in.; 7–10 cm.) This is the most difficult time during childbirth. The contractions are stronger, last longer, and are closer together. These contractions have been compared to the ocean waves on a beach during a storm, with one coming in on top of another. Feelings of irritability, discouragement, loss of control, and panic are common. Other difficulties include hot and cold flashes, disorientation, nausea, and vomiting. The mother usually feels a strong desire to push, comparable to having a bowel movement. Fortunately the transition phase is relatively short, lasting 30 to 60 minutes for primaparas, and about 20 to 30 minutes for multiparas (Hassid, 1984).

Expulsion

The second stage of labor begins as soon as the cervix is completely open. This stage is usually a welcome relief after the difficult transition phase. The time between contractions decreases to 3 to 5 minutes, and the mother has a chance to recover her equilibrium. The mother can now use her abdominal muscles and diaphragm to help push the baby out of the birth canal. The baby is usually born within 1 to 2 hours after this stage begins. For multiparas, however, expulsion may last only about 20 minutes (Hamilton, 1984).

If the baby is in the head-first position, the head advances through the birth canal with each contraction and recedes slightly as the uterus relaxes, as if taking two steps forward and one step back. The baby's head must rotate to move through the mother's pelvic structure. The top of the head eventually becomes visible at the vaginal opening. The term **crowning** is used when the largest part of the scalp appears and does not recede between contractions.

About the time an inch (3 centimeters) of the baby's head is visible, the physician usually makes a surgical incision (**episiotomy**) in the perineum—the tissue between the vagina and rectum. The routine performance of episiotemies is controversial and has been questioned as unnecessary surgery (Thacker & Banta, 1983). Some physicians argue, however, that a neat, controlled surgical incision is easier to repair and heals better than a ragged, uncontrolled natural tear (Pritchard et al., 1985).

Once the baby's head is out of the birth canal, the head rotates to become aligned with the baby's shoulders. The shoulders must also rotate to pass through the pelvic structure. First one shoulder emerges and then the other, followed by the buttocks and lower limbs. This part is relatively easy, since the larger head has paved the way.

When the baby emerges from the uterus, the umbilical cord is still attached. Some physicians keep the baby below the vaginal opening and wait about 30 seconds before clamping the cord (Pritchard et al., 1985). Others wait until the cord stops pulsating (Parfitt, 1977).

Placental Expulsion

The third stage of labor begins as soon as the baby is completely out of the birth canal and ends with the expulsion of the placenta and fetal membranes (the afterbirth). This stage usually lasts about 10 to 30 minutes. If it extends beyond 30 minutes, the danger of excessive bleeding becomes a problem.

As soon as the baby is born, the contractions usually stop for a few minutes and then start again to expel the placenta. The uterus shrinks dramatically so that the implantation site of the placenta is reduced. Since the placenta stays the same size, it separates or "peels off" from the lining of the uterus and is expelled during the final contractions.

Recovery

The recovery stage usually lasts for about an hour after the delivery of the placenta is complete. However, the length of this stage varies with hospital and cultural practices. During this period, the mother and baby are carefully observed for complications of the birth process. The episiotomy and any tears in the vaginal tissue are stitched and repaired. The stage of expulsion and the first hour after birth are considered to be the most dangerous period in the birth process for the mother because of the danger of excessive bleeding.

CAESAREAN DELIVERY

A variety of conditions can prevent or interfere with a vaginal childbirth. When something does happen, the baby is removed through a surgical incision in the abdomen and uterus, called a **Caesarean section** (C-section). The transverse position of the fetus, failure of the cervix to dilate, obstructions in the uterus or pelvis, and signs of fetal distress are some of the conditions that might necessitate a Caesarean delivery (Hawkins & Higgins, 1981).

The number of Caesarean births has more than quadrupled in the last sixteen years, rising from 5.5 percent of all deliveries in 1970 to 24 percent in 1986 (Greenville Daily Reflector, 1987). This trend has been accompanied by the use of local anesthesia in uncomplicated cases, allowing the mother to be awake and aware of the child's birth. In some cases, the father can also be present for the delivery. The increase in C-sections has been attributed to (1) improved techniques in surgery and anesthesia, (2) more concern about handicaps resulting from complications in vaginal deliveries, and (3) use of more sophisticated fetal monitoring techniques to indicate fetal distress (Hawkins & Higgins, 1981).

Even under ideal conditions, the surgical procedures involved in C-sections are a greater risk for the mother than normal vaginal delivery (Brengman & Burns, 1983). Consequently, the rising number of Caesarean births has become a concern among physicians and public health officials. Approximately one-third to one-half of all C-sections are performed because the mother had a previous delivery by this method (Jarrell, Ashmead & Mann, 1985). In the past, obstetricians took the position that once a C-section is performed, the mother must have all future deliveries in the same way, to avoid the possibility of the uterus rupturing during labor at the site of the previous incision. The results of recent studies indicate that normal labor and delivery are possible for the majority of carefully screened patients who had a previous Caesarean delivery (Brengman & Burns, 1983; Jarrell et al., 1985).

MULTIPLE BIRTHS

Labor and delivery of more than one fetus presents special problems. The extra crowding of the uterus frequently results in early rupture of the membranes, leading to premature labor. Although labor and delivery proceed satisfactorily in most cases, the overstretching of the uterus sometimes causes weak and inefficient contractions, delaying the progress of labor. There is also an increased risk of maternal bleeding after the birth process has been completed (Oxorn, 1980).

The birth of twins and other multiple conceptions may be complicated by the position of the fetuses. Usually both twins are in the ideal head-first position when labor begins, but other combinations of positions are possible. The second twin faces a greater risk because it occupies the less favorable position, and the uterine capacity to supply oxygen to the placenta may be reduced after the first twin is born. In most cases (80 percent) the second twin is born within 30 minutes of the first twin (Oxorn, 1980).

USE OF FORCEPS

Obstetrical forceps are used in some deliveries to rotate the baby's head and help the baby through the birth canal. Forceps are generally shaped like salad tongs, but they come in a variety of designs for specific applications. A physician may resort to the use of forceps when the mother cannot push the baby out because of exhaustion or the effects of medication. This instrument may also be used to speed delivery in case of an emergency such as fetal distress.

The use of forceps is controversial because of the risk of injury to the baby or mother (Hassid, 1984). The possibility of injury is greatest when forceps are applied before the baby's head is engaged in the pelvic opening. Numerous studies have consistently documented the adverse effects of using forceps before the baby's head has reached the vaginal opening. The problems identified include physical injuries and reduced long-range intelligence scores (Freedman et al., 1984; Painti, 1982). In recent years, the trend has been away from the use of forceps (Traub et al., 1984).

POSITION OF THE MOTHER

Women in different cultures labor and give birth in a variety of positions, including kneeling, squatting, standing, sitting, or on hands and knees (Capalbo-Moore & Jacobellis, 1983; Rosser, 1983). In American culture the mother usually labors and delivers while lying on her back in what is sometimes called the "stranded turtle" position. During delivery, the head of the delivery table is raised and the mother's knees are bent toward the abdomen with the feet flat on the surface or in stirrups (Hamilton, 1984).

Some physicians now encourage the mother to choose the position that is most confortable for labor and delivery (Rosser, 1983). Researchers are beginning to study the effects of various maternal positions on the length of labor and on the safety and comfort of the mother and baby. A few studies have found that when women stand, sit, walk around, and explore various positions, labor is often easier and faster (Hawkins & Higgins, 1981; Kurokawa & Zilkoski, 1985). Not all studies (e.g., McManus & Calder, 1978; Williams, Thom, & Studd, 1980) support this conclulsion, however.

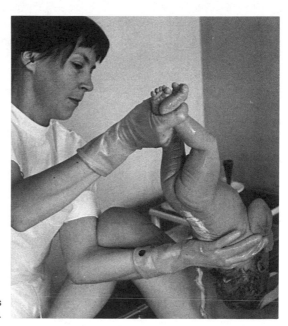

This baby was born while the mother was in a semi-reclining position on her back.

PAIN AND LABOR

The reality of childbirth pain is universal and well documented. Melzack (1984) reviewed studies that found that labor ranks among the most intense types of pain recorded by women in all cultures. There are many causes of pain during labor and delivery, including both physiological and psychological. The contractions of the uterus restrict the blood supply to the muscles, creating a painful shortage of oxygen. Pain signals are sent to the brain by the stretching of the cervix and other organs, as well as the pressure and friction on sensitive nerve endings by the baby's descent through the birth canal.

People vary widely in their anatomy as well as in their sensitivity to pain. The mother's pelvic structure and the size of the baby affect the extent to which labor is painful. In addition, the amount of pain actually experienced may be increased or diminished by the mother's emotional state. Fear, anxiety, and stress create muscle tension and may initiate chemical changes that intensify the pain of labor and delivery.

METHODS OF PAIN RELIEF

Before the discovery of ether and chloroform in the mid-1800s, people resorted to chants, rituals, body contortions, and folk medicine in attempts to find relief from the pain of childbirth. Currently, there are numerous obstetric medications as well as hypnosis and prepared childbirth training that alleviate childbirth pain. A total of fifty-three drugs that are used during labor and delivery have been identified (Brackbill, McManus, & Woodward, 1985). Depending upon their functions, obstetric medications can be broadly classified as analgesics, sedatives, tranquilizers, and anesthetics. In many cases, various types of drugs are combined to produce multiple effects.

Analgesics

Medicines such as aspirin, which prevent or relieve pain without causing a loss of consciousness, are called **analgesics**. Narcotics are considered to be the most effective analgesics available (Brackbill, 1979) and are widely used during labor and delivery. Meperidine (Demerol) is the most popular obstetric pain killer in the world (Brackbill, 1979; Pritchard et al., 1985). Unfortunately, narcotics rapidly cross the placenta and may impair respiratory functions of the newborn infant. In some cases a type of drug known as narcotic antagonists is administered to the newborn after birth to counteract these effects.

Sedatives and Tranquilizers

A variety of sedatives and tranquilizers are given during labor to reduce the mother's anxiety and excitement. When taken in sufficient doses, sedatives and some tranquilizers induce drowsiness or sleep. Sedatives and tranquilizers are frequently used to heighten the effects of other medications and to reduce the total amount of medication needed. For example, meperidine (analgesic) and promethazine (tranquilizer) are frequently used together (Pritchard et al., 1985). Promethazine (Phenergan) is a tranquilizer that is used widely for obstetric purposes, but hospitals and physicans vary widely in the specific medications they prefer to administer.

Anesthesia

Anesthetics are used to bring about partial or complete loss of sensation, either by inducing unconsciousness or by blocking the conduction of nerve inpulses. Anesthetics are classified as general or regional (local), depending upon their effect.

General anesthesia affects the entire body and usually induces partial or total unconsciousness. This type of medication is administered in the form of gas or an intravenous solution. Heavy doses of general anesthesia are seldom used during normal labor because it adversely affects the central nervous system of both mother and baby. In addition, they can cause the mother to choke on her own gastric juices. In some cases, light doses of inhalent anesthesia are self-administered through a small face mask for a few seconds during the strongest contractions.

Regional anesthetics   are substances that cause loss of feeling in a particular area of the body. A drug similar to Novocain is administered in a single injection or by continuous conduction through a small tube. The major advantage of regional anesthesia over other obstetric medications is that it allows the mother to remain conscious and alert during the birth process. As with any medication, the main disadvantage of a regional anesthetic is the side effects. Mothers who receive regional anesthesia sometimes experience reduced blood pressure, severe headaches, and convulsions. If given too early, or in large doses, these substances interfere with contractions, delay labor, and increase the need for the use of forceps.

EFFECTS OF OBSTETRIC MEDICATION

Women consume an average of seven different drugs during labor and delivery (Doering & Stewart, 1978). Most drugs rapidly cross the placenta and accumulate in the bloodstream and in organs of the baby. The detrimental effects on the respiratory efforts of the baby immediately after birth are clearly observable. Scientists have been concerned about possible temporary or permanent behavioral effects on the developing infant.

Numerous studies have examined the effects of obstetric medications on infant behavior. The results of the research reports have been summarized as follows (Brackbill et al., 1985): (1) Forty-seven of the studies found that obstetric medication adversely affected one or more infant behaviors, such as information processing efficiency and attention. (2) None of the studies showed that the medication enhanced or improved infant behavior. (3) The extent of the behavioral effects was related to the potency of the drug. General anesthesia was the worst offender, whereas regional anesthesia had the least impact on the behaviors studied. (4) Few studies tested for the effects of medication beyond 6 weeks of age, and none of the studies tested beyond the first year. Therefore, long-term effects cannot be ruled out.

PREPARED CHILDBIRTH TRAINING

Many women attempt to avoid or minimize the use of medication during child birth through childbirth preparation classes. Prepared childbirth training has gained popularity since the 1960s as the result of concerns about the undesirable effects of medication and the desire of both mothers and fathers to partaicipate more actively in the birth process (Gordan & Haire, 1981). There are several specific methods of prepared childbirth. The two most widely used approaches are the Read and the Lamaze methods. But many others, such as the Bradley method, are also used.

Read Method

Prepared childbirth training was introduced in the United States in the

1940s by Grantley Dick-Read, an English obstetrician (Feldman, 1978). Dick-Read believed that childbirth pain is intensified by the mother's fear and anxiety, which cause the muscles to become tense. If the muscles are tense, the contractions are more difficult and painful. The increased pain leads to greater anxiety, which in turn causes more muscle tension, creating a cyclical effect. The Read method, which is sometimes called *natural childbirth*, interrupts the fear-tension-pain cycle through mental and physical preparation for childbirth. The training sessions include information about the physiology of labor and delivery, abdominal breathing exercises, relaxation techniques, positions for labor, and various body-conditioning exercises. The presence and encouragement of the father, who serves as a coach during labor and delivery, is considered important but not mandatory (Dick-Read, 1972).

Lamaze Method

The Lamaze method was developed by French obstetrician Fernand Lamaze (Lamaze, 1970). His approach is similar to the Read method but includes a much more structured and systematic set of instructions. Lamaze based his method on Pavlov's theory that responses can be conditioned and controlled through learning. The mother typically goes through a series of six lessons during which she learns a combination of breathing and relaxation exercises to use during the various stages of labor and delivery. As in the Read method, physical exercises and information about the physiology of labor are also included. Lamaze stressed the importance of the father (or a substitute) participating in the classes with the mother and serving as the labor leader or coach, providing emotional support and physical assistance during labor and birth.

Lamaze (1970) believed that "the pain of childbirth is neither necessary nor inevitable (p. 41)." Although contemporary Lamaze instructors do not emphasize the pain of childbirth, they recognize its reality. The goal of Lamaze training is not necessarily to eliminate pain, but to control it and make childbirth a positive experience (Ewy & Ewy, 1982). Medication for pain relief is available if needed. The Lamaze method is the most widely used approach to preparation for childbirth (Burroughs, 1986).

Bradley Method

The Bradley method of prepared childbirth (Bradley, 1974) is much less structured or specific than either the Lamaze or Read method. Relaxation, physical and breathing exercises are demonstrated in a series of eight sessions. However, each couple is expected to find its own ways to relax and cope with the labor and delivery processes. Emphasis is placed on creating darkness and quiet and controlling other environmental variables to facilitate relaxation (Burroughs, 1986). The method is also referred to as husband-coached childbirth because the supportive role of the husband is an essential part of the process. Advocates of the Bradley method are very strongly opposed to the use of any type of medication during the birth process (Feldman, 1978).

Hypnosis

Some mothers elect to use hypnosis as an alternative to medication to control childbirth pain. There are different methods of hypnosis that vary with practitioners. The benefits of hypnosis have been favorably compared with those of prepared childbirth training (Parfitt, 1977). However, this approach is not widely used because obstetric personnel usually do not have the special training and skills needed to use hypnosis.

EFFECTS OF PREPARED CHILDBIRTH TRAINING

Research studies generally support claims that women who participate in prepared childbirth training tend to (1) experience reduced pain during labor and delivery, (2) have less need for medication, (3) have lowered rates of forceps delivery, and (4) demonstrate a more positive attitude toward childbirth than women who do not receive such training (Cogan, 1980). However, the results of prepared childbirth training vary widely with instructors and individual patients. Although such classes are effective in reducing pain, most participants eventually request medication during labor or delivery (Melzack, 1984). Childbirth educators are sometimes criticized for minimizing the reality and individual variability of childbirth pain (Lumley & Astbury, 1980).

LEBOYER METHOD

The methods of prepared childbirth discussed up to this point are procedures designed to control pain during labor and delivery. The Leboyer method is different from the others in that it involves procedures for controlling the environment in the delivery room and for handling the infant during the first few minutes after birth. French obstetrician Frederick Leboyer (1975) believes that the process of birth is traumatic for the infant and potentially leads to emotional difficulties later in life. Leboyer's method of gentle birth, sometimes called "birth without violence," is designed to help minimize the shock of the birth experience and make the transition from the uterus to the outside world easier. The delivery room is warm and quiet. The lights are dim as the baby emerges from the uterus. The newborn baby is handled gently and placed on the mother's stomach, where it is lightly massaged until the umbilical cord stops pulsating. The baby is then moved to a tub of warm bath water designed to resemble the uterine environment.

One of the first follow-up studies (Rappoport, 1976) of babies born with the Leboyer procedures indicated that they walked sooner than the average

age, were easily toilet trained, and developed self-feeding skills earlier than average. Many displayed ambidextrous use of their hands. However, additional studies (Maziade et al., 1986; Nelson et al., 1980) have found no differences between Leboyer babies and babies born in traditional environments on measures of crying, motor performance, cognitive functioning or temperament. Consequently, further evidence is needed before the effectiveness of Leboyer's approach can be assessed more completely.

FATHERS' PARTICIPATION

An important outcome of the prepared childbirth movement in the United States has been increased participation by fathers in the birth process. A few years ago hospitals were very reluctant to allow fathers to go into the delivery room because of concerns about increasing the risk of infection and about legal issues that might arise. Hospital personnel also feared that the husband would faint or otherwise interfere with the birth process. However, most hospitals now routinely allow the father to enter the labor and delivery room if he wishes. Approximately 75 percent of fathers are now present during hospital deliveries (Philips & Anzalone, 1982). The use of local anesthesia makes it possible for the father to attend even a Caesarean birth.

ALTERNATIVES IN CHILDBIRTH AND HOSPITAL CARE

Rooming-In

The traditional hospital routine for postpartum (afterbirth) care, has been to keep the baby in the nursery while the mother stays in a separate room, except at feeding and visitation times. This arrangement allows the mother to rest and recover from the birth process before assuming full-time care of the baby.

Hospitals have responded to parental demands for family-centered childbirth and maternity care as well as professional concerns about the effects of early separation of mother and infant. Most hospitals now allow patients to choose a "rooming-in" arrangement in which the baby stays in a private room with the mother immediately after birth or as soon as she desires. Proponents of rooming-in believe that it facilitates parent-child attachment while allowing new parents to practice child care skills under the supervision of the hospital staff. In this arrangement, the father is allowed to visit and participate in the care of the baby. Also, more and more hospitals are allowing siblings to visit the mother and baby. Such practices help other members of the family feel included in the birth process and help in the transition of accepting the new arrival.

Home Delivery

Until 1940, more than half of all babies in the United States were born at home. By 1979, however, 99 percent of all births were carried out in hospital settings (National Center for Health Statistics, 1984). In recent years there has been a resurgence of interest in home births, especially among middle-class parents.

Advocates of childbirth at home believe that women should have the choice of giving birth in the privacy of a relaxed environment where obstetric medication is not encouraged and where the support of family members makes the birth experience a more satisfying personal event (Sagor et al., 1983). From their perspective, a home delivery is as safe as a hospital and possibly safer because of the absence of elective invasive surgical procedures. Opponents of planned home birth believe that the hospital is the safest place to give birth. If an unexpected emergency should occur, medical equipment and expertise are immediately available.

Mehl and Peterson (1981) compared home births with hospital births and found no significant difference in the death rates or other risk factors, such as prolonged labor or fetal oxygen deprivation. The risk of a serious emergency occurring in a home delivery has been estimated as less than 1 in 1,000 cases for low-risk pregnancies (Sagor et al., 1983). Women considering having a home delivery must thus weigh the small risk in relation to the anticipated benefits. In any event, a planned home birth without the support of a competent attendant increases the risk and is not advisable.

Midwives

In recent years there has been an increased interest in the use of midwives for childbirth, both at home and in the hospital (National Center for Health Statistics, 1984). People who call themselves midwives can be classified either as lay midwives or as nurse midwives. A lay midwife is a person who has learned by experience and apprenticeship to help mothers give birth. They vary widely in knowledge and skill and typically have little formal training or credentials. A midwife who has completed nurse's training plus a special program in obstetrics is certified as a nurse-midwife by the American College of Nurse-Midwives. Research studies have found that skilled midwives who are backed up by medical resources have records of successful births comparable to those of physicians (Gordon & Haire, 1981; Devitt, 1979b).

Birthing Centers

The increased interest in home births and family-centered labor and delivery has led some hospitals to develop birthing rooms and maternity centers. These facilities more closely resemble the home environment and are usually less expensive than the standard hospital labor and delivery rooms. The mother labors and delivers in the same room, with the father and possibly other family members present.

Some birthing centers are located in conventional hospital settings, whereas other units are structures built separately from the main hospital. In each case, the facilities attempt to combine the best of both the home and the hospital. The safety of maternity care in both types of birthing centers is comparable to that in a conventional hospital setting (Baruffi et al., 1984; Klein et al., 1984).

SUMMARY

1. Scientists do not clearly understand what causes the onset of the birth process. The most promising explanation is that the labor is triggered by chemical substances called protaglandins. When the mother has a prolonged pregnancy or other problems, the physician may induce labor.

2. The process of childbirth begins with involuntary contractions of the uterus. As labor progresses, the contractions occur closer and closer together. Before labor actually begins, the mother may experience "false labor," sometimes referred to as Braxton Hicks contractions.

3. For the mother to have a vaginal delivery, the cervix has to go through the process of effacement (thinning out) and dilation (opening).

4. Some of the signs that labor is about to begin are lightening of the fetus, a bloody show, diarrhea, increased Braxton Hicks contractions, a sudden spurt of energy, and spontaneous rupture of the amniotic sac.

5. Normal labor and delivery consists of three basic stages—dilation, expulsion, placental—plus a recovery period. Dilation is the longest and most difficult stage of labor. It is divided into the latent, active, and transition phases. The stage of expulsion begins when the cervix is completely dilated and ends with the birth of the baby. After the baby is born, the umbilical cord is cut and the placenta is expelled during the final stage. The recovery stage, which lasts for approximately an hour after the placenta is expelled, is a very dangerous period for the mother because of the risk of excessive bleeding.

5. Almost all babies are born in the head-first position. A few babies are born in one of four different breech positions: complete, frank, footling, or kneeling. If the baby is in a transverse (crosswise) position when labor begins, the baby has to be turned or surgically removed through a Caesarean delivery. Caesarean sections may also be performed if the cervix fails to dilate properly or if other complications occur.

6. Multiple births are more difficult and complicated than single deliveries. In most multiple births, the babies are born head first, but a variety of position combinations are possible.

7. Current trends in childbirth management include the decreased use

of forceps in delivery and the use of a variety of positions for the mother during labor and delivery.

8. Women vary widely in the amount of pain they experience during labor and delivery, but childbirth pain is universal. A variety of analgesics, sedatives, tranquilizers, and anesthetics are available for the treatment of labor pains. The use of regional anesthetics is popular because the mother can be awake during the birth process. The disadvantage of all obstetric medications is that they adversely affect the baby's behavior, at least temporarily.

9. In recent years, classes in prepared childbirth for expectant parents have become popular. Approaches to prepared childbirth training include the Read, Lamaze, and Bradley methods. These methods differ somewhat in theory and specific procedures, but they are similar in their goal of achieving a relatively pain-free childbirth without the use of medication, while involving the father as an integral part of the birth process. Prepared childbirth is generally effective in reducing the pain of labor, decreasing the amount of medication needed, and increasing the father's participation in the birth process.

10. The Leboyer method of "gentle" birth is designed to minimize the trauma of the birth experience for the infant through a carefully prepared delivery room environment. The Leboyer method differs from other prepared childbirth procedures in that it deals with what happens after the baby is born rather than events which occur during the birth process.

11. Current alternatives to traditional hospital procedures used in childbirth and postpartum care include rooming-in, sibling visits, home delivery, the use of midwives, and the use of homelike birthing centers.

3

The Newborn

Be careful with that new baby—it leaks.
—*American Greeting Cards*

In comparison to other mammals, the human infant is one of the more help-less creatures at birth. We should not assume, however, that the newborn is totally unprepared for life outside the uterus. Years ago William James, a famous psychologist, described the newborn infant's reaction to the world as "one great blooming, buzzing confusion" (James, 1890, p. 488). We now know that James greatly underestimated the sensory capacities of the newborn baby.

In this chapter we explore the ability of babies to make adjustments to life after birth. We consider the newborn's physical features, sensory and perceptual capacities, and behavior states. Part of the chapter is devoted to preterm and low-birthweight babies. Finally, procedures for assessing the health and well-being of babies during the first few minutes, hours, and days after birth are described.

The neonatal (newborn) period begins with the cutting of the umbilical cord and ends when the part that remains attached to the baby falls off to form the navel. Normally this takes about two weeks. However, not everyone agrees on when the newborn period ends, so infants as old as 4 to 6 weeks of age are often classified as newborns. In this text, the neonatal period is defined as the first two weeks of life after birth. You should keep in mind, however, that when the results of research studies on the neonate are discussed, the subjects may be babies who are a little older.

ADJUSTMENTS TO BIRTH

Respiration

Most infants begin to breathe within 20 to 30 seconds after birth (Cock-burn, 1984). The first breath is largely reflexive. It is probably initiated by stimulation in the brainstem triggered by skin contact with the cold air, along with decreased oxygen and higher levels of carbon dioxide (Vulliamy, 1982). The newborn may have difficulty breathing because of fluid in the lungs from the amniotic sac. Normally, much of the amniotic fluid is squeezed out of the lungs as the baby passes through the birth canal. In addition, the physician removes fluid and waste products from the mouth and throat by gentle suction immediately after birth. Babies who are born through Caesarean section tend to have more difficulty breathing at first because excessive fluid remains in their lungs.

Temperature Regulation

At the time of birth, the infant's temperature, which is slightly higher than the mother's, drops immediately. Normally, the body temperature goes back up within 2 to 4 hours if the temperature-regulating mechanism located

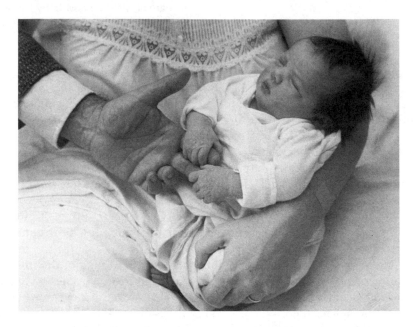

This baby is only a few hours old. Notice the grasp reflex. She is in a state of regular sleep with the eyelids tightly closed. (See Sleep States.)

in the hypothalamus of the brain is functioning properly (Lowrey, 1978). However, even at best, temperature control in the newborn is not well established. Adults shiver or sweat to get warmer or cooler, but these mechanisms are not very efficient in the newborn. In addition, the newborn has a larger skin surface area in proportion to body size than older children and adults. There is also less fat beneath the skin for insulation. A newborn baby thus loses heat about four times as fast as an adult (Bruck, 1961).

A newborn baby must rely largely on a special kind of adipose tissue called "brown fat" for the production of body heat. This tissue is used up rapidly in babies who are exposed to cold or prolonged illness. It is deficient in preterm babies (Cockburn, 1984). Obviously, newborns should not be exposed to temperatures that are too cold or too hot. A room temperature as warm as 65 to 68 degrees is recommended as a minimum for newborns who weigh as much as 5 pounds (Spock & Rothenberg, 1985).

Eating and Digestion

Within a few hours after birth, the baby needs to begin eating or to receive nourishment through other means. Many babies show signs of hunger and are ready to utilize their sucking, rooting, and swallowing reflexes as soon as they are born. However, eating and digestion are not very efficient, so babies tend to lose a few ounces of weight during the first two weeks of life. Spitting up is common among newborn infants because of air that is swallowed during feeding. Occasional vomiting is also not unusual during the neonatal period.

Elimination

The kidneys are functional even before the baby is born. Two out of three infants urinate within the first 12 hours after birth, although it may take up to 48 hours for some babies (Vulliamy, 1982). The frequency of urination gradually increases during the first few days after birth to about once an hour. The volume of urine also increases but varies with fluid intake. The newborn's kidneys do not function at full efficiency, which means that the ability to withstand dehydration or process a large amount of salty substances is very limited (Vulliamy, 1982).

The first bowel movement usually takes place within 24 hours after birth. The material eliminated is called **meconium.** This is a greenish black, semi-solid substance consisting of amniotic fluid, mucus, bile, and other body secretions. If the baby is in distress during prolonged labor, elimination may occur in the amniotic fluid before birth. When that happens, there is a danger that some of the particles of meconium can be inhaled into the baby's lungs, possibly leading to pneumonia. The number of daily bowel movements varies with individual babies. The frequency may vary from one in three days to as many as ten per day (Vulliamy, 1982). The frequency tends to decrease to one or two a day as the baby gets older (Spock & Rothenberg, 1985).

PHYSICAL APPEARANCE

As seen through the eyes of the typical parent, the newborn infant is simply beautiful. Many other people, however, have images of the newborn that are not quite as flattering. Shakespeare pictured the infant as "mewling and puking in the nurse's arms." G. Stanley Hall's (1891) classic description of the newborn as "an ugly creature with its red, shriveled, parboiled skin . . . squinting, crosseyed, pot-bellied, and bow legged" has been widely quoted. The beauty of the neonate is thus likely to lie in the eyes of the beholder.

At birth, the baby may be covered with a cheeselike vernix that is especially noticeable in the folds and crevices of the skin. The baby may also be splattered with spots of blood, along with bruises, scratches, and skin discolorations from the birth process. The head may be elongated, lopsided, or otherwise misshapen from the passage through the birth canal. Fortunately, the skull is soft and pliable, with separate pieces of cartilage designed to overlap during the birth process. Thus, the only problem from the normal molding of the head at birth is one of temporary appearance.

The color of the Caucasian newborn's skin ranges from pale to bright pink. It may have a bluish tint if there has been a decrease in oxygen. Some babies have large red patches of skin, called **strawberry nevi,** which become especially noticeable during crying episodes. These and other skin discolorations tend to disappear within a few days after birth. Black infants and infants from other racial and ethnic groups tend to have lighter-than-normal skin at birth. The skin reaches its natural hereditary coloring within a few days after it is exposed to light. The individuality of the infant is obvious at birth. Some babies are born with a head full of hair, whereas others have the appearance of being bald. In addition, some of the prenatal lanugo may remain on parts of the body for a few days after birth. Permanent hair develops within a few weeks after birth. The newborn's hair may eventually change color. The pigment of the baby's eyes may also change to a darker shade or a different color.

SENSORY AND PERCEPTUAL ABILITIES

In normal infants, the five basic senses—sight, hearing, touch, taste, and smell—are functioning at birth. The idea that infants are passive creatures with a mind that is comparable to a blank slate (or computer disc) is no longer widely accepted. Babies are currently viewed as being partially programmed at birth to participate actively in their experiences of the world. The notion that the neonate's sensory experiences amount to only "buzzing confusion" has also been replaced with the view of the infant as capable of organizing and processing discrete impressions. However, the quantity and quality of information newborns obtain through the senses and how it is organized and interpreted continue to be the subject of scientific debate and investigation.

Visual Competency

Acuity and Accommodation.   The eyes of the newborn are shorter and flatter than those of an adult. The ciliary muscles that control the lens do not function well. These characteristics affect the ability of the infant to see objects clearly (acuity) and to bring objects into focus at various distances (visual accommodation). Estimates of the visual acuity of the newborn range from 20/800 to 20/150. The best estimate appears to be 20/500 (Aslin & Dumais, 1980). Thus a newborn infant needs to be as close as 20 feet to clearly see an object that a person with perfect vision (20/20) can see at 500 feet. Infants achieve almost adult levels of visual acuity by approximately 6 months (Rose & Ruff, 1987).

Visual accommodation in newborn infants is not well understood. On the basis of a study by Haynes, White, and Held (1965), it is widely believed that neonates and very young infants see objects best at a distance of about 8 to 10 inches from the face. At this stage, the eyes are like a camera that can take a clear picture only at one distance. However, criticism of the researchers' methodology, along with more recent investigations, indicate that this assumption may not be correct (Banks & Salapatek, 1983). It now appears that newborns have the ability to keep objects in focus between 5 inches and 59 inches and are not limited to fixed-focus vision (Salapatek, Bechtold, & Bushnell, 1976).

Tracking and Scanning. Newborns can locate and follow a single moving object with their eyes (tracking) for about 90 degrees. However, their eye pursuit is slow and jerky. Tracking movements become smoother and more coordinated with age. Most infants develop the ability to track an object from one side to the other (180 degrees) by 3 months of age.

Newborn infants also engage in visual scanning of stationary objects. They apparently scan the environment, even in the dark, to find something to look at. Haith (1979) believes that neonates operate according to the following "rules" in their attempts to locate and look at interesting things:

1. When awake and the light is not too bright, open eyes.
2. If it is dark, look for a light.
3. When an object is found, look for the edges on it.
4. When the edge, or contour, is found, look up and down or back and forth across it.

From birth until about 2 months of age, infants scan the edges of objects and have an aversion to looking at the internal features. Apparently some contours are more appealing than others. Newborns tend to prefer angles over straight lines. When given a choice between horizontal and vertical contours, they prefer the vertical (Banks & Salapatek, 1983). They appear to be captivated by a single feature of a complex figure.

The looking patterns of newborns indicate that they do not perceive whole forms and simple relationships among the elements of an object. At about 2 months of age, an infant is more likely to look at the internal elements of an object and scan it more extensively. By around 3 months of age, infants apparently begin to appreciate the total shape, or visual gestalt, of an object (Lamb & Campos, 1982).

Visual Preferences. Some of the early studies in infant vision (e.g., Fantz, 1961, 1963) found that newborns prefer to look at human faces over other stimuli. They also prefer real faces over photographs of faces, blank or scrambled faces, or the face of a mannequin (Goren, 1975). On the basis of findings such as these, some researchers have concluded that infants are born with an innate visual preference for human faces over other things in the environment. Additional studies, however, have not supported this conclusion. No preference for human faces is demonstrated when infants are given a choice between objects of equal size, brightness, contrast, and contours (Cohen, DeLoache, & Strauss, 1979). Apparently the border of the face provides a high-contrast boundary that is more appealing to the baby than many other objects.

Newborn infants are capable of responding to variations in brightness of lights. Infants as young as 2 to 4 days old prefer to look at lights of medium brightness rather than at brighter or dimmer lights (Hershenson, 1964). The ability to discriminate among different degrees of brightness increases rapidly.

By 2 months of age, infants appear to be able to make discriminations among degrees of brightness almost as well as adults (Peeples & Teller, 1975).

The visual preferences of infants change with age as their capacity to attend to more distinct features and discriminate among similar stimuli emerges. For example, Fantz and Nevis (1967) found that until 1 month of age, infants would rather look at a grating of horizontal bars than at a bull's-eye target. By 2 months of age, a strong preference for the bull's-eye appeared. Some researchers (e.g., Brennan, Ames, & Moore, 1983; Hershenson, Munsinger, & Kessen, 1965) claim that infants prefer visual patterns with greater complexity as they get older. However, the evidence is not sufficient to support such a conclusion (Banks & Salapetek, 1983). There are many unanswered questions about what visual patterns infants prefer to view as well as the reasons for their preferences.

Depth Perception.   Much of the research on visual capabilities of infants has been directed toward finding out when depth perception develops. Depth perception involves such things as seeing objects in three dimensions, judging the size and distance of objects, and perceiving heights of drop-offs.

One approach used to study depth perception is to observe the responses of infants to a "looming stimulus." An object is placed in the visual field and gradually moves closer as if it is going to hit the infant in the face. When babies respond with eye blinks, raise their arms, or move their heads to defend against the impending collision, it is assumed that the infant is capable of a type of depth perception based on movement. Generally, such studies have found this type of depth perception to be present in the 3-month-old infant. There are some indications that it may be present as early as 1 month of age (Yonas & Granrud, 1985). However, studies have not reliably found this ability in younger infants.

Other studies have used a visual cliff to test when depth perception develops by linking it to the fear of heights. A visual cliff is created by using a special table with a checkerboard-patterned surface covered by a sheet of clear Plexiglas. One side of the table has a drop-off of several feet. The infant is placed on a board between the shallow and deep sides. Infants who can crawl typically avoid the side with the drop-off even though it is covered by Plexiglas (Gibson & Walk, 1960).

Precrawling infants are tested by measurements of their heart rate. Infants who are between 1½ and 3 months of age respond differently to the drop-off than they do to a level surface (Campos, Langer, & Krowitz, 1970). However, the babies may simply be responding to two different visual patterns without any appreciation for the differences in depth. Newborns are considered too immature to respond to the visual cliff.

In summarizing the results of research, Rosenblith and Sims-Knight (1985) concluded that newborn infants demonstrate only very primitive traces of depth perception. Their perceptual abilities develop rapidly, though, so that depth perception has improved considerably by 1 to 3 months of age. By 4 to 6 months of age, infants are capable of a sophisticated ability to perceive depth in various ways (e.g., visually guided reaching, visual cliff drop-off).

Color Vision.   Do newborn infants have the ability to see color, or is their vision limited to a black-and-white view of the world? Adams and Maurer (1983, 1984) found that 3-day-old infants distinguish red, yellow, green, and blue from gray. On the basis of studies such as these, it is possible to conclude that even newborns are capable of color vision (Bornstein, 1985). However, the babies may be responding to different degrees of brightness along the color spectrum, rather than color, per se. Therefore, further research with controls for brightness is needed before questions about color visual capacities of newborns can be answered conclusively.

In any case, the ability to perceive color and to make distinctions develops fairly rapidly during early infancy. Even the most skeptical scientists (e.g., Werner & Wooten, 1985) generally agree that by 2 months of age, infants can perceive the difference between two of the primary colors. Many of the fundamental aspects of color vision are reasonably adultlike by 3 months of age (Banks & Salapatek, 1983).

Hearing

Contrary to early theories that infants are born deaf, we now know that babies hear and respond to sounds even before birth. The development of the hearing apparatus is basically complete around the fifth or sixth month of fetal life (Bredberg, 1985). Researchers have noted movements (Fleischer, 1955) and changes in heart rate (Murphy & Smyth, 1962) following auditory stimulation of 7- to 9-month-old fetuses. At birth, the hearing capacity of the baby is diminished for two or three days until the amniotic fluid drains from the ear canals.

Structurally, the size and shape of the external ear, the ear canal, and the middle ear cavity continue to change into early childhood. Thus, changes in sensitivity to sounds are to be expected throughout the infancy period. In addition, the meanings infants associate with sounds also change with age. The part of the brain in which sound is interpreted is quite immature at birth, so the infant's early responses to sound may be largely reflexive (Muir, 1985).

Sound Localization.   In spite of their limitations, newborn infants are amazingly sensitive to sounds. Several studies (Aslin, Pisoni, & Jusczyk, 1983) have shown that neonates are capable of sound localization (that is, detecting the spatial position of sounds). Babies as young as 2 to 4 days turn their head toward the correct location of a sound (Muir & Field, 1979). However, for reasons not altogether understood, the ability to orient toward sounds apparently declines during the second and third months. It reappears by 4 months of age (Aslin et al., 1983).

Sound Discrimination.   Newborn infants are able to distinguish between sounds of different pitch, loudness, and duration (Leventhal & Lipsitt, 1964). They are capable of distinguishing the difference between tones that are about one note apart on a musical scale (Weir, 1970). Moderately low-pitched sounds and continuous or rhythmic sounds have a soothing effect on newborns. Very-low-frequency and high-pitched sounds produce an opposite effect (Appleton, Clifton, & Goldberg, 1975). In addition, newborns apparently are more attentive to sounds that are of moderate duration (5 to 15 seconds) than shorter or intermittent sounds (Eisenberg, 1976).

Neonates demonstrate a preference for sounds within the range of the human voice (Eisenberg, 1976). They have been observed moving their arms and legs in rhythm to voices (Condon & Sander, 1974; Bernhardt, 1987) and tend to prefer music that is accompanied by vocal sounds (Butterfield & Siperstein, 1974). Given a choice, newborns prefer their mother's voice to other female voices (DeCasper & Fifer, 1980). They also would rather listen to the voice of a female than the voice of a male. However, they do not prefer their father's voice to those of other males, even though they can detect the differences in the voices (DeCasper & Prescott, 1984). The preference for female voices in general and the mother's voice in particular may originate with their prenatal auditory experiences. DeCasper and Spence (1986) found that newborn infants whose mothers had read "The Cat and The Hat" to them during the prenatal period preferred that story to "The King, the Mice and the Cheese," after they were born.

The ability to make some fairly sophisticated distinctions between similar speech sounds develops rapidly. Between 1 and 4 months of age, infants can distinguish between consonants such as p and b (Eimas et al., 1971) as well as d and t (Eimas, 1975). They also hear the difference between a variety of vowel sounds, such as a and e (Kuhl, 1981). Furthermore, very young infants are capable of discriminating practically every phonetic contrast on which they have been tested (Aslin et al., 1983). If infants are not born with this adultlike ability to make sound distinctions, they acquire it very quickly after birth.

Taste

The sense of taste appears to be well developed at birth. A newborn infant will smile with satisfaction when a drop of sugar water is placed on its tongue and will frown with distaste in response to a drop of lemon juice, bitter quinine (Steiner, 1977), or a salty solution (Beauchamp, 1981). Thus, newborns discriminate between the four basic tastes (sweet, sour, bitter, salty) to which adults respond.

The newborn's taste for sweet is by far the dominant taste. Researchers have consistently reported that newborn infants all over the world prefer sweet substances to plain water or other substances, including milk. Their hearts beat faster (Lipsitt, 1977), and they suck faster, longer, and stronger (Crook, 1977) when they are given sweet substances as opposed to others. Apparently the sweeter the solution is, the better they like it (Desor, Maller & Greene, 1977). Even premature infants prefer sweetened liquids over unsweetened liquids (Tatzer et al., 1985). Many scientists believe that the "sweet tooth" infants have at birth is an innate characteristic.

Newborns find sour flavors distasteful. They reduce their intake of a sweetened liquid when a sour substance is added (Desor, Maller & Andrews, 1975). Surprisingly, they respond indifferently to salty and bitter solutions. When salty and bitter substances are added to a sweetened liquid, the amount consumed does not change (Desor et al., 1977). Salt was accidentally substituted for sugar in the formula of newborns fed in a hospital nursery. All of the infants drank the formula until they became quite ill (Finberg, Kiley & Luttrell, 1963). We still are not able to explain why newborn infants react negatively to salty and bitter substances placed on their tongues but do not stop sucking when these flavors are mixed with water or other solutions (Weiffenbach, Daniel, & Cowart, 1979).

Researchers are just beginning to investigate how taste sensitivity and preferences change during infancy. Beauchamp and Cowart (1986) found that infants younger than 4 months old did not detect the difference between plain and salty water. However, between 4 and 20 months of age, they actually enjoy sipping salty water. By 2 or 3 years of age, they, like adults, prefer water plain and food with salt. Other studies also indicate that 2-year-olds prefer salted to unsalted foods, and this preference continues throughout childhood (Weiffenbach et al., 1979).

The available research supports the idea that the infant's early taste experiences affect later preferences. Freitas (1984) found that infants who tasted a wide variety of foods early in life were more accepting of new foods and preferred a wider range of foods than infants who had tasted only a few foods early in life. Two-year-old infants who had been regularly fed sugar water by their mothers consumed more sucrose solutions, but not more water, than infants who were not fed sugar water (Beauchamp & Moran, 1984).

Smell

There is relatively little research on the development of the sense of smell during infancy. Some researchers (e.g., Guillory, Self & Paden, 1980) argue that the ability to discriminate odors does not develop until 1 month of age. However, the bulk of evidence indicates that infants have the ability to smell, at least some odors, as soon as they are born. For example, a newborn smiles pleasurably when a piece of cotton with a banana odor is waved under its nose, but frowns in protest at the smell of rotten eggs. Like adults, newborns prefer the smell of vanilla to the odor of fish (Steiner, 1977).

The sense of smell improves rapidly during the first few days of life. Babies are able to detect weaker odors as they get older. Lipsitt, Engen, and Kaye (1963) discovered that the amount of asafetida odor needed to elicit a response in newborns gradually decreases with age. Breast-fed babies soon learn to detect the difference between the odor of milk from the mother's breast and milk from the breast of a stranger. MacFarlane (1975) found that such distinctions could be made by 6-day-old infants but not by 2-day-old infants. However, Russell (1976) concluded that this ability did not occur until 6 weeks of age. In any case, the sense of smell may play a role in the formation of attachments in humans, just as it does in animals (Lamb & Campos, 1982).

Touch

Touch has been referred to as the "mother of the senses" (Montagu, 1971). Between 7½ and 14 weeks of gestational age, almost the entire surface of the embryo becomes sensitive to tactile stimulation (Hooker, 1952). It is the first sensory system to develop (Gottfried, 1984). Touch is the most complex of the senses and the most difficult to study as a separate modality. The word *touch,* and its synonyms *contact* and *feel,* usually refer to sensations that occur when receptors in the skin are stimulated. The sense of touch also encompasses perceptions of pain, temperature, pressure, weight, texture, firmness, and many other feelings. Touch is closely linked with sensations of the muscles and joints and with sensations of movement (Rose, 1984).

Touch plays a very important role in infant development. One of the most effective ways to soothe crying babies is to pick them up and hold them close to the body or to swaddle them tightly in a blanket. Researchers have found that low-birthweight and preterm babies gain weight faster and go home from the hospital sooner if they are stimulated with gentle stroking (Korner, 1984).

There are indications that touch, or related sensations, influences parent-infant attachment, cognitive development, sociability, ability to withstand stress, and immunological development in infants (Gottfried, 1984). Touching an infant can have a positive or negative effect. The type of touching, as well as when it occurs, are important factors. A sick infant responds differently to vigorous stroking than does a well infant. The precise effects of touch are not entirely clear because of the difficulty encountered in separating touch from other sensations (Gottfried, 1984).

Perception of Pain

For many years, doctors have performed surgery on newborn infants with little or no anesthesia. The rationale for this practice is that anesthesia increases the risk, and the immaturity of the infant's brain blocks out significant perceptions of pain. Evidence is beginning to accumulate, however, to indicate that newborn infants respond to pain in ways that are similar to those of adults. Harrigan-Hamamoto (1983) observed crying, facial expressions, fist clenching, changes in color, blood pressure, and other vital signs in newborns during a procedure used to draw a sample of blood. Lipsitt and Levy (1959) found that newborn infants are sensitive to the pain of a mild electric shock at birth. Their responsiveness gradually increased over the first four days of life.

The American Academy of Pediatrics (1987) now recommends using anesthesia whenever possible in operating on newborn infants.

Cross-modal Perception

When infants recognize that an object that is seen can also be touched, they are engaging in cross-modal perception, or intersensory integration. As part of perceptual development, infants transfer information between the various sensory systems. When infants recognize an object with one of the senses (e.g., vision) through the use of information obtained by a different sensory mechanism (touch) they are engaging in cross-modal transfer.

The question of how and when cross-modal perception develops has been a subject of debate and represents a current area of research emphasis. Some theorists, such as Bower (1977) believe that infants are born with the senses integrated so that cross-modal perceptual development is innate and develops fairly soon after birth. On the other hand, other theorists, such as Piaget (1929; 1952) believe that the senses are separated at birth and that cross-modal perception develops later in infancy through experience.

In a rather ingenious experiment, Meltzoff and Borton (1979) provided 1-month-old infants with a smooth object attached to a pacifier and a rough, nubby one attached to another pacifier. The infants were allowed to suck, but not view, each of the two objects. They were then given the pacifiers to look at, along with new objects larger than those used for sucking. The infants showed a definite preference for looking at the objects with which they had become familiar through sucking. This experiment indicates that young infants have the ability to engage in cross-modal transfer.

According to Rose and Ruff (1987), newborn infants are more interested in visually tracking objects that make a sound as they move than they are in silent objects. By 1 month of age, infants can match the mother's voice with her face. At the age of 3 or 4 months, infants can match pictures with recorded sounds. This ability is determined by showing infants separate films of two events at the same time. As the moving pictures are projected side by side, a sound track that matches only one of the films is played. When infants look longer and more often at the pictures that are synchronized with the sounds, it is assumed that they have made a correct match. Evidence from research supports the view that infants have at least a limited capacity to coordinate and integrate information from different sensory modalities soon after they are born. This ability improves with age (Rose & Ruff, 1987).

STATES OF AWARENESS

The responses of a newborn to people and various stimuli are affected by its level of alertness, attentiveness, and activity. These conditions reflect the baby's needs and availability for contact with the outside world and are referred to as

infant states. Wolff (1966) identified seven states that are characteristic of newborn infants.

1. *Regular sleep.* The baby lies very still with the eyelids firmly closed. Breathing is smooth and even. Facial muscles are relaxed and the skin is pink.

2. *Irregular sleep.* The baby may jerk and startle. Facial expressions change frequently and include smiling, frowning, and pouting. The eyelids remain closed but sometimes move. Breathing is irregular and the skin may become flushed during activity.

3. *Periodic sleep.* This state occurs between regular and irregular sleep. The baby engages in bursts of rapid breathing and muscle movements, followed by a period of slow breathing and inactivity.

4. *Drowsiness.* This is a transition period from waking to sleeping and from sleeping to waking. The eyelids open and close intermittently and are unfocused. Breathing is regular but rapid.

5. *Alert inactivity.* The baby is awake, with bright, shiny eyes. The face is relaxed; breathing is regular but faster than it is during sleep. The baby is happy, alert, and curious.

6. *Waking activity.* There are frequent bursts of vigorous movements. The skin becomes flushed and breathing is very irregular. The baby may moan, grunt, or whimper.

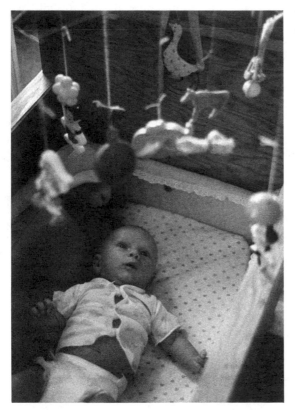

This infant is in a state of waking activity, gazing intently at the crib mobile.

7. *Crying.* The baby cries consistently and engages in vigorous movements. The face is twisted into a cry grimace and becomes flushed.

Newborns typically spend most of their time (67 percent) in one of the states of sleep or drowsiness (7 percent). They are alert and quiet about 10 percent of the time, and awake and active approximately 11 percent of each day (Berg, Adkinson, & Strock, 1973). Although it probably seems longer to parents, babies spend about 5 percent of their time crying. However, babies vary widely in the amount of time spent in each state. While one infant may sleep and wake at regular intervals, another may be very irregular. Infant states can be altered by caregiving activities and environmental conditions. For example, infants are roused from sleep by sudden movement or temperature changes and are quieted by soothing voice tones, cuddling, and rocking.

As they get older, infants change their patterns of sleep-waking activities. When the baby is approximately 1 month of age, the amount of time it sleeps decreases markedly (Emde, Gaensbauer, & Harmon, 1976). Some infants begin sleeping through the night about this time, but infants typically do not establish such a pattern until they are about 4 months old (Parmelee, Wenner, & Schulz, 1964). Another dramatic reduction in the amount of sleep an infant needs may also be observed between 5 and 7 months of age (Emde et al., 1976). These changes may correspond with the physiological maturation of the brain.

BIRTHWEIGHT AND GESTATIONAL AGE

Two of the most important factors affecting the newborn's ability to survive in the outside world are birthweight and gestational age. Birthweight is easily and routinely measured, but gestational age is more difficult to ascertain. An estimate of gestational age can be made from the first day of the last menstrual period. However, this information is frequently unreliable because of reporting inaccuracies and irregular menstrual cycles. An ultrasound scan prior to 18 weeks of pregnancy can provide a fairly good estimate of gestational age. Chemical analysis of substances found in the amniotic fluid can also be used for estimating gestational age. The Dubowitz Scale (Dubowitz, Dubowitz, & Goldberg, 1970) is frequently used to assess gestational age after the baby is born. In this test, the baby's physical flexibility, muscle tone, and physical appearance are observed to obtain a maturity rating.

Newborn infants are usually classified according to gestational age, weight, and weight for age. The following three classifications are used to designate babies by their age of gestation:

Preterm (or premature) = less than 37 weeks of gestation

Full-term = between 37 and 42 weeks of gestation

Postterm (or postmature) = 42 weeks or more of gestation

Approximately 90 to 95 percent of all infants born each year are full-term babies.

A baby who weighs less than 5½ pounds (2,500 grams) at birth is classified as **low-birthweight** (LBW), regardless of gestational age. The term *low-birthweight infant* has begun to replace the term *premature infant* in general usage (Lowrey, 1986). Two additional categories that are sometimes used to designate babies according to weight are *very low-birthweight* (VLBW), which describes babies weighing less than 3 lb. 5 oz. (1,500 grams); and *extremely low-birthweight* (ELBW), for babies less than 2 lb. 2 oz. (1,000 grams). In developed countries, 5 to 8 percent of all births are LBW infants, including VLBW and ELBW categories (Hall, 1985).

Scientists (e.g., Lubchenco et al., 1963) have developed growth charts to classify newborns on the basis of birthweight by age of gestation. Notice in Figure 3-1 that infants who rank between the 10th and 90th percentiles are considered *appropriate for gestational age* (AGA). Birthweight below the 10th percentile is ranked as *small for gestational age* (SGA), whereas birthweight above the 90th percentile is designated as *large for gestational age* (LGA). For example, a preterm infant born at 30 weeks of gestation and weighing 2 lb. 10 oz. (about 1,200 grams) would be AGA. Another infant of 30 weeks' gestation with a birthweight of 1 lb. 12 oz. (about 800 grams) would be SGA.

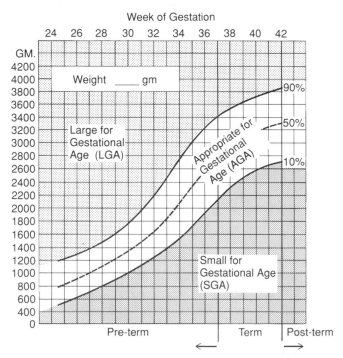

FIGURE 3-1 Classification of Newborns: Birthweight by Gestational Age.
Source: F. Battaglia and L. Lubchenco, (1967), Classification of newborns by birthweight and gestational age. *Journal of Pediatrics, 71,* p. 161. Copyright by C. V. Mosby Co. Reprinted by permission (as adapted by Mead Johnson & Co.).

PRETERM AND LOW-BIRTHWEIGHT BABIES

Most (75 percent) LBW babies are also preterm (Lowrey, 1986). In this section we consider preterm and low-birthweight infants together because they share many of the same characteristics, risk factors, and problems. Low-birthweight infants who are products of full-term pregnancies are discussed in a separate section on SGA infants.

Physical Characteristics

Preterm and low-birthweight babies are not just smaller versions of a full-term baby, but continue to be a fetus developmentally. The youngest of these babies are covered with the downy hair (lanugo) that normally is lost before birth. The skin is paper thin and transparent. Since little fat has accumulated beneath the skin, the baby looks scrawny and has the wrinkled appearance of a wizened, elderly person. The ears are wrinkled and lie flat against the head, since the cartilage is not well formed. The nipples on the breast may be barely visible. The genitals are not fully developed but may be swollen and abnormal in appearance. The relatively large head and abdomen are particularly striking.

In contrast to those of full-term infants, the movements of preterm infants are wild and bizarre. When lying on the stomach, the knees are stretched out to the side of the body rather than drawn underneath the abdomen. These babies do not attempt to change position very often. Their limbs are very limp and floppy and are not likely to resist forced movement.

A preterm infant in a neonatal intensive care isolette.

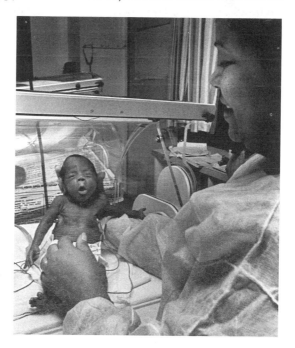

Preterm infants sleep most of the time. The cries of preterm infants are comparatively weak, short, and infrequent. These infants cannot be relied on to demand food. They have difficulty swallowing and sucking.

Problems and Complications

In recent years, medical specialists have made remarkable progress in helping preterm and low-birthweight babies survive. Neonatal intensive care units now available in many hospitals can save 80 to 85 percent of the preterm VLBW babies (Vulliamy, 1982). About half of the ELBW infants (1.6 to 2.2 lb.) born as early as 28 weeks of gestation survive (Henig, 1982). Even so, in comparison to full-term normal-birthweight infants, preterm low-birthweight infants are almost forty times more likely to die in the neonatal period. The risk for VLBW infants is almost 200 times greater than it is for full-term infants (Committee to Study the Prevention of Low Birthweight, 1985). A number of problems make survival difficult for infants born too early and too small.

Respiratory Distress Syndrome. The most frequent cause of death among preterm infants is *respiratory distress syndrome* (RDS), sometimes referred to as *hyaline membrane disease*. About 8000 to 10,000 infants in the United States die each year of RDS. The death rate increases as birthweight and gestational age decrease (Henig & Fletcher, 1983). RDS occurs more frequently in male infants than in female infants (Lowrey, 1986). The problem is caused mainly by the lack of a chemical called **surfactant.** Without surfactant, the air sacs in the lungs tend to collapse between breaths. This makes breathing more difficult and inhibits the efficient exchange of oxygen and carbon dioxide. Infants do not usually have adequate levels of surfactant until about the thirty-fourth or thirty-fifth week of gestation (Lowrey, 1986).

A premature infant is placed in an incubator, where the oxygen supply is carefully controlled. If the baby develops RDS, an oxygen hood may be placed over the baby's head. In extreme cases, a mechanical respirator or ventilator does the breathing for the baby. Improved treatment methods have reduced the number of deaths from RDS dramatically. Ten years ago, almost three out of every four infants with RDS died. Today the large majority of infants recover from RDS within ten days to two weeks.

In the future, it may be possible to prevent RDS from occurring. In some cases, to stimulate the baby's lungs to make surfactant, steroids are injected into a mother about to have a preterm delivery. Researchers have also extracted a substitute form of this chemical from the lungs of calves, and this substitute may soon be available for injection in preterm infants at birth (Stark & Frantz, 1986).

Temperature Regulation. One problem faced by preterm and low-birthweight infants is maintaining a stable, normal body temperature. The layer of fat needed for insulation has not yet developed, and the skin surface area from which heat can be lost is relatively large. Preterm infants cannot sweat to keep cool because their sweat glands are not completely developed. In addition, the temperature-control mechanism in the brain is not sufficiently mature to regulate the body's responses to environmental temperature changes. At birth, these babies are placed in an incubator, where the temperature can be carefully maintained.

Heart Problems. Before birth the infant's heart circulates the blood through the placenta, where it receives a supply of oxygen. Most of the blood bypasses the baby's own lungs. In full-term infants a blood vessel (ductus arteriosus) closes automatically soon after birth so that the full blood supply is channeled into the lungs. In preterm and low-birthweight infants it may remain open much longer. If this happens the infant will have an insufficient oxygen supply. The condition can be life threatening, and emergency surgery may be necessary. However, in recent years a new drug has been developed that frequently is successful in stimulating the duct to close on its own (Sammons & Lewis, 1985).

Bleeding in the Brain **(Intracranial Hemorrhage).** In preterm infants, the small blood vessels in the brain are more immature and have fewer supporting cells in the surrounding tissue. Therefore, sudden changes in blood pressure or blood oxygen levels may cause blood vessels to rupture and bleed inside the skull (Sammons & Lewis, 1985). The younger and smaller the infant, the more likely this problem is to occur. Intracranial bleeding occurs in 50 percent of infants who are less than 32 weeks of gestational age and with a birthweight less than 3 lb. 5 oz. (Kopelman, 1982). In some cases, the bleeding is so slight that it has little or no impact on the functions of the brain. More massive bleeding may result in long-term motor and mental difficulties or even death.

Retrolental Fibroplasia. A common problem resulting from the intensive care of very small and immature newborns is **retrolental fibroplasia** (RLF). This disorder causes scarring of the retina, which may lead to visual impairment or blindness. RLF is generally attributed to excessive oxygen. Physicians are frequently faced with the dilemma of giving supplemental oxygen to preterm infants to keep them alive, even though they know it may lead to RLF. The problem seems to be more prevalent in ELBW infants who weigh less than 2 lb. 3 oz. because they need high oxygen concentrations for an extended period of time (Sammons & Lewis, 1985). However, RLF sometimes occurs in full-term infants who were not given supplemental oxygen (Harley, 1983). Consequently, oxygen toxicity may not be the only factor involved in RLF (Sammons & Lewis, 1985).

Excess Bilirubin.   Preterm and low-birthweight infants frequently have a yellow-orange skin color similar to a fading tan. This condition, referred to as *jaundice,* is caused by an excess accumulation of bilirubin in the bloodstream and body tissues. Bilirubin is a pigment formed when red blood cells are destroyed. Preterm infants are especially susceptible to jaundice because the liver is likely to be too immature to remove the bilirubin from the blood. Normally, this problem can be corrected by placing the baby under a special light. In some cases a blood-exchange transfusion may be required. Extremely high bilirubin levels can eventually lead to brain damage.

Nutrition.   Meeting the nutritional needs of preterm and LBW infants is a special problem because of the immaturity of sucking and swallowing abilities as well as the digestive system. The stomach is small and the passage of its contents is very slow. The infant's capacity to metabolize fat and protein is inefficient. Hypoglycemia (low blood sugar) is a common problem in SGA infants (Lowrey, 1986). Preterm infants who are too immature to suck are usually fed through a tube inserted through the nose or mouth into the stomach. They also may be given intravenous solutions of glucose (Redshaw, Rivers, & Rosenblatt, 1985).

Infections and Other Problems.   Preterm infants are very susceptible to infections from bacteria and viruses. Immunity to diseases, which the infant receives from the mother, is not present until 28 weeks of gestational age, and the level of immunity is rather limited at first (Vulliamy, 1982). Some of the problems, such as blood poisoning, probably result from the invasive procedures used in inserting tubes, taking blood samples, and other routines used in intensive care nurseries. Necrotizing enterocolitis, a life-threatening disease that affects the bowel wall, is a special hazard of prematurity. Other problems preterm infants face include apnea (prolonged pause in breathing) and inefficient kidney function.

Risk Factors

In most cases it is not possible to determine exactly why a mother has given birth to a preterm or low-birthweight baby. Many diverse factors may increase a pregnant woman's chances of giving birth to such an infant, including the mother's age (less than 17 or over 34), poor nutritional status, inadequate prenatal care, low socioeconomic status, alcohol or drug abuse, smoking, infections, and diseases (Committee to Study the Prevention of Low Birthweight, 1985). Other possible risk factors include multiple pregnancy, high blood pressure during pregnancy, premature opening of the cervix, hormonal deficiency, fetal malformations, premature rupture of the amniotic sac, and unusual physical or psychological stress. Many of these conditions are interrelated. For example, low socioeconomic status is associated with poor nutrition, stress, lack of prenatal care, and other adverse conditions. Not all of the factors carry the same weight; and even if one or more factors are present, the mother is still likely to give birth to a full-term AGA infant (Redshaw et al., 1985).

Prevention

Research studies have consistently shown that prenatal care is very effective, especially among women in high-risk categories, in preventing low birthweight and prematurity (Committee to Study the Prevention of Low Birthweight, 1985). Pregnant women are less likely to smoke or to use alcohol, drugs, and other harmful substances when they are aware of the adverse effects on the baby. They also are more likely to maintain better nutrition and health when they receive appropriate prenatal care. In some cases the mother can be hospitalized and treated with labor-stopping drugs if the beginning of premature labor is detected early enough (Herron, Katz, & Creasy, 1982). However, there are some factors, such as early rupture of the bag of waters, that are beyond the ability of medical science to control.

SMALL FOR GESTATIONAL AGE BABIES

An infant who weighs less than 90 percent of other infants of the same gestational age is, by definition, small for gestational age (SGA). The majority of these infants are born at term, although some are classified as preterm SGA or postterm SGA (Cockburn, 1984). Full-term SGA births are usually caused by intrauterine growth retardation. Known causes of this problem include genetic conditions, congenital infections, maternal malnutrition, placental abnormalities, and maternal ingestion of adverse substances.

The majority of full-term SGA infants appear to have starved in the uterus. SGA infants tend to have even less fat and muscle tissue than preterm infants. The head appears to be larger and even more out of proportion to the rest of the body. The skin is loose and dry with very little lanugo or vernix. Typically such babies have more hair than preterm infants (Sammons & Lewis, 1985). These infants are often very active and cry vigorously (Cockburn, 1984).

SGA infants face some of the same problems as preterm infants, such as temperature regulation, but they have some special complications of their own. They are more likely to have problems such as asphyxia (low oxygen and high carbon dioxide blood level) before they are born. SGA infants also frequently have trouble with hypoglycemia (low blood sugar). Since they are stressed, these infants tend to inhale meconium, which they excrete into the amniotic fluid before birth. Inhaled meconium causes breathing difficulties after birth and often leads to pneumonia. The stress placed on the heart by these breathing difficulties may result in death (Vulliamy, 1982).

EFFECTS OF PREMATURITY AND LOW BIRTHWEIGHT

The vast majority of preterm and low-birthweight infants grow up to be normal, healthy infants with little or no traces of their former condition. Unfortunately, though, some of these infants will suffer physical handicaps and other problems. Approximately 5 to 15 percent will have serious or moderate degrees of such problems as visual impairment, hearing loss, epilepsy, cerebral palsy, or mental retardation (Kopp & Parmelee, 1979). The risks increase with decreasing age and birthweight. Some reports indicate that the handicap rate is about 18 percent for VLBW infants, and about 20 to 25 percent for ELBW infants (Hall, 1985).

Healthy AGA premature or low-birthweight infants who have adequate nutrition usually catch up to full-term infants of the same birth date by 40 to 42 weeks of age. After that time, AGA preterm infants grow at the same rate as full-term infants (Desmond et al., 1980). SGA infants are the most likely to grow up to be smaller than their full-term peers (Hall, 1985). For example, Willie Shoemaker, the famous jockey, was an SGA baby (2½ pounds at 36 weeks' gestation). His parents kept him in a shoe box in the oven with the door open during the neonatal period (Shoemaker & Tower, 1970). Shoemaker's adult height is only 4 feet 11½ inches.

During the first two or three years of life, preterm infants typically display deficiencies in behavioral organization, visual attention, information processing, motor skills, and language acquisition. Most of these problems tend to disappear with age, but the effects on cognitive performance may be permanent for some children. Children who were born prematurely may not be quite ready to begin school at age 6 (Desmond et al., 1980). Some premature and low-birthweight infants are therefore more likely to have problems in academic achievement than their full-term peers (Kopp, 1983).

Holmes, Reich, and Pasternak (1984) believe that, as a group, low-birthweight children "perform more poorly on assessments of mental skills, with the size of the deficit increasing as birth weight declines" (p. 169). They estimate that very low birthweight babies may have, on the average, an IQ deficit of about 10 points. However, this may be because a small group of severely retarded children tends to pull down the group average; the other low-birthweight children may actually be unaffected. Preterm infants now tend to have higher intelligence test scores than those of previous generations (Kopp, 1983).

POSTMATURE BABIES

Babies born after 42 weeks of gestational age are considered to be postmature. The main risk these babies face is the aging of the placenta. After about 40 to 42 weeks' gestation, the placenta loses efficiency in supplying nutrition and carrying off waste products. The amount of amniotic fluid also tends to diminish in a postterm pregnancy. As a result, postmature babies are long and skinny and have dry skin that may be cracked and peeling. Asphyxia, inhalation of meconium, pneumonia, and hypoglycemia are typical problems they experience at birth (Cockburn, 1984; Vulliamy, 1982). With more accurate methods of assessing gestational age, physicians are now better equipped to prevent pregnancies from continuing too long.

NEWBORN SCREENING TESTS

Apgar Scale

Many physicians routinely use the **Apgar Scale** to evaluate the vital signs of newborn infants in the delivery room. The scale is administered within the first 60 seconds after birth to check the baby's heart rate, breathing, muscle tone, reflex irritability, and color (Table 3-1). A second assessment is usually made about 5 minutes later. Infants who are in the best condition score in the 8–10 range. A score from 5–7 warns the doctor that the baby may need help and should be carefully observed. If the score is 4 or below, the infant is in critical condition and requires emergency care. The large majority of infants score in the 7–10 range.

TABLE 3-1 Apgar Scale

SIGN	0	1	2
A—appearance (color)	blue, pale	body pink (extremities blue)	completely pink
P—pulse (heart rate)	absent	below 100	over 100
G—grimace (reflex irritability, response to stimulation of sole of foot by a glancing slap)	no response	grimace	cry
A—activity (muscle tone)	limp	some flexion of extremities	active motion
R—respiratory (respiratory effort)	absent	slow, irregular	good strong cry

Source: J. Butterfield, and M. Covey, (1962). Practical epigram of the Apgar Score. *Journal of the American Medical Association, 181,* 353. Copyright 1962, American Medical Association.

The Brazelton

The *Brazelton Neonatal Behavior Assessment Scale* (BNBAS) was designed to assess the newborn infant's responses to the environment (Brazelton, 1973). One section of the test contains twenty items that measure the intactness of the nervous system through elicited reflexes such as rooting and sucking. The examination also contains items that score an infant on twenty-six kinds of behavior, including sensory responses (e.g., vision, hearing), motor maturity, alertness, self-quieting activity, and social interaction (cuddliness). The Brazelton scale is about 80 percent effective in detecting abnormalities of development in newborns (Heidelise et al., 1979). The device has been used widely in research and is also used in teaching parents about the behavior of their baby (Heidelise et al., 1979).

FACILITATING NEONATAL DEVELOPMENT

The most important thing parents and caregivers of newborns can do is to meet the infant's basic needs, including adequate nutrition, good health care, and affection. Burton White (1985) believes that giving an infant a "feeling of being loved and cared for" is the best thing parents can do to get their child off to a good start (p. 26). He recommends the following child-rearing practices during the first six weeks of life:

1. Handle the newborn frequently and respond promptly to its cries. A crying infant who is not hungry or in need of a diaper change can usually be calmed by swaddling (wrapping tightly in a blanket), rocking, holding and cuddling, gently bouncing, humming, providing a pacifier, or adjusting the temperature.

2. A crib mobile with contrasting colors is about the only enrichment material a newborn needs. The mobile should be designed so that it can be enjoyed from the perspective of an infant looking up rather than an adult looking down.

3. The position and location of the baby should be changed several times. A baby should be placed on its stomach frequently during the day. This position induces head lifting and increases the visual field.

4. Develop the habit of talking to the baby when it is alert. Diaper changing and other caregiving activities are usually good times to get the baby's attention and engage in play.

Caring for Preterm or Low-Birthweight Infants

Parents should maintain regular contact with preterm and other newborn infants who must stay in the hospital for an extended period. Hospitals encourage parents to hold the baby and participate in feeding and other caregiving activities as conditions permit. The importance of touching, massaging, cuddling, rocking, and talking to the baby is emphasized (Redshaw et al., 1985).

The following special stimulation activities are sometimes used with preterm infants:

1. Water beds with built-in rocking mechanisms are provided in some hospitals. When medical conditions permit, these infants are also rocked by caregivers at regular intervals.

2. Sound recordings of the mother's heartbeat and other intrauterine noises, parental voices, and even classical music are provided. However, recorded sounds are not used to substitute for human contact and live voices.

3. High-contrast pictures and other materials are placed in the infant's field of vision.

4. Infants' bodies (back of the head, neck, and back) are gently massaged, and their arms and legs are slowly moved.

Parents and other caregivers should take their time and avoid rushing or overstimulating the infant. Stimulation should be withdrawn if the baby appears to be stressed. These babies need more time to warm up and respond to touch than full-term infants. Although proper care is important, parents should avoid the tendency to overprotect the infants.

SUMMARY

1. The newborn period is defined as the first two weeks after birth. Adjustments newborn infants have to make include breathing, temperature changes, taking in nourishment, and eliminating body waste.

2. Infants vary widely in physical appearance at birth, but the effects of the birth process are usually obvious. Skin discolorations, bruises, and a misshapen skull are some of the features displayed by many infants.

3. The five basic sensory systems—vision, hearing, touch, taste, and smell—are normally functioning at birth. Babies actively seek sensory stimulation, and their perceptual abilities improve with age and experience.

4. Visual acuity is limited but reaches adult capacity around 6 months. Newborns scan the edges of objects and do not look much at the overall shape of objects until around 3 months. Newborns prefer to look at high-contrast objects such as human faces, but their visual preferences change with age. Although depth perception is very limited at birth, it is well developed by 4 to 6 months of age. Newborns are capable of limited color vision, but their ability to discriminate between colors of various shades improves rapidly.

5. Newborn babies are sensitive to sounds and are capable of distinguishing between sounds of different pitch, loudness, and intensity. They prefer to listen to sounds within the range of the human voice. Between 1 and 4 months of age, infants develop the ability to discriminate between very similar sounds.

6. Newborns apparently have the capacity at birth to distinguish between the four basic tastes. The taste for sweet substances is predominant over other taste preferences and is probably innate.

7. The sense of smell may be the least developed sense in the newborn. Infants can detect strong odors at birth but do not respond to weaker odors until they are a few days older. Like adults, infants prefer pleasant to unpleasant odors.

8. The sense of touch is one of the earliest and most important senses to develop. It is the most complex of the senses to study and understand.

9. Contrary to previous opinion, newborns respond to pain in ways that are to similar to the ways adults respond to pain.

10. The responses of infants to sensory stimulation are affected by their particular state of awareness. Seven states exhibited by newborns have been identified: regular sleep, irregular sleep, periodic sleep, drowsiness, alert inactivity, waking activity, and crying.

11. The infant's birthweight and gestational age are important factors that have a major impact on growth and development. The term *low-birthweight* is used to designate infants who weigh less than 5½ pounds at birth. Infants who are born at less than 37 weeks of gestation are called preterm or premature infants. Most preterm infants fall into the low-birthweight category.

12. Preterm and low-birthweight infants have many of the same problems and characteristics. Some of their problems include respiratory distress syndrome, temperature-regulation difficulties, heart problems, intracranial bleeding, retrolental fibroplasia, excess bilirubin, and poor nutritional metabolism.

13. Preterm and low-birthweight infants usually catch up with the physical development of their full-term peers by the end of the infancy period. The risk of handicaps increases as the gestational age and birthweight decrease. The majority of preterm and low-birthweight infants grow up to be normal, healthy infants.

14. The Apgar Scale and the Brazelton Neonatal Behavior Assessment Scale are assessment instruments that are widely used to determine the developmental status of newborn infants.

4

Physical Development

As surely as life continues outside the uterus, the baby grows. At no other time period following birth is growth so rapid, dramatic, and clearly observable as it is during infancy. Adults are constantly amazed at how quickly an infant changes in physical appearance. Physical growth results from two processes—cell division and the increase in the size of existing cells. Before birth, cell division is the main type of growth activity. After birth, the process shifts to the enlargement of existing cells. This does not mean that no new cells are formed, but the main growth function is to build on existing structures and to replace cells that are lost through aging, wear and tear, and physical injury.

In this chapter we consider physical changes that occur during infancy. Clearly observable changes in height, weight, head circumference, teeth, and skin are discussed. We also give attention to less obvious growth processes occurring in the internal organs such as the brain, muscles, skeleton, and cardiovascular system. Finally, procedures for evaluating and enhancing physical growth are considered.

FACTORS INFLUENCING PHYSICAL GROWTH

Human growth is an extremely complicated process that is affected by numerous forces including heredity, hormones, health, nutrition, socioeconomic status, sex, race, and emotional stress. Some of these factors are considered in connection with specific aspects of growth in other chapters (e.g., Chapter 7), whereas others are discussed at this point. Keep in mind, however, that the precise influence of each factor is almost impossible to determine because of the complex ways in which heredity and environmental conditions intermix.

Socioeconomic Status

Children from higher social class groups are taller, heavier, and grow faster than children from lower socioeconomic groups in the same part of the country. Children of fathers employed in professional jobs average about three-fourths of an inch taller at age 3 than those of fathers working in unskilled occupations (Tanner, 1978; Hamill, Johnston, & Lemeshaw, 1972). Infant mortality and health problems are most common among children of lower socioeconomic status. Social class differences simply reflect the nutrition, health care, and other environmental conditions to which infants are exposed.

Illness

The effects of garden-variety childhood diseases (measles, colds, viruses, etc.) on the growth rate of well-nourished children are hardly noticeable. The growth of undernourished children may be slowed down slightly, but once the disease is cured, the growth rate resumes and the infant makes up for "lost time" (Tanner, 1978). In all children, major diseases delay growth, but the effects on body size are seldom lasting. However, some of the illnesses to which infants are exposed have the potential to cause severe sensory or nervous-system impairments leading to physical disabilities.

Culture and Race

Many aspects of physical growth during infancy, such as height and weight, vary widely around the world, depending upon genetic pools, nutrition, and other environmental factors. At 1 year of age, infants living in different regions of the world differ as much as 5.5 inches in average height and 9 pounds in average weight. The shortest and lightest infants come from South-Central and Southeast Asia (India, Vietnam, Pakistan). The tallest and heaviest infants come from the United States and Europe (Werner, 1979).

In the United States, black infants tend to be slightly smaller at birth than white infants, but their skeletal development is slightly more advanced. Black infants soon surpass white infants in size and are a little taller and heavier throughout childhood as long as socioeconomic factors are equivalent (Eichorn, 1979). The largest physical differences in races are those of body proportion (Tanner, 1978). However, differences in shape are more observable in later years than in infancy.

Hormonal Influences

Hormones secreted directly into the bloodstream by the endocrine glands play a major role in physical growth. Although numerous hormones affect all growth throughout the life cycle, the hormones that are particularly influential during infancy are thyroxine and human growth hormone (HGH).

Thyroxine. The thyroid gland releases thyroxine in response to chemical messages from the pituitary gland. Adequate quantities of this hormone are necessary for cell multiplication and subsequent growth in size. Thyroxine also is important for the stimulation of brain growth during the fetal and early infancy periods (Lowrey, 1978). To meet this need, it is secreted in greater quantities during the first two years of life, after which the amount is reduced until adolescence (Tanner, 1978). Insufficient quantities of thyroxine (hypothyroidism) leads to brain growth failure and mental subnormality. If hypothyroidism is discovered and treated within the first 3 months of life, an infant has an 85 percent chance of developing an IQ of at least 85. The outlook is more dismal if treatment is delayed.

Human Growth Hormone. Normal physical growth from late infancy to maturity depends upon an adequate supply of human growth hormone (HGH), which also comes from the thyroid gland. HGH is apparently not necessary for normal prenatal growth. It becomes most influential during late infancy and early childhood. HGH affects cell multiplication and expansion in all organs of the body except the central nervous system and some of the endocrine glands (Lowrey, 1978).

The extent of growth retardation is related to the amount of HGH available. Children grow only about 1½ inches after the age of 2 without HGH. Their bodies are normally proportioned, but they become miniature adults. Fortunately, injections of HGH can be given that will result in normal growth. The supply of HGH has been limited since its discovery in 1956, because it could be obtained only from the glands of human cadavers. However, scientists have now developed a synthetic form of HGH, which should increase the drug's availability. The ability of the body to use growth hormone is limited by the genetic potential, so HGH supplements will not stimulate a genetically small child to grow larger.

Emotional Disturbances

Disturbances in the parent-child relationship or other causes of continuing severe emotional stress result in growth failure. This condition is sometimes referred to as *psychosocial* or *deprivation dwarfism*. Apparently, young children respond to stress by reducing or completely inhibiting the secretion of growth hormone. When the stress is alleviated, the child resumes growth and usually catches up with age mates (Tanner, 1978). Short-term emotional stress connected with normal daily family living has no marked impact on growth patterns.

BODY SIZE

The three major indicators of normal body growth during infancy and childhood are weight, height, and head circumference. Measurements of these body features should be made periodically as a part of a child's routine health care. The curve of normal body growth for male and female infants can be found in Appendices 1–4.

Weight

Body weight is probably the best single indicator of growth in infancy because it represents a summary of all changes in size. Typically, a newborn baby is expected to gain about 1 ounce (30 grams) each day, averaging about 2.2 pounds (1 halogen) each month for the first six months of life (Silver, 1984). During the latter half of the first year, the weight gain slows down to about ½ ounce per day. Healthy infants usually double their birthweight by 4 or 5 months, triple it by 1 year, and quadruple it by 2 years of age. Thus the average infant who weighs 7.25 pounds at birth will probably weigh about 14.5 pounds at 4 months, 22.5 pounds at 1 year, and 29 pounds at 2 years of age.

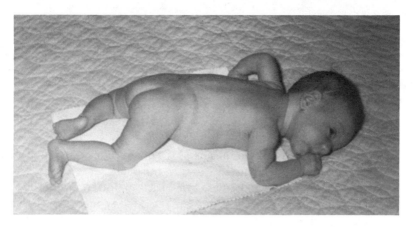

This infant weighed 7 lb. and 7 oz. and was 19 inches long at birth. At two months of age, when this picture was taken, she weighed 11 lb. and 7 oz. and was 23 inches long.

During the remainder of infancy and early childhood, the average annual weight gain is about 5 pounds.

The growth of the skeleton, muscles, and body organs contribute to weight gains in infancy, but much of the body weight is due to the addition and enlargement of fatty tissue. The layer of fat beneath the skin of the fetus begins to develop approximately the thirtieth week of the prenatal period. Body fat continues to increase until reaching a peak in growth rate from 6 to 9 months after birth. The rate of fat cell growth then gradually declines throughout infancy.

Male infants, on the average, weigh a little more than female infants, but females tend to have slightly more fat. Although male and females do not differ in their number of fat cells, they differ in the size of the cells. The differences tend to persist throughout life (Tanner, 1978). At birth, the average male infant (7.25 lb.) usually weighs about one-fourth of a pound more than the average female infant (7 lb.). The difference in weight gradually increases throughout infancy until 2 years of age, when the average male (27.75 lb.) weighs about 1½ pounds more than the average female (26.25 lb.).

Height

The first year of postnatal life brings rapid change in height. By the first birthday, an infant has usually increased the birth length by approximately 50 percent. Thus, the average infant (50th percentile) who measures 20 inches at birth would be about 30 inches tall at the end of the first year. During the second year, the increase is less dramatic, with a gain of about 4.5 to 5 inches, or about 24 percent of the full length. On the average, infants grow about 3 to 4 inches in the third year and measure about 3 feet tall (Silver, 1984). Typically males remain about ¼ to ½ inch taller than females throughout the infancy period.

Tanner's (1978) relative maturity percentages are sometimes used as a rough estimate of adult height. At 2 years of age, a boy will be 49.4 percent as tall as he will grow to be as an adult. A girl of the same age has reached 52.7 percent of her mature height. However, it is not possible to accurately predict the final body size of an infant because there are too many unknown variables that can affect growth.

Head Growth

The circumference of an infant's head is a major index of normal growth during infancy. At birth, head circumference normally ranges from 12 to 15 inches, with an average of 13.75 inches. The head circumference of the typical (50th percentile) 6-month-old infant measures about 17 inches, increasing to around 18 inches at 1 year of age, and around 19 inches at 2 years. Males usually have a slightly larger head (¼ to ¾ inch) than females during the infancy period.

The shape of the young infant's head is noticeably different from that of an adult (Fig. 4-1). The cranium, or top of the head, is proportionately larger and more prominent in the infant. The face constitutes a much smaller part of the head. At birth, the head of an infant is approximately one-fourth of the total body length, whereas for an adult the head is only about one-eighth of total height. During infancy, the head grows slower, so there is a noticeable change in its proportion to body length.

The shape of an individual's skull is influenced by sex, race, and other factors, but the facial size is closely related to the overall growth of the head. If the brain grows normally, the head circumference will equal the expected measurements. An extremely small or large head may be an indicator of brain subnormality. However, the total body size should be considered, because a

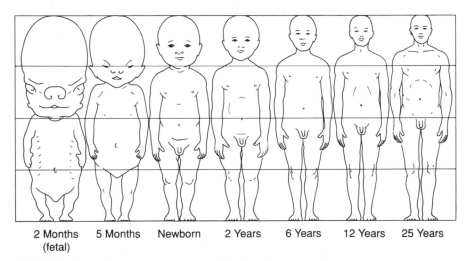

2 Months (fetal)	5 Months	Newborn	2 Years	6 Years	12 Years	25 Years

FIGURE 4-1 Proportionate Changes in Growth of the Head, Trunk, and Limbs.
Source: B. Anson, (Ed.) (1966). *Morris' human anatomy* (12th ed.). New York: McGraw-Hill. Used by permission.

large baby will typically have a larger head and a small baby will usually have a small head (Illingworth, 1983). If the head circumference measures below the 3d percentile or above the 97th percentile, the infant should be carefully evaluated for such problems as microcephaly (underdeveloped brain) or hydrocephaly (excess fluid on the brain) (Valadian & Porter, 1977).

Fontanels.   The skull of an infant consists of eight pieces of bone held together by softer cartilage and connecting tissue. At birth the bones are soft and movable and may overlap so the head can more easily move through the birth canal. The narrow seams of cartilage are called **sutures,** while the wide sections of cartilage are called **fontanels,** or "soft spots." Normally four sutures and six fontanels are present at birth.

The two larger fontanels can easily be felt with the fingertips as soft spots in the skull. The sutures are more difficult to find and usually cannot be felt after the first few weeks. However, the sutures are not completely closed until adolescence. The largest fontanel is located in the front of the cranium. It is typically diamond shaped and measures about 0.4 to 2.5 inches at birth (Nelms & Mullins, 1982). The front fontanel is usually closed by 18 to 20 months of age (Valadian & Porter, 1977). The fontanel on the back of the skull is typically shaped like a triangle and measures about 0.2 inches in diameter at birth. As the skull hardens, this fontanel gradually gets smaller and is completely closed by 3 or 4 months in most infants. In some infants it may already be closed at birth (Behrman & Vaughan, 1983).

The Face.   The most noticeable and complex growth of the head can be observed in the facial features. The front view of the newborn infant reveals a broad, flat appearance in comparison to the face of an adult. The flat facial appearance is a result of the baby's small, almost bridgeless nose, and cheek-bones that are barely distinguishable. The profile (side view) is dominated by the cranium and forehead since the lower jaw is underdeveloped and receded (Ranly, 1980). Lorenz (1965) has noted that these facial features, in combination with the infant's small size, form the "cuteness" that attracts adults to infants. This infant shape triggers nurturing behaviors, including human affection for the young of other species.

With age, the lower part of the face undergoes "catchup growth" that changes the infant's overall appearance. The length of the face is about 40 percent complete at birth. Facial growth proceeds very rapidly during the first three years of life, after which growth is slower and steadier until maturity (Ranly, 1980). The middle of the face emerges from beneath the cranium and grows forward and downward. The bony bridge and soft tissue of the nose grow while the front sinus cavities expand so that the flat appearance of the face diminishes. In spite of the rapid growth, however, the face of an infant remains considerably less mature in appearance than an adult face.

The Eyes.   One of the most striking features of an infant's face is the eyes. The eyes dominate the face of the infant until the nose becomes large

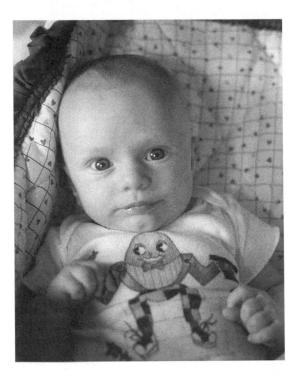

The eyes are the dominant feature of the young infant's face. Notice, also, the relatively large skull and small jaw.

enough to provide a definite separation between them. Apparently, the infant is equipped with a small nose to prevent the mother's breast from pressing against it and cutting off the air supply. In the normal full-term newborn, the eyes are approximately three-fourths of normal adult size. They grow rapidly during the first year and at a rapid but decelerating rate until the third year. Although growth of the eyes continues after infancy, it is at a much slower rate.

Various parts of the eye have different growth rates. The front part of the eye is relatively larger at birth and grows less than the structures in the back of the eye. The cornea is large at birth and reaches mature size at about 2 years of age. It tends to flatten with age (Behrman & Vaughan, 1983). Overall, the shape of the eye becomes more clearly spherical with growth. The color of the eyes tends to get darker with age in many children. In Caucasians, the eyes are typically light blue at birth but get darker and may change color as pigment is added (Behrman & Vaughan, 1983). Non-Caucasian infants typically have dark eyes at birth, so the addition of pigment is not as noticeable.

Catchup Growth

An individual's potential body size is controlled by several genes, each of which has a small effect. Some genes do not begin to function until after birth. During the prenatal period the baby's growth is affected by the size of the mother's uterus. The uterus of a small mother thus may have a restraining effect on a baby who has the genetic potential to grow larger than average. On the other hand, an infant born to a larger mother may be larger than average even though genetically programmed to reach a relatively small adult height.

After birth, small infants who have the genetic heritage to be tall adults will usually grow faster than average for the first 5 months of life. Such rapid growth after a period of intrauterine growth restriction is called **catchup growth** (Tanner, 1978). By the same genetic principle, larger-than-average infants who are destined to be small adults will grow slower than average. Thus, the baby's length at birth is not a good indicator of height at maturity.

SKELETAL GROWTH

At birth an infant's skeleton is made up mostly of semihard, gristlelike tissue called **cartilage.** The skeleton is softer and more flexible in the joints. As the baby grows, the skeleton becomes harder and less flexible. The process by which minerals and other substances are added to the cartilage so that it hardens into bones is called **ossification.** Bone growth and ossification are largely dependent upon an adequate supply of nutritional and hormonal substances. Different parts of the skeleton grow and ossify at different rates.

Girls are more typically advanced in skeletal ossification than boys at birth. The sex difference tends to increase with age because female infants mature at a faster rate during infancy. In addition, the rate of ossification is less variable for girls than for boys (Sinclair, 1978).

The Limbs

The bone-hardening process begins in an ossification center in each piece of cartilage. At birth, primary ossification centers have begun in all of the long limb bones. Shortly before and immediately after birth, secondary ossification centers, or **epiphyses,** form near each end of each separate piece of cartilage. Ossification then proceeds from the end of each bone to the middle.

New ossification centers appear continuously throughout the skeleton until maturity is reached. At the same time ossification is proceeding, new layers of bony tissue are deposited on the outside of the basic structure so that the bones grow in width. The bones also grow in length and change in shape as cells are added to the epiphyses. At birth, the bones of the lower limbs and pelvic area are proportionately shorter and less advanced than the upper limbs and shoulders. However, the lower limbs grow at a faster rate and catch up with the upper part of the skeleton (Sinclair, 1978).

The Feet

The feet of the normal newborn infant are proportionately longer and thinner than those of older children. The toddler's feet are somewhat chubbier and wider than the feet of older children. The bottom typically appears flat because of external fullness of the foot pad.

Since the ankle joints are very flexible, the toes may appear to be turned too far in or out. Intoeing, a condition in which the front part of the entire foot turns in, is a common problem in young infants. This condition can result from confinement in the uterus, sleeping on the stomach, or genetic predisposition. When the baby begins to stand and walk, the problem tends to correct itself. In some cases, however, a special orthopedic examination and treatment may be necessary (Behrman & Vaughan, 1983).

Muscles

The muscle tissue makes up about 20 to 25 percent of an infant's weight at birth. The muscle fibers are small, watery, and underdeveloped. As the baby grows, the proportion of water in the muscles decreases as protein and other substances are added. These changes result in an increase in strength and stamina. Growth of the muscle fibers is influenced by nutrition, hormones, metabolism, exercise, and health (Valadian & Porter, 1977).

Scientists generally believe that the total number of muscle fibers the human body needs are present at birth or develop shortly afterward (Tanner, 1978). Muscle fibers become longer and thicker throughout infancy and childhood. Muscles grow at about twice the rate of bones. The muscles in the top part of the body develop a little faster than those in the lower part of the body.

Skin

A newborn infant usually comes equipped with five complete layers of skin. However, the outer layers are thinner and more delicate. The baby's outer layers of skin are also more loosely connected to the inner layers than are those of an adult. Although all of the sweat glands are present at birth, they function poorly. The glands that produce the oily secretions that form the vernix caseosa covering the baby at birth decrease production and remain relatively inactive until puberty (Lowrey, 1978). The infant's skin is thus normally dry and may flake or peel easily. Diaper rash, heat rash, allergic reactions, and skin infections are common in infants because of their delicate skin (Valadian & Porter, 1977).

In comparison to older children and adults, the skin of an infant contains less pigment (color). Infants of dark-skinned parents thus tend to have lighter skin coloring than they will have at maturity. Pigment in the skin of infants of all races increases throughout the infancy period, but the process proceeds more slowly in children with light skin (Nelms & Mullins, 1982).

Infants have a larger skin surface in proportion to their body weight than adults. Thus, an infant loses more water through the skin and has more potential for heat loss and dehydration than an adult. In proportion to adults, a baby needs more calories for maintaining basal metabolism (Eichorn, 1979).

Teeth

Ordinarily humans grow two sets of teeth in the course of a lifetime. The first set includes twenty teeth that are referred to as the *primary* or **deciduous** teeth. The word *deciduous* literally means to "fall off." Primary teeth are also called *milk teeth, baby teeth,* or *temporary teeth.* Unfortunately such names lead parents to mistakenly think that these teeth are not important (Woelfel, 1984). Some of the primary teeth begin to develop beneath the gums as early as the twelfth week of prenatal life. The buds of some of the permanent teeth also begin to form around the fourth or fifth month of the prenatal period (Beedle, 1984).

The development of a tooth begins with a bud that forms the crown and grows downward to form the root. The enamel (outer portion) is formed slightly ahead of the dentin (inner portion). The enamel develops in microscopic layers, comparable to the rings of a tree. Severe nutritional deficits, hormonal imbalances, and prolonged or serious illnesses may disturb the formation or hardening of the teeth. For example, a 30-month-old child who has measles may develop a weakness in the enamel of the permanent teeth that are calcifying at that time.

Usually none of the infant's teeth are visible at birth. The first tooth normally begins to appear around 8 months. The central incisors (front and center teeth) are typically the first teeth to cut through the gums, followed by the lateral incisors. The sequence and approximate ages at which the primary teeth erupt are presented in Figure 4-2. The lower front teeth and second molars tend to cut through the lower jaw before their counterparts are visible in the upper jaw. The lateral incisors, canines, and first molars tend to emerge in the upper jaw earlier than in the lower jaw (Lunt & Law, 1974).

Infants vary considerably in the order as well as the timetable of tooth development. Variations of as much as six months from the average dates, either earlier or later, are considered normal (McDonald & Avery, 1983). The 12-month-old typically has six to eight teeth, the 18-month-old has from twelve to fourteen teeth, and the 2-year-old usually has approximately fourteen to sixteen teeth. The complete set of twenty deciduous teeth is present by 30 to 36 months in most infants.

Infants also vary in their responses to teething. Some babies are very cranky and fussy when they are cutting a tooth, whereas other babies appear to be affected very little by the process. Teething usually causes the gums to be sore, but contrary to popular opinion, teething does not cause fever or diarrhea (Beedle, 1984). Babies try to bite on objects placed in their mouths during this stage. When teeth begin to erupt, the biting behavior may present problems for the nursing mother, who may then decide to wean the baby at that point.

Good dental care is important even for the temporary teeth. These are the only teeth a child will have until around the sixth birthday. Young children need primary teeth for chewing of food, normal appearance, and clear

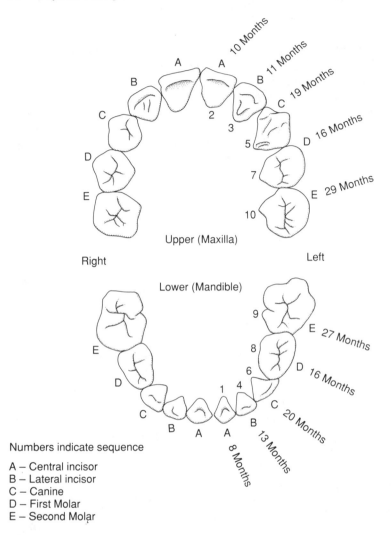

FIGURE 4-2 Eruption of the Primary Teeth—Age and Sequence.
Data from R. Lunt and D. Law, (1974). A review of the chronology of eruption of deciduous teeth. *Journal of the American Dental Association, 89,* 872–879. Used by permission.

speech. They may reject food needed for a proper diet, such as raw fruits and vegetables, because of missing or decayed teeth. Also, decay and abscess in a primary tooth may cause the permanent tooth developing beneath it to have a dark spot (Woelfel, 1984). More importantly, premature loss of primary teeth may result in problems with the timing of the eruption, spacing, and occlusion (bite) of the permanent teeth. An infant should begin regular visits to the dentist by the time all of the primary incisors have erupted, or at least by the age of 2.

BRAIN AND NERVOUS SYSTEM

The tissue of the human brain is made up of basic nerve cells (**neurons**), supporting cells called **neuroglia,** myelin, and various chemical substances called neurotransmitters. Neurons carry impulses from one part of the body to another. The cell body of each neuron grows treelike branches called dendrites, and a longer extension called an axon. Dendrites are receptors of nerve impulses, and axons are the transmitters (Fig. 4-3). Dendrites and axons of separate neurons lie close together but do not touch each other. These connecting gaps, called synapses, are where nerve impulses are passed from one neuron to another by releasing small amounts of chemicals.

The brain of a newborn infant is relatively large and well developed. All major lobes (sections of the brain) are clearly distinguishable. At birth, the brain typically weighs about 1 pound (DeKaban, 1970), which is roughly 15 percent of the total body weight. By comparison, the adult brain weighs 3 pounds and makes up only approximately 2 percent of the total body weight. By 1 year of age, the brain is about two-thirds as large as the adult brain. Growth of the brain is slower during the second year, during which it reaches about 75 percent of mature size (Tanner, 1978).

Scientists have tried to identify critical periods of very rapid brain growth, sometimes referred to as brain growth spurts. Dobbing (1976), one of the major investigators of brain growth, has identified two periods of rapid growth during which the brain is particularly vulnerable to environmental influences. The first period is the embryonic and fetal period, when the brain cells, particularly the neurons, are forming. The second period begins during late fetal life and continues through early infancy, when the brain cells increase in size and complexity. Not all scientists agree, however, about the peak, or critical periods, of brain growth. Epstein (1978) proposes that postnatal brain growth occurs mainly during two periods—3 to 10 months of age and 2 to 4 years of age.

Regardless of when the critical periods occur, scientists generally agree

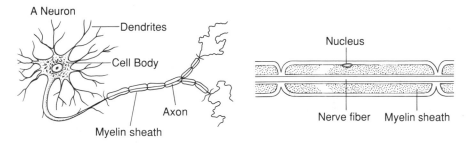

FIGURE 4-3   Myelination of a Neuron.
Source: I. Valadian and D. Porter, (1977), *Physical growth and development*. Boston: Little, Brown & Co. p. 134. Copyright by Little, Brown, & Co. 1977. Adapted by permission.

that environmental deficits or hazards occurring during that time are likely to result in permanent reduction in brain size, total number of brain cells, quantity and complexity of cell connections, chemical composition, and functional capacity of the brain (Williams, 1983). There is also some evidence that appropriate environmental stimulation can increase the growth of the dendrites, thereby affecting the complexity of the nervous system (Parmelee & Sigmon, 1983).

Neuroglial cells continue to be formed for approximately two years after birth in some parts of the brain. These cells serve as support links between the neurons and the blood supply. They are smaller and more numerous than neurons but do not carry messages (Tanner, 1978). Once they are formed, nerve cells grow to about 200,000 times their original size. Thus, most postnatal brain growth occurs because of an increase in the size of the neurons and the addition of neuroglial cells.

Different parts of the brain develop at different rates. The lower part of the brain develops and becomes functional before the higher structures. The parts of the brain that control the basic body functions and early reflexive activity are most fully developed at birth. The upper part of the brain, which controls voluntary movements, speech, and other cognitive processes, is comparatively undeveloped at birth. As the upper hemispheres develop, the motor and sensory centers develop quickly. By the end of the third month of postnatal life, the brain has developed sufficiently for the infant to establish control over the upper parts of the body. The part of the brain controlling thought and learning processes develops rapidly from the sixth through the fifteenth month (Hanson and Reynolds, 1980).

The process of **myelination** is a very important part of brain development. Myelin is a fatty substance that forms a sheath around the nerve fibers (see Fig. 4-3). The myelin sheath functions like the insulation on an electric wire to prevent short circuits. It also affects the rate at which impulses travel through the nervous system. Apparently, myelin begins to form on the nerve cells in the spinal cord and some areas of the brain before birth. The process continues rapidly during infancy, slowing down after the fourth or fifth year of life. Myelination is not complete in some parts of the nervous system until adulthood. Immediately after birth, myelination is most rapid in the upper part of the brain.

The appearance of certain motor abilities and muscle control corresponds with the formation of the myelin sheath in the area of the brain that controls those functions. Since myelination of the nerve fibers throughout the nervous system tends to proceed in a downward direction, the infant acquires control over the upper limbs before the lower limbs (Valadian and Porter, 1977). The increase in the myelin content of the brain cells is accompanied by the addition of connections between neurons.

CARDIOVASCULAR SYSTEM

Heart

Growth of the heart during the first four to six weeks after birth is very slow. Following this period, the heart grows steadily and rapidly throughout infancy. At the end of the first year, the weight of the heart has doubled; by the second year it has tripled (Moore, 1978). The shape of the heart also matures rapidly. By the second or third year of life, the outline of the infant's heart is very similar to that of an adult (Lowrey, 1978).

The heart rate of the newborn infant is rapid and subject to wide fluctuations. The 120 to 140 beats per minute is about twice the normal rate of an adult. The heart rate decreases to about 110 beats per minute between 1 and 2 years, and to 105 beats per minute between 2 and 4 years of age (Stangler, Huber, & Routh, 1980). Heart rates are more variable in infants than in adults, and heart murmurs are common. In most cases, such murmurs do not indicate a serious problem and usually disappear by age 1 (Lowrey, 1978).

Blood Pressure

Normally blood pressure increases throughout infancy. For example, the blood pressure of the full-term newborn is 75/50 as compared with the typical 100/60 of an infant 2 to 4 years of age (Stangler et al., 1980). Premature infants typically have lower blood pressure readings than full-term infants. Blood pressure is more variable in infants than it is in adults. However, some of the variability reported in blood pressure is probably a result of the difficulty of obtaining accurate and consistent measurements. Some of the fluctuations may be attributed to rapid shifts in infant states, such as sleeping or crying, which tend to cause the blood pressure to change.

EVALUATING PHYSICAL GROWTH

Records of an infant's height, weight, head circumference, and height:weight ratio should be maintained and compared periodically with normative growth standards. Various tables and growth charts are available for this purpose, but the tables and growth curves produced by the National Center for Health Statistics (1976) are the best ones currently available. The norms are based on nationwide studies of large numbers of infants of various ages. The growth status of any infant in the United States can be compared with that of other children of the same sex and age, but not the same race.

The child's status is interpreted according to percentile rankings. Various measurements can be plotted on a growth-curve chart (see Appendices

1–4), which gives a graphic illustration of the child's relative standing in comparison to that of other infants of the same age. To use one of the charts, find and point with one index finger to the child's weight in the vertical column. With the other index finger, point to the child's age in the horizontal row. Move the two fingers along the two lines until they meet. The intersection represents the child's percentile ranking. Measurements should be plotted at three- to six-month intervals throughout infancy to obtain the growth curve.

Infants with measurements between the 25th and 75th percentiles are considered to be growing normally. Rankings between the 10th and 25th percentiles, or between the 75th and 90th percentiles may or may not represent normal growth. Infants who fall above the 95th percentile or below the 5th percentile should be evaluated for nutritional, health, or other problems that might be affecting their growth trajectory (Stangler et al., 1980). About 10 percent of children who are normal fall outside the 10th and 90th percentiles (Behrman & Vaughan, 1983). Many children change percentile rankings over time.

FACILITATING PHYSICAL GROWTH

The infant's basic physical needs include food, elimination, warmth, sleep, rest, exercise, cleanliness, health, and safety. As long as caregivers consistently meet these basic needs, infants usually grow to fulfill their full genetic body size potential. Facilitating physical development thus means routinely providing adequate nutrition, bathing, diapering, dressing, and sleep and rest periods for an infant (Gonzalez-Mena & Eyer, 1980). In addition, regular health-maintenance checkups (including appropriate dental care) and prompt medical treatment for illnesses are extremely important.

The infant's social, emotional, and other psychological needs are closely linked to the physical needs. Therefore, the manner and attitude with which caregivers meet the infant's physical needs are important. Infant caregivers should not be aloof or indifferent as they provide routine physical care. Rather, parents and other caregivers should touch, cuddle, and talk to the infant in tender, loving ways as they meet basic physical needs.

SUMMARY

1. Physical growth is influenced by a variety of environmental factors. The factors discussed in this chapter are socioeconomic class, illness, emotional disturbances, hormonal influences, and race.

2. The three major indicators of body growth are height, weight, and head circumference. Male infants usually weigh a little more and are slightly taller than female infants at birth and throughout the infancy period. Infants normally double their birthweight during the first four or five months, triple it

by the end of the first year, and quadruple it during the second year of life. Infants usually increase their birth length by 50 percent during the first year and an additional 24 percent during the second year of life.

3. The average head circumference increases from 13.75 inches at birth to approximately 19 inches by the end of two years. Two soft spots, called fontanels, may be felt on the newborn infant's head. The fontanel on the back of the head is usually closed by 3 or 4 months of age. The larger fontanel in front is closed by approximately 20 months of age.

4. The infant's facial features are broader and flatter in appearance than an adult's. The lower jaw is underdeveloped and receded. The eyes are the most noticeable feature of an infant's face because of the relatively small nose. The infant's eye color tends to darken during the early months of life.

5. Normally, the infant's feet are proportionately thinner and longer than those of older children, but the feet of toddlers are somewhat chubbier and wider.

6. Muscle tissue makes up about one-fourth of the newborn baby's weight. All the muscle fibers the infant will need throughout life are present at birth or soon afterward.

7. The infant's deciduous teeth begin to develop as early as the twelfth prenatal week. The first tooth, however, is not visible until approximately eight months after birth. The complete set of twenty temporary teeth is usually present by 30 to 36 months.

8. The brain of the newborn infant is relatively large and well-developed but continues to grow rapidly during infancy, reaching 75 percent of its mature size by the end of two years. The infant brain may be especially vulnerable to environmental disturbances. Brain growth after birth consists primarily of increases in the size of the neurons, the growth and formation of neuroglial cells, plus the myelination of the nerve cells.

9. The heart of the infant grows rapidly during infancy and triples in size by the second year. The heart rate gradually decreases, while the blood pressure increases during infancy.

10. Standardized growth charts can be used to monitor an infant's height, weight, and head circumference. Infants who are ranked above the 95th percentile or below the 5th percentile on one or more aspects of growth should receive further evaluation. If the basic physical needs of infants are adequately met, they are likely to fulfill their potential for normal body growth.

5

Motor Development

The loving mother teaches her child to walk alone. She is far enough from him so that she cannot actually support him, but she holds out her arms to him. She imitates his movements, and if he totters, she swiftly bends as if to seize, so that the child might believe that he is not walking alone. . . . And yet, she does more. Her face beckons like a reward, an encouragement. Thus, the child walks alone with his eyes fixed on his mother's face, *not* on the difficulties in his way. He supports himself by the arms that do not hold him and constantly strives towards the refuge in his mother's embrace, little suspecting that in the very same moment that he is emphasizing his need of her, he is proving that he can do without her, because he is walking alone.

–Søren Kierkegaard

As soon as an infant is born, or perhaps even before, the struggle to establish control over the body begins. The changes that occur in the infant's ability to control the movement of the muscles of the body are referred to as motor development. During the first three years of life, the child progresses from a relatively helpless infant state of motor activity to a state of independence and mobility. The development of basic motor skills during infancy forms the foundation for the more elaborate and refined motor acts of later childhood.

The numerous motor behaviors that emerge during the infancy period can be classified under the following general headings: (1) reflex movements, (2) eye–hand coordination, (3) achievement of an upright position and loco-motion, (4) self-care activities. This chapter focuses on the characteristic patterns and processes of motor development in each of these categories. In addition, the factors that influence the acquisition of motor skills are discussed. Before proceeding, however, let us consider how motor development is inter-related with other areas of infant development.

INTERRELATIONSHIPS OF DEVELOPMENTAL AREAS

The development of motor skills is a complicated process involving coordination between the nervous system, the skeleton, muscles, and sensory mechanisms. Consequently, motor development influences and is influenced by other components of the growing infant.

During infancy the most important indicator of mental functioning may be the ability to carry out motor acts (Tanner, 1978). At the same time, the acquisition of motor skills allows the infant to move and explore the environment, a process necessary to satisfy curiosity and obtain knowledge. In Piaget's (1952) view, the sensorimotor activities of infancy provide the foundations of intelligence (see Chapter 8).

Experiments with kittens (Held & Hein, 1963) have shown that movement is necessary for adequate perceptual development. By the same token, sensory and perceptual processes play a key role in motor development. All voluntary motor acts are preceded by information perceived through one or more of the senses and interpreted by the brain (Williams, 1977). Studies of institutionalized infants suggest that lack of opportunity for movement and perceptual stimulation may retard the attainment of motor milestones and possibly change the order in which certain motor abilities develop (Robertson, 1984).

Lamb and Campos (1982) point out that motor activities play an important role in emotional development. Infants do not become afraid of heights until they are able to move around. Crawling apparently allows the infant to judge height more accurately or to experience more parental reactions to near-falls. Infants thus develop the impression that heights are dangerous and should be avoided.

The development of an infant's body awareness and self-image are derived to some extent from information obtained through sensorimotor activities (Williams, 1983). As infants use their bodies and experience success or failure in motor acts, they form self-opinions that are inextricably interrelated with overall personality development. The establishment of physical independence through motor control leads to feelings of self-confidence, psychological security, and independence. On the other hand, feelings of dependency and inadequacy tend to inhibit the acquisition of motor control.

FACTORS INFLUENCING MOTOR DEVELOPMENT

Genetics

The genetic structure of the infant's body provides the foundation for motor development. Research studies have found greater similarity of motor development among identical twins than among fraternal twins (Freedman & Keller, 1948; Gesell, 1954). Twin studies generally support the view that genetics provide the infant with the capacity to acquire motor skills while limiting the potential for progress and performance (Malina, 1973b). Specific genetics effects are difficult to determine, however, because scientists cannot completely separate the importance of environmental factors.

Maturation and Learning

A question closely related to genetic influences is the extent to which physical growth and maturation control motor development. Several classic research studies indicate that motor development is largely controlled by the process of maturation. For example, Gesell and Thompson (1934) gave one identical twin six weeks of practice in a variety of motor tasks, while they gave the other twin no opportunity for practice. Within a three-week period after the training ended, the twin who had not been given special instruction made more progress than the twin who had been trained. The researchers concluded that practice does not make any difference until a child is biologically ready to acquire a particular motor skill.

Another classic study, by Dennis (1941), reached a similar conclusion. Hopi Indian infants who were tied to a cradleboard on their mother's backs for much of the first nine months of life were compared to a group of infants from Western culture who were allowed relatively unrestricted movement. Since both groups of infants began to walk at about the same age, Dennis concluded that walking must be maturationally determined.

On the other side of the question, T. G. R. Bower (1977), a Scottish psychologist, believes that opportunities for learning "have a great deal to do with the rate and direction of motor development" (p. 91). In one of Bower's experiments, babies were given practice in reaching for a dangling object. These babies obtained a more mature pattern of reaching and grasping several weeks earlier than a control group of infants who had no comparable experience. Learning experiences were thus considered to have been influential in the acquisition of these particular skills.

Cratty (1979), a widely respected authority on motor development, has concluded that some motor skills may be accelerated by systematic training during late infancy and early childhood. However, before 18 months of age, normal milestones of basic motor development such as walking and climbing are not likely to be accelerated through early training. Obviously, the role of maturation and growth of the brain and nervous system in motor develop-

In some cultures, infants are carried on the mother's back for several months.

ment during infancy is of crucial importance. However, appropriate opportunities for learning at the time the child is maturationally ready are also very important in promoting optimum and timely acquisition of motor skills.

Body Size

The sizes of the various parts of the body affect its resistance to movement (Newell, 1984). Body size and proportions are apparently related to the age at which some of the motor milestones are achieved. The relationships are not simple, however, and are most clearly observed in infants who represent extreme differences in body measurements (Malina, 1973b). For example, slender infants with relatively long legs walk earlier than shorter infants with shorter legs (Bayley, 1935; Shirley, 1931). Garn (1966) found that leaner infants attained better scores on a variety of early motor tasks than heavier infants.

Cultural Influences

Cross-cultural studies consistently show that traditionally reared infants from underdeveloped countries are more accelerated in motor performance than infants from Western culture (Werner, 1979). Their advanced motor development was attributed to such child-rearing practices as frequent sensorimotor stimulation through participation in adult activities, exposure to multiple caregivers from extended families, and freedom from restrictive clothing and playpens. Infants reared in cultures where they were restricted by heavy clothing and where interactions with caretakers were quiet and passive tended to lag behind in motor activities. There is some evidence that black infants demonstrate precocity in motor development (King & Seegmiller, 1973). This advanced motor ability may be accounted for by environmental variables, including permissive and accepting attitudes on the part of black families. Differences in motor development that result primarily from cultural influences tend to disappear by the end of the infancy period.

Nutrition

Nutrition may affect motor development in two ways. First, inadequate nutritional intake may cause damage to the nervous system, resulting in impairment of intersensory functioning. The child may thus have problems in processing and efficiently utilizing sensations, perceptions, memory, and attention in acquiring motor skills. Second, nutrition affects strength and energy level. Undernourished infants are apathetic and lack sufficient physical vigor and endurance to pursue motor activities (Smoll, 1982).

The relationship of nutrition to motor development is dramatically illustrated by cross-cultural studies of infants from poverty-stricken environments where breast feeding is heavily utilized. During the first six months of life, infants from these cultures compare very favorably with infants from more economically advantaged environments. However, during the second half of the first year, when breast milk alone becomes insufficient to meet nutritional needs, there is a steady decline in the psychomotor performance of these infants. Motor development begins to decline even earlier if the period of breast feeding is shorter (Werner, 1979).

DEVELOPMENTAL TRENDS

Motor Biases

Infants demonstrate preferences or biases in motor activities. They generally prefer to work on developing new motor skills. Levin (1983) points out that babies tend to give themselves homework assignments such as "work on crawling," or "practice standing now." For example, once infants discover that the hand can be used to touch an object, they practice over and over until they have achieved and refined their ability to reach, touch, and pick up an object. Fourteen-month-old Kristin tried to make a lid fit on a small plastic bottle. She had formed the idea that caps go on bottles if you twist them. However, she could not quite get the threads on the cap to fit the threads on the bottle. She would twist and turn until she became frustrated. Then she would throw the pieces away in anger. She returned to the same task over and over until she had mastered the skill.

Infants can be observed engaging in repetitive movements such as rocking on hands and knees, head banging, kicking, and scratching. These patterns of movements are sometimes referred to as **rhythmical stereotypies** (Thelan, 1981). Infants tend to use stereotypies as a means of preparing for later, more coordinated movements. Thelan (1981) believes that infants are programmed at birth to engage in rhythmic movements. These activities are viewed as normal responses that facilitate motor development.

Mass to Specific

General movements develop before specific movements. In the newborn, the legs and arms usually move at the same time. As the baby grows, the capacity to make specific movements with individual body parts increases. An infant can eventually move the arms without moving the legs, then one arm without the other, and finally one finger at a time. For example, if a newborn's foot is touched with an ice cube, the whole body moves in a generalized response. An older infant responds to the ice cube by withdrawing the specific foot that has been touched.

Hierarchical Integration

The simplest and most elementary skills develop first and become more complex as they are combined to form more elaborate movements. An infant who grasps a raisin between the thumb and index finger and places it in a bottle is integrating four basic skills—reaching, grasping, placing, and releasing—to complete a more difficult pattern of activity.

Developmental Direction

Motor development generally follows the laws of developmental direction. According to the **cephalocaudal principle,** the infant obtains control of the arms before the legs. Reaching develops before walking. Following the **proximodistal** trend, control of the arms is established before control over the wrist and fingers is obtained. Cratty (1979) notes that while the laws of developmental direction are generally true, there are exceptions, particularly in the proximodistal trend. In his estimation, the laws of developmental direction need further refinement and examination in the light of current research studies.

REFLEXES

The first movements newborn infants exhibit consist mostly of reflex activities. A reflex is an automatic or involuntary response to a specific stimulus. The reflexes are controlled by the lower brainstem and spinal cord. As the upper part of the brain matures, the reflexes are mostly replaced with voluntary movements. The newborn infant is equipped with seventy or more primitive reflexes (Illingworth, 1983).

Some of the reflexes, such as sucking, have obvious survival value. However, the importance of many of the reflexes is not clear. In general, the reflexes are considered to be indicators of the maturity and normalcy of the nervous system. Several reflexes can be easily observed in young infants. If a reflex fails to appear or disappear at the appropriate age, some type of neurological problem may exist. A few of the key reflexes are described below.

Rooting and Sucking

Newborn infants are equipped with rooting and sucking responses that allow them to obtain nourishment. Touching a newborn infant in the corner of the mouth will trigger a rooting or searching response in which the head is turned in the direction of the stimulus in search of something to suck, preferably a breast or a bottle containing milk. In concert with the rooting reflex, the newborn begins sucking reflexively as soon as a finger or a nipple touches the mouth. The rooting reflex begins to disappear by 3 months of age. The sucking reflex is gradually replaced by voluntary sucking.

Grasp

The palmar grasp reflex is easily elicited by placing a finger or small object in the palm of the baby's hand. The grasp may be so tight that the baby's weight can be supported for an instant. The palmar grasp becomes weaker after the first month and is replaced by voluntary grasping by 3 or 4 months of age.

Moro

The Moro reflex is a response to a loud noise or sudden loss of support. It may be elicited by holding an infant with one hand supporting the head and the other behind the back. The hand supporting the head is lowered abruptly, allowing the infant's head to fall an inch or two. The baby responds by quickly stretching the arms outward and bringing them together in a hugging motion. The back is arched and the hands curl slightly, while the knees are drawn toward the stomach. The Moro, sometimes called the embracing reflex, is normally present at birth and begins to disappear around 3 months of age. It cannot be observed in most infants after 5 or 6 months of age. The Moro is one of the most widely used reflexes in the neurological examination of infants (Bench et al., 1972).

Babinski

If a finger or a pencil is rubbed along the inner side of the young infant's foot from heel to toe, the big toe will move upward while the other toes fan inward toward the bottom of the foot. This is the Babinski reflex, which is present as early as the third or fourth prenatal month and disappears between 12 and 18 months in most infants.

Tonic Neck

There are two types of tonic neck reflexes: the asymmetrical, in which one side of the body is dominant, and the symmetrical, in which both sides of the body are balanced. Of the two, the asymmetrical tonic neck reflex (ATNR)

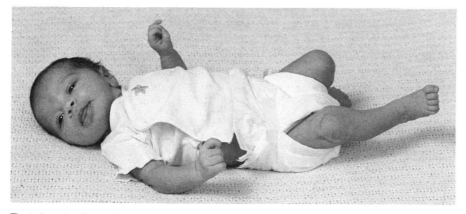

The tonic neck reflex position.

is the most widely known. It can be elicited by placing an infant on its back. The baby's head turns toward one side. One arm and leg are extended in the direction in which the head is facing. The other arm is bent at the elbow with the hand placed near the head. This is similar to a "fencing" position. The ATNR is most commonly observed during the first two or three months of life. It is usually gone by six or seven months.

The symmetrical tonic neck reflex (STNR) may be observed by holding the infant under the stomach and bending the head up and down. When the head goes up the arms go down while the legs are raised. Raising the head has the opposite effect. The reflex must disappear before an infant can learn to crawl, since the arms and legs must move independently of the head.

Stepping

Infants typically exhibit a stepping or walking reflex at birth or soon afterward. When held upright with bare feet touching a flat surface, an infant will take rhythmic steps forward. The stepping reflex usually disappears by the fifth month of age.

Influence of Reflexes on Voluntary Movement

The extent to which reflexes facilitate or interfere with voluntary movement is a major question in infant motor development. From one point of view, reflexes form the basis for all voluntary motor activities (Newell, 1984). Reflexes are considered to be responses that an infant may incorporate efficiently into the process of establishing voluntary motor skills. In support of this position, researchers have found that exercise of the stepping reflex during the first nine weeks of life can lead to an earlier beginning of voluntary walking (Zelazo, Zelazo, & Kolb, 1972). Similar effects of reflex exercise have been found for crawling (Lagerspetz, Nygard, & Strandwick, 1971) and grasping (Bower, 1977).

On the other hand, reflexes are sometimes viewed as behaviors that inhibit the onset of voluntary movements (Newell, 1984). According to this position, a reflex response must disappear before a related voluntary motor movement can be established. For example, the plantar reflex must disappear in the feet before an infant can stand and walk. Otherwise the bottoms of the feet tend to curl up and fail to provide a firm foundation for walking.

The relationship between the establishment of voluntary motor skills and reflex activities is obviously a complex issue. Both points of view have some validity. Apparently some of the reflexes evolve into voluntary motor responses, and with practice, facilitate their early onset. At the same time, other reflexes stand in the way of emergence and development of some motor skills.

DEVELOPMENT OF HAND CONTROL

Eye-Hand Coordination

The development of the ability to locate, grasp, and manipulate objects is a major task in motor development. This very complex task requires the voluntary coordination of eye, arm, hand, and finger movements. There are two major stages in the development of eye-hand coordination, which include a variety of changes during the infancy period.

Stage 1: Prereaching. Some scientists (Cratty, 1979; Trevarthen, 1978; Williams, 1983) believe that infants are equipped at birth with an underlying "motor prewiring" through which vision and kinesthetic sensations work together to produce reaching and grasping movements. Newborn infants apparently reach for or swat at objects in their visual field (Bower, Broughton, & Moore, 1970; Von Hofsten, 1982). Such movements, however, are referred to as **prereaching** (Bushnell, 1985; Von Hofsten, 1984), in contrast to later reaching.

Researchers have identified several characteristic features of prereaching activities. During this stage, infants are rarely successful in touching, not to mention grasping, the target object. They move their arms very rapidly, withdrawing the hand immediately without making corrective adjustments in the trajectory or path of the hand (Bower, 1982; Bushnell, 1985). Prereaching infants do not appear to look at both the reaching hand and the target object in their reaching attempts. Rather, the eye-hand coordination of newborn and very young infants seems to be based on a primitive combination of kinesthetic (sensations of movement from the muscles and joints) and visual responses.

Prereaching movements are *visually elicited* rather than visually guided (Bushnell, 1985). That is, an infant sees an object and reaches out for it automatically as part of the same response pattern. The reaching response is apparently triggered by the sense of vision rather than the thought of obtaining and manipulating the object. The main function of prereaching behavior is thus considered to be attentional rather than intentional (Von Hofsten, 1982).

The quantity and quality of prereaching activities change with age. Major changes become evident by 7 weeks of age (Von Hofsten, 1984). The amount of reaching activity declines while the intensity of staring increases. A baby seems to grasp an object with the eyes, mentally dropping it and picking it up again (Williams, 1983). Around this age, infants have a tendency to spend a lot of time looking at their hands. Apparently the increased visual attention inhibits and alters reaching behavior. Burton White (1975) believes that the visual discovery of the hands around 6 or 7 weeks is a major milestone in infant development.

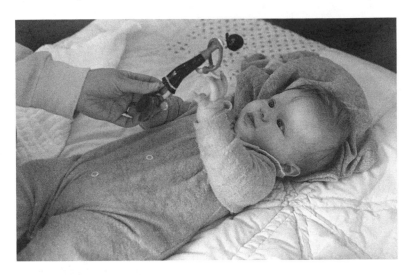

This baby is engaged in visually directed reaching.

When the 7-week-old infant occasionally reaches for an object, the form is different from neonatal reaching. The hand is held with the fist closed during reaching rather than remaining open as it was earlier. As the infant gets older, the amount of reaching activity goes up again, and the hand opens as it reaches an object. The changes that occur in reaching activities have been attributed to reorganization of the systems of the brain as the baby matures and moves from reflexive to voluntary responses (Von Hofsten, 1984).

Stage 2: Visually Directed Reaching.   The infant begins to acquire the ability to engage in visually directed reaching some time between 3 and 5 months (Bushnell, 1985). Williams (1983) describes this stage as "the regulation of grasping/manipulative responses through intensified visual activity." The infant first locates an object with the eyes and attempts to pick it up. Frequently, the baby loses sight of the object and fails as in earlier eye-hand coordination efforts. However, when this happens, the baby intensifies visual fixation, adjusts the reaching movements, keeping the object in view until the goal is obtained. As the infant builds on previous experiences, visually directed reaching becomes smoother and more successful with age.

Prehension

After the grasp reflex disappears at approximately 4 months of age, the infant begins to work on prehension—grasping an object between fingers and thumb. Halverson (1931) identified ten stages that occur between 26 and 52 weeks of age in the acquisition of adultlike grasping skills (see Table 5-1 and Figure 5-1). In the early stages, the infant uses only the fingers and the palm in picking up an object, such as a small cube. Initially an infant rakes at a tiny

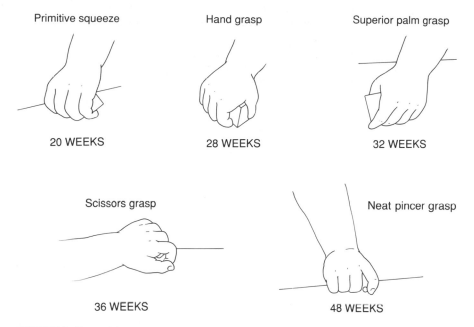

Primitive squeeze   Hand grasp   Superior palm grasp

20 WEEKS   28 WEEKS   32 WEEKS

Scissors grasp   Neat pincer grasp

36 WEEKS   48 WEEKS

FIGURE 5-1 Types of Grasping Behavior.
Sources: H. Halverson, (1931). *Genetic Psychology Monographs, 10*, 107–286. Reprinted with permission of the Helen Dwight Reid Foundation. Published by Heldref Publications, 4000 Albemarle St., N.W., Washington, DC 20016. Copyright 1931; Knobloch, H., Stevens, F., & Malone, A. (1980). *Manual of Developmental Diagnosis.* New York: Harper and Row. Used by permission.

object, such as a pellet, without picking it up. As soon as the ability to use the thumb (finger-thumb opposition) is acquired at approximately 9 months, grasping skills develop faster. By approximately 1 year of age, an infant can pick up cubes and pellets in an adultlike fashion, with a thumb and forefinger pincer grasp.

Object Manipulation

Once infants develop the ability to grasp and pick up objects, they spend a large amount of time engaging in manipulative activities. The way in which an infant interacts with an object varies according to age. Uzgiris (1967) observed how infants between the ages of 2 and 24 months manipulate a variety of objects including a rattle, a small doll, and a piece of aluminum foil. She identified the following patterns at various ages:

1. *Mouthing,* or attempting to get an object in the mouth, dominates the early interactions with objects (2 months).
2. *Visual inspection,* i.e., gazing intently at an object held almost motionless for considerable periods of time (3 months).
3. *Hitting* or banging an object on a surface or waving it in the air as if making contact (4–7 months).

4. *Shaking* an object in a side-to-side movement of the lower arm and hand (5–7 months).

5. *Examining* an object by turning it around, poking, tearing, pulling, crumpling, squeezing, rubbing, sliding, pushing it, or moving its various parts while observing the effects of the manipulations (6–10 months).

6. *Letting go* of an object by dropping or throwing it to watch it fall or hear a sound when it hits (8–11 months).

7. *Showing* or extending an object to another person to initiate an interaction.

8. *Naming* an object after viewing or examining it (18–24 months).

These characteristic patterns of using objects apparently develop sequentially, with earlier behaviors continuing into later stages.

Hand Preference

Many organisms display a preference for one side of the body in performing certain movements. Rats tend to exhibit a paw preference, and even grasshoppers have a favorite scratching leg (Hecaen & Ajuriagurra, 1964). Human beings may begin to demonstrate a preference for one hand or the other in reaching and grasping as early as the infancy period.

Although infants prefer to use one hand more than the other at times,

TABLE 5-1   Milestones of Fine Motor Development

MOTOR ACTIVITY	AVERAGE AGE (MONTHS)	MOTOR ACTIVITY	AVERAGE AGE (MONTHS)
Prehension of cubes		Prehension of pellets	
Reaches—no contact	4	Rakes with whole hand	5.5
Reaches—makes contact	5	Inferior scissors grasp	7.4
Primitive squeeze	5	Scissors grasp	8.2
Squeeze grasp	6	Inferior pincer grasp	9.2
Hand grasp	7	Neat pincer grasp	11
Palm grasp	7	Inserts pellet in bottle	12
Superior palm grasp	8	Other	
Inferior forefinger grasp	9	Turn pages, two or three	
Forefinger grasp	12	at one time	18
Superior forefinger grasp	12	Inserts shoelace through	
Voluntary release of cube	11	safety pin	24
Builds tower of four cubes	18	Turns single page	30
Builds tower of seven			
cubes	24	Tries to cut with scissors	36
Aligns train of four cubes	24		
Builds tower of ten cubes	36		

Sources: H. Halverson, (1931). *Genetic Psychology Monographs*, 10, 107–286. Reprinted with permission of the Helen Dwight Reid Foundation. Published by Heldref Publications, 4000 Albemarle St., N.W., Washington, DC 20016. Copyright 1931; Knobloch, H., Stevens, F., & Malone, A., (1980). *Manual of Developmental Diagnosis*. New York: Harper and Row. Used by permission.

they frequently display an irregular pattern of usage, shifting preference from one side to the other or to an interchangeable pattern. Gesell and Ames (1947) observed that the hand used most frequently by infants in reaching for objects tends to alternate from left to right during the first year. Between about 56 and 80 weeks of age, there is considerable interchangeability. A definite hand preference is established in many children by 2 years of age (Illingworth, 1983). For many others, though, hand dominance is not observable until a year or two later.

Questions about whether hand preference is controlled by heredity or environmental influences have been debated for a long time. A few years ago a widely used child development text included the opinion that "training and social conditioning determine handedness and, therefore there is no such thing as *natural handedness*" (Hurlock, 1972, p. 144). However, the prevailing opinion now tends to favor hereditary and biological explanations. Boklage (1980) believes that hand preference is linked to the organization of the brain, which is established early in the prenatal period. Evidence from his study of 800 twins reveals that if either one or both parents were left-handed, they were 50 percent more likely to have a left-handed child. Left-handedness occurs almost twice as often in twins as in singletons.

Throwing and Catching

Infants do not develop much proficiency in throwing. However, the ability to throw objects begins to emerge as early as 6 months, when babies accidentally release and hurl objects they are waving about or shaking (Espenschade & Eckert, 1967). As voluntary release is established, infants soon learn that dropping objects has an interesting effect. They delight in dropping or throwing spoons and other objects from the highchair to hear the noise as well as to watch someone pick them up. The first attempts at throwing are usually a stiff underhand motion (Cratty, 1979). Most infants (75 percent) develop the ability to throw a small ball overhanded by 22 months of age (Frankenburg, Dodds, & Fandal, 1973).

The ability to catch an object requires much more eye-hand coordination and perceptual ability than does throwing. Consequently, infants make little progress in this area. The baby's first efforts at catching are typically trying to stop a rolling ball (Hottinger, 1977). The first successful attempts to catch an object thrown into the air usually occur around 3 years of age (Williams, 1983).

POSTURE AND LOCOMOTION

Posture represents the adjustments of the body in relation to the forces of gravity. Postural abilities an infant must develop include achieving head control, sitting, and standing. Posture provides the base of support for body movements. Locomotion is the ability to move from place to place. The

TABLE 5-2   Milestones of Gross Motor Development

MOTOR ACTIVITY	AVERAGE AGE (MONTHS)
Rolls over	2.8
Sits with support—head steady	2.9
Sits alone—steadily	6.6
Crawls	7.0
Stands—holding on	8.6
Creeps or hitches	9.0
Walks holding on	9.2
Stands alone	11.0
Walks alone	11.7
Throws ball	13.3
Walks up steps—with help	16.1
Walks downstairs—with help	16.4
Jumps in place	22.3

Sources: Taken from the Bayley Scales of Infant Development. Copyright © 1969 by the Psychological Corporation. All rights reserved. Frankenburg, Dodds, & Fandal, 1973; Knobloch, H., Stevens, F., & Malone, A. (1980). *Manual of Developmental Diagnosis*. New York: Harper and Row. Used by permission.

achievement of mobility increases the infant's opportunities for exploration and is necessary for the development of independence. Although learning to walk is the most dramatic and important locomotor task of infancy, it is preceded and followed by an orderly progression of several other significant milestones (see Table 5-2).

Head Control

Establishing control of the head is the first step toward achieving an upright position and independent locomotion (Gesell, 1954). Head control is defined as the ability to keep the head steady in an upright position and move it at will. The neck muscles of the newborn are not strong enough to support the weight of the disproportionately large head for more than a few seconds. In addition, the relative immaturity of the nervous system makes voluntary control of head movements difficult for the newborn.

The beginning of head control may be observed when the baby raises the head far enough to clear the chin from the surface for a few seconds. Most infants (90 percent) accomplish this task by 3 weeks of age. When lying on the stomach, an infant can routinely hold the head so that the face makes a 45-degree angle with the surface at approximately 2½ months of age (Frankenburg et al., 1973). On the average, infants acquire the ability to hold their head steady when held in an upright position at around three months (White, 1975).

Rolling

The infant's first attempt at locomotion is rolling from one side to another. Ordinarily an infant can roll from stomach to back around 16 weeks of age, although occasionally a newborn can accomplish this task. The more difficult task of rolling from back to stomach is typically performed about 6 weeks later (Knobloch, Stevens, & Malone, 1980).

An infant rolls by turning the head, twisting the trunk, and using a leg to push the body over. Cratty (1979) believes that the body-righting reflex and visual-tracking reflexes are responsible for the infant's first attempts to roll over. The baby catches sight of a moving object and turns the head to follow it. The turned head triggers the righting reflex, which causes the body to flip over.

Sitting

As the infant gradually gains control over the muscles in the trunk of the body, sitting alone becomes possible. Most babies are able to sit alone momentarily without support around 5 months of age (Bayley, 1969). During their first attempts at sitting alone, infants lean forward to gain added balance and support (Gallahue, 1982). By 6 or 7 months an infant can maneuver into a sitting position and sit alone steadily (Bayley, 1969).

Crawling

About the time an infant can sit alone and roll onto the stomach, crawling movements are likely to follow. In crawling, the head and chest are raised

This baby is just beginning to make crawling movements on his hands and stomach.

while the stomach maintains contact with the surface. The weight of the head and shoulders rests on the elbows and hands, which are used to slide the body forward or backward. The legs usually drag, although they may sometimes be used to push or pull. Most infants begin crawling around 7 months (range = 4.5 to 9.5 months) (Burnett & Johnson, 1971).

Creeping

As the baby becomes a proficient crawler, and muscle strength increases in the legs, efforts are made to advance to the creeping stage. Infants begin to creep around 8.5 months (range = 5 to 14.5 months) (Burnett & Johnson, 1971). Creeping is defined as locomotion on the hands and knees or hands and feet. The technical definitions of crawling and creeping may be confusing because the meanings are usually reversed in common usage. Thinking of the terms alphabetically—*crawling* before *creeping*—may help you remember their sequence and therefore the definitions.

When infants first attempt to creep, they slowly and deliberately move one limb an inch or two at a time. With practice, the movements become smoother, more efficient, and faster. Most babies exhibit a pattern in which the arm movement is followed by movement of the opposite leg. However, about 20 percent of all infants follow the arm movement by moving the knee on the same side of the body (Cratty, 1979). Infants are individuals, though, and tend to use a variety of positions and movements in creeping and other forms of locomotion.

For reasons not altogether understood, some infants never crawl and some do not go through the creeping stage (Illingworth, 1983). A few theorists believe that failure to go through these stages may result in later problems such as learning disabilities. However, the prevailing scientific opinion is such claims have no basis and that crawling and creeping are not essential for normal development.

Hitching

A few infants learn to move around by an unusual method referred to as hitching, or scooting. Hitching is defined as locomotion in a sitting position. The baby uses the legs, heels, and sometimes the hands to slide the buttocks along the floor. Some infants can scoot along quite rapidly and may use hitching as a substitute for creeping or walking. For example, at 20 months of age, Sue was attending a nursery-toddler class in which she was the only child who had not learned to walk. However, she could participate in the activities and keep up with the others by skillful hitching movements. Although her parents and teachers were concerned, physical and neurological examinations revealed no problems. She was walking by 2 years of age.

Standing

Infants typically begin to stand by pulling themselves up and holding onto furniture. One of the infant's motivations for standing is to extend the range of grasping and reaching for attractive objects above eye level. Most infants begin to pull themselves to a standing position by using chairs or other furniture between 6 and 10 months of age (Frankenburg et al., 1973).

Standing up to furniture is followed by *cruising*. This activity consists of moving around, usually sideways, holding onto furniture or other objects. As infants gradually gain stability in pulling up and cruising, they develop enough confidence to let go of their support for a few seconds. Most infants accomplish the task of standing alone with stability between 10 and 14 months (Frankenburg, et al., 1973). Once they achieve this milestone, they soon proceed to the more interesting task of walking alone.

Walking

From the parents' point of view, the baby's first independent steps may represent the most significant accomplishment of infancy. From the baby's perspective, walking opens up a new world. The average age for walking alone is 12 months. However, the normal range is from 9 months to as late as 17 months (Bayley, 1969). Infants are often referred to as **toddlers** from the time they begin to walk until they achieve a stable pattern of walking around 24 months of age.

In the initial stage of walking, the legs are spread apart for a wide base of support (Cratty, 1979). The toes are pointed outward with the knees slightly bent. The arms are held out for balance as the legs move in rigid, high-stepping, halting movements. The baby has difficulty maintaining balance and falls easily (Gallahue, 1982). Some infants may walk sideways as a carry-over from early cruising movements.

Toddlers progress to a more advanced stage of walking rather quickly, although for several weeks they may resemble a "duck out for a jog" (Fogel, 1984, p. 207). With practice, the walking pattern becomes more balanced and smoother, the toes point straight ahead, and heel-to-toe contact replaces flat-footed slipping (Gallahue, 1982). The length of the steps tends to increase with age. Walking improves throughout the infancy period, but a mature, adultlike pattern does not emerge until around 4 to 7 years (Scrutton, 1969).

Running

Young children begin to run soon after they begin to walk. Toddlers may take a few rapid steps to maintain balance even before they master walking. The toddler just beginning to walk sometimes moves the feet as rapidly as possible to reach the next base of support (Williams, 1983). Running is defined as "a series of smoothly coordinated jumps during which the body weight is borne on one foot, becomes airborne, is then carried on the opposite foot and again becomes airborne" (Slocum & James, 1968). The feature that distinguishes running from fast walking is the phase in which the body briefly leaves the supporting surface (Wickstrom, 1983).

Running begins its developmental course around 18 months of age. In the initial stage of running, the leg swing is short and limited. The stride is stiff and uneven. There is no observable time when the feet are not in contact with the surface. By 2 years of age, most infants can run well enough to meet the minimum standards of true running (Gesell, 1940). They can move a little faster and the length of the stride has increased. There is a limited but clearly observable flight phase. The arm and leg movements are more balanced and coordinated (Gallahue, 1982). Although a mature running pattern is not established during the first three years of life, infants make a remarkable amount of progress.

Climbing

An infant may attempt to go up stair steps on all fours before developing the ability to stand alone or walk. These initial climbing efforts are an extension of creeping and generally coincide with early attempts to stand. After they begin to walk, infants will attempt to climb stairs in an upright position with the assistance of an adult. These early efforts consist of a "mark time" pattern in which the child leads with the same foot on each step. Wellman (1937) found that children can climb a long flight of stairs and a ladder by 24 months of age using this same pattern. Climbing with an alternating foot pattern begins to occur around 3 years of age (Cratty, 1979).

Jumping

The first attempts to jump (off low steps) may be observed in infants at about 18 months of age (McClenaghan & Gallahue, 1978). Infants like to jump off the last step as they are descending stairs with assistance. This seems to be a preliminary phase in development before they obtain the ability to jump up and down from a standing position (Williams, 1983). The average age for jumping off the floor with both feet is 28 months (Bayley, 1969).

SELF-CARE ACTIVITIES

Self-care skills such as dressing, toileting, and eating (see Chapter 7) vary widely among toddlers. The development of these abilities is largely dependent upon biological maturation but is also related to internal motivation and parental influences. Some infants insist on doing things for themselves very early, whereas others are more passive and dependent.

This baby can take the sock off but is not successful in putting it back on.

Dressing

Gesell (1940) observed that infants learn many things in reverse order. This observation is especially applicable to dressing skills. Infants begin to remove articles of clothing long before they can put them on. During the first 12 to 18 months of infancy they are more concerned about taking clothes off than putting them on. They take special delight in pulling off their shoes, tied or untied, as well as their socks. By 19 months, most infants (75 percent) can remove at least one article of clothing (Frankenburg et al., 1973).

Infants begin to push their arms through sleeves and hold out their feet for shoes shortly before they are 1 year old. However, most of their dressing skills develop between 18 months and 3 years. During this period, most infants begin to put on their shoes, shirts, sweaters, and most other articles of clothing. Most infants (75 percent) accomplish the task of self-dressing with supervision by 36 months of age (Frankenburg et al., 1973), except for tying shoes and buttoning or zipping difficult garments.

Elimination Control

A major developmental task that begins during infancy is the establishment of control over the sphincter muscles, which control bowel and bladder movements. At birth, elimination is a reflexive act that is subject to conditioning. Infants can be conditioned to empty the bladder or bowels as early as a month or two. However, infants are not usually ready to begin to establish voluntary control over these functions until they are 15 to 18 months old (Illingworth, 1983).

Many child development experts advise parents to wait until an infant is at least 2 years old before beginning toilet training. White (1975) believes that toilet training should not be attempted between 14 and 24 months of age, because the infant is entering a period of negativism. Two-year-olds are more cooperative and usually train themselves in a short period of time. Elimination control is usually established in the following sequence: bowel control, daytime bladder control, nighttime bladder control.

HANDICAPPING CONDITIONS

Blind Infants

Vision is obviously a very significant factor in motor development. Surprisingly, though, blind infants tend to achieve some of the tasks of motor development at about the same time and in the same sequence as infants who can see. Blind infants look at their hands with their unseeing eyes (Illingsworth, 1983), begin to sit alone, roll from back to stomach, take stepping movements when their hands are held, rise to their hands and knees, and stand alone within the normal age range (Adelson & Fraiberg, 1974). However, blind infants experience considerable delay in achieving self-initiated mobility and in reaching for objects.

Fraiberg and her colleagues (Fraiberg, 1971; Fraiberg, Smith, & Adelson, 1969) developed a guidance program to help blind infants with the achievement of reaching and mobility. Their program focused on the coordination of the ear and hand in reaching for objects, parent-child games, and the use of sound lures as incentives to mobility. Bower (1977) equipped a 16-week-old blind infant with a device that produced echoes from objects. The baby was able to reach accurately and grasp silent objects, even distinguishing two different objects. Scott, Jan, and Freeman (1977) have produced a guidebook for parents of visually impaired infants and toddlers that contains suggestions for helping these children with motor skill development.

Mentally Retarded Infants

Research findings generally indicate that infants with lower-than-average intelligence experience delay in achieving the normal milestones of motor development (Wickstrom, 1983). The extent of the delay depends on the level of retardation and physical or nervous-system handicaps. In some areas of motor functioning, however, mentally retarded children may be more alike than different from other children. For example, Kaminer and Jedrysek (1983) recorded the age of walking in 200 infants representing all levels of mental retardation. The majority of children walked by the normal age of 17 months. Only when the children were extremely retarded was walking delayed beyond 17 months. However, early walkers were found even among this group.

FACILITATING MOTOR DEVELOPMENT

A variety of infant-stimulation programs have been developed to assist parents and other caregivers in helping infants enhance their motor skill development. Some of these programs have been designed specifically for handicapped infants (e.g., Connor, Williamson, & Siepp, 1978), and others are intended for use with normal infants (e.g., Gerber, 1981; Prudden, 1964; Levy, 1973). Ridenour (1978) advises parents to avoid motor-stimulation programs that claim to greatly enhance an infant's future motor or intellectual performance. The following principles are recommended for use by parents and caregivers:

1. Activities and materials should be developmentally appropriate within the various stages of motor development (Weiser, 1982).

2. Caregivers should not try to hurry development. Babies get ready for the next stage by mastering what they are doing in the present stage (Gonzalez-Mena & Eyer, 1980).

3. Stimulation activities, such as games and exercises, should be provided in each area and stage of motor development (Weiser, 1982). The Uzgiris-Hunt (1975) Scales of Psychological Development suggest many age-appropriate motor activities.

4. Movement activities should be staged so that infants can solve them without adult help or interference (Weiser, 1982).

5. A variety of toys and materials designed to facilitate motor development should be made available to an infant. However, such objects should usually be placed within the infant's reach rather than directly in the hands (Pikler, 1968).

6. Infants should be placed in situations where they are most free and least helpless during the waking hours (Gonzalez-Mena & Eyer, 1980). Playpens, infant seats, highchairs, swings, and jump chairs should not be used for extended periods of time (Gerber, 1981; Prudden & Sussman, 1972). Parents should carefully supervise infants who are using such equipment because of the risk of injury (Ridenour, 1978).

7. Infants should frequently wear as little clothing as temperature and social settings allow in order to facilitate maximum freedom of movement (Pikler, 1968; Prudden, 1964).

SUMMARY

1. Motor development plays an important role in the development of intelligence, perceptual skills, emotional development, self-awareness, and other aspects of infant development.

2. Factors influencing motor development include heredity, maturation and learning, body size, cultural practices, and nutrition.

3. Infants display a tendency to practice a new motor activity until it becomes a skill. Motor development proceeds from general to specific responses and from simple to complex skills. Motor development follows the cephalocaudal law of developmental direction, and with some exceptions, the proximodistal law as well.

4. Newborn infants are equipped with numerous reflexes, such as sucking, rooting, and grasping. Many of the reflexes normally disappear at specific ages. Some of the reflexes apparently facilitate the development of motor skills with practice, whereas others tend to inhibit the emergence of voluntary control.

5. Eye-hand coordination is established in two stages between birth and 3 to 5 months of age. Prehension, the ability to grasp an object between fingers and thumb, develops in several stages between 4 months and 12 months of age. The infant who has developed prehensory skills spends a lot of time mouthing, visually inspecting, examining, and manipulating objects in numerous ways.

6. Hand preference is established in most infants by 2 years of age. Current professional opinions tend to favor the theory that handedness is controlled by heredity.

7. To achieve an upright position, the infant establishes head control (3 months), sitting alone (5–6 months), and standing alone (6–10 months). The development of locomotion begins with rolling (16–22 weeks) and progresses through the stages of crawling, creeping, and sometimes hitching. Infants usually begin to walk alone by around 12 months of age. Climbing, running, and jumping develop toward the end of the infancy period.

8. Infants typically accomplish most of the skills needed in undressing and dressing themselves between 8 months and 3 years of age. Parents are advised to wait until the infant is 2 years old before beginning toilet training.

9. Some of the conditions that delay motor development include blindness and mental retardation.

10. Numerous programs have been developed to facilitate motor development during infancy. However, parents should use developmentally appropriate activities and not try to hurry motor development.

6

Health And Safety

Eat no green apples or you'll droop
Be careful not to get the croup
Avoid the chickenpox and such
And don't fall out the window much.
—*Edward Anthony*

Every two seconds somewhere in the world a child dies before reaching the fifth birthday (Colburn, 1986). Approximately 11 out of each 1,000 infants die in the first year of life (U.S. Bureau of the Census, 1987). Countless others suffer serious illnesses and injuries. The life-threatening situations infants face include congenital malformations, birth injuries, infectious diseases, accidental injuries, sudden infant death syndrome, and child abuse. When the numerous potential health and safety hazards infants may encounter are considered, it is amazing that the death rate is not higher.

In the first part of this chapter we consider the immunizations and other precautionary measures that can be taken to protect infants and prevent the spread of deadly communicable diseases. We also look at the major symptoms of illness in infants along with some of the most frequent, garden-variety illnesses of infants for which no permanent immunizations are available. The second part of this chapter is devoted to a discussion of the leading causes of accidental death among infants and how accidents can be prevented.

IMMUNIZATIONS AGAINST COMMUNICABLE DISEASES

We are fortunate in having vaccines available to provide immunity against many of the life-threatening communicable diseases infants and young children face in growing up. Immunization is begun early in life so that the baby will have time to build up the level of protection necessary to avoid getting the diseases. Information about the diseases for which vaccines are available is given in Table 6-1.

Immunization against certain communicable diseases is required in each state before a child can enter school or a child care program. Unfortunately, many infants do not get their vaccinations early enough to prevent the outbreak and spread of the diseases. On a worldwide basis, 2 million children die each year because of measles; 600,000 die because of whooping cough. Nearly 1 million newborn infants die from tetanus contracted through the umbilical cord incision; and 30,000 to 50,000 are crippled because of polio (Colburn, 1986).

Natural Immunity of Newborn

Newborn infants have some resistance to a number of infectious diseases because of the antibodies they receive from the mother during the prenatal period. The mother may be immune to communicable diseases such as diphtheria, German measles, mumps, and polio because she has had either the

TABLE 6-1 Communicable Diseases: Vaccines Routinely Given

DISEASE	SYMPTOMS	CAUSE OF SPREADING	INCUBATION PERIOD	PERIOD OF CONTAGION	POTENTIAL COMPLICATIONS AND DEATH RATE
Diphtheria	Sore throat, fever, headache, vomiting	Diphtheria bacteria in respiratory or nasal secretions	2–5 days	About 2 to 4 weeks after symptoms begin	Respiratory distress, central nervous system damage, blood poisoning, 12% death rate
Haemophilus influenzae, Type B[a]	Fever, vomiting, irritability, convulsions	Bacteria in environment on normal sites such as skin or mucosal surfaces	NK[b]	NK[b]	Pneumonia, croup, meningitis, arthritis, inner ear disease, Death rate = 10%
Measles (Rubeola)	Fever, cough, red watery eyes, runny nose, white spots inside cheek, red rash	Virus in respiratory or nasal secretions	7–14 days (average = 10 days)	4 days before rash appears until 4 to 5 days after rash appears	Inner ear disease, pneumonia, inflammation of brain. Death rate = 1 out of 1,000 cases
Mumps	Fever, headache, pain in chewing and swallowing, 30–40% have no symptoms	Virus in respiratory secretions, saliva, and urine	14–21 days	7 days before symptoms to 9 days after	Deafness, hearing loss, central nervous system inflammation (rare). Fatalities are rare.
Pertussis (Whooping Cough)	Coldlike symptoms, low grade fever, "whooping-like" cough	3 types of bacteria in respiratory secretions, airborne	5–21 days	7 days after exposure to 3 weeks after coughing begins	Bronchitis, pneumonia, brain damage. Death rate = 0.5% (most are infants)
Poliomyelitis (Infantile Paralysis)	Fever, sore throat, headache, nausea, vomiting, abdominal pain	3 types of polio viruses in respiratory secretions and fecal matter, congenital	7–12 days	Duration of infection	Paralysis (mostly from type 1 virus) in 1 out of 100 to 850 cases
Rubella (German Measles)	Usually mild and brief: Low grade fever, headache, sore throat, swollen lymph nodes, 3 day rash	Virus	14–21 days	7 days before to 5 days after rash begins	Main danger is to pregnant women. Can cause congenital malformations in fetus
Tetanus (Lockjaw)	Progressive stiffness of muscles, painful muscle contractions, paralysis of jaws	Bacteria grows in animal fecal matter; spread through contact with puncture wounds; newborn unbilical cord	4 days to 3 weeks	Not communicable from person to person	Death rate exceeds 50%

a New vaccine available; not recommended by all physicians routinely.
b Not Known.

Sources: Marks, 1985; Krugman et al., 1986 Reprinted by permission.

disease or a vaccine (Reinisch & Minear, 1978). If the mother does not have immunity against the disease, no protection can be passed on to the baby. In any case, the immunity provided for the baby lasts only from approximately 6 weeks to 6 months and may offer only partial protection.

Immunization Schedule

Recommendations and guidelines for the immunization of infants and young children have been developed by the American Academy of Pediatrics and the United States Public Health Service. The guidelines are revised as new scientific information becomes available. The schedule currently recommended for the routine immunization of normal, healthy infants is given in Table 6-2. Delays and deviations from the schedule may be recommended by an infant's doctor because of health concerns, reactions to previous immunizations, or an infant's individual needs. To establish the maximum level of immunity, it is extremely important for parents to obtain the complete series of immunizations for an infant as recommended by the child's doctor.

In addition to the regularly scheduled immunizations, a tuberculin skin test is recommended at 1 year of age. This is a simple screening test to determine whether the baby has been exposed to tuberculosis. If the test is positive, additional testing will be done to determine whether or not the baby actually has an active case of the disease. In the United States, the chance of an infant's having tuberculosis is very small, but the test is very important because of the seriousness of the disease. A vaccine (B.C.G.) is available but is not usually

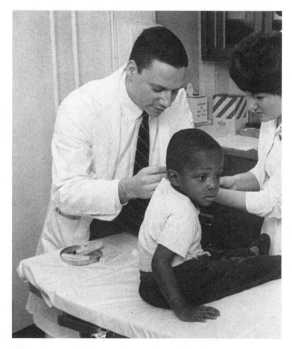

This toddler is being prepared for a booster immunization.

given unless an infant lives in an area or in a family where tuberculosis is prevalent.

The immunization schedule no longer includes routine vaccination for smallpox. Fortunately, smallpox has disappeared to the extent that it is no longer considered a threat. Actually, health officials consider the risk of complications from the vaccine to outweigh the risk of catching the disease. If 95 percent or more of infants worldwide can be immunized, it may be possible to eliminate many other communicable diseases (Fulginiti, 1984).

Some of the vaccines such as diphtheria, pertussis, and tetanus (DPT) are combined and given in a single injection. One advantage of this practice is that the baby has to be stuck with a needle only once instead of three times. The practice also saves time and is therefore less expensive. The main disadvantage of giving combined vaccines is in determining which vaccine is the cause if a reaction occurs.

Adverse Reactions

Modern vaccines are extremely safe and effective, but a slight risk of side effects exists with all vaccines. Minor reactions such as a fever, swelling around the site of the injection, and general discomfort for a few hours are common. However, there is a slight risk of severe complications. In very rare instances (1 in 8,000,000), oral polio vaccine has resulted in paralytic poliomyelitis. The greatest amount of concern centers around the potential risk of the pertussis (whooping cough) vaccine. There is a slight risk (1 in 100,000 cases) of convulsions or other side effects that may cause brain damage (Robinson, 1981).

Scientists are currently working on a safer pertussis vaccine. However, until a better vaccine is developed, the risk of no immunization must be

TABLE 6-2 Recommended Schedule for Immunization of Normal Infants and Children

RECOMMENDED AGE	VACCINE
2 months	DPT;[a] TOPV[b]
4 months	DPT; TOPV
6 months	DPT; TOPV[c]
1 year	Tuberculin test[d]
15 months	MMR[e]
18 months	DPT; TOPV
18–24 months	*Haemophilus influenzae* Type b vaccine
4–6 years	DPT; TOPV
14–16 years	Td[f]—Repeat every 10 years for life

[a]Diptheria, tetanus, and pertussis vaccines.
[b]Trivalent oral poliovirus vaccine, Types 1, 2, and 3.
[c]A third dose of TOPV is optional but may be given in areas of high endemicity of poliomeylitis.
[d]Test should be done at the time of, or preceding, the measles immunization.
[e]Measles, mumps, and rubella vaccine.
[f]Combined tetanus and diphtheria toxoids (adult type).
Sources: Immunization Practices Advisory Committee, 1983; 1986.

weighed against the potential adverse effects of the vaccines currently available. The American Academy of Pediatrics (Committee on Infectious Diseases, 1986) recommends that infants continue to receive the pertussis vaccine as scheduled unless there are certain medical problems, such as a history of progressive neurological disorders or a previous adverse reaction to the vaccine. The benefits of the protection far outweigh the risks associated with immunization.

SYMPTOMS OF ILLNESS IN INFANTS

Numerous symptoms accompany illness in infants. Some of the more common symptoms parents and other caregivers should attend to include general discomfort (malaise), loss of appetite, vomiting, congestion, runny nose, fever, cough, diarrhea, skin rash, listlessness, crying, and irritability. An infant may exhibit one or more of the symptoms, and the symptoms could be caused by one problem or a combination of problems. Generally, parents tend to be concerned most about coughs, colds, fever, diarrhea, and vomiting.

Fever

A temperature over 100° F (37.8 C) by mouth, or above 101° F (38.4 C) by rectum is usually considered to be a fever (Radetsky, 1984). The degree of fever is not always a good indication of the extent of an illness, however, especially for infants younger than 2 or 3 months of age. Some mild illnesses such as measles may be accompanied by a temperature as high as 105° F. On the other hand, a very severe infection such as meningitis in a young infant may result in a low-grade fever or no fever at all (Austin, 1978).

A major concern associated with fever in young children is the danger of convulsions and brain damage. The risk of convulsions is the greatest between 1 and 3 years of age. However, only around 3 percent of children with fever are affected by convulsions. Even if convulsions occur, brain damage is rare (Leach, 1984). Although fever in an infant should always be considered important, it is often dramatic without being serious. Even high fevers in the range of 104 to 105° (oral) are rarely harmful. The most frequent causes of fever in infants under 2 years of age are upper respiratory infections, viruses, gastroenteritis, and ear infections. Examples of more serious, but less common, illnesses that cause fever are septicemia (blood poisoning) and pneumonia (McCarthy, 1979). Parents are usually advised to call a doctor if an infant has a temperature of 102° or above (Kunz, 1982).

Vomiting

Some infants vomit easily and frequently; others vomit only in response to extreme stomach distress. Vomiting may result from one or more of a long list of causes, ranging from food reactions to motion to viral infections. The decision about when to seek medical attention is not always clear. Generally parents are advised to contact a doctor if

1. The baby vomits repeatedly.
2. Vomiting is accompanied by diarrhea or a fever.
3. The baby has ingested something unusual that may be poisonous.
4. Vomiting is preceded by a fall or blow to the head.
5. There are indications of stomach pain or other discomfort (Leach, 1984).

Diarrhea

Diarrhea is defined as an increase in the frequency, fluidity, and volume of bowel movements. One or two watery bowel movements a day is not unusual for an infant, but three to five is considered mild diarrhea (Austin, 1978). Diarrhea is one of the most frequent problems encountered by infants and young children. During the first three years of life, an infant is likely to experience at least one to three severe episodes of significant diarrhea (Gellis & Kagan, 1986).

Viruses are the most frequent cause of diarrhea in infants under 2, especially during the winter months. Diarrhea is often preceded or accompanied by other symptoms, such as respiratory congestion or cough (Gellis & Kagan, 1986). Food is usually not the source of the problem in most severe cases of infant diarrhea in the United States. However, dietary changes sometimes result in mild diarrhea. The symptoms usually subside in 72 hours. An infant is in danger of dehydration if severe diarrhea continues for several days. Worldwide, 4 to 5 million children under 5 years of age die each year from fluid loss due to diarrhea that goes untreated (Colburn, 1986).

Oral rehydration therapy is a simple but highly effective means of treating diarrhea. Infants who show signs of dehydration are given a special solution to drink containing water, salt, glucose, and other ingredients to replace fluid losses. The World Health Organization (1985) operates oral rehydration therapy programs in undeveloped countries for preventing infant mortality due to diarrhea.

COMMON ILLNESSES OF INFANTS

While many of the life-threatening infectious diseases of infants can be controlled through immunizations, there are numerous other illnesses and health problems which cannot be. It is not possible in this chapter to consider all the diseases to which infants are susceptible, but the disorders that occur most frequently are briefly discussed. Parents should obtain a medical guide such as Spock and Rothenberg's *Baby and Child Care* (1985) or *The Child Care Encyclopedia* by Leach (1984).

Common Colds

Infants who live in families with school-age children have approximately six common colds each year. More than 150 different viruses have been identified as possible causes of colds and coldlike illnesses. Infants are more likely than adults to have a fever with a cold (Marks, 1985). They have special difficulty with the nasal congestion caused by a cold because of the inability to blow their nose and clear the nasal passage. Furthermore, very young infants are often instinctive nose breathers and have a great deal of difficulty breathing through the mouth when the nasal passage is obstructed. The main concern about colds is not so much the cold itself, but the potential side effects, such as ear and throat infections, bronchitis, and pneumonia. Although there is no prevention or cure for the common cold, secondary infections can be treated with antibiotics.

Otitis Media (Middle-Ear Infection)

The most common infectious illness of infancy is otitis media, an infection in the middle ear (Schmitt and Berman, 1984). Approximately 75 percent of all infants in the United States have at least one middle-ear infection before they are 2 years old (Marks, 1985). The highest incidence is in children 6 to 24 months of age.

Otitis media is a secondary infection caused by bacteria that are usually not associated with the primary illness. Streptococcus, pneumonia, and haemophilis influenzae are the most common infecting bacteria. The infection produces a sticky fluid that may gradually accummulate because the tubal passage tends to be swollen and blocked. The symptoms include earache, drainage, hearing impairment, and fever. However, many infants exhibit only general signs of distress, such as irritability, crying, diarrhea, and loss of appetite. The condition may persist for weeks without any signs of ear pain or other symptoms. Otitis usually clears up within a week or two of treatment with antibiotics. If the condition goes undetected and untreated for a long time, there is a danger of permanent hearing impairment (Krugman et al., 1986). In infants with chronic otitis, the infection may also cause hearing loss, which can interfere with language acquisition.

Croup

Influenza, colds, and common respiratory viruses often produce an infection of the air passage leading to the lungs. This condition is commonly referred to as croup. The swelling and irritation result in hoarseness, labored breathing, and the characteristic cough, which has been compared to the bark of a seal (Marks, 1985). Croup is usually accompanied by symptoms common to all infectious diseases such as general discomfort, loss of appetite, and fever. Croup occurs mostly in infants 3 months to 3 years old and is seen mainly during the fall and winter (Davis et al., 1981).

Croup can be very frightening to children and to parents because of severe coughing and breathing difficulties. The disease is rarely life threatening unless it goes untreated. Doctors typically treat mild croup by adding moisture to the air to aid breathing. More serious and complicated cases may be treated with medications as indicated by the originating infection. The most severe cases may require hospitalization (Marks, 1985).

Pneumonia

The term *pneumonia* is used to refer to a variety of reactions of the lungs to infectious and noninfectious agents (Krugman et al., 1986). There are several types of pneumonia, which vary with the location and extent of the affected lung. Approximately 80 percent of all pneumonia cases occur among children under 7 years of age, with the peak incidence in 2- to 4-year-olds. Boys are more susceptible to pneumonia than girls (Marks, 1985).

Pneumonia is usually caused by viruses and bacteria, but it may also result from ingesting fungi, food, powder, or other foreign substances into the lungs. Infants who have pneumonia develop a cough and have difficulty breathing. Fever is usually present, but infants tend to have a lower fever than older children. With modern medical treatment, death and long-term complications are rare.

Streptococcal Infections

Streptococcus is a type of bacteria that causes several diseases in infants, including strep throat and skin infections. Strep infections in infants are hard to distinguish from a cold or other respiratory-tract infections unless a lab test is done (Krugman et al., 1986). In the past, strep infections were often followed by complications such as rheumatic fever, kidney disorders, pneumonia, or blood poisoning. Today, the use of antibiotics has dramatically reduced the incidence of serious complications from strep infections.

Hepatitis

Most cases of hepatitis are caused by a virus that enters through the mouth and makes its way into the bloodstream. There are at least six viruses that cause hepatitis (Krugman et al., 1986). Hepatitis causes an inflammation of the liver, leading to jaundice. Symptoms of hepatitis include loss of appetite, stomach pain, nausea, vomiting, and loss of energy. Generally, hepatitis is milder in infants than in adults, with most infants having no symptoms of the disease (Marks, 1985).

Hepatitis is extremely contagious in group child care situations, especially in large day care centers. Lack of sanitation, particularly hand washing, is one of the major factors contributing to its spread. Immune globulin is sometimes given to high-risk infants and their caregivers to provide temporary immunity or to lessen the effects of the disease. Vaccination is usually recommended for infants and children in day care and for their families if they have been exposed to one or more cases of viral hepatitis (Krugman et al., 1986). With proper treatment, serious complications from hepatitis are rare.

Roseola Infantum

Roseola is a mild disease that affects mainly infants from 3 months to 3 years of age. The disease begins with a high fever which drops after three to five days. A rash of small, separate pink spots usually appears on the upper part of the body as the fever decreases. Roseola is believed to be the most common cause of fever and rash in infants under 2 years of age. Approximately 30 percent of all infants develop this disease (Krugman et al., 1986). Apparently, the only risk it poses to infants is convulsions from the high fever. Roseola is probably caused by a virus, but the specific type has not been identified.

Thrush

A common infection that attacks young infants is thrush. White patches, resembling milk curds, develop inside the baby's cheeks and on the tongue. The mouth becomes sore, which causes difficulty in sucking and eating. Thrush is caused by a yeast (candida), which is a normal and usually harmless inhabitant of the mouth. Infants are particularly susceptible to thrush because of their low immunity and tender skin. Malnutrition, antibiotics and other drugs lower the resistance to thrush infections. Newborn infants may develop thrush from the yeast acquired from the birth canal during delivery. Thrush is not serious, but like other yeast infections, it may be difficult to cure.

Diaper Rash

Sooner or later, most infants have diaper rash. The skin covered by the diaper becomes red and irritated. Most cases of diaper rash are mild with no serious risks. However, if untreated, a skin infection can develop. Diaper rash is usually produced by prolonged contact with urine or feces. Soap and detergents left on the skin or in the diapers also contribute to the problem. If the rash lasts more than 72 hours, a type of fungus called candida is likely to invade the skin and make the condition worse (Weston, Lane, & Weston, 1980).

The treatment of diaper rash includes frequent changes of diaper, careful washing, and exposing the affected area to air as much as possible. Protective ointments, antibacterial creams, or antiyeast preparations are often prescribed. If cloth diapers are used, boiling or soaking them in an antiseptic solution and rinsing them in vinegar may help. The use of boric acid or any ointment containing mercury is not recommended (Weston et al., 1980).

Allergies

An allergy is the body's response to substances that an individual has difficulty tolerating. Substances (allergens) that commonly cause allergic reactions include food, things that are inhaled (pollen, dust, mold, mildew, etc.), things that touch the skin (chemicals, soaps, plants, fabrics, etc.), insect bites, and nonspecific factors such as health and emotions (Crook, 1975). Almost any substance is a potential allergen to someone. Allergic reactions include a runny nose, sneezing, congestion, watering and itching eyes, skin rashes, headaches, and wheezing (asthma). Infections from other diseases interact with allergies so that an allergy may make an infection worse, or an infection may make an allergy worse.

Allergies have been ranked as the sixth-leading cause of doctor's visits for infants under 1 year of age and the fifth-leading cause between 1 and 14 years of age (Allergy Foundation of American, 1971). About one in five infants develops allergies (Leach, 1984). Development of an allergy requires time, so infants usually do not exhibit adverse reactions to substances the first time they are exposed. For example, an infant who becomes allergic to penicillin may receive one course of treatment with the drug without any ill effects. The second or third treatment may make the infant very ill because the body has manufactured antigens to fight off the offending substance. An allergic illness that occurs during the infancy period depends largely upon the environmental factors to which an infant is exposed. (Food allergies are discussed in Chapter 7.)

In infants, allergy most often takes the form of eczema. Three-quarters of all childhood eczema develops in the first year of life (Price, 1984). The first signs of eczema are bright red, itchy patches of inflamed skin on the cheeks. The rubbing and scratching lead to runny sores on the face and scalp. In some babies the eczema spreads to other parts of the body. Babies with severe eczema are subject to serious secondary infections (Price, 1984).

SUDDEN INFANT DEATH SYNDROME

Sudden infant death syndrome (SIDS) is defined as the sudden death of any infant or young child which cannot be explained by medical history and for which no adequate cause can be found (Golding, Limerick, & Macfarlane, 1985). The terms *cot death* and *crib death* are also used to describe this phenomenon. Approximately 8,000 deaths (2 out of 1,000 live births) in the United States each year are attributed to SIDS. (Golding et al., 1985). Although unexplained sudden death has affected infants throughout human history, SIDS was not identified as a medical syndrome until the early 1960s.

SIDS is the leading cause of death among infants between 1 month and 1 year of age (Merritt & Valdes-Dapena, 1984). Ninety-five percent of all SIDS deaths occur within the first eight months of life (Foundation for the Study of Infant Death, 1985). Within that age range, the greatest number of cases are found between 1 and 4 months of age (Kelly & Shannon, 1982). SIDS rarely occurs before 1 month of age. Death rates vary from country to country and from state to state.

Factors Associated with SIDS

For many years, infants who died suddenly in the night were thought to have been smothered when their parents rolled on top of them during the night, or by their own pillows or bed coverings. Eventually, this theory was disproved when sudden infant death victims were found on their backs with their faces uncovered (Russell-Jones, 1985).

During the past twenty-five years a massive amount of information has been accumulated in the search for an answer to the SIDS mystery. Scientists have identified a number of factors that are statistically associated with an increased risk of SIDS. The following trends have been reported:

1. SIDS occurs more frequently among economically disadvantaged families, teenage parents (younger than 20), mothers who smoke or use drugs, or who have had a previous fetal loss (Kelly & Shannon, 1982).
2. The risk of SIDS increases with the number of children in a family (Golding et al., 1985).
3. More male infants are affected by SIDS than female infants, but this is also true of infant deaths from known causes (Kelly & Shannon, 1982).
4. Preterm, low-birthweight infants and infants of multiple births tend to have an increased risk of SIDS (Golding et al., 1985).
5. Black and Native American infants are two to three times more likely to be affected by SIDS than white infants (Adams, 1985).
6. SIDS occurs at increased rates during the winter months, when respiratory infections are more prevalent (Public Health Service, 1986).

Possible Causes

Genetics.   Although SIDS tends to be more prevalent in some families than in others, scientists generally do not believe that SIDS is caused by a genetically transmitted defect (Kelly & Shannon, 1982). Current evidence suggests that prenatal and postnatal environmental conditions interact to exert substantially more effect than genetics in increasing the risk of SIDS (Russell-Jones, 1985). However, further research is needed to rule out genetics as the major factor.

Viruses.   In many cases (40–75 percent), SIDS victims have a mild respiratory infection or stomach upset (Kelly and Shannon, 1982). These statistics have suggested that a virus, possibly interacting with the climate, may be the cause of SIDS. There is no evidence that a particular virus is responsible for SIDS. However, it is possible that the infection may in some way trigger an allergic response that results in death (Golding et al., 1985).

The Apnea Theory. Some infants are susceptible to episodes of prolonged apnea during which breathing stops for 20 seconds or longer. Brief episodes when infants stop breathing for about 20 seconds or less are normal and are not dangerous unless accompanied by a decreased heart rate. However, prolonged apnea can lead to death. Apnea has been attributed to an abnormally soft larynx or to a malfunction in the central nervous system, which regulates breathing (James, 1985), but no one knows for sure why it occurs. Preterm infants are particularly susceptible to apnea.

The risk of SIDS is somewhat greater for infants who have experienced prolonged apnea than it is for infants in the general population. However, apnea and SIDS are currently considered to be separate medical problems (American Academy of Pediatrics, 1985). Most infants who die from SIDS have no history of apnea, and most infants who have episodes of apnea are not affected by SIDS (Fan, 1984).

Other Theories. Numerous other theories about the cause of SIDS have been proposed, including errors in metabolism, toxic levels of one or more chemicals, deficiency of essential vitamins and minerals, failure of the immune system, house-mite allergy, botulism, hypernatraemia (high sodium in the blood), abnormal lung surfactant (substance necessary for breathing), hypothermia (chilling), hyperthermia (overheating), abnormalities of heartbeat or heart defects, central nervous system defects, or faulty reflexes affecting various vital functions (Golding et al. 1985; James, 1985; Kelly & Shannon, 1982; Russell-Jones, 1985). In spite of the proliferation of theories and research studies, there is no generally accepted explanation for why SIDS occurs. Scientists are beginning to doubt whether the cause of SIDS will ever be found. In general, the evidence indicates that there is probably no single cause of SIDS, but that "several factors come together in a given time to cause death" (Russell-Jones, 1985, p. 281).

Preventing SIDS

Until the cause of sudden infant death is determined, no effective means of treatment or prevention can be developed. Currently the main approach to the prevention of infant death due to SIDS or apnea is the use of a monitoring device that sounds an alarm if the baby stops breathing or the heart stops beating. Unfortunately, there are no reliable ways to identify infants who should be equipped with such devices. Physicians frequently recommend monitoring for infants who have had a life-threatening episode of apnea or "near-attack" of SIDS. Infant siblings of SIDS victims are also sometimes equipped with a monitor.

The use of monitoring devices has been controversial. The monitors currently available are not totally reliable because they sometimes give false alarms or fail to alarm appropriately. Research studies conducted to date on the effectiveness of home monitors in preventing SIDS are somewhat contradictory. Experts generally agree that SIDS monitoring may be useful in selected situations, if only to give reassurance to parents (Milner, 1985). However, the American Academy of Pediatrics (1985) cautions physicians to advise parents that monitors cannot guarantee that SIDS will not occur.

CHILD ABUSE AND NEGLECT

Every year more than 1 million children in the United States are estimated to be victims of child abuse and neglect. Between 2,000 and 5,000 die from the injuries they receive (American Medical Association, 1985). Approximately one-third of the child-abuse and neglect cases reported each year involve children under 5 years of age (Solomons, 1984). Abuse is the most frequent single cause of death in infants between 6 and 12 months of age. Almost all murders of children younger than 3 years of age are the result of child abuse by a parent or caretaker (Heins, 1984).

Physical Abuse

Child abuse and neglect are difficult to define precisely because of disagreements about the difference between discipline and abuse, as well as how to distinguish between intentional and unintentional injury. One widely accepted definition of an abused child is "any child who receives nonaccidental physical injury (or injuries) as a result of acts (or omissions) on the part of his parents or guardians" (Kempe and Helfer, 1972, p. xi).

Physical abuse takes many forms. Abused children are beaten severely, burned, poisoned, and punished in many other ways. The extent of injuries varies from minor bruises and abrasions to broken bones, permanent nervous-system damage, and death. Reports of child abuse similar to the following appear frequently in the news:

> He was only three years old . . . and by the time police arrived with a document declaring Michael M. to be a neglected child, it was too late. He was already dead. . . . The mother's live-in boyfriend allegedly beat the child for wetting his pants. The beatings were allegedly administered with a large belt buckle and lasted through the morning into early afternoon. . . . The mother lead police to a muddy ditch where the dead child had been buried (Slater, 1983, p. 26).

A form of abuse frequently reported is the severe shaking of an infant resulting in the Whiplash Shaken Infant Syndrome (Eagan, Whelan-Williams, & Brooks, 1985). Although there are no external injuries, the shaking results in traumatic bleeding in the brain and eyes as well as whiplash injury to the neck bones and muscles. The following is an excerpt from a case report: "An 11-month old female was taken to the emergency room after she was found lying on the floor unconscious. The stepfather reported that the child fell from the couch but later admitted that he had "shaken" the child to wake her from her nap in an attempt to adjust her sleep schedule and 'slapped' her to gain her attention" (Eagan et al., 1985). This type of injury is very difficult to label as child abuse.

Neglect

Child neglect refers to the willful failure of parents to provide the basic needs of food, clothing, shelter, and medical treatment (Krugman, 1984). This type of maltreatment occurs three or four times more frequently than physical abuse (Solomons, 1984). Child neglect does not typically receive as much public attention as physical abuse. However, the following is a case that made the news:

> Four children, ages one through four, were found crying from hunger and thirst in an apartment where they had been left alone for 45 hours. Police reported the children were filthy and the stench from human waste was almost unbearable (Family Life Council of Greater Greensboro, 1973, p. 1).

Emotional and Sexual Abuse

Emotional abuse involves verbal assaults, unreasonable demands, scapegoating, and other treatment that undermines the child's self-esteem. It also includes ignoring the child and withdrawing love and nurturance needed for normal growth and development (Word, 1985). Emotional abuse is the most difficult kind of abuse to legally define, detect, and prosecute. Due to the lack of a uniform definition, emotional abuse is not illegal in some places. No one knows to what extent it occurs.

Sexual abuse is the exploitation of a child for financial benefit or emotional gratification of an adult (American Medical Association, 1985). Sexual abuse includes fondling, oral-genital contact, exhibitionism, intercourse, and child pornography (Word, 1985). This form of abuse occurs mainly among older children, although it occasionally happens to infants.

Characteristics of Child Abusers

Why does child abuse occur? How could any sane parent abuse a helpless child? Attempts to find answers to such questions have focused largely on the characteristics of abusive parents. Many abusive parents have little knowledge of normal child growth and development, and their ignorance results in unrealistic expectations of a child. They also tend to be afraid of spoiling their children, or they strongly believe in the value of physical punishment as a means of discipline (Mayhall & Norgard, 1983).

The belief that child abusers were themselves abused as children by their own parents is widespread. However, after reviewing research studies on this issue, Kaufman and Zigler (1987) concluded that unqualified acceptance of the theory that child abuse is usually transmitted from generation to generation is unfounded. Although being maltreated as a child puts a person at risk for becoming abusive, the majority of mistreated children do not grow up to be abusive parents. Approximately one out of three people who were abused or neglected as children will mistreat their own children (Kaufman & Zigler, 1987).

Infants are most often abused by their biological parents. However, foster parents, adoptive parents, stepparents, grandparents, siblings, other relatives, friends, baby sitters, and other child care providers, inside and outside the home, are frequently involved (American Medical Association, 1985). Most incidents of abuse occur at home, and the abusive parent is more likely to be the mother than the father (Ghent, DaSylva, & Farren, 1985).

Child abusers cannot usually be distinguished from their neighbors and are generally classified as "normal" people. Only about 10 percent of abusive parents are likely to be insane or have criminal tendencies (Baxter, 1985). No two abusive parents are exactly alike, but they are often characterized as being immature, lacking in self-esteem, impulsive, self-centered, and rigid (Mayhall & Norgard, 1983). Alcoholism is frequently a part of the picture.

Child abuse occurs among parents of all religious persuasions, race, and socioeconomic status. However, child abuse tends to be reported more frequently in families from the lower social classes. The link between economic stress and child abuse is clearly seen in the rise in child-abuse cases in periods of high unemployment. Families involved in child abuse are often isolated, without friends and support from relatives (Krugman, 1984).

Characteristics of Abused Children

In searching for answers about why child abuse occurs, researchers have attempted to identify physical and behavioral characteristics of child-abuse victims that may contribute to their own mistreatment. Infants, from birth to age 3, are more likely to be victims of child abuse than children in any other age group (Mayhall and Norgard, 1983).

Young infants are unable to escape and are totally dependent on their caretakers. They often trigger an adult's violent response through inconsolable colicky crying. Older infants evoke abusive behavior by their inability to obtain or maintain control over elimination or impulsive behavior. Difficulties in eating and sleeping are other typical behaviors that abusive parents report as evoking their anger (Krugman, 1984).

Crittenden (1985) found that abused infants are often mildly developmentally delayed and difficult to manage and that they react more angrily when stressed than do nonabused infants. Neglected infants tended to be more passive, significantly delayed, and somewhat lifeless when stressed. The maltreated infants were not inherently different from other children but probably learned the behaviors in response to abuse.

Prematurity and low-birthweight have frequently been associated with child abuse. Theoretically, parents have more difficulty in becoming emotionally attached to these infants because they are isolated during the important early days after birth. Although some studies have found evidence to support claims that prematurity and low-birthweight are risk factors for child abuse, other studies have not found this to be so. More recent studies, which have controlled for social class and other important variables, have found that premature and low-birthweight babies are no more frequently involved in child abuse cases than other infants (Leventhal, Edgerter, & Murphy, 1984).

Usually only one infant in each family is a child abuse victim. It appears that the child becomes the focal point and thus a scapegoat for all the parental anger and frustration (Solomons, 1984). Statistically, the abused child is likely to be a male infant (Straus, Gelles, & Steinmetz, 1979). Boys are generally perceived as being more active and difficult to manage and thus more likely to invite abuse than girls.

Effects of Child Abuse

The effects of child maltreatment are devastating and long-lasting in most cases. If they survive, abused infants suffer long-lasting physical and mental handicaps. Damage to the brain leaves them with mental retardation, seizures, learning disabilities, and hearing or other sensory impairments. Even when severe physical impairments are not obvious, mistreated children may have lower-than-average intellectual, language, and motor abilities, leading to lower academic achievement and developmental delays (Mayhall & Norgard, 1983). Abused children also suffer emotional scars, which may make them extremely shy and withdrawn. Many abused children have difficulty trusting other people and forming close relationships. They may become excessively aggressive, growing up to commit violent or criminal acts against society (Baxter, 1985).

Child-Abuse Laws

Child abuse and neglect are criminal offenses everywhere in the United States. Although legal definitions and penalties vary, each state has a law against child maltreatment. Physicians and other professionals who have contact with infants and children are required to report cases of suspected child abuse.

Treatment and Prevention

The complexities of child abuse require a wide range of treatment and prevention strategies. Efforts to treat abusive parents and their victims include individual therapy, family counseling, placing children in foster care or crisis nurseries, and short-term residential treatment for the entire family (Starr, 1979). Parents Anonymous is a volunteer organization that has been very effective in working with abusive families. The large majority of abusive parents can be helped with appropriate treatment and support. Approaches to the prevention of child abuse include parent-education programs, and hospital maternity ward practices to facilitate parent-child bonding. Researchers are attempting to develop measures to screen and predict potential child abusers and victims.

INFANT SAFETY

Nearly all children are involved in one or more accidents while growing up. In most cases, the accidents are minor and have no long-term effects. However, accidents can result in a permanent handicap or death. Accidents happen in strange and unexpected ways before caregivers realize what is happening. A letter that appeared in "Dear Abby" (1981) described how a toddler fell into an ice chest and drowned. The same letter-writer reported another incident, in which her 14-month-old grandson wiggled down and hanged himself from the strap of his highchair when the baby sitter left the room for a few minutes.

Approximately 3 out of each 1,000 infants born in the United States die from accidental causes before they reach 4 years of age (National Safety Council, 1987). The first year of life is the most dangerous. Accidents take the lives of more babies during this period than any other year of life. About one-half of all fatalities among infants occur before 5 months of age, and more than two-thirds occur by 7 months. During later infancy, the number of accidental deaths levels off (Metropolitan Life Insurance Co., 1985).

At every age of life, the rate of accidents is larger for males than for females. Accidental death rates tend to be about 25 percent higher for male infants than for female infants (Metropolitan Life Insurance Co., 1987). Either by nature or nurture, boys are typically more active and aggressive in exploring their environment. Thus they are more likely to be exposed to hazards. Parents also tend to be more protective of female infants.

Causes of Accidents

Motor Vehicles. By far the leading cause of accidental deaths and injuries during infancy is automobile accidents (Table 6-3). Approximately 1,100 infants (0–4 yr.) die each year in motor vehicle accidents (National Safety Council, 1987). Another 70,000 infants are injured (Davis, 1985). The death rate is highest for infants less than 6 months of age. Very young infants are more likely to be riding in the front seat held in someone's arms (Kane, 1985). They are especially vulnerable to head injury because of the soft spots in the skull and a top-heavy body.

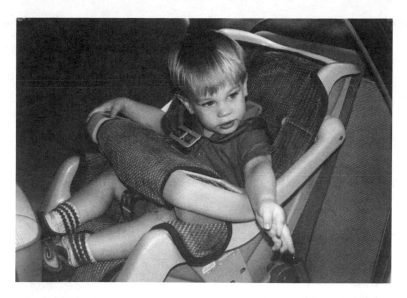

An infant in a car safety seat.

Most motor vehicle deaths and serious injuries could be prevented through the proper use of infant safety seats. A ten-year research study conducted in the state of Washington found safety seats to be 80 to 90 percent effective in preventing deaths and major injuries to infants and children under 5 years of age (Scherz, 1981). Yet fewer than 50 percent of all children are protected with safety seats while riding in a car (Davis, 1985).

Every state has a law requiring the use of automobile safety restraints for infants and children. The laws have succeeded in increasing the use of infant safety seats, thereby decreasing the death rate. For example, since legislation was passed in North Carolina in 1982, the use of safety seats has increased from 31 percent in 1982 to 56 percent in 1984 (Orr et al., 1984). The National Safety Council (1987) estimates that the number of infants killed in automobile collisions dropped from 1,300 in 1981 to 1,100 in 1986. This can be attributed mainly to the increased use of safety seats.

Fires and Burns. Fires and burns are the second-leading cause of accidental death during the first four years of life (see Table 6-3). Most fire victims die from asphyxiation and inhalation of poisonous substances rather than from burns. However, infants are more sensitive to heat from flames than older children and adults because of their thin, tender skin. Infants also suffer burns from hot water, grease, steam, heating and cooking appliances, and electrical shocks. Numerous injuries occur when unattended toddlers turn on the hot water faucet. Although such burns are not likely to cause death, the injuries can be serious. Most accidents involving fires and burns occur in the home (Kane, 1985).

TABLE 6-3   Leading Causes of Accidental Deaths Among Infants (0–4 years) in 1986

RANK	CAUSE	NUMBER
1	Motor vehicles	1,100
2	Fires and burns	750
3	Drownings	750
4	Suffocation[a]	250
5	Poisoning	150
6	Falls	110
7	Firearms	40

[a]By ingestion or inhalation of food or other objects; excludes mechanical suffocation.

Source: National Safety Council. (1987). *Accident facts.* Chicago: Author. Used by permission.

Drowning.   Water is another safety hazard for infants. Drowning is the third-leading cause of accidents during infancy. Drowning accidents are most likely to happen when infants are left in bathtubs or near swimming pools. Infants drown even in ice chests and toilets. Dr. Jay Arena, Professor of Pediatrics at Duke University Medical Center, wrote to newspaper columnist Ann Landers asking her to warn parents about the danger of 1- and 2-year-olds drowning when the toilet seat is left up. He reported three cases in which toddlers stumbled and drowned in the toilet bowl (*The News and Observer,* 1985).

Suffocation.   During the first four years of life, suffocation is the fourth-leading cause of accidental deaths. However, for infants who are under 1 year of age, choking is the leading cause of fatal injuries. Suffocation accounts for one-fourth of all accidental deaths during the first year of life. The first two months are especially hazardous (Metropolitan Life Insurance Company, 1985).

Young infants choke primarily on food or vomit because of their immaturity in swallowing and the tendency to cough up substances that obstruct the respiratory passages. Crawling infants take special delight in finding small objects such as safety pins, buttons, or small parts of toys. Everything small enough to fit is automatically placed in the mouth, where it may be swallowed. Some infants are able to pull off and swallow pieces of the plastic coverings on their disposable diapers, which can result in choking.

Infants also suffocate by getting their heads trapped in plastic bags and between the rails of baby cribs and playpens. A ten-year study conducted by the U.S. Consumer Product Safety Commission found that 45 percent of all the victims of head-entrapment accidents were under 12 months of age (Miles, Rutherford, & Coonley, 1983). Babies are also found strangled by drapery cords or cords from toys or other objects. The period when this type of strangulation is most likely to occur is between 9 and 12 months of age (Rutherford & Kelly, 1981).

Poisoning. Each year about 2 million children under 5 years of age swallow or breathe potentially dangerous substances (Kane, 1985). Poisoning ranks as the fifth-leading cause of accidental death among infants (National Safety Council, 1987). Fortunately, most cases of poisoning do not result in death. The list of poisonous substances found in homes and yards is almost limitless. Medicines are the toxic agents most frequently swallowed by children (Kane, 1985). Other substances frequently ingested include cleaning products, cosmetics, pesticides, petroleum products, alcoholic beverages, and plants. Lead paint chips, which flake off the walls of old buildings, are especially dangerous. The toxic effects of poisons are more damaging to infants than to adults because of the immaturity of infants' organs (Kane, 1985).

Infants and toddlers between 1 and 3 years of age have the highest rate of injuries from accidental poisoning of any age group. They are especially vulnerable because they are curious, active, and capable of getting into cabinets, drawers, and other places where toxic substances are likely to be kept. Adults find it difficult to anticipate and control the children's growing ability to get into things.

Since 1970, the federal government has required child-resistant packaging for medicines and numerous other potentially harmful substances commonly used in the home. The number of children poisoned by aspirin and

This toddler is in a very dangerous situation which could have been avoided if these toxic substances had been properly stored in a "child-proof" location.

other medicines has declined substantially because of the use of safety containers. However, safety experts warn parents not to be lulled into a false sense of security. Containers are frequently left open, and young children can be very resourceful in finding ways to open "child-proof" containers.

Falls.   Accidental deaths due to falls have been declining in recent years (National Safety Council, 1987). However, countless infants continue to receive cuts, bruises, fractures, and other types of injuries from falls each year. Falls from highchairs and cribs are frequent causes of injuries to infants under 2 years of age. Babies also fall from tables, cabinets, and other high places when parents leave them momentarily. Crawling infants and toddlers are more likely to fall down stairs, out of windows or grocery carts, off playground equipment, and from numerous other places. Toddlers who live in high-rise apartments are especially at risk. Falls occur mainly when caregivers leave them unattended in hazardous places.

Baby-proofing the Environment

One of the most important steps an infant caregiver can take to prevent accidents is to make regular safety checks of the home and other places where infants live and play. For example, medicines, cleaning supplies, and other substances with toxic-warning labels should be kept in a locked cabinet or a place that is not accessible to an active toddler. Plants should be kept out of reach. Razor blades, knives, and other sharp objects should be removed from drawers within the reach of infants and toddlers. Electrical outlets not in use should be covered with a safety plug. Cords on appliances should not be accessible to infants. Floors should be checked regularly for small objects such as coins, tacks, pins, paper clips, and marbles.

Equipment or furnishings may need to be moved, added, removed, or modified. For example, stair railings, baby cribs, or playpens which might trap a baby's head should be modified. Stairs should be blocked at the top and bottom. Play yards should be fenced in. Severe burns can be avoided from tap water by lowering the thermostat setting below 130 degrees. Numerous other things can be done to provide a hazard-free, "baby-proof" environment. However, there is no substitute for constant vigilance.

Toy Safety

All toys and play materials for infants should be selected with safety precautions in mind. Toys that have small parts which can come off and become lodged in the windpipe, ears, or nostrils are among the most hazardous. Materials such as buttons, marbles, and chalk should not be available to young infants. An inexpensive device called a "no choke testing tube" can be used to determine if an object is large enough to give to an infant. (Available from Toys to Grow On, P.O. Box 17, Long Beach, CA 90808).

Toys for infants and toddlers should not have sharp edges or points, should not be made of glass or brittle plastic, should not have cords or strings over 12 inches long, and should not be put together with easily exposed straight pins, wires, or nails (USDHEW, 1972). Even carefully selecting toys, adults should supervise their use and examine them from time to time to be sure that wear and tear has not made the toys unsafe.

In Case of an Accident

Infant caregivers should be prepared to act quickly in case an accident occurs. Emergency telephone numbers, including the number of a poison-control center, should be posted on or near the telephone. A first-aid kit and an emergency-action chart should be readily available. The Duke University Poison Control Center recommends the following in case a poisoning occurs: (1) remove any remaining substance from the skin or mouth; (2) call the doctor or a poison control center immediately; and (3) follow their instructions. A bottle of ipecac syrup should be kept on hand to induce vomiting. However, it should be used only if recommended by a medical specialist.

SUMMARY

1. Approximately 11 out of each 1,000 infants die before they reach 1 year of age from birth defects and injuries, diseases, accidental injuries, sudden infant death syndrome, and child abuse.

2. Newborn infants usually have some temporary resistance to a number of communicable diseases as the result of antibodies obtained from the mother during the prenatal period.

3. Infants should receive a complete series of immunizations against diphtheria, pertussis, poliomyelitis, measles, and mumps. The immunizations should be given at the scheduled age recommended by medical authorities.

4. The pertussis vaccine has been controversial because it carries a slight risk of adverse reactions. However, the benefits of immunization far outweigh the risks.

5. The most common symptoms of illness in infants are general discomfort, loss of appetite, vomiting, congestion, runny nose, fever, coughing, diarrhea, skin rash, listlessness, crying, and irritability. Parents are usually most concerned about fever, diarrhea, vomiting, and coughing.

6. Common illnesses and health problems of infancy include diarrhea, colds, otitis media, croup, pneumonia, strep infections, hepatitis, roseola, thrush, diaper rash, and allergies.

7. The leading cause of death of infants between 1 month and 1 year of age is sudden infant death syndrome. A number of factors, such as prematurity and low socioeconomic class, statistically increase an infant's chances of being affected by SIDS. The reason infants die suddenly and unexpectedly remains a scientific mystery.

8. Each year thousands of infants are victims of physical abuse, neglect, and emotional and sexual abuse. Factors associated with child abuse include unrealistic expectations of infants, low socioeconomic class, alcoholism, teen-age or single-parent status, and such personal characteristics as immaturity. More mothers than fathers abuse their children. Many child abusers were abused by their own parents. Child abuse occurs more frequently among infants than any other age group. Usually only one infant in each family is abused, and that infant is more likely to be a male than a female. Infants who survive child abuse may suffer long-lasting physical, mental, and emotional problems.

9. Each year many infants are seriously injured or killed in an accident. The first year of life is the most dangerous, but at every age more boys than girls are involved in accidents. The six leading causes of accidental death and injury during infancy are automobile accidents, burns, drowning, suffocation, poisoning, and falls.

10. Parents and infant caregivers should take careful steps to prevent accidents by baby-proofing the environment and selecting toys that are free of safety hazards.

7

Nutrition And Feeding Practices

A baby is fed with milk and praise.
—Mary Lamb

Nutrition is fundamental to growth and development. The maintenance of nutritive balance during the early months of life is especially important because it lays the foundation for physical health and mental functioning throughout life. Prenatal and infant nutrition affect the quality and quantity of body cells and fluids, skeletal and dental development, and the body's susceptibility to disease. It is difficult to think of any aspect of infant growth and development that is not directly or indirectly influenced by nutrition.

In this chapter we consider the nutritional needs of infants and how these needs can best be met during various stages of the infancy period. Nutritional concerns and feeding problems such as anemia, food allergies, and obesity are discussed. We also take a look at the consequences of malnutrition and signs of nutritional adequacy. Suggestions for feeding infants are also provided.

NUTRITIONAL NEEDS

Nutrition is the process by which the body uses food and other substances in the digestive system (McLaren & Burman, 1982). Infants need nutrients for the maintenance and growth of the skeletal system and body tissues, as well as for energy. Technically, human nutritional needs are stated as Recommended Dietary Allowances (RDA), which include the following categories: energy (calories), protein, vitamins, minerals, and water. The RDA listed in Table 7-1 represent the average daily intake of nutrients considered adequate to meet the needs of normal infants and young children.

Nutritionists have had difficulty determining the exact quantities of nutrients needed by infants or humans in general, so the recommendations best represent scientific estimates rather than absolute requirements. The Food and Nutrition Board (1980) of the National Research Council, which publishes the RDA information, points out that the allowances are averages that need to be adjusted to individual needs. Body size, age, activity level, and environmental conditions such as temperature are factors that affect individual requirements.

Energy

An infant must have sufficient energy in the diet to maintain physical activity, growth, and physiological processes such as breathing, digestion, and blood circulation. Energy needs, expressed as calories, kilocalories, or kilojoules, are met by foods containing fats, carbohydrates, and protein. Infants need to be provided with calories throughout the day because of their limited intake capacity. If energy needs are not met, infants grow at slower-than-normal rates and may lose weight. Excessive caloric intake may result in an overweight baby.

TABLE 7-1 Recommend Daily Dietary Allowances for Infants

NUTRIENT	AGE		
	0–6 MONTHS	6–12 MONTHS	1–3 YEARS (29 LB.)
Calories	115 kcal/kg.	105 kcal/ kg.	1,300 kcal
Protein	2.2 grams/kg.	2.0 grams/kg.	23 grams
Vitamin A. (R.E.)	420	400	400
Vitamin D (I.U.)	400	400	400
Vitamin E (mg)	3	4	5
Ascorbic acid (mg)	35	35	45
Folacin (mg)	30	45	100
Niacin (mg)	6	8	9
Riboflavin (mg)	0.4	0.6	0.8
Thiamin (mg)	0.3	0.5	0.7
Vitamin B_6 (mg)	0.3	0.6	0.9
Vitamin B_{12} (mg)	0.5	1.5	2.0
Calcium (mg)	360	540	800
Phosphorus (mg)	240	360	800
Iodine (mg)	40	50	70
Iron (mg)	10	15	15
Magnesium (mg)	50	70	150
Zinc	3	5	10

Adapted from Recommended Dietary Allowances, Food and Nutrition Board. Washington, D.C.: National Academy of Sciences, National Research Council, 1980.

Protein

Protein needs vary according to age, growth rate, body size, and caloric intake from fats and carbohydrates. The protein requirements decrease in proportion to body weight as the infant gets older and the growth rate decreases (see Table 7-1). Infants who do not receive enough protein in their diet to meet their individual needs grow more slowly than normal. Severe protein deficiency continuing over an extended time results in the cessation of growth. On the other hand, too much protein may also inhibit growth or, for young infants, overload the kidney capacity (Cox & Gallagher-Allred, 1980; Woodruff, 1978).

Vitamins

A vitamin is defined as an organic substance in food which is essential for growth and maintenance of life. Vitamins perform a variety of functions in the human infant. Many of the vitamins participate in the metabolism of energy and protein, whereas others interact with various nutrients to produce growth of bones and mucous membranes, and the synthesis of vital compounds (Pipes, 1985). The estimated vitamin requirements for normal infants are shown in Table 7-1. Care should be exercised to prevent infants from consuming large quantities of vitamins (in excess of the RDA).

Vitamin deficiencies can lead to a variety of nutritional disorders, depending upon the specific vitamin. For example, a deficiency of vitamin C may result in scurvy. The small blood vessels become so fragile that they break and bleed at the slightest pressure. Vitamin D deficiency causes rickets, a softening of the bones possibly resulting in bowlegs or other malformations. Vitamin K is especially important for normal blood coagulation.

Minerals and Water

Minerals are inorganic nutrients that are important in the regulation of body fluids and metabolic processes. They are also structural components of the skeletal system, teeth, and body tissues (Pipes, 1985). Recommended intake levels of minerals (except fluoride) are listed in Table 7-1. Excessive intake should be avoided because some of the minerals can be stored in the body and reach toxic levels.

Water is also an essential component of the body. The body of the newborn infant is approximately 75 percent water. The total body water as a percentage of body weight decreases throughout the first year of infancy to 60 percent, which is comparable to the adult proportion (Pipes, 1985). Infants need water to replace liquid lost from skin, lungs, and the eliminative organs, and to provide a small amount for growth needs (Foman, 1974). Infants need more water in proportion to their body weight than adults. Under normal conditions the amount of water in breast milk or properly diluted formula is adequate to meet the nursing infant's needs. Care should be taken to replace water lost during periods of very hot weather and illness. Infants who can communicate their needs should be given water on demand.

STAGES OF INFANT FEEDING

The Committee on Nutrition (1980) of the American Academy of Pediatrics recommends that infant feeding be considered in three stages: (1) the nursing period, (2) the transitional period, and (3) the modified adult period. The nursing period is the time, usually the first six months of life, during which breast milk or formula is the source of all nutrients. The transitional period begins around 4 to 6 months with the addition of specially prepared semisolid food to the diet. The modified adult period corresponds to the toddler age (1 to 2 years), during which the majority of the nutrients come from the family table. The stages overlap so that an infant typically begins one stage before finishing another. Ideally, the rate at which an infant progresses through the stages is determined by the growth rate and developmental changes in the nervous system, by digestive capacity, and by kidney function. In most cases, however, prevailing sociocultural attitudes tend to be more powerful sources of influence than scientific information in determining the rate at which infants are encouraged to move from one stage to another.

Stage 1: The Nursing Period (Birth to 6 Months)

During the nursing period the baby is given a liquid diet of breast or formula milk. Newborn babies are equipped with rooting, sucking, and swallowing reflexes which facilitate the intake of liquids. In addition, an extrusion reflex causes the infant to push solid food out of the mouth when it is placed on the back of the tongue. The feeding reflexes gradually diminish during the first three or four months of life and are replaced by voluntary control over sucking and swallowing, as well as tongue and lip movements. The nursing period is also characterized by immature kidney and digestive capacity and by the absence of teeth with which to chew.

Choice of Feeding Method. The most important question to be answered during the nursing period is whether the baby will be fed with breast milk or a milk-based formula. At the turn of the century, almost all infants in the United States were breast fed (Martin & Beal, 1978). Over the years, cow's milk formula gradually replaced breast milk as the most frequently used alternative for meeting nutritional needs during the early months of life (Committee on Nutrition, 1976a).

During the last decade, a resurgence of interest in breast feeding has occurred. Statistics indicate that more mothers from all socioeconomic classes are breast feeding and continue to do so for a longer period of time (Martinez & Dodd, 1983). As might be expected, the incidence and duration of breast feeding are reduced among working mothers, especially among those in higher socioeconomic groups.

The growing number of mothers who are choosing to breast feed may be attributed, in part, to its increased emphasis in scientific publications as well as in popular magazines and books. Medical and health societies in the United States, Canada, and England have published statements emphasizing the superiority of breast milk and recommending that mothers be encouraged to breast feed, if possible (American Academy of Pediatrics, 1978; Canadian Paediatric Society Nutrition Committee, 1979). In addition, the LeLeche (pronounced LaLaychay) League promotes breast feeding through the development of local support groups and the publication of "how-to" information.

ADVANTAGES OF BREAST FEEDING. A variety of arguments have been used to convince mothers that "breast is best." The reasons include both physiological and psychological advantages for the infant and the mother as well. The major arguments are summarized below.

1. *Nutritional superiority.* Until recently human milk and cow's milk formula were reported to be nutritionally equivalent. Recent investigations, however, have emphasized the very different properties of the two types of milk (Jelliffe & Jelliffe, 1972; 1977). The protein and other ingredients in

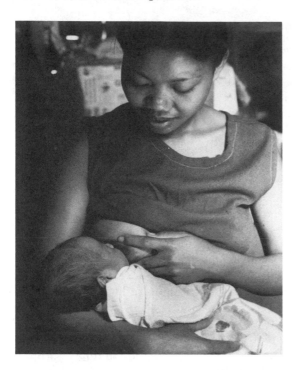

An increasing number of mothers are choosing to breastfeed.

human milk differ qualitatively from the protein in cow's milk and other milk substitutes. Breast milk proteins are easier for the body to digest and absorb. In addition, the waste products are more easily processed by the immature kidneys of the infant. Human milk is used as the standard for determining the nutritional needs of the infant for the first six months of life. In spite of these arguments, however, there is no evidence to prove that bottle-fed babies are less well nourished than breast-fed infants.

2. *Formula contamination and dilution.* Breast milk is sterile and is not subject to contamination. In mixing formula for bottle feeding, there is a possibility of using contaminated water or the wrong amount of water. Problems resulting from improper formula mix may not occur very often among well-informed mothers with adequate resources. However, the proper use of bottle milk is a problem of major concern in underdeveloped countries where bacterial contamination, underdilution, or overdilution of formula mixture is more likely to occur (WHO/UNICEF 1981).

3. *Infections.* There is increasing evidence that breast-fed infants are more resistant to infections and communicable diseases than bottle-fed infants. Newborn infants acquire antibodies from breast milk which increase their resistance to a variety of intestinal microorganisms while their own immune systems mature (Mata & Wyatt, 1971). Respiratory infections, ear infections, viral infections, meningitis, and diarrhea are also reported to occur less fre-

quently among breast-fed babies (American Academy of Pediatrics, 1978; Addy, 1976; Wood & Walker-Smith, 1981). This added protection can be achieved by only a few days of breast feeding.

4. *Allergies.* Breast-fed infants are apparently less susceptible to allergic reactions such as eczema and asthma than bottle-fed infants. Studies have reported a reduced number of allergic reactions for breast-fed babies in infancy as well as in later childhood and adult life (Gerrard et al., 1973; Eastham & Walker, 1977). Since cow's milk protein is the most common allergenic substance in infancy, breast feeding may be the best preventive for food allergy during infancy.

5. *Economic benefits.* Proponents of breast feeding argue that it is cheaper to breast feed an infant than to purchase formula for bottle feeding. Attempts to compare the economic advantages of breast feeding to formula feeding have produced contradictory results (Satter, 1983; Homan, 1973; Jelliffe & Jelliffe, 1977). Variations in food choices (e.g., peanut butter or steak), food costs, appetites, and choice of formula are factors that make questions about cost comparisons difficult to answer. The costs of bottle feeding are probably more important considerations in poor families in which a larger percentage of the family income is needed for formula milk than in families with more discretionary income.

6. *Health of the mother.* There is general agreement among physicians that breast feeding causes the uterus to contract after pregnancy, facilitating return to its normal size and reducing the danger of hemorrhage (Martin & Beal, 1978). It has also been suggested that breast cancer is rarer in countries in which breast feeding is common (McLaren & Burman, 1982). Researchers have found indications that prolonged lactation reduces the risk of breast cancer (Byers et al., 1985). However, the evidence is not sufficiently strong at this point to advise women to breast feed specifically to decrease the risk of cancer (Byers et al., 1985).

7. *Psychological benefits.* Some people believe that breast feeding offers a superior psychological intimacy that results in emotional and cognitive advantages over other feeding situations. Since the mother has to hold the infant close to her body, there appears to be a certain amount of warmth, nurturing, and skin contact inherent in breast-feeding situations. Klaus and Kennell (1982) believe that breast feeding is one of the procedures that facilitates the development of mother-infant bonding. However, claims that there is a relationship between breast feeding and bonding have been disputed. Analyses of mother-infant interactions have shown that breast feeding does not necessarily provide a comfortable or nurturing relationship with the mother (Kulka, Walter, & Fry, 1966).

Through the years, researchers have tried to find a relationship between infant-feeding methods and later psychological functioning. Strong evidence that breast feeding results in superior cognitive performance and personality adjustment has not been forthcoming. After reviewing the research literature on the effects of infant feeding published before 1964, Caldwell (1964) concluded:

> The fragments of evidence that can be mustered in support of possible psychological advantages of breast-feeding are not convincing because of the failure to control such factors as duration of total nutritive sucking and degree of physical intimacy offered the nonbreast-fed subjects. However, it is worth noting that while research which has claimed to demonstrate psychological advantages associated with breast-feeding is generally unconvincing, no single piece of research has ever produced evidence of any psychological superiority of formula-feeding (p. 79).

Little research on the issue has been published since Caldwell's review, and those studies which have been (e.g., Young et al., 1982) are not significant enough to alter the validity of Caldwell's conclusion.

FORMULA FEEDING AS AN ALTERNATIVE.   The evidence favoring breast milk as the food of choice for young babies is very compelling. Consequently, few people argue for the superiority of formula feeding over breast feeding. However, many people (e.g., Homan, 1973) believe that formula feeding is an equally good alternative. Pro-choice advocates point to the healthy growth and development of generations of infants and children who have been bottle fed as evidence of the adequacy of breast milk substitutes.

In some instances, mothers prefer not to breast feed because of psychological aversions resulting from feelings of revulsion, embarrassment, fear, uncertainty, and concerns about having an adequate milk supply. In other cases, mothers may wish to breast feed, but should not because of such factors as illness (e.g., tuberculosis), alcoholism, use of certain medications, or insufficient milk production. When such difficulties cannot be overcome, formula feeding is the preferred method (Waletzky, 1979).

In addition, the following problems and disadvantages have been associated with breast feeding:

1. Difficulties for working mothers. There are usually restrictions placed upon working mothers which make it difficult or impossible for them to breast feed satisfactorily. While some mothers are willing to fight for the right to unrestricted breast feeding during working hours, others are less assertive. Statistics show that the incidence and duration of breast feeding are lower for working mothers than for non-working mothers in the United States (Martinez & Dodd, 1983). This trend probably reflects the difficulties perceived and encountered by mothers who work. Some mothers pump the milk out of their breasts and store it for bottle feeding when they are not available for nursing. Other mothers provide formula to substitute for breast feeding at such times.

2. Fathers are left out of the feeding process. When the mother nurses the baby, the father has little role, if any, in feeding the baby. In some

instances, feelings of jealousy and other psychological difficulties experienced by a husband may result in a negative and nonsupportive attitude toward breast feeding (Waletzky, 1979). However, at least one father found a way to play a role in the breast-feeding process. A medical journal article (Wollman, 1981) reported a case in which a father successfully breast fed his daughter after receiving hormone injections. Most fathers, though, would not consider such an approach to be a viable alternative.

3. Drugs and toxins in breast milk. Breast-fed babies are susceptible to the harmful effects of certain drugs and toxins ingested by the mother (Committee on Nutrition, 1976a). Lactating mothers are advised to take medication only under the supervision of a physician. Examples of drugs that should not be taken are anticoagulants, most laxatives, radioactive drugs, and tetracycline (Foman, 1974). Environmental contaminants such as PCB may also get into the mother's milk supply.

BREAST FEEDING AND FORMULA FEEDING IN PERSPECTIVE. The American Academy of Pediatrics (1982) has concluded that the benefits of breast feeding are so numerous that pediatricians and other professionals should strongly promote the practice. Breast feeding is especially important in underdeveloped countries, where poor sanitation, poor nutrition, and a high incidence of infectious diseases exist. However, it must also be recognized that the choice of breast or formula feeding involves multiple and complex factors. In any case, mothers who cannot or do not wish to breast feed should not be reprimanded or criticized. They should be given assurance that normal growth and development are possible with the proper use of substitute formulas (Committee on Nutrition, 1976a; Foman et al., 1979).

CHOICE OF FORMULA. The mother who bottle feeds her baby has several options in the selection of formula. Premodified milk formulas are available in powdered, concentrated, and ready-to-feed cans and bottles. Formulas are available under different brands, with or without iron fortification and with slight variations in nutrient content. Several milk substitute formulas, usually made from soy milk, are available for infants who are allergic to cow's milk protein. Goat's milk is another possibility, provided appropriate vitamin supplements are given. The two most popular formulas are the concentrated liquid and ready-to-feed formulas (Johnson, Purvis, & Wallace, 1981). Condensed milk, skim milk, and low-fat milk are not nutritionally acceptable for infant feeding during the first two years. Regular whole cow's milk should not be given to infants under 6 months of age because it may cause a small amount of intestinal bleeding resulting in iron deficiency anemia (Committee on Nutrition, 1985).

Dietary Supplements. Nutritionists generally agree that some dietary supplementation is necessary during the nursing period. Opinions vary, however, as to the specific feeding schedule and the amounts and types of supplements needed. Infants are typically given supplements of vitamins C and D, iron, and fluoride, depending upon age, whether the infant is breast or bottle fed, formula choice, and fluoride content of the water. Infant caregivers should very carefully follow the physician's instructions to avoid excessive or inadequate amounts of vitamins, fluoride, and iron.

Schedule versus Demand Feeding.   Another decision that must be made in feeding infants is whether to schedule feedings every three or four hours, or to follow a baby-led, self-demand approach. Over the years, recommendations in the child-rearing literature have variously emphasized feeding babies on a rather strict schedule, or feeding them any time they get hungry. For example, all of the articles published in 1920 recommended tight feeding schedules, but in 1948, 100 percent of the articles advised self-demand schedules (McCandless, 1967). In recent years the emphasis has continued to favor demand feeding and self-regulation by the infant.

Out of 455 pediatricians who responded to a nationwide survey (Snow, 1982), the majority (63 percent) preferred feeding infants on a demand basis. In addition, approximately 20 percent recommended a modified demand approach in which the baby is allowed to eat when hungry, but only if there is a minimum time interval between feedings. The modified demand approach represents a compromise between schedule and demand feeding. The results of the survey are generally consistent with the recommendation of the American Academy of Pediatrics (1978) that infants should be fed on a demand basis rather than on a rigid three-to-four-hour schedule.

It may appear unrealistic to expect demand-fed babies to eat with restraint and self-control. However, years ago, Gesell and Ilg (1937) called attention to the ability of infants to regulate their own food intake with respect to both quantity and frequency. They published extensive data from individual cases of infant feeding to support their contention. Foman (1974) fed two groups of infants formulas with different caloric content. After about 6 weeks of age, infants in both groups adjusted the amount of milk consumed to the point where they were getting the same caloric intake. In addition, a study of 668 demand-fed babies (Aldrich & Hewitt, 1947) revealed no particular feeding difficulties and a generally restrained pattern of eating. Most of the infants placed themselves on a three-meals-per-day schedule by the time they were 10 months old.

Other studies have supported the practice of providing food to babies in small, frequent feedings rather than in larger amounts at more widely spaced intervals. Experiments with rats fed on an ad libitum (without restraint) basis revealed that they accumulate less body fat than rats fed larger meals at less frequent intervals (Fabry & Tepperman, 1970). The effects of feeding frequency on infants have not been determined, but the available research tends to favor demand feeding over schedule feeding. It may not be best to get an infant to sleep through the night as early as possible or to adapt early to a pattern of three meals a day (Foman et al., 1979).

Stage 2: Transitional Period (4–12 Months)

The second stage of infant feeding is called the transitional period because the baby is changing from a completely liquid diet to a diet consisting mainly of soft or semisolid baby food. The baby is "in transition" between a milk diet and adult table food. The major issues to be considered during this period are (1) developmental characteristics of the infant, (2) the process of weaning, (3) when to introduce semisolid food, and (4) what foods and supplements to include in the diet.

Developmental characteristics. The 4- to 6-month-old infant who is ready to enter the transitional period has matured physically enough to eat and digest soft, semisolid foods comfortably. By 4 or 5 months of age, the feeding reflexes have been replaced by voluntary muscle control. Sucking and rooting are voluntary, and the extrusion reflex has diminished or disappeared. The mouth is larger in proportion to the tongue and more easily accommodates a spoon. The normal infant is able to maintain a sitting position and hold the head erect without support. By 6 months the digestive system is more mature and can process a wider range of protein, fats, and carbohydrates. The kidneys have a greater capacity to handle increased eliminative loads with less water.

Weaning. The World Health Organization (WHO/UNICEF, 1981) defines weaning as the process by which milk-fed infants gradually become accustomed to the range of foods characteristic of the society into which they are born. For parents, the term most likely means the process of taking away the breast or bottle. Weaning is difficult to define with precision because there are a variety of transitions that may be made. The process of weaning may include a partial transition from breast to bottle, from a bottle to cup, from liquids to solids, and from caretaker-administered feeding to self-feeding (Gesell & Ilg, 1937).

For thousands of years, weaning in most cultures was started between 2 and 3 years (Ford, 1945). Some babies wean themselves easily, while others are more reluctant to give up the breast or bottle. Whether weaning is easy or difficult depends upon the readiness of the infant and the pressure exerted by the parent. Professionals in the field of child care tend to favor gradual weaning rather than an abrupt "cold turkey," approach (Wood & Walker-Smith, 1981). Some people advocate "baby-led" weaning, which allows infants to nurse until they are ready to give up the breast or bottle. Babies who are allowed unrestricted nursing typically wean themselves between 18 months and 3-1/2 years (Waletzky, 1979). Some babies lose interest in breast feeding as early as 6 months of age. However, other children may act as if they will never wean on their own, as the following anecdote illustrates.

A mother was sitting in the reception room of her pediatrician's office. As she was waiting her turn, she was breast feeding her baby. Another lady waiting beside her was observing the process with great interest. Finally, when she could restrain herself no longer, she said to the nursing mother, "Isn't that baby a little too old to still be breast feeding?" Before the mother could respond, the baby paused momentarily, then raised itself up and said, "Mind your own business, lady!" (Wood & Walker-Smith, 1981, p. 170).

Mothers who breast feed are encouraged to continue the process for at least 6 months. Some pediatricians believe there is no reason for discontinuing breast feeding before 18 to 20 months of age as long as other foods are introduced into the diet by 5 or 6 months to achieve an adequate nutritional balance (Foman et al., 1979). On the other hand, it is possible that prolonged breast or bottle feeding can promote undesirable nutritional habits whereby milk replaces other important nutrients in the diet. Infants who are bottle fed over an extended time may expose their teeth to sweetened liquids for longer periods of time, leading to tooth decay (Satter, 1983). Unfortunately, there is relatively little scientific research on weaning, so advice on weaning is based primarily on feelings and intuitions.

Freudian theorists have hypothesized that weaning practices may influence the development of habit patterns and personality traits such as non-nutritive sucking, aggressiveness, and impatience. Various researchers have attempted to test this hypothesis. However, studies have failed to demonstrate any consistent relationship between the time of weaning from breast or bottle and the development of child or adult personality patterns (Caldwell, 1964).

Age to Begin Semisolid Food.   The German word **beikost** (pronounced beiˊkost) is sometimes used to refer to baby foods other than milk or formula (Foman, 1974). The terms *semisolid, nonliquid, strained,* and *supplementary food* are also commonly used to mean the same thing as *beikost*. The appropriate age to begin *beikost* has been the subject of debate and controversy through the years. Currently, there is wide agreement among health-care professionals and nutritionists that the best time to introduce semisolid food is from 4 to 6 months of age.

In practice, it appears that many infants in the United States as well as other countries are fed semisolid food as early as 1 or 2 months of age (Foman et al., 1979; Canadian Paediatric Society Nutrition Committee, 1979; Sleigh & Ounsted, 1975). The early introduction of semisolid food has been attributed to prevailing sociocultural attitudes, aggressive advertising by baby food companies, and the erroneous belief that the additional food will help infants sleep through the night (Pipes, 1982; Foman et al., 1979).

Various medical groups (Committee on Nutrition, 1980; Canadian Paediatric Society Nutrition Committee, 1979; Addy, 1976) have expressed concern about possible harmful effects of introducing semisolid food at 1 or 2 months of age. The practice of feeding infants any food other than breast or formula milk before 4 to 6 months of age is strongly discouraged. The reasons for delaying the introduction of semisolids until that time are

1. The extrusion reflex (tendency to push food out of the mouth) does not disappear until 3 or 4 months of age.

2. The neuromuscular coordination necessary for the swallowing of semisolids is not fully developed until 16 to 18 weeks of age.

3. The nutritional values of solids are inferior to milk or formula in meeting specific needs of infants for the first 5 to 6 months of life.

4. Semisolid foods impose a higher eliminative load upon immature kidneys.

5. The addition of solids may diminish the immune protection conferred by breast milk.

6. The addition of solids increases possible sources of allergic reactions.

7. Introduction of solids before the infant is able to indicate a desire for food probably represents a type of forced feeding.

8. There is no evidence of obvious nutritional benefits.

9. The early introduction of semisolid food may interfere with establishing sound eating habits and may contribute to overfeeding.

10. There is no evidence that the addition of semisolid food helps babies sleep through the night.

There are no absolute guidelines for timing the introduction of semisolid foods, except that the decision should be individual in relation to the developmental level and needs of each infant. According to the American Academy of Pediatrics (Committee on Nutrition, 1980), supplemental foods should be introduced when the infant can sit with support and has good neuromuscular control of the neck and head at about 4 to 6 months of age.

Order of Introduction of Different Foods.   From a nutritional standpoint, the order of introduction of various foods appears to be relatively unimportant (Foman et al., 1979). However, caregivers are advised to introduce one new single food ingredient at no less than weekly intervals. The purpose of the procedure is to identify specific food allergies as they occur (Committee on Nutrition, 1985).

The typical sequence for the introduction of various types of food is given in Table 7-2. Infant cereals, which provide additional energy and iron, are usually introduced as the first semisolid food. Some pediatricians recommend the use of single-grain, rice-based cereals first because they are the least likely to cause an allergic reaction. Iron-fortified cereal is frequently given to satisfy iron requirements. Vegetables may be better accepted if they are introduced before fruits (Canadian Paediatric Society Nutrition Committee 1979), but this is not a widespread opinion among infant nutritionists (Foman et al.,

TABLE 7-2 Suggested Ages for the Introduction of Semisolid Foods and Table Foods

FOOD	AGE (MONTHS)		
	4 TO 6	6 TO 8	9 TO 12
Iron-fortified cereals for infants	Add		
Vegetables		Add strained	Gradually delete strained foods, introduce table foods
Fruits		Add strained	Gradually delete strained foods, introduce chopped well-cooked or canned foods
Meats		Add strained or finely chopped table meats	Decrease the use of strained meats, increase the varieties of table meats
Finger foods such as arrowroot biscuits, oven-dried toast		Add those that can be secured with a palmar grasp	Increase the use of small-sized finger foods as the pincer grasp develops
Well-cooked mashed or chopped table foods, prepared without added salt or sugar			Add
Juice by cup			Add

Source: Reproduced by permission from: Peggy L. Pipes, *Nutrition in infancy and childhood* (3rd. ed.). St. Louis, 1985, The C. V. Mosby Co.

1979). Juices should be given to the baby when the ability to drink from a cup has developed (Committee on Nutrition, 1980). Meats and other high-protein foods, such as eggs, are usually introduced last because they place more strain on the digestive and eliminative processes. Home-prepared strained foods are just as nutritious as commercially prepared baby food. Precautions must be taken to avoid spoilage of any type of food provided (Committee on Nutrition, 1985).

Stage 3: Modified Adult Period (1 to 2 years)

Children begin to imitate adults very early in life, even in eating patterns. Although there is considerable individual variation, many babies move away from infantile eating schedules and baby food by the time they are 1 year of age. The modified adult period is characterized by (1) the development of self-feeding skills; (2) the change from chopped (junior) baby food to food from the family table; and (3) the increasing significance of the psychosocial value of food. This period overlaps with the transition period (second stage) because infants may be eating baby food and adult food at the same time. Some infants may even continue to nurse (stage 1) from breast or bottle during this stage.

This one-year-old infant has begun to feed himself with a spoon, but at this age he gets more food on his face and hands than in his mouth!

Development of Self-feeding Skills. Beginning around 1 year of age, many of the skills that are essential for self-feeding are being developed and refined. The average baby has changed the pattern of eating from sucking to rotary chewing movements. Some of the teeth have developed to the point of being useful in biting and chewing solid food. Control of the lips and tongue, which is essential in drinking from a cup, has developed. Infants usually manage to hold a cup and drink with only minor spilling early in the second year.

Voluntary hand-to-mouth movements, a finger-thumb grasp, and the ability to hold and let go of eating utensils have developed around 7 or 8 months of age. Wrist control, essential in using a spoon efficiently, develops between 12 and 18 months. According to Gesell and Ilg (1937), the 2-year-old is relatively efficient at spoon feeding. The willingness of the parent to allow the baby to practice self-feeding is a very important factor in determining when the skill is accomplished.

During the modified adult period, the baby moves from the caretaker's lap, or an infant seat, to the highchair for meals. The rapidly developing language skills and cognitive capacities play an expanded role in the feeding process. The baby learns to recognize different foods by such features as taste, texture, aroma, and name. Specific foods are given verbal labels, which facilitate requests for food and the statement of food preferences. The feeding process thus takes on an added social and psychological significance during this period.

Nutritional Requirements and Food for the Older Infant. When the infant changes from baby food to table food, it is important to take another look at nutritional requirements. During the 1- to 2-year period, the infant's caloric needs are relatively low, but protein needs for the growth of muscles and tissue remain high (Anderson, Chin, & Fisher, 1982). Protein, caloric, and other basic nutritional requirements can be met with menus prepared from the four basic food groups, which include milk, meat, fruits and vegetables, and bread and cereals (Table 7-3).

An adequate supply of iron (15 mg./day) should be included in the diet during this period. Meats and iron-enriched cereal products are major sources of iron. Some nutritionists advise that the use of iron-fortified infant cereals be continued through the second year of life as the best source of easily digestible iron (Committee on Nutrition, 1976b). Consumption of more than 16 to 24 ounces of milk per day and sugary snacks may result in inadequate intake of iron-containing foods (Satter, 1983).

Unless adequate fluoride is available in the water supply, the continuation of fluoride supplements is recommended until age 16. However, the fluoride intake should be carefully monitored to avoid tooth pitting and discoloration. For maximum absorption by the body, fluoride should be given between meals (Committee on Nutrition, 1985). Additional mineral or vitamin supplements are not needed during this feeding period if a balanced diet is provided.

Social and Psychological Aspects of Infant Feeding.   Although research studies have failed to find a definite relationship between infant feeding practices and personality adjustment, the psychosocial implications of food and the process of eating during infancy are still considered to be very important. Bruno Bettleheim (1970) believes that "the ability to control oneself, to wait, to work now for future rewards," as well as one's "entire attitude to the world" is conditioned by the eating experience (p. 16). According to Erikson (1963), the regularity and procedure with which an infant is fed are very important ingredients in the establishment of basic trust. "The first demonstration of social trust in the baby is the ease of his feeding . . ." (p. 247).

From the beginning, feeding a baby is not simply a one-way process, something that a caretaker does to a child. Rather, it is a process which occurs

TABLE 7-3   Basic Four Food Plan for Infants

FOOD GROUP	DAILY SERVINGS BY AGE	
	6 TO 12 MONTHS	18 TO 36 MONTHS
Milk (and dairy products)	16–24 oz.	2–3 cups
Meats, fish, eggs	2 (½ oz)	2 (½ oz)
Fruits-vegetables	4 (1–2 tbsp)	4 (2–3 tbsp)
Bread-cereal	4 (¼ adult size)	4 (⅓ adult size)

Source: E. Satter, (1983). *Child of mine: Feeding with love and common sense.* Palo Alto, CA: Bull Publishing Co. Adapted by permission.

as a concert between caretaker and baby. Even the newborn is an active partici-
pant in the feeding situation. Individuality is expressed early in the infant's
own unique approaches to nursing and feeding styles (Barnes et al., 1953).
Caretakers also bring their own personality characteristics, expectations, and
attitudes to the feeding situation. The underlying parental attitudes are likely
to be more potent than actual parental practices in feeding infants (Caldwell,
1964). In any event, the success in feeding and the psychosocial consequences
of the feeding process ultimately depend upon the interactions between infant
and caretakers.

As the infant grows older and moves to the highchair, new opportunities
for social interchange with the family at mealtimes are provided. The process
of eating takes on increasing meaning in the establishment of autonomy and
self-control. The toddler's refusal of new food and the insistence on particular
food preferences is one way of expressing the need for autonomy and individuality.

There is a danger that food will become a battleground between parent
and child and take on a negative dimension. Infants learn early that food may
be used as a means of controlling behavior and attracting attention. Usually
relaxed parents who are willing to give their child choices and freedom to
establish food preferences avoid unnecessary power struggles and get through
the period with minimum frustration.

SPECIAL NUTRITIONAL CONCERNS AND FEEDING PROBLEMS

A number of problems are related to infant nutrition and feeding practices.
Special concerns that are the focal point of current discussion and research
activity include iron deficiency anemia, food allergies, dental caries, infantile
obesity and its relationship to adult obesity, and the effects of sodium intake in
early life on the development of hypertension in adulthood.

Iron Deficiency Anemia

Iron deficiency is the most common specific nutritional deficiency usually
encountered in infants and young children in the United States (Woodruff,
1978). The condition is most prevalent in infants between 4 and 24 months of
age (Foman, 1974; Pipes, 1985). Small, premature infants become more susceptible to iron deficiency when their prenatal nutritional iron stores are
depleted after about 2 months of age. The risk period for full-term infants
begins around 4 to 6 months of age. The highest incidence of the condition is
found among lower socioeconomic populations and low-birthweight infants
(Committee on Nutrition, 1976b). Symptoms of iron deficiency anemia
include poor appetite, irritability, poor skin color, and listlessness. Anemia also
reduces the child's resistance to infectious disease (Pipes, 1985).

Food Allergies

The incidence of food allergies in children is highest during the infancy period (Pipes, 1985). A wide range of symptoms have been associated with allergic reactions to food, including skin rashes, abdominal pain, vomiting, diarrhea, respiratory distress, headaches, and hyperactivity. Because the symptoms are varied and may also result from other sources, the specific foods that are the culprits are hard to identify. To further complicate the problem, children may outgrow certain food allergies but become susceptible to new food intolerances with changing age. Food allergies tend to run in families.

Milk, wheat, eggs, corn, and citrus fruits are foods most frequently identified in allergic reactions in babies (Speer, 1973), but any food is a potential offender. Milk allergy is a problem for an estimated 3 to 7 percent of formula-fed infants (Goldstein & Heiner, 1970). Some children also react adversely to breast milk. In some cases the elimination of cow's milk from the mother's diet has solved the problem (Jakobsson & Lindberg, 1978) for breast-fed babies. The usual procedure for identifying the cause of an allergic reaction is to remove a suspicious food from the diet and introduce it again a week or so later to determine if the symptoms recur. Blood tests are widely used for assessing food allergies. Skin tests are sometimes used in extreme cases, but they present special problems for infants.

Dental Caries

Dental caries represent one of the most common problems resulting from nutritional and feeding inadequacies. Although dental caries are more prevalent among older children, approximately 25 percent of all 2-year-old infants worldwide develop them (Foman, 1974). Nutrition plays a critical role in the development of healthy teeth from the sixth week of the prenatal period through the adolescent period. The state of dental health is, to a large extent, a reflection of dietary adequacy. The major nutrients required for normal tooth development are protein, calcium, phosphorus, Vitamin A, Vitamin D, and ascorbic acid. The value of fluoride, in combination with an adequate diet, in the prevention of dental caries has been well documented (Committee on Nutrition, 1979).

A characteristic pattern of dental caries which is frequently observed in infants and young children is bottle-mouth syndrome (also called nursing-bottle syndrome). The problem is characterized by extreme damage to the upper and sometimes the lower front teeth. The teeth decay and may break off at the gum line. The pattern of decay results from the pooling of milk around the teeth. Children who are habitually given a bottle while going to sleep are particularly susceptible to bottle caries. The use of pacifiers coated with sugary substances, or bottles containing sweetened beverages or fruit juice also increase the risk of bottle-mouth disease.

Obesity

Obesity is a problem of special concern during infancy because the fat infant tends to become the fat child, who, in turn, becomes the fat adult. Obesity can result from an increase in fat cell numbers (hyperplasia) or an increase in fat cell size (hypertrophy). Theoretically, there are two critical periods for the development of fat cell numbers—infancy and adolescence. Excessive weight gain during a critical period may result in excessive numbers of fat cells, which may be permanent. Thus, later weight loss is difficult, if not impossible, because it can be accomplished only through reduction in cell size (Knittle, 1972).

Strong new evidence, however, indicates that whether an infant grows up to be fat or skinny depends largely upon genetic factors. Research studies of adopted infants and twins suggest that human fatness and obesity are more closely related to heredity than to early eating habits. Stunkard and his associates (1986) studied 540 adults in Denmark who had been adopted as infants. The adoptees tended to develop a body weight that more closely resembled that of their biological parents than of the parents who reared them. In another study, Stunkard, Foch and Krubec (1986) found the incidence of obesity to be twice as high in identical twins as in nonidentical twins. The results of both studies are consistent with earlier findings (Mayer, 1965) that only 14 percent of the offspring of two normal-weight parents become obese. In comparison, 40 percent of infants with one overweight parent and 80 percent of those with two overweight parents become obese.

None of these studies should be interpreted to mean that infants of overweight parents inevitably become obese. Neither do the studies mean that parents do not have to pay attention to what infants are fed. The research does suggest, however, that parents who are overweight need to make special efforts to keep their infants from overeating. In addition to dietary control, parents need to develop other strategies to prevent obesity, such as providing increased opportunities for age-appropriate exercise activities. Obesity is not inevitable and can be prevented.

The growth of infants should be carefully monitored by a physician's growth chart to avoid obesity (see Chapter 4). In the event that obesity has developed, the infant is usually not placed on a weight-loss diet. Rather, the emphasis is placed on restricting further excessive weight gain until normal body proportions are obtained with normal increments in height (Canadian Paediatric Society Nutrition Committee, 1979).

Sodium and Hypertension

An increasing amount of concern has been expressed in recent years that the amount of sodium usually included in the diets of infants may be excessive. Cross-cultural studies have found that population groups with high sodium diets have a higher incidence of hypertension than groups with low sodium intake. Studies on rats show certain genetic strains developing hypertension in adulthood when subjected to high sodium diets in infancy (Dahl, 1972).

Subsequent research studies (e.g., Whitten & Stewart, 1980) using human subjects have failed to establish that sodium intake in infancy is a contributing factor in adult hypertension. Yet there remains a reasonable possibility that controlling sodium intake during infancy and childhood may be a preventive measure for the people who are susceptible. Statistics show that 20 percent of the infants in this country will develop hypertension by the time they reach adulthood (Committee on Nutrition, 1974).

Baby food manufacturers have responded to the concern about controlling sodium intake and no longer add salt to commercially prepared infant foods. Parents are advised to avoid adding salt to baby food that they buy or prepare at home (Committee on Nutrition, 1980). Salt is an acquired taste, and babies will eat salted and unsalted foods equally well (Foman et al., 1970).

CONSEQUENCES OF MALNUTRITION

Malnutrition is a condition in which there is either a deficit or an excess of one or more essential nutrients needed by the body tissues (Santos, Arrendo, & Vitale, 1983). Malnutrition can result from either insufficient or excessive nutrient intake. There are various degrees of malnutrition, ranging from mild to severe. Malnutrition is considered to be the most widespread and serious problem affecting infants and young children in the world (Santos et al., 1983). Its effects are numerous and varied. Specific symptoms or conditions resulting from varying nutritional problems include growth delay or failure, rickets, anemia, dental caries, obesity, and lowered resistance to disease. Malnutrition also has serious behavioral consequences such as listlessness, withdrawal, and mental retardation. The ultimate outcome of malnutrition depends upon its timing, severity, and duration.

Protein Energy Malnutrition

On a worldwide scale, the most serious and common nutritional problem is protein energy malnutrition (PEM). This condition results in growth retardation or failure and possibly mental retardation (McLaren & Burman, 1982). Cases of PEM become evident between 4 months and 2 years of age, when infants from cultures of poverty have been weaned from breast milk. The main features of mild to moderate PEM are growth retardation, lowered resistance to infectious diseases, and a diminished activity level. The first effects on growth are characterized by

1.   a slower rate of linear growth and weight gain
2.   delayed bone maturation, resulting from low protein and calcium intake

3. a decrease in midarm circumference, due to muscle wasting
4. normal or diminished weight:height ratio
5. normal or diminished skin-fold thickness, which reflects loss of fat stores (McLaren & Burman, 1982, p. 114).

Growth retardation may be compounded by the higher incidence of infectious diseases that occur in an infant subjected to PEM. The lack of sufficient calories (energy) in the diet causes the baby to be listless and apathetic. There is a danger that caretakers will interpret this quiet behavior as a sign of a "good" baby and fail to see it as a problem.

The moderate to severe forms of PEM include the conditions known as kwashiorkor and marasmus. Kwashiorkor is caused primarily by an insufficiency of protein in the diet and usually occurs in the second, third, or fourth year of life (Wood & Walker-Smith, 1981). The child who suffers from kwashiorkor has a swollen appearance (edema) but has little muscular tissue under the skin. Skin ulcers, loss of hair, irritability or lethargy, weakness, and growth failure are other characteristics of the condition.

Marasmus is caused by insufficient food intake (starvation) in general, but a deficiency of calories in particular. Marasmus typically appears in the early months of life. The marasmic child has lost most of the subcutaneous fat and appears to be mostly skin and bones. The condition may include chronic diarrhea, vomiting, irritability, or apathy (McLaren & Burman, 1982). Either marasmus or kwashiorkor leads to death if left untreated. These diseases are usually not found in the United States, although rare cases are found from time to time.

Catchup Growth.

Obviously, the effects of malnutrition can be devastating to the human

These children are suffering from Kwashiorkor. Notice the swollen stomach, skinny arms, and loss of hair.

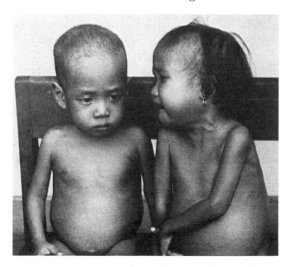

body. To what extent do children have the capacity to recover from severe PEM that has resulted in stunted growth? There is reasonably strong evidence that human beings have an amazing "catchup" capacity. A group of Johns Hopkins University doctors (Graham & Adrianzen, 1972) studied children in Lima, Peru, who had been hospitalized for malnutrition between 3 and 15 months of age. The children eventually achieved normal physical growth after they were removed from their impoverished environments and placed in homes where they were given adequate nutrition and medical care. Other studies (e.g., Garrow, 1967; Winick, Meyer, & Harris, 1975) have found similar results.

The evidence is not conclusive, however, and not all researchers are equally optimistic about the possibility of reversing the effects of nutritional growth failure. It is possible that stunted growth that begins with even a moderate degree of PEM in infancy might have adverse consequences in old age or even in the next generation (Gurney, 1979; Eddy, 1973).

Malnutrition and Brain Growth

The effects of malnutrition on brain growth and mental functioning have been the subject of speculation and intensive investigation. Evidence is accumulating to show that severe early malnutrition is likely to alter the structure and function of the brain. Both animal and human studies have found that early malnutrition of the marasmus type reduces the number of brain cells, brain size, and head circumference. In addition, the myelinization, structural organization, and biochemical composition of the brain are adversely affected (Winick, 1979).

The period of growth when the brain is most vulnerable to damage by starvation probably begins with the last trimester of fetal growth and continues through the first 18 months after birth (Martin, 1973). Nutritional deficits that occur during this period of rapid brain growth tend to cause permanent damage (Winick, 1976). Whether or not the effects are permanent is likely to be determined by the timing, duration, and severity of the malnutrition. The effects of mild to moderate short-term malnutrition on brain growth are thought to be inconsequential, but on the basis of current knowledge, no one can say for sure.

Malnutrition, Learning, and Behavior

To what extent does malnutrition in infancy adversely influence learning and intellectual performance over the course of a lifetime? Various researchers have tried to assess the impact of nutritional deficits on psychological development. One of the first studies was conducted in the early 1960s in Mexico City by Cravioto and Robles (1965), who tested twenty infants hospitalized for kwashiorkor. All of the infants were found to be below the age norms for physical and mental development. The study revealed that infants with the earliest (ages 3 to 6 months) and most severe degree of malnutrition showed fewer signs of recovery from developmental deficits than infants with later (15 to 42 months) and less severe nutritional deficits.

In general, research studies tend to show that severe protein caloric malnutrition that occurs during the first year of life plays a major role in impaired intellectual development. The more severe the nutritional deficits and the longer they continue, the greater the chances of persistent intellectual impairment. On the other hand, if intervention occurs early in the first year, the chances of recovery of normal or near-normal intellectual functioning appear to be very good (Ricciuti, 1973).

Researchers have had difficulty separating the effects of limited nutrition from the effects of other environmental factors. Malnutrition may exert its major influence on learning indirectly by causing changes in attention, motivation and responsiveness (Beal, 1980). The undernourished baby is listless, easily tired, and less inclined to seek or be responsive to mental stimulation. The infant's inactivity and lack of responsivity may result in decreased social interchanges with parents, other caregivers, and peers. The malnourished child's greater susceptibility to illness also increases the social isolation.

SIGNS OF NUTRITIONAL ADEQUACY

Generally, the signs of nutritional adequacy are related to growth rate, appetite, muscle tone, activity pattern, and appearance of the oral cavity (Lewis, 1979). One of the best indicators of good nutrition is a consistent, steady growth rate, which, when recorded on a standard growth chart, generally parallels the normal curve. Usually the appetite will correlate positively with the growth rate, allowing for temporary variations for illness and changes in routines. The muscles should be firm to the touch and should have good motor reactions. Behaviorally, the baby should be alert, inquisitive, happy, and responsive. Malnourished children are listless, withdrawn, and often irritable. The mucous membranes inside the mouth as well as the lips, tongue, and gums should be reddish pink. The tongue normally has a slightly rough appearance. Any teeth that are present should remain bright and free of cavities or pitting (Lewis. 1979).

SUGGESTIONS FOR FEEDING INFANTS

Unfortunately, feeding infants is not an exact science and the advice given to parents is often contradictory and controversial. Parents should make decisions about feeding practices only after obtaining current information from their pediatrician and other professional sources. The following are some examples of generally recommended, less controversial feeding practices for each feeding stage (Hinton & Kerwin, 1981; Lewis, 1979; Satter, 1983).

Nursing Infants

1. Engage in eye contact and cuddle the infant during feeding sessions.
2. Avoid using bottle props to replace a caretaker's lap.
3. Allow infants to decide how much to eat. Discontinue feeding when the infant loses interest in eating. Avoid giving infants breast or bottle to stop crying resulting from needs other than hunger.
4. To avoid bottle-mouth syndrome, do not allow an infant to go to sleep with a bottle containing anything but water. Sweetened liquids should not be given in a bottle.
5. Avoid giving an infant honey in any form because of the risk of botulism.

Transition Infants

1. Do not mix cereal or other foods with milk and give it from a bottle.
2. Make the first solids thin and smooth. Use a small spoon to place the food on the middle of the tongue, but do not exert pressure. Give very small amounts of any new food at the beginning.
3. Introduce new foods one at a time at one- or two-week intervals and observe for allergic reactions. Do not mix foods until each has been introduced separately.
4. Allow all infants to have food preferences. Offer infants a variety of foods over time.
5. Do not add salt or sugar to an infant's food.

Toddlers

1. Serve food at lukewarm temperature in bite-size pieces and small portions. Provide child-size utensils and comfortable seating.
2. Encourage self-feeding as soon as the infant can hold a spoon and manage a cup. Be tolerant of spills and messiness.
3. Provide meals in a pleasant, relaxed atmosphere. Keep mealtime conversation happy and pleasant. Allow for a premeal rest period when possible.
4. Avoid rigid rules about the amount of food to be eaten. Do not force toddlers to eat by coaxing or by offering treats or bribes.
5. Give toddlers between-meal snacks; toddlers need more frequent feedings than adults. Snacks should consist of nutritious, low-sugar foods. They should be carefully spaced, usually midway between meals.

SUMMARY

1. For healthy growth and development, infants need a diet that provides a daily balance of calories, protein, vitamins, minerals, and water.

2. The three stages of infant feeding are the nursing period (birth–6 months), the transitional period (4–12 months), and the modified adult period (1–2 years).

3. The percentage of mothers who breast feed their babies has been

increasing in recent years. The scientific arguments and professional opinions favor breast feeding over bottle feeding. However, mothers who cannot or do not wish to breast feed should be assured that formula feeding is still an acceptable alternative where public health is generally good.

4. Generally, professionals recommend feeding infants on demand rather than on a predetermined schedule.

5. Recommendations on the age for weaning infants vary widely among professionals. In the United States, most infants are likely to be weaned by the end of the first year of life.

6. The recommended age for the introduction of semisolid food into the diet of an infant is from 4 to 6 months. However, in the United States, many infants begin eating semisolid food much earlier.

7. Infants develop the motor-coordination skills for efficient self-feeding by 2 years of age.

8. The infant's basic nutritional needs during the modified adult period can be met with menus planned from the basic four food groups: milk and dairy products, meat, fruits and vegetables, bread and cereal.

9. Food and mealtime become increasingly significant for socioemotional development as the infant gets old enough to sit in a highchair.

10. The most common nutritional problem of infants in the United States is iron deficiency anemia. Food allergies, dental caries, obesity, and excessive sodium intake are other nutritional problems and concerns during infancy.

11. Protein energy malnutrition (PEM) is the most common nutritional problem among infants throughout the world. The physical effects of PEM include retardation of physical growth, lowered resistance to infectious diseases, kwashiorkor, and marasmus.

12. Very severe malnutrition occurring during the prenatal period and early months of life is likely to result in permanent damage to the developing brain. Malnutrition may also cause learning deficits as the result of a diminished level of responsiveness and exploratory behavior.

13. Some of the signs that infants are receiving adequate nutrition are a normal growth rate, good appetite, firm muscle tone, curiosity, and alertness.

8

Intellectual Development

> What is the little one thinking about?
> Very wonderful things no doubt! . . .
> Who can tell what a baby thinks.
>
> —J. G. Holland

When do infants begin to think? How do they think? How soon do learning and memory begin? What does an infant know? These and other questions about the development of intelligence in infants have been the target of numerous inquiring minds. One of the characteristics of human intelligence is to try to find out how that intellectual capacity evolved. During a child's infancy, we have opportunities to observe the development of intelligence almost from the very beginning. Although we have only scratched the surface, our knowledge of cognitive development has increased dramatically during the past thirty years.

This chapter focuses on some of the factors that influence intelligence, Piaget's theory of cognitive development, some of the ways infants learn, and the development of infant memory. We also look at some of the instruments that are used to assess infant intelligence. Finally, suggestions for facilitating cognitive development during the infancy period will be considered.

DEFINITIONS

Definitions of intelligence are numerous and varied. Wechsler (1958) defined intelligence as "the capacity of the individual to act purposefully, think rationally and deal effectively with the environment" (p. 7). Piaget (1954) defined intelligence in terms of an individual's capacity to adapt to the environment. Most definitions emphasize one or more of three common themes: the capacity to think, learn, and solve problems; the capacity to accumulate knowledge (memory); and the ability to adapt to the environment (Robinson & Robinson, 1965).

Cognition is a term that is closely associated with intelligence. The two terms are frequently used to mean the same thing (e.g., Wadsworth, 1979). Technically, though, cognition refers to all the mental processes, such as thinking, remembering, use of language, problem solving, and concept formation. The cognitive processes thus make up the functional component of intelligence. In this chapter the terms **intelligence** and **cognition** are used interchangeably.

INFLUENCES ON INTELLIGENCE

The extent to which intelligence is controlled by heredity or environment has been the subject of intense debate for centuries. The most widely accepted point of view today is that heredity and environment interact in complex ways to shape intelligence. Researchers have attempted to determine the relative contribution of each factor.

Genetic

In recent years, the position that heredity is the dominant force in intellectual development has been represented most vigorously by Arthur Jensen (1969). Jensen claims that approximately 80 percent of the *differences* in IQ scores is the result of genetic factors. Thus if one child obtains an IQ score of 120 and another obtains a score of 100, sixteen points of the twenty-point difference (0.80 × 20) are the result of heredity.

Other researchers (Plomin & Defries, 1980) have suggested that Jensen's estimate is too high, and the difference in IQ scores which can be attributed to genetic factors is no more than 50 percent. Most scientists have been reluctant to accept either conclusion as valid because of the difficulties involved in separating genetic from environmental factors. Scientists such as Scarr and Weinberg (1978) believe that it is impossible to assign a specific percentage to the contribution of heredity to intelligence.

Environmental

Numerous environmental influences potentially affect intellectual development. Most of these factors, including health, nutrition, and prenatal and perinatal influences, are covered in other chapters. At this point we need to consider three additional potential sources of influence during infancy: the family environment, cultural factors, and socioeconomic factors.

Family Environment.   Research studies have tended to confirm the assertion that family influences play a very important role in the development of intelligence. In the Harvard Preschool Project, White and his associates (1973) conducted extensive observations of the home environment of thirty-one infants through the first three years of life. They concluded that the infants who were assessed to be the most intellectually competent experienced superior parent-child interactions in contrast to the infants who were less competent. A four-year longitudinal study of 193 mothers and their infants (Bee et al., 1982) found that measures of home environmental quality and parent-infant interaction taken in the first year of life are good predictors of later IQ and language development.

Cultural Factors.   Cross-cultural studies have generally found more similarities than differences in cognitive development of infants throughout the world. After reviewing numerous investigations, Super (1981) concluded that infants from one particular culture or race generally do not show more rapid cognitive development than infants from other cultures or races, except for conditions of minimal stimulation or malnutrition. Kagan and Klein (1973) found that infants living in an isolated village of Guatemala were delayed two to three months in achieving a variety of cognitive milestones such as object permanence and symbolic aspects of play. The delays were attributed to the inadequate stimulation they experienced during their first year.

Socioeconomic Status.   Children from low socioeconomic backgrounds consistently score lower on measures of intelligence than do their middle-class peers. However, these differences do not begin to appear until after the first eighteen months of life (Golden & Birns, 1976). By 3 years of age, the child's IQ score has been affected by such socioeconomic indicators as parental education, occupation, and income (Bayley & Schaefer, 1964).

Infancy as a Critical Period

Since the rate of intellectual growth catapults rapidly during the first three years of life, many people believe that infancy is the critical period in the development of intelligence. Benjamin Bloom (1964) has concluded that about one-half of a person's intelligence is developed by age 4. Burton White is convinced that the period of life that is likely to be the most decisive for the development of intelligence is 10 to 18 months (White & Watts, 1973).

Both Bloom's and White's conclusions have been widely publicized to support the critical importance of infancy in cognitive development. However, Rutter (1985) argues that "There is no marked critical period for cognitive growth" (p. 683). His conclusion is based on the follow-up studies of ten infants who suffered gross physical and cognitive deprivation until they were rescued at ages ranging from 30 months to 13 years. Even though the children were severely mentally retarded, seven of the ten eventually obtained normal IQ scores. Rutter notes, however, that the effects of extremely bad experiences can be reversed only through big changes in the child's environment (Rutter, 1985).

PIAGET'S THEORY

The theory of Jean Piaget has most widely influenced contemporary understanding of the development of infant intelligence. Piaget did not agree with the nativist view that infants are born with basic concepts and knowledge structures. He also disagreed with the environmentalist position that the newborn infant's mind is a *tabula rasa* (blank slate) and all knowledge is acquired through experience. Instead, Piaget's theory is based on the belief that intelligence develops through an interaction between internal (genetic) and external (environmental) factors.

Key Concepts

For Piaget (1952), making progress in cognitive development is based on **scheme** building. A scheme is a basic pattern of action, thought, or knowledge that is used to interact with the environment. Schemes can be classified as either motor or mental. Motor schemes are organized patterns of action such as sucking a bottle, picking up a toy, or walking. Mental schemes are concepts, ideas, or images that make up the thought processes. Mental and motor schemes are used together and are difficult to separate, as when an infant produces a sound (motor) to form a word (mental). For Piaget, the schemes are the building blocks of intelligence. They make up the structure of the mind and serve as basic units of behavior. At any given age, a person's intelligence is based upon the number, complexity, and flexibility of the available schemes.

Schemes are built and modified through the process of **adaptation.** As a biologist, Piaget studied how organisms adapt to their surroundings, particularly when they are moved to a new environment. He once transferred a species of snails from a calm pond to the rocks on the shore of a turbulent lake. Piaget observed how the snails adapted over time by changing their shapes from an elongated form to a shorter, rounder body. This enabled the snails to get a better grip on the rocks so they would not be washed away. Piaget came to believe that adaptation is the key to intellectual functioning just as it is to biological processes (Pulaski, 1980).

Adaptation takes place through two related processes—**assimilation** and **accommodation.** Assimilation is making the environment fit you. In assimilation, the individual makes use of substances or information through existing schemes. A young infant who spots a new object will probably pick it up and try to eat it or bang it on something. If the toy is small enough, the baby can exploit it without making any modifications in existing behaviors. In some cases an infant assimilates information (perceptions) from the environment by forcing it to conform or fit in with existing ideas or understandings (schemes). For example, an infant may learn the word *cat* and associate it with a four-legged, furry animal. The infant may then use that particular scheme (cat) to apply to a dog or other animals. Thus, in assimilation, the infant uses and tries to preserve existing structures.

Accommodation is making yourself fit the environment. It is the process whereby an individual's schemes are altered to fit new information or experiences. When a breast-fed baby is given a bottle for the first time, the sucking scheme has to be modified to fit the shape, size, and milk flow of the new nipple before it is effective. The infant who calls all four-legged animals "cat" will eventually learn that the "cat" scheme only applies to certain animals. In some cases a new scheme has to be created because there is no existing scheme available into which new information can be accommodated. Accommodation is the mechanism through which variability, growth, and change occur.

Assimilation and accommodation are complementary processes that usually operate in concert. The two processes may be observed when an infant adjusts the mouth (sucking) to accommodate the shape of a new nipple while at the same time taking in or assimilating nourishment and pleasurable sensations. In this instance, assimilation and accommodation have reached a state of **equilibrium** or balance. The infant has reached a state of adaptation to the environment. However, the equilibrium or state of balance between assimilation and accommodation does not last, and one process or the other dominates temporarily. When assimilation and accommodation are out of balance, the

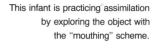

This infant is practicing assimilation by exploring the object with the "mouthing" scheme.

result is usually cognitive conflict. The infant is then motivated to restore equilibrium by searching for a solution. Cognitive development advances as the baby produces more sophisticated schemes in order to adapt and change.

Piaget's Stages

According to Piaget, cognitive development proceeds through a series of orderly stages. Although the approximate age at which each stage occurs has been identified, not everyone goes through the stages at the same rate or chronological age. In some instances, a person may "straddle," or be in two stages, at the same time. However, the order in which people progress through the stages does not vary. The basic stages Piaget identified are the *sensorimotor period* (birth to 2 yr.), the period of *preoperational thought* (2 to 7 yr.), the period of *concrete operations* (7 to 11 yr.), and the period of *formal operations* (11 to 15 yr.). The sensorimotor period, which corresponds with infancy, is considered further.

Sensorimotor Period. The first two years of life are called the sensorimotor period because the baby relates to the world by coordinating information from the senses with motor activities of the body. Piaget (1952) introduced the idea that thought arises from action. In the beginning of life, knowledge is not separated from activities. The young infant looks at an object and reflexively reaches for it without thinking about the process. As the baby

TABLE 8.1 Development during Piaget's Sensorimotor Period

STAGE	DEVELOPMENTAL UNIT	INTENTION AND MEANS-END RELATIONS	MEANING	SPACE	TIME	CAUSALITY	IMITATION	OBJECT PERFORMANCE
1	Exercising the ready-made sensorimotor schemes (0–1 mo.)							
2	Primary circular reactions (1–4 mo.)		Different responses to different objects				Pseudo-imitation begins	
3	Secondary circular reactions (4–8 mo.)	Acts upon objects	"Motor meaning"	All modalities focus on single object	Brief search for absent object	Acts; then waits for effect to occur	Pseudo-imitation quicker, more precise. True imitation of acts already in repertoire	Brief single-modality search for absent object
4	Coordination of secondary schemes (8–12 mo.)	Attack barrier to reach goal	Symbolic meaning	Turns bottle to reach nipple	Prolonged search for absent object	Attacks barrier to reach goal; waits for adults to serve him	True imitation of novel acts not visible on own body	Prolonged, multimodality search
5	Tertiary circular reactions (12–18 mo.)	"Experiments in order to see"; discovery of new means through "groping accommodation"	Elaboration through action and feedback	Follows sequential displacements if object in sight	Follows sequential displacements if object in sight	Discovers new means; solicits help from adults	True imitation quicker, more precise	Follows sequential displacements if object in sight
6	Invention of new means through mental combinations (18–24 mo.)	Invention of new means through reciprocal assimilation of schemes	Further elaboration; symbols increasingly covert	Solves detour problem; symbolic representation of spatial relationships, mostly internal	Both anticipation and memory	Infers causes from observing effects; predicts effects from observing causes	Imitates (1) complex, (2) nonhuman, (3) absent models	Follows sequential displacement with object hidden; symbolic representation of object

Source: Adapted with permission from *The origins of intellect: Piaget's theory,* (2nd ed.) by John L. Phillips, Jr. Copyright 1969, 1975, pp. 58–59. W. H.

gets older, the repetition of motor activities provides the basis for development of mental schemes, or ideas of the mind.

The period of sensorimotor intelligence is divided into six stages. The infant is working on several tasks during the various substages. These tasks include imitating the behavior of others, developing intentional behavior, and understanding object permanence, cause-effect relationships, and time and space concepts. A summary of the cognitive changes that occur during the sensorimotor period is included in Table 8-1.

STAGE 1: EXERCISING REFLEX SCHEMES (BIRTH–1 MO.). A newborn infant is equipped with some basic reflex schemes such as sucking, looking, and crying. The baby's actions during this stage consist primarily of exercising these innate reflexes. The newborn does not have the capacity to make meaningful associations between the sensations obtained through different sensory capacities. For example, sounds and sights are not perceived as belonging to the same object. The information obtained (sights, sound, smells, internal body sensations) is processed at the reflexive level. Piaget claims that infants are totally dominated by **egocentrism** at this point. That is, they cannot distinguish themselves from the rest of the environment.

The main accomplishment during this substage is the increased efficiency and complexity of reflexive behaviors. For example, the baby uses the sucking scheme on different objects and assimilates taste and other pleasurable sensations in the process. With experience and practice, the sucking reflex becomes more efficient and adapted to satisfying both nutritive and non-nutritive sucking needs. The other reflexes are also modified and become more efficient and discriminating if the infant has opportunities for practice.

STAGE 2: PRIMARY CIRCULAR REACTIONS (1–4 MO.). The reflex schemes have become more complex through repeated use and now serve as the basis for new patterns of behavior. Piaget labeled these new schemes *primary circular reactions.* Responses in this stage are called *primary* because they are centered in the baby's own body, and because they are the first of a series of circular reactions. A **circular reaction** is a response that stimulates its own repetition.

At the beginning of this stage, the baby may be observed repeating over and over interesting and pleasurable behavior patterns that have been accidentally discovered. One of the first primary circular responses an infant demonstrates is thumb-sucking. The baby gets the thumb into the mouth by accident and finds that it is good for sucking. The pleasurable sensation serves as a stimulus to trigger more sucking. This pattern of behavior will continue until the infant gets tired or finds something more interesting. Later the baby recognizes the stimulus that triggered the pleasurable sucking activity and tries through trial-and-error movements to get the thumb back into the mouth. This is an indication that reflex behaviors are beginning to be gradually replaced with voluntary actions.

A major accomplishment in this stage is the infant's growing ability to coordinate and combine various schemes. Piaget (1952) observed his daughter Jacqueline turning her head to locate the sound of his voice at age 2 months and 12 days. Her action represents the intercoordination of the looking and hearing schemes.

At this stage, the infant also begins to anticipate the occurrence of events on the basis of past experience. An infant may begin sucking movements the minute it is picked up and placed in the position to nurse. In so doing, the infant demonstrates an elementary understanding that there is a sequence to certain events. This forms the basis for the infant's understanding of time.

STAGE 3: SECONDARY CIRCULAR REACTIONS (4–8 MO.).   The circular reactions are now labeled as *secondary* for two reasons. For one thing, this stage represents the second in the series of circular reactions. The main reason, though is that the infant's repetitive behaviors now focus on events or objects outside the body. The stage 3 infant is concerned with a result produced in the external environment. Unlike primary circular reactions, these are not reflexive behaviors, but schemes that have been acquired through learning.

Secondary circular reactions are the result of accidental or random behaviors which produce something that attracts the infant's attention. The following is an example:

> One day when Dimitri was 4 months old, he was lying on his back in his crib looking at his multicolored animal mobile . . . when he suddenly kicked one of his feet and banged the side of the crib. The movement of his leg against the crib bars caused the mobile to sway . . . Dimitri watched the mobile's movement until it stopped. As soon as the mobile was still, he looked away and then looked back at it again. No movement. Now he again looked away, but this time catching sight of his foot. Then he kicked his foot again but not hard enough to make the crib, and hence the mobile move. He became slightly agitated and kicked both feet, this time with success. Dimitri lay perfectly still, his eyes fixed on the dancing animals. When they stopped moving, he kicked both feet and waved his arms until he moved the crib enough to activate the mobile. (Sherrod, Vietze, & Friedman, 1978, p. 104)

When Dimitri made the connection between the moving mobile and his own movements, he repeated the action and established a secondary circular response.

Dimitri was more interested in the result of his action than in the action itself. At this point, the baby is beginning to develop the capacity to separate the means from the end. In the previous stage, action, such as thumb-sucking, was repeated as an end in itself (to suck). Now an action is repeated to produce interesting results. A subtitle Piaget used in labeling stage 3 is "procedures destined to make interesting spectacles last."

The stage 3 infant begins to develop an awareness of the object concept. Infants have to learn that objects are external or separate from themselves and continue to exist even though they are not visible (object permanence). At this point the infant will search for an object if it is partially visible. When Piaget's son Laurent was 7 months old, Piaget showed him a bottle of milk. Piaget then hid the bottle, but left one end sticking out. Laurent screamed and tried to get the bottle. If the bottle was completely hidden, Laurent acted as if it no longer existed and did not struggle to find it, even though he saw the bottle being hidden. If an infant drops an object and loses sight of it, the infant will attempt to visually anticipate its new location. This usually happens only if the baby has caused an object to disappear. The concept of object permanence thus is only partially developed in stage 3.

STAGE 4: COORDINATION OF SECONDARY CIRCULAR REACTIONS (8–12 MO.). For the first time, the infant exhibits behaviors that Piaget called truly intelligent. Schemes are now mobile and flexible enough to be generalized to new situations. Babies can use existing schemes to overcome obstacles or solve simple problems. The infant can also combine and coordinate several different schemes to reach a goal. This stage is thus called *coordination of secondary circular reactions* (schemes).

Stage 4 infants demonstrate intentional, goal-directed activity, which is one of the first signs of intelligent behavior. Piaget described how he placed his hand in front of a matchbox Laurent was trying to obtain. Laurent hit his father's hand to move it aside in order to get the box. When Piaget replaced the hand with a cushion as an obstacle, Laurent also hit the pillow so that he could grasp the box. In this example, we see how an existing scheme is adapted to apply to a new situation. The "hitting" scheme that Laurent used to make a mobile move in stage 3 was applied to obtain the desired object.

We can also see in Laurent's means-to-an-end behavior a major step in the understanding of cause-effect relationships. Up to this point, an infant acts and waits for something to happen, but with no real understanding of how effects occur. It was as if things happened by "magic" or that objects obeyed the baby's wishes. At this stage, however, infants begin to be aware that their own actions create results. If you hit a mobile, it moves.

The development of the object concept takes another step forward in this stage. The infant's increased understanding of the permanence of objects is evident when the infant searches for an object that has disappeared. If a ball rolls under a chair, the infant will try to find it there. An infant will also remove a cover from an object that is completely hidden. At this stage, infants love to play "peek-a-boo" and "hide-and-seek" games based on the disappearance and reappearance of people and objects.

The concept of object permanence is not completely established, though. Limited by egocentrism, the infant cannot think of an object as having an independent existence apart from the actions performed on it. If an object is placed under one cover (A) and then under another (B), the infant will look only under the first cover (A). The infant will find a ball that is hidden under a handkerchief but will continue to look under the handkerchief if the ball is hidden the second time under a pillow even while the infant watches. At this stage, the object is still connected with the infant's previous success in locating it at point A, so the search ends at that location. Piaget believed that the infant thinks there is more than one object involved in the game. In other words, there is an object at A and another just like it at B.

According to Piaget, the beginning of true imitation occurs in this stage. Imitation involves the capacity to copy the actions, sounds, or other characteristics exhibited by a model. Before stage 4, infants engage in what Piaget called *pseudoimitation*. This is an early form of imitation that is based on a response the child has already demonstrated or finds easy to mimic. For example, an infant will readily imitate cooing and other sounds the infant has already made. Infants can be taught to imitate adults waving "bye-bye" and performing other actions, but Piaget did not call these behaviors true imitation because they require constant practice and encouragement.

Now, at stage 4, infants can imitate actions that involve movements they cannot see themselves perform, such as wrinkling the nose. They also begin to imitate new sounds. For example, one mother was surprised after she angrily hung up the phone to hear her 1-year old mimic her perfectly with the word "Damn!" (Pulaski, 1978).

STAGE 5: TERTIARY CIRCULAR REACTIONS (12–18 MO.).   *Tertiary* means third-order, or third in a series. Piaget used this term to describe how the baby's intellectual activities reach a more complex and advanced level of proficiency. The infant still engages in repetitive activity, but deliberately makes variations to see what happens. The stage 4 infant was satisfied with producing the same result over and over. The stage 5 infant wants to use a familiar combination of schemes to produce something new and different. This marks the beginning of curiosity and creative activity.

Piaget (1952) described how Laurent dropped pieces of bread and other objects from various body positions and locations. In the previous stage he would have been interested simply in the act of letting go, to observe the same result over and over. At stage 5 he was more interested in observing where the object landed, particularly in relation to the position from which he let it fall. Piaget referred to this type of activity as *directed groping*.

The subtitle which Piaget used for this stage is the "discovery of new means through active experimentation." Through the use of tertiary circular reactions, the infant solves simple problems by trial and error. Like a budding scientist, the infant experiments to find new ways to accomplish a goal or solve a problem. New combinations and variations of schemes are attempted until the infant finds one that works. For example, babies discover that they can obtain an object that is out of reach by pulling on the tablecloth on which the object is resting. Such behavior indicates that the stage 5 baby displays a certain amount of practical intelligence.

The infant continues to make progress in understanding the various features and functions of objects. The stage 5 infant is able to walk, which brings increased opportunities for contact with more objects and opportunities to see their relationship to one another in space. The baby learns more about physical properties such as size, weight, and texture. During the previous stage, the infant was interested in taking objects apart, putting them into containers, and dumping them out. Now the infant is interested in putting the pieces of an object together and exploring the relationship between different objects and their containers.

The understanding of cause-effect relations reaches a new level during this stage. Infants now begin to recognize that actions result from the behavior of other people as well as their own. They are thus becoming slightly less egocentric. When an object moves, they may look for the source of the movement outside their own activities. For example, Piaget (1954) slowly moved Laurent's stroller with his foot. Laurent leaned over to the edge of the carriage to find what was making it move. As soon as he saw his father's foot on the wheel, he gave a smile of understanding.

The concept of object permanence also improves. The infant can now follow and locate an object that has been hidden in three successive locations. However, the infant must see the movements. If a baby is not allowed to watch where the object disappears at any point, the baby becomes confused and will look for it only at the first location. Apparently it is not yet possible for the infant to imagine what might be happening to an object while it is out of sight.

Like the object concept, the development of imitation parallels cognitive development. Stage 5 infants are capable of more accurate and extensive imitations. They can imitate behaviors that are not in their repertoire, but they require some "groping," or trial and error. In keeping with the tendency to experiment, they vary the actions or sounds of the model to observe the result.

STAGE 6: INVENTION OF NEW MEANS THROUGH MENTAL COMBINATIONS (18–24 MO.).   At last the infant begins to think before acting. The ability to represent objects and events by mental images (symbols) develops during this stage. The infant no longer has to "discover" solutions to problems through trial and error, but is capable of inventing solutions by combining mental schemes.

Piaget (1952) gave Lucienne a matchbox containing his watch chain. He left a small opening so that she could see the chain inside. Her first efforts to get it out with her index finger were unsuccessful. Next, she looked at the opening and began to open and close her mouth, wider and wider. She then put her finger into the opening of the box and slid the cover back far enough to reach the chain. Lucienne gave an indication of what she was thinking when she opened and closed her mouth. Piaget concluded: "This new type of behavior pattern characterizes systematic intelligence" (Piaget, 1952, p. 331).

The ability to represent actions through mental pictures makes it possible for an infant to imitate a model faster and more accurately. The infant can, for the first time, imitate a model that is no longer present. Jacqueline observed a little boy stamping his feet while engaging in a temper tantrum. The next day she screamed and stamped her feet in a similar fashion (Piaget, 1962). This is called *deferred imitation.*

The concept of the object permanence is fully developed at this stage. The baby now has a mental image of the object which is independent of an immediate sensory impression of the object itself. The object has an independent, enduring existence even though it cannot always be seen. Infants are not as easily fooled when an object disappears, even though part of the process may be invisible. They search in various places where they have found objects hidden before. At this stage, the symbolic aspects of language begin to take on meaning.

SUMMARY OF SENSORIMOTOR PERIOD. The basic accomplishments that take place during the first two years of life can be summarized as follows:

Most of the reflexes are replaced by voluntary movements and intentional behavior.

The infant has progressed from an "out-of-sight, out-of-mind" consciousness of objects to an understanding of objects as having permanence in time and space even when they cannot be seen.

The use of schemes simply to perpetuate an interesting activity is replaced by an expanded ability to engage in activities to create something new and different.

The infant has advanced from discovering activities and solutions to problems by accident to trial-and-error learning. By the end of the period, simple problems are solved through foresight and planning.

The infant's ability to imitate a model advances from pseudoimitation to deferred imitation.

By the end of the sensorimotor period, infants have moved from thinking that objects move by "magic," to an understanding that they are the cause as well as the recipient of actions.

Evaluation of Piaget's Theory

Presently, there is sufficient evidence to support the basic sequences of development outlined in Piaget's sensorimotor stages. On the other hand, researchers have found evidence to challenge some of Piaget's assumptions. There is an increasing amount of research indicating—but not conclusively— that infants accomplish some of the cognitive tasks earlier than Piaget's timetable suggests. Bower (1982) found that infants could coordinate the looking and reaching schemes as early as 2 weeks of age. Piaget claimed this ability develops gradually over the first three or four months of life (Lamb & Bornstein, 1987). Bower's (1982) studies also strongly suggest that infants acquire the concept of object permanence as early as 5 or 6 months of age. Other evidence suggests that imitation (see Chapter 3) may take place ahead of Piaget's schedule.

HOW INFANTS LEARN

Learning is the acquisition of knowledge or skills through experience. Infants begin to learn even before they are born. However, for a number of reasons, learning is generally more limited during infancy than at other stages. For one thing, the brain and nervous system are very immature. The interconnections between the various cells have not yet been completely established. The sensory organs that affect the infant's perceptual capacity have not reached their peak functional capacity. The infant's limited attention span, motor skills, and language ability are additional factors affecting the capacity to learn. All of these limitations affect the infant's ability to collect, process, store, and retrieve information. In spite of these immaturities, however, much learning takes place during infancy. The ways in which infants learn are numerous and varied.

Conditioned Responses

Behavioral psychologists believe that all learning is the result of conditioned responses. This theory is based on the principle that infants learn through actions that are reinforced, punished, or ignored. There are two types of conditioned responses—**classical** and **operant.**

Classical Conditioning (Respondent).   Infants frequently exhibit the same response to a particular stimulus each time it is encountered, such as turning the head when the cheek is stroked (rooting reflex). In classical conditioning, an infant learns to transfer the response to a different stimulus that does initially elicit the response. This type of conditioning is based on the principle that when two different stimuli appear close together, the response to one of them will be transferred to the other (Baldwin, 1967). For example a buzzer can be set off each time the cheek is stroked to elicit the rooting reflex. A baby will eventually turn its head in response to the buzzer alone. An infant thus learns to associate a new stimulus (buzzer) with an old response (rooting reflex). This is referred to as a new stimulus-response connection.

Researchers have observed classical conditioning in unborn infants during the last three months of the prenatal period. Spelt (1948) found that a loud sound would cause a fetus to move each time the noise was made. The loud sound was paired with a vibration of the mother's abdomen. After a number of simultaneous repetitions, the vibratory stimulus alone was effective in causing the infant to move. A more recent study using ultrasound images has confirmed Spelt's conclusion (Birnholz & Benacerraf, 1983).

Researchers have also demonstrated classical conditioning in infants soon after birth. Connolly and Stratton (1969) paired the Babkin reflex, in which the mouth opens when pressure is applied to the palms, in 2- to 4-day-old infants, with a neutral buzzing noise. When the noise was presented by itself, the infants exhibited mouth-opening movements characteristic of the Babkin reflex. The use of classical conditioning is limited to the responses that infants already exhibit.

Younger infants are harder to condition than older infants. The emotional responses of older infants are particularly susceptible to classical conditioning. Numerous environmental encounters become sources of infant fears. Carla, a toddler, was stung by a bee while she was playing on her swing set. After that she was afraid of all flying insects. Babies frequently begin crying as soon as they see a doctor or anyone else dressed in a white coat. They have learned to associate the coat, initially a neutral stimulus, with painful examining or treatment procedures such as an injection.

Operant Conditioning (Instrumental).   If a response to a stimulus is followed by reinforcement, the chances are increased that the response will be repeated when the stimulus is repeated. By the same token, responses that are punished or receive no reinforcement are less likely to be repeated. In operant conditioning, the reinforcement follows the response that, in the beginning, occurs spontaneously. In classical conditioning, the infant has no control over the events through which stimuli occur. However, in operant conditioning the infant's response, or lack of response, determines whether a reinforcer will follow (Sameroff & Cavanagh, 1979).

Researchers have not found a method by which operant conditioning can be studied in the unborn infant. However, there is ample evidence that newborn infants can be conditioned. In fact, operant conditioning is easier to obtain in newborns than classical conditioning. Examples of this type of learning are found in experiments that have successfully conditioned newborns to alter their head-turning (Siqueland, 1968) and sucking (Sameroff, 1968) responses to receive a reinforcer.

Operant conditioning, like classical conditioning, depends upon the ability of an infant to emit a specific response. Consequently, the variety of behaviors that can be conditioned in infancy is limited. As with classical procedures, the operant-conditioned responses are obtained easier and faster as the infant gets older, especially after 6 months of age (Lamb & Bornstein, 1987). Sameroff and Cavanagh (1979) believe that there is a *seven- to nine-month shift* in the behavioral organization of an infant. During this time, changes occur in the emotional, cognitive, and physiological domains which greatly facilitate conditioned responses as well as other types of learning.

In older infants, operant conditioning procedures are often used to shape behavior. This involves reinforcing gradual changes, or successive approximations, in the infant's behavior until the desired behavior is obtained. Parents often use this procedure with their infants. An example is found in the infant's use of the word "Da-da." When the baby first says "Da-da," it is reinforced by praise, hugs, and other positive responses no matter when the sound is made. Later, parents respond positively only if "Da-da" is repeated in the presence of the father. Finally, the term is reinforced only when the infant uses it to designate the father.

Imitation

One of the most easily observed ways that infants learn is through imitation. At around 6 weeks of age, imitation begins to play an increasingly important role in learning (Rosenblith & Sims-Knight, 1985). Older infants imitate actions from a variety of models, including adults, children, and television characters. Parents are primary models, as the following example indicates: At 15 months, Candy is very imitative. "Often when she picks something up from the floor, she wipes it on her dress. That's what her mother does with anything Candy will put in her mouth again" (Peterson, 1974, p. 37).

Imitation is frequently combined with operant conditioning in the learning process. An initial response is produced by an infant because it has been copied from a model. If the behavior is considered desirable, the infant receives responses that are rewarding so the behavior will continue. At 2 years of age, Kristin was encouraged to observe her mother use the bathroom as a way to begin toilet training. As soon as Kristin began to imitate her mother's behavior she was reinforced with verbal praise, "Good, Kristin! That's good!" The verbal reinforcement that was used in facilitating toilet training was so effective that Kristin began to imitate her mother in the use of praise. One day, while observing her mother use the bathroom, Kristin said, "Good, Mommy! That's good!"

An example of imitation.

Learning Through Play

Play is one of the basic ways infants learn. To an infant, "play is learning and learning is play" (Sroufe, 1977, p. 93). No one needs to teach infants to play. Their play is voluntary, intrinsically motivated, and freely chosen (Johnson & Ershler, 1982). Piaget (1962; 1971) viewed play as opportunities for infants to test reality through acts of assimilation. Sounds, objects, and other stimuli are freely manipulated to serve the infant's own particular needs. Piaget divided cognitive play during infancy into two basic stages: sensorimotor play and symbolic play. Within each stage, the complexity of play changes with the baby's cognitive maturity and competence.

Sensorimotor Play.   During the first three or four months of life, infant play is focused on body movements that provide sensory pleasure. Repetitious kicking movements and sucking the fist are typical activities. Infants also begin to play with cooing and other sounds as soon as they are capable. At approximately 6 months of age, an infant typically plays with one object at a time (Fenson et al., 1976). This earliest object play involves mouthing, shaking, banging, inspecting visually, and shifting from one hand to the other.

After about 9 months of age, the simple, undifferentiated type of play declines and is gradually replaced by **function-relational play** with two or more objects (Belsky and Most, 1981). The infant begins to figure out how some objects "work" (e.g., a toy telephone dial). At first, two objects may be used together indiscriminately, without regard to their appropriate relationships (e.g., placing a hairbrush in a cup). Later the infant learns to combine objects in ways that exploit their appropriate relationships, such as placing a lid on a pot. During this stage, infants usually prefer new toys to old ones (Ross, 1974), and complex toys to simple ones (McCall, 1974).

Pretend (Symbolic) Play.   The earliest form of symbolic play begins around 12 months of age when the infant begins to perform simple "pretend" activities. In the beginning, pretend play involves activities directed toward the self, such as making drinking sounds using an empty cup, or using a doll brush on the infant's own hair (Belsky & Most, 1981). As infants get older, their pretend play is directed toward others (dolls are fed "pretend" bottles of milk) and they begin to substitute "pretend" objects for the real thing (a stick becomes a bottle of milk). The most sophisticated level of pretend play is called **double substitution** (Belsky & Most, 1981). This happens when a toddler uses two "pretend" materials in a single play sequence. Thus, a stick becomes a "doll" and a bottle cap is used as a cup to feed the "doll."

Learning Through Sensory Experiences

The infant's five senses are pathways to the mind. As their sense organs mature and become fully functional, the quality of sensation and perception improves. "With their sensory capacities, infants learn not only to look but to

Infants are sensory creatures who use simple, everyday experiences, such as bathing, for play and stimulation.

see, not only to hear but to listen, not only to touch but to feel and grasp what they touch. They taste whatever they can get into the mouth. They begin to smell what they encounter" (Frank, 1968, p. 435).

Lamb and Bornstein (1987) believe that, in emphasizing the importance of motor activity, Piaget failed to recognize the vital contributions of perceptual and sensory experiences to cognitive development. Their position is supported by a study (Decarie, 1969) of babies born without limbs because of prenatal exposure to the drug thalidomide. In spite of the lack of normal motor capacity, these infants scored in the normal range of intelligence. They were apparently able to learn adequately through looking, listening, and the use of other intact sensory mechanisms.

Infants who receive too little sensory stimulation fail to develop their full intellectual potential. On the other hand, too much sensory stimulation can be as bad as too little. Wachs (1982) found that too much noise is especially detrimental to cognitive development of infants. Apparently, when infants become overstimulated they begin to block out sensory input. If this happens too frequently, they suffer deprivation, as if the stimulation did not exist.

MEMORY

Do infants remember what they learn? How soon does memory begin? How long do infants remember? Questions such as these are significant because memory is one of the most important components of intelligence. Memory involves the capacity to encode (take in) information, store it, and selectively bring it to mind as needed. Various terms are used in discussing different aspects of memory development, including *sensory, short-term, long-term, recognition,* and *recall.*

Sensory Memory

Sensory memory consists of the immediate sensory impressions that persist for less than a second after a stimulus is gone. The information is stored for just an instant. It is replaced by other sensory stimulation unless it receives further attention so that the information is transferred to the short-term memory. Sensory or temporary memory is one type of memory that apparently changes little with age (Hoving et al., 1978).

Memory Length

Short-term memory consists of information that is stored only temporarily. The amount of time involved is generally considered to be about a minute (Helms & Turner, 1976).

Long-term memory involves the ability to recall information after days, weeks, and even years have passed. Some information and experiences are stored permanently. Short-term memory develops ahead of long-term memory. Both improve with age during the infancy period. Memory length will be discussed further, in connection with two basic types of memory—recognition and recall.

Recognition Memory

The ability to recall whether a stimulus has been previously experienced is referred to as **recognition memory.** An infant who, upon request, selects a picture of a cat from an animal book is demonstrating this type of memory. There is little doubt that newborn infants display recognition memory. The ability to recognize a stimulus that triggered a response is not possible without a minimum working memory. The conditioned responses that have been demonstrated in numerous experiments with newborns constitute evidence of their capacity to remember (Olson & Strauss, 1984). The ability to store information in short-term memory increases dramatically in infants from all racial and ethnic groups around the world between 8 and 12 months (Kagan, 1981b).

There is also evidence that newborns have the capacity for long-term memory. Babies less than 55 hours old remembered a specific reinforcement schedule for as long as ten hours after a single learning session (Panneton & DeCasper, 1982). However, due to the immaturity of the nervous system, the newborn's capacity to remember is limited to a very primitive form of recognition memory.

Within the first month or two, infants show signs of an emerging capacity for long-term retention of information. Researchers have found that 1-month-old infants can remember a conditioned response for about two days in some experiments (Ungerer, Brody, & Zelazo, 1978) and for as long as ten days in others (Little, Lipsitt, & Rovee-Collier, 1984). By 2 months of age, infants have demonstrated that they remember for almost three weeks how to move a crib mobile (Davis & Rovee-Collier, 1983). However, the infants remember the response only if they receive some prompting (called *reactivation*). As you would expect, 2-month-olds forget more rapidly than 3-month-olds, who remember the procedure for a month or more with prompting (Greco et al., 1986).

The period between 3 and 7 months of age is a time in which memory shows a dramatic improvement (Olson & Strauss, 1984). The information-processing skills have improved remarkably as the result of physiological maturation, increased attention span, improved motor skills, and the acquisition of a substantial amount of knowledge. The infant can learn more complex information faster and remember it for longer periods of time. Fagan (1971) found that 6-month-old infants recognize a variety of stimuli for as long as fourteen days without prompting. Long-term recognition memory is routinely displayed by infants between 3 and 6 months of age (Daehler & Greco, 1985).

Recall Memory

Recall memory is the ability to remember something that is currently not available to direct sensory perception (Mandler, 1984). A baby who can tell you the name of the family dog is demonstrating recall memory. The ability to think begins with recall memory. Piaget linked recall memory with deferred imitation and symbolic thinking (mental images), and the use of language. Piaget thus argued that this type of memory does not emerge until 18 to 24 months of age. However, there is an increasing amount of evidence that infants are capable of elementary recall memory much earlier.

One method researchers have used to study recall memory has been to ask parents to keep diaries of their child's memory behavior over a period of time. Using this approach, Ashmead and Perlmutter (1980) found examples of recall memory in infants between 7 and 9 months of age. In one case, a 9-month-old girl kept some ribbons that she played with in the bottom drawer of a chest. One day she opened the drawer but could find no ribbons. She opened all the drawers until she found her ribbons in the top drawer. The next day she looked for her ribbons in the top drawer. Anecdotal records such as this seem to provide evidence of long-term recall memory. However, other researchers believe that this type of research lacks scientific objectivity (Daehler & Greco, 1985).

Mandler (1984) points out that the examples of early recall in infants are based on "retrieval through reminding" (p. 83), or situational cues. This is a more primitive type of recall memory than self-instigated or deliberate recall. In his discussion of recall memory, Piaget was probably referring to active attempts to remember rather than to the type of memory that results from situational reminders. As yet, there is little evidence that the more sophisticated and deliberate type of recall memory occurs earlier than 18 months.

ASSESSING INFANT INTELLIGENCE

"Intelligence is what the tests test" (Boring, 1923, p. 35). This widely quoted definition of intelligence, is an indication of the importance that has been attributed to testing intelligence. The assessment of intelligence in infancy is viewed as especially important in the early detection of mental deficiency as well as in determining the extent to which intelligence changes from infancy to adulthood.

The accurate measurement of infant intelligence has proved to be very difficult, from the standpoint of both test construction and test administration. Eliciting an infant's attention and cooperation can be a major obstacle to testing, especially when the infant is being tested by a strange person in a strange place. Intelligence tests for children and adults typically have a large verbal-skills component, whereas intelligence tests for infants are comprised primarily of sensorimotor functions. Scarr-Salapatek (1983) believes that the type of intelligence displayed by infants during the first two years is not comparable to the cognitive skills that evolve later in life. Thus, infant test scores are not reliable predictors of intellectual functioning in later years.

In spite of these problems, though, infant intelligence scales (sometimes referred to as *developmental schedules*) have proved to be reliable and useful for specific purposes. They are widely used in screening programs to identify infants with potential mental handicaps. Researchers have also found these measures useful for a variety of purposes such as assessing the influence of certain factors on the development of intelligence during the infant years.

Gesell Developmental Schedules

Arnold Gesell (1925) was one of the pioneers in the assessment of infant development. Gesell and his co-workers at Yale University made extensive observations on the normal developmental patterns of infants and young children. Gesell's schedules were designed primarily for the purpose of determining the integrity and functional maturity of the nervous system between 1 month and 6 years of age.

The schedules are divided into five major areas: adaptive (e.g., problem solving), fine motor (e.g., grasping and manipulating objects), gross motor (e.g., creeping), language (e.g., vocalizations), and personal-social (e.g., smiling, feeding abilities). A separate score is obtained for each of the five areas plus an overall score that is labeled the Developmental Quotient (DQ). Gesell intended for the score to be used as an indicator of total development rather than intelligence, per se. A short version of the test is available for use as a developmental screening inventory.

Cattell Infant Intelligence Scale

Psyche Cattell (1940) used Gesell's schedules as the starting point for the development of a new test specifically designed to measure intelligence. The

Cattell scale covers the age span of 2 months to 30 months. It includes five items and one or two alternate items for each age level tested. An overall score, referred to as the infant's Mental Age (MA), is obtained.

Bayley Scales of Infant Development

The Bayley Scales of Infant Development (BSID) are the result of many years of work by Nancy Bayley (1969). The BSID is currently considered to be "the best and most widely used general instrument to evaluate infant developmental status" (Horowitz, 1982, p. 109). It is used in both clinical and research settings. Like the Cattell test, the BSID (Bayley, 1969) is administered by trained psychologists to infants from 2 months to 30 months of age.

The BSID is divided into three separate scales that can be used independently or in combination for assessment purposes. The Mental Scale is designed to assess such functions as memory, learning, language development and problem-solving ability. This scale results in a standard score which is labeled the Mental Development Index (MDI). The Motor Scale measures body control, large and fine motor skills, as well as manipulatory ability. The results of this scale are expressed as the Psychomotor Development Index (PDI) score. The third scale, the Infant Behavior Record, is a report based on the examiners' observations of the infant's attitude, interests, emotions, alertness, and other behaviors expressed during the assessment process.

Denver Developmental Screening Test

One of the most widely used screening tests for infants and children up to 6 years of age is the Denver Developmental Screening Test (DDST) (Frankenburg et al., 1973). Although the DDST is not an intelligence test, it is widely used for detecting early indications of mild developmental retardation. The test covers four areas of development: gross motor, language, fine motor-adaptive, and personal-social. Infants who do not pass a sufficient number of age-appropriate items are referred for further testing. An abbreviated version (DDST-R), which is easier to use as a part of a well-child medical exam, is available (Frankenburg et al., 1981).

Uzgiris-Hunt Scales

The most recently developed instrument for assessing cognitive functioning in infancy is the Uzgiris-Hunt Ordinal Scales of Psychological Development (Uzgiris & Hunt, 1975). The scales are based on Piaget's description of cognitive development during infancy. The term *ordinal* indicates that the test items are arranged, or ordered, according to the level of difficulty. The first items on the scale should be passed at an earlier age than subsequent items. The scales reflect Piaget's belief that all infants go through the tasks involved in sensorimotor development in the same specific order, although not necessarily at the same age.

The Uzgiris-Hunt Scales consist of six subscales: (1) the development of visual pursuit and the permanance of objects; (2) the development of means of obtaining environmental events; (3) the development of vocal and gestural imitation; (4) the development of operational causality; (5) the construction of object relations in space; and (6) the development of schemes relating to objects. Each scale includes seven to fourteen steps in the developmental progression from birth to 2 years of age. The highest step achieved on each of the six subscales forms an infant's developmental profile. No single, overall score is provided.

According to Horowitz (1982), the Uzgiris-Hunt Scales are considered to provide the most in-depth assessment of cognitive development of any instrument available. The scales may be especially useful in early-intervention programs because they measure very small steps in sensorimotor development. This instrument has not been used as widely as other infant assessment scales, but it appears to be increasing in popularity.

FACILITATING INTELLECTUAL DEVELOPMENT

Some of the research and theoretical information currently available on the development of intelligence in infants has been translated into suggestions for caregiving activities. Piaget did not develop practical applications of his theory, but others have. For example, Lehane (1976) has produced a guidebook of 100 Piaget-based activities for helping infants learn. Numerous other resources offer suggestions for facilitating cognitive development during infancy (e.g., Fowler, 1980; Leach, 1976; Marzollo, 1977; Painter, 1971; Sparling & Lewis, 1979).

Greenfield and Tronick (1980) have developed a list of techniques for use in teaching babies how to use play materials, solve problems, and develop specific skills. Some of these techniques, listed in order from the simplest to most complex, are as follows:

1. Simplify the activity. For example, in introducing nesting cups, give the infant only the smallest and largest ones in the set. This is the main teaching technique to use with infants under 6 months of age.

2. Point to and touch the important parts of a new activity, such as the space on a puzzle board that matches the piece of puzzle the baby is holding.

3. Show the infant how to do an activity or solve a problem (after about 6 months). For example, let the infant watch you place one block on top of another.

4. Tell the baby what to do next in an activity. This technique, obviously, is only appropriate when words are used that an infant can understand. Use short, simple phrases, such as "Turn it over" and "Put it here." The other techniques may be used in combination with telling.

5. Allow infants to use self-teaching as much as possible. Avoid interfering in activities when help is not needed or wanted.

Parents and other caregivers are advised to avoid the pressure-cooker approach to early learning in an attempt to create a "super-intelligent" baby. Doman (1982, 1984) believes that parents can teach an infant math or almost any subject. However, too much emphasis on early intellectual achievement can result in the "hurried-infant syndrome" (Elkind, 1981). When infants are expected to achieve too much, too soon, a level of stress is created that may result in behavior problems at the time or at a later stage of development. White (1985) believes that superiority in the intellectual domain is frequently obtained at the expense of progress in other areas of equal or greater importance. Infants learn more efficiently with better results when they are developmentally ready to master a task.

SUMMARY

1. Intelligence consists of the ability to think, to solve problems, to learn, to remember and to adapt to the environment. In this text, cognition and intelligence are used to mean the same thing.

2. Intelligence is influenced by heredity and environmental influences. The family environment and socioeconomic background are two important environmental factors.

3. There is widespread agreement that infancy is a very *important* period for the development of intelligence. However, researchers have failed to find convincing evidence that infancy is a *critical* period for intellectual development.

4. The theory of Jean Piaget has been widely influential in the contemporary understanding of intellectual development during the infancy period. Piaget's theory is based on the development of schemes through the process of adaptation and two related processes: assimilation and accommodation.

5. Piaget identified four basic stages in the development of intelligence. The stage that corresponds with the first two years of life is the sensorimotor period. This period is divided into six substages: (1) exercising reflex schema; (2) primary circular reactions; (3) secondary circular reactions; (4) coordination of secondary circular reactions; (5) tertiary circular reactions; and (6) invention of new means through mental combinations.

6. By the end of the sensorimotor period, infants have typically developed the ability to understand cause-effect relationships, object permanence, simple problem solution through insight, and deferred imitation.

7. Infants are capable of learning through both classical and operant conditioning processes from birth. Imitation is another mechanism through which infants learn, beginning at approximately 6 weeks of age. Infants also learn through play, which progresses through two basic stages: sensorimotor and pretend, or symbolic, play. The infant's sensory organs are pathways through which learning takes place.

8. Newborn infants are capable of both short- and long-term recognition memory at a very elementary level. The memory capacity improves with age, especially between 3 and 7 months. Recall memory develops later than recognition memory. Infants are capable of the recall memory based on situational cues at approximately 7 to 9 months of age. The more difficult, deliberate type of recall is first observed around 18 months of age.

9. Infant intelligence test scores are not reliable predictors of intellectual functioning in other stages of life. However, infant intelligence scales, or developmental schedules, are used for screening programs and research purposes. The most widely used tests of mental development in infancy are the Gesell Developmental Schedules, the Cattell Infant Intelligence Scale, the Denver Developmental Screening Test, and the Bayley Scales of Infant Development. The newest test for assessing cognitive functioning in infancy is the Uzgiris-Hunt Scales.

10. A variety of materials and recommended activities are available for stimulating the development of infant intelligence. However, parents and other caregivers are advised to avoid early learning activities that attempt to create "super-intelligent" infants.

9

Language Development

Out of the mouths of babes and sucklings
Thou hast brought perfect praise.
—*Psalm 8:2; Matthew 21:16*

One of the most fascinating and exciting things to observe about babies is the process of language development. Parents and scientists alike are captivated by how children learn languages. For parents, language represents a communicative link with their child and the key that opens the door to the child's inner world. Communication is at the center of the relationship between the parent and child.

Language is a complex system of mutually agreed-upon symbols used to express and understand ideas and feelings. In its broadest meaning, language refers to an act or acts that produce some kind of interchange or communication between two or more people (Bangs, 1982). The symbols used in language include vocal utterances, written expressions, and body movements such as hand gestures and facial expressions. **Speech** is the vocal or oral component of language and refers to the production of spoken words or other meaningful sounds. The terms *speech* and *language* are frequently used interchangeably, but technically they are not synonymous.

Scientists have been astonished at the predictability of language development and at how easily babies learn to talk. Normally, all children pass a series of "milestones" at approximately the same age, regardless of the language they acquire (McNeil, 1970). For a long time, observers of language development were content to plot these major milestones and record children's utterances. More recently, however, they have been concerned with why and how language is acquired. This chapter summarizes the processes involved in language acquisition, the progress infants make in developing language competence, and some of the biological, psychological, and social influences.

THEORIES OF LANGUAGE DEVELOPMENT

There are three major theories on how human language is acquired. At one extreme is empiricist or behavioral theory. According to this position, language is simply the product of experience. The opposite point of view is found in rationalist or nativist theory, which claims that language is controlled by biology. A third theory, one that occupies the middle ground, is the cognitive development position. According to this theory, language development grows out of intellectual development, which is controlled by both environment and experience.

Behavioristic Theory

Skinner (1957) proposed that language, like any other behavior, can be explained as conditioned responses. When infants make sounds that resemble adult speech, such as "ma ma," adults reinforce them with smiles, hugs, or other positive responses. Other behaviorists (e.g., Bandura, 1977) add imitation as a factor that plays a key role in language acquisition. These behaviorists stress the importance of having speech models to copy. Behaviorism has been criticized, among other things, for failing to adequately explain the creative use of language, the production and comprehension of novel utterances (Bryen, 1982), and the rapid rate of language development during infancy.

Nativistic Theory

There is little doubt that human infants are uniquely equipped to acquire language. However, the extent to which language development is controlled by biology has been the subject of extensive debate. Nativists argue that progress in language development is closely linked to the maturation of the brain. Language acquisition is remarkably predictable and similar among humans. Children normally pass a sequence of milestones at about the same age, regardless of the language or cultural conditions. In addition, progress in language development during the early years appears to be synchronized with progress in motor development. The two functions thus appear to be commonly controlled by the maturation of the central nervous system.

Nativistic theory is based on neurological studies that have shown that verbal function in humans is controlled by specific speech centers in the brain. For most people, perhaps as many as 95 percent, language is located in the left cerebral hemisphere. Lenneberg (1967) asserts that there is a critical period for language acquisition beginning around the age of 2 and ending at puberty. He maintains that speech functions have not been localized in a particular region of the brain as early as infancy. His theory is based on studies showing that if injury occurs to the left side of the brain in infancy or childhood, the right side of the brain apparently takes over the language functions so that normal speech is possible. As the child grows older, the speech functions become increasingly lateralized, with less flexibility to compensate for damage. Other theorists (Krashen, 1973; Kinsbourne, 1978) assert that lateralization of the brain occurs much earlier than Lenneberg proposed.

Chomsky (1968), another leading proponent of nativism, has proposed that human infants are equipped at birth with a Language Acquisition Device (LAD). This device is analogous to a computer that is prewired or programmed to acquire language. Babies are programmed to sort out the underlying rules and principles of their native language. Although the concept of the LAD has fascinated scientists, there is little evidence to support Chomsky's theory (Bruner, 1978).

Cognitive Developmental Theory

According to Piaget, language development is rooted in the cognitive development that occurs during the sensorimotor period (see Chapter 8). The infant has to develop the concept of self as a distinct person separate from other objects and understand the concept of object permanence before speech can begin. In Piaget's view, development of language also depends upon the acquisition of knowledge through touching, tasting, manipulation, and other experiences with objects and people. As the child's cognitive capacities and thoughts become more elaborate and complex through the years, language acquisition becomes more sophisticated and complete.

Not all cognitive developmental theorists agree with Piaget's view that thought precedes language development. Whorf (1956) took the opposite view when he hypothesized that the language we learn determines the way we think. For example, we view an orange as a round piece of fruit because we have attached those verbal labels to it. If oranges had originally been labeled as square, purple smalzes, we would perceive oranges in those terms. Thinking is thus dependent upon language.

Still another group of theorists, including the Russian psychologist Vygotsky (1962), believes that language and thought develop at the same time and eventually become interdependent. In early infancy, language and thought develop along parallel lines because they are both related to the same underlying cognitive ability. However, at about 2 years of age, language and the thought processes merge as the infant acquires the capacity to understand the symbolic meanings of words. Language then begins to facilitate thought, and the two processes become interdependent.

The debate about the relationship between thought and language involves another "chicken-and-egg" question that is practically impossible to resolve. There is some validity in each position. As Jenkins (1969) concluded, "Language is dependent upon thought, thought is dependent upon language, each is dependent upon the other and in some circumstances the two may be unrelated" (p. 36).

STRUCTURAL COMPONENTS OF LANGUAGE

To understand the process of language acquisition, we must first know something about the nature and structure of language. All spoken languages consist of five basic components:

1. Phonology: the distinctive sound features of speech and their combinations.
2. Morphology: the way sounds are combined to form words and other units of meaning.
3. Syntax: the way words are combined to form sentences.
4. Semantics: the definitions of words and the meanings of sentences.
5. Pragmatics: the ways language is used to communicate.

These components overlap and are interrelated in usage. Each language has a set of rules governing the components and their relationships. Developing language proficiency involves mastering these rules.

TABLE 9-1 Milestones in Language Development

AGE	PHONOLOGY	MORPHOLOGY AND SEMANTICS	SNYTAX	PRAGMATICS
Birth	Crying			
1 Month	Attends and responds to speaking voice			
2 Months	Cooing, Distinguishes phoneme features			
3 Months	Vocalizes to social stimulus			
4 Months	Chuckles			Pointing and gestures
6 Months	Babbling			
9 Months	Echolalia	Understands a few words		Understands gestures: responds to "bye-bye"
12 Months	Repeated syllables, Jabbers expressively	First word		Waves "bye-bye"
18 Months		Comprehends simple questions, points to nose, eyes, and hair, Vocabulary of 22 words	Two-word utterances, Telegraphic speech	Uses words to make wants known
24 Months		Vocabulary of 272 words	Uses pronouns and prepositions; uses simple sentences and phrases	Conversational turn-taking

Sources: Taken from the Bayley Scales of Infant Development, Copyright © 1969 by the Psychological Corporation. Reproduced by permission. All rights reserved. *Biological Foundations of Language.* Lenneberg, E. Copyright © 1967. John Wiley and Sons, Inc. Reprinted by permission of John Wiley and Sons, Inc. McCarthy, D. "Language Development in Children." In *Manual of Child Psychology.* L. Carmichael (ed.). Copyright © 1954 by John Wiley and Sons, Inc. Reprinted by permission of John Wiley and Sons, Inc.

Considering the complexities involved, human infants normally make remarkable progress toward mastering their native language. Infants are mostly occupied with developing phonological proficiency. However, they also work on the other features of language, sometimes separately and sometimes simultaneously, until the five components are combined in an elementary fashion by the end of the infancy period. A summary of the major milestones in language development, shown in Table 9-1, illustrates the progress made in the various components during the first two years of life.

Phonological Development

Each spoken language is made up of a set of basic, distinctive sounds, sometimes referred to as **phonemes,** which are used to form words. There are two major classes of phonemes—segmented and suprasegmented. The segmented phonemes consist of the vowels and consonants. The suprasegmented phonemes include the sounds of pitch, intonation, juncture, and stress, which constitute the "melody" of a language (Bryen, 1982). To master the sound system of a language, infants must learn to discriminate and combine the phonemes into meaningful words. Apparently infants master the phonemes of their language by discovering the contrasting or distinctive features. Each phoneme is learned in context with another sound rather than one at a time. The first distinction infants make is between vowels and consonants.

Early Sound Perception.   Most babies are born with the sensory capacity to hear distinction between sounds. Within a few days after birth, infants are responsive to speech and other sounds resembling the human voice. They prefer to listen to recorded speech or vocal music over instrumental music or rhythmic sounds (Butterfield & Siperstein, 1974). In addition, babies prefer female voices at the time they are born. Within a few weeks they can discriminate between their mother's voice and other voices (Eimas, 1975).

Numerous studies have demonstrated that very young infants can make distinctions between very similar sounds. One group of researchers (Eimas et al., 1971) taught two groups of four-week-old babies how to turn a tape player on by sucking on a pacifier connected to a control device. While one group of babies was allowed to listen to "pa pa pa" sounds, the other group heard "ba ba ba" sounds. The babies in both groups soon habituated to the sounds and stopped sucking, which turned off the speakers. When the taped sounds were reversed between the two groups, renewed sucking was generated to keep the new sound going. The researchers concluded that the infants could discriminate between the very similar sounds of *p* and *b*. Studies have also confirmed that babies not only discriminate between very similar speech sounds (Moffitt, 1971; Eilers & Minifie, 1975), but are also aware of differences in voice inflection (Morse, 1972) and pitch (Moffitt, 1971).

Development of the Speech Mechanism. The production of meaningful utterances involves the complex coordination of the respiratory system and vocal tract by the nervous system. To produce a desired sound, we transmit a set of instructions, usually unconsciously, from the brain to our respiratory system and vocal tract. When we are ready to speak, an airstream is released from the lungs into the vocal tract, which includes the throat, mouth, tongue, nasal cavity, and other organs. The type of sound produced depends upon the tautness of the vocal cords, the position of the tongue, the shape of the lips, whether the air passes through the mouth, nasal cavity, or both, and the speed and continuity of the airstream (Lindfors, 1980). Obviously defects in the speech mechanism, such as a cleft palate or brain dysfunction, will affect sound production.

The speech mechanism of an infant is in an almost constant state of anatomical change. According to Kent (1980):

> The infant's vocal tract differs from that of an adult in four major respects: The infant's tract is shorter; the pharynx is shorter and wider in relation to its length . . . ; the mouth is flatter than in the adult because of the absence of teeth, and the tongue more evenly fills the mouth (p. 39).

The vocal tract lengthens and changes its relative anatomical relationship as the baby grows. These changes affect the patterns of sound produced, which means that the motor control of speech has to be continuously modified during the course of development.

Crying. The first sound a baby makes is likely to be a cry. In the beginning, crying and "vegetative noises" such as burps and hiccups are involuntary behaviors that are biologically rooted (Lenneberg, 1967). The crying of the newborn thus serves no intentional communicative purpose. However, as the baby grows older, crying becomes associated with specific stimuli, such as hunger pains, and is a signal to the caretaker that the baby has a need to be met.

Wolff (1969) studied the cries of infants during the first six months of life to identify the emotional quality conveyed by sounds. Out of the four main types of cries identified, the "basic," or hunger, cry was the type which occurred most frequently. Other types of cries were a "mad" or angry cry, a cry caused by pain, and a "fake" cry. Fake crying is a more purposeful type of crying behavior that begins around the third week and is described as "of a low pitch and intensity; it consists of long drawn out moans which occasionally rise to more explicit cries, and then revert to poorly articulated moans" (Wolff, 1969, p. 98).

Both adults and children can distinguish between various types of cry sounds. In one study, adults were able to distinguish between tape-recorded

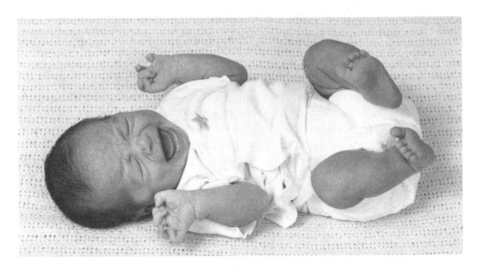

Crying usually means that the baby is trying to get the attention of the caregiver.

cries of pain and cries indicating hunger (Zeskind et al., 1984). Even children as young as 7 years of age are capable of distinguishing different types of cries (Berry, 1975). There is some indication that mothers are more skillful than nonmothers in identifying infant cries (Sagi, 1981), but not all studies support this conclusion (Rosenblith & Sims-Knight, 1985). However, parents are more accurate in identifying the different types of cries of their own babies than those of a strange baby (Wiesenfeld, Malatesta, & DeLoache, 1981).

Other researchers have studied the cries of babies with developmental abnormalities. In one such study, (Wasz-Hocket et al., 1968), the cries of brain-damaged babies were compared with the cries of normal babies. The researchers concluded that the sounds produced by the babies with abnor-malities were quite different from the cries of normal infants. Such differences are apparently obvious to parents. Zeskind (1983) found that the cries of high-risk infants could be distinguished from low-risk infants' cries by Anglo-Amer-ican, Cuban-American, and Black American mothers, regardless of their pre-vious experience with infants.

Cooing. Sometime between 1 and 3 months of age, the types of pre-speech sounds commonly referred to as "cooing" begin to emerge. In contrast to crying sounds, which are signals of distress, cooing sounds are usually sounds of contentment and happiness. Babies everywhere cry and coo alike. The appearance of cooing is related to physical and sensory changes that take place around 6 or 8 weeks of age, including increased visual attention, and greater control of the tongue (Mussen et al., 1974).

Cooing sounds are open, vowel-like, gurgling noises, such as "aaah" and "oooh." Unlike crying, cooing involves the use of the tongue and lips in sound production. The earliest cooing sounds consist of vowels that come from the front of the mouth and use the tongue, such as /e/ as in bee and /u/ as in blue (Irwin, 1948). The term *cooing* most likely arises from the predominance of the /u/ sound (Dale, 1976). A few consonants formed in the back of the mouth appear in cooing, such as /k/ as in kite and /g/ as in goat (Cruttenden, 1970). Vowel sounds are frequently preceded by a consonant to form sounds like *coo* and *moo*.

Babbling.　Between 6 and 10 months of age, the infant's vocalizations take on an increasingly speechlike quality. At this point, the baby enters the babbling period. Babbling is the repetition of consonants and vowels in alternating sequences ("ba ba ba," "ga ga ga," "da da da"). These sounds are sometimes referred to as reduplicated babbling (Stark, 1979). Babbling is distinguished from cooing by a closer resemblance of sounds to the syllables of words. The transition from cooing to babbling is due to increasing control over the vocal mechanisms (Menyuk, 1982). However, babies continue to coo and tend to shift back and forth between cooing and babbling in their vocalizations for several weeks.

During the babbling period the repetition of syllables (e.g., "na na na") is accompanied by distinctive intonational patterns as babies begin to explore the suprasegmental aspects of phonology. The sounds take on a definite rhythmic and melodic quality. The sound play of this period has been compared to practicing scales on a piano (Hopper & Naremore, 1978).

The predominance of vowel sounds continues during the babbling period, but consonants increase in frequency with age (McCarthy, 1954). Sounds and sound combinations never heard from parents have been identified in the babblings of infants. As strange as it may seem, sounds that babies find difficult to produce later in words are produced frequently in babbling (Ervin-Tripp, 1966). Toward the end of the babbling period, the sounds that are not included in the native language begin to drop out of the infant's repertory. Many infants go through a period when they babble less frequently, immediately before the onset of speech.

The babbling sounds of infants from all language backgrounds are remarkably similar. The babbling of an American infant cannot be distinguished from that of Chinese or Mexican infants (Olney & Scholnick, 1976; Oller & Eilers, 1982). Although we cannot say for sure that no differences in babbling occur, studies suggest that differences are hard to find in the light of overwhelming similarities and rare occurrence of nonuniversal sounds.

Even deaf infants babble (Lenneberg et al., 1965). Babbling begins at about the same age in deaf children as in hearing children and is similar, though perhaps a little more monotonous. Deaf children tend to stop babbling earlier than hearing children because of the lack of auditory feedback (Whetnall & Fry, 1964).

Echolalia.　Beginning around 9 months of age, infants begin to repeat, or "echo," some of the sounds they hear from others as well as their own vocalizations. This tendency to repeat sounds for their own pleasure is referred to as **echolalia.** Intonation, pitch, and stress are included in the infant's imitations.

According to Piagetian theory, the echolalic behavior of this period results from the universal ability to coordinate the hearing and vocal schema as well as to imitate new sounds. Although echolalia functions mainly as self-stimulation and sound play, these vocalizations take on an increasing ability to attract adult attention and serve as vehicles for communication (Bryen, 1982).

Significance of Prespeech Sounds.

The relationship of crying, cooing, and babbling to each other and to later stages in the acquisition of speech has been the subject of debate and controversy. Some theorists believe that crying sounds have no relationship to cooing and babbling, and that none of the prespeech sounds are important in the development of speech. Jakobson (1968) strongly believes that babbling is simply a period of vocal play and has little effect on later speech.

Research evidence now suggests that each stage and substage of language development are connected (Hopper & Naremore, 1978). Stark (1978) found indications that early crying and later cooing vocal behaviors are integrally related. Sound features present in crying and reflexive vocal tract activity are apparently incorporated in vocal expressions of pleasurable cooing. The voice and breath control developed during crying and fussing are important factors in the emergence of cooing.

Other researchers (Oller et al., 1976) also offer support for the significance of babbling in the development of speech. For example, the phonetic content of babbling indicates that infants exhibit preferences for certain consonant-vowel clusters that are later found in meaningful words. Although the role of babbling and other prespeech utterances in language development is still not clear, this experience appears to be an important preliminary step in gaining articulatory control of the vocal apparatus. In addition, these sounds provide practice in the production of certain sound sequences, intonations, and pragmatic aspects of speech.

Morphological Development

When an infant has learned to pronounce phonemes, the next task is to combine them into units of meaning, or morphemes. At this stage the child begins to work on the morphological component of language—the formation of words with the proper endings to express grammatical elements such as tense, gender, number, person, and case. Morphemes are "the smallest meaningful units of language" (Gleason, 1985, p. 19). Some words consist of a single morpheme, while others are composed of multiple morphemes. For example, the word *boy* is a single morpheme, *trustworthy* consists of two morphemes, *trust* and *worthy,* and the word *opened* consists of the morphemes *open* and *ed.* A sentence is a collection of morphemes, but there may be more morphemes than words.

The First Word. Near the end of the first year of life, babbling consists largely of reduplicated monosyllables, (e.g., "na na" or "ma ma"). These sophisticated babbling sounds are rich in intonation and are frequently made with gesture and eye contact. Such sounds are sometimes referred to as *expressive jargon*. At this point, the baby begins to make the transition from the prespeech to the speech stage, with the combination of sounds into words. The baby's first word is generally considered one of the most significant milestones in speech development. The first word is likely to be a syllable such as "ma-ma" or "da-da," which becomes associated with a specific person.

Different ages for the appearance of the first word have been reported by researchers. Generally, the average age cited in these reports is about 11 to 12 months. The range of 8 to 18 months includes most observations recorded for normal children (Darley & Winitz, 1961; McCarthy, 1954). If the first word does not appear by 18 months, there may be reason to suspect problems in the physiological, cognitive, or environmental foundations of language (Whitehurst, 1982).

CHARACTERISTICS OF FIRST WORDS. The first words produced by infants are mostly nouns and references to things that move, things that can be acted upon, or objects of particular interest or familiarity (e.g., ball, car, cat). Verbs, adjectives, adverbs, and prepositions are acquired later, usually in that order. While vowels dominate the cooings and babblings of the infant, consonants occur more frequently than vowels during this phase (Bryen, 1982). In addition the first words tend to

1. be single syllable words such as "go" or "no";
2. be reduplicated (repeated) monosyllables such as "ma-ma" or "bye-bye," or
3. end with *ie* or *y* (birdie, doggie, sissy);
4. begin with consonants such as /s/, /b/, /d/, /t/, /m/, or /n/ followed by a variety of vowel sounds that are made at the front of the mouth (Beck, 1979);
5. appear one at a time;
6. refer to objects or events familiar to the child.

The repetitive quality of the babbling period carries over into many of the child's early words. Babbling continues during this period but diminishes in frequency as the repertory of meaningful words expands.

Development of Meaning (Semantics)

Mastery of the semantic features of a language includes vocabulary development and understanding word meanings and relations among words and sentences. Infants concentrate mainly on the first task of developing a mental dictionary of individual word definitions. As the baby grows, new words are added and definitions of old words are revised and expanded. Toward the end of the second year of life, infants demonstrate a developing cognitive sophistication that provides the basis for the development of meaning (Bangs, 1982).

Vocabulary Development.   From the time the infant utters the first word, vocabulary development proceeds at an increasingly rapid rate. The vocabulary grows rather quickly during the last half of the second year with the infant's increasing mobility and expanding knowledge and experience with people, objects, and events. The rate of spoken vocabulary acquisition is depicted in Table 9-2.

Vocabulary development involves expansion and elaboration of the various meanings of words already acquired. Many words used by infants are overextended or overgeneralized to apply to situations, objects, or persons not included in the conventional adult meaning. The word *horse*, for example, might be used to name a dog, a cow, or all four-legged animals.

Infants also underextend words by using them too narrowly and specifically. A child may think that the word *car* applies only to the family car rather than to cars on the street or to cars in picture books. According to Clark's semantic features hypothesis (Clark, 1973), underextensions are the first stage in the process of learning new words. The child begins by identifying one or two meanings of a new word and adding more features until the word, over a period of time, corresponds to the adult definition. Thus, in the process of adding new meanings to words, children often use words too broadly.

One of the most interesting aspects of vocabulary development is the way infants create their own versions of adult words. A child's version of "Santa

TABLE 9-2   How the Infant's Vocabulary Grows

AGE (MONTHS)	NUMBER OF WORDS	GAIN
8	0	
10	1	1
12	3	2
15	19	16
18	22	3
21	118	96
24	272	154
30	446	174
36	896	450

Adapted from M. E. Smith (1926). An investigation of the development of the sentence and the extent of vocabulary in young children. *University of Iowa Studies in Child Welfare, 3*, (5), p. 54. Used by permission.

Reading to a child and naming pictures is an excellent way to enhance language development.

Claus" may be "Slaus Slaus," or a bottle may be a "baber." Obviously, such words are the product of mispronunciations or simplifications of adult usage. However, other words are the result of the child's own creation for which there is no adult version. The infant who called a pacifier a "bye" and money "bee" was not approximating adult word sounds.

Why babies simplify adult words is not clearly understood, but it probably results from their limited articulatory skills (Clark & Clark, 1977). Children have been observed simplifying words by omitting final consonants ("out" = "ou"), reducing consonant clusters ("step" = "dep"), or reduplicating syllables ("water" = "wa wa") (Bryen, 1982; Smith, 1973). In other instances, infants create their own words from sounds or features associated with an object. A bell is called a "ding-ding," or a cow a "moo-moo."

Receptive Speech: Word Comprehension. The meaning the infant attaches to what other people say is called **receptive speech.** Babies usually understand more words than they can say at all stages of language development. Infants typically understand a few words such as *mommy, daddy, bye-bye,* and *no* well before they say their first word (Ervin-Tripp, 1966). After they begin to say their first words, infants demonstrate the ability to follow simple directions and commands (Sachs & Truswell, 1978). Toward the end of the second year, 2-year-olds usually can understand and carry out two or three related requests combined in a single utterance (Bzoch & League, 1971). Children usually comprehend most of the words they will ever need to use in ordinary conversation by the time they are 3 years old (White, 1975).

Mastery of Syntax

Children learn the syntax of a language when they (1) can join words into sentences and (2) understand multiple-word sentences said by others (Wood, 1976). Infants begin to put two words together around 18 months. This stage represents an important milestone in language acquisition. The infant's utterances become more representative of formal grammar as many of the rules of syntax are applied without explicit guidance.

Holophrastic Speech.   **Holophrases** are single-word utterances that are roughly equivalent to whole phrases or complete sentences (McNeil, 1970). For example, when baby Jane says "ball," she may mean "There is a ball" or "Bring me the ball." Children normally use variations in voice inflections or gestures to help the listener distinguish between ambiguous meanings. In some instances, however, such words are hard to interpret without gestures or situational cues.

The extent of children's knowledge about sentence structure in using holophrastic utterances has been the subject of debate and controversy for several years. From one point of view, the one-word sentence implies a certain grammatical structure that cannot be represented in a single-word utterance. By definition, a single word cannot be a sentence. On the other hand, other investigators maintain that holophrases are the product of the child's increasing cognitive awareness and limited verbal skill for self-expression (de Villiers & de Villiers, 1978).

Two-Word Utterances.   At approximately 18 months of age, the infant begins in a halting and uncertain manner to put two words together. The transition from one-word to two-word utterances has begun. In keeping with this developmental progression, deaf infants who are learning sign language begin to use two signing combinations at around 18 months of age (Bates, O'Connell, & Shore, 1987). Many infants go through a brief phase in which strings of single words are produced in succession with pauses and separate intonations for each word. When the child reaches that point, the appearance of two-word utterances is imminent, and "Baby. Chair." becomes "Baby chair." (Bloom, 1973). The appearance of two-word combinations typically coincides with the time when the child has acquired a vocabulary of about fifty words (Lenneberg, 1967).

Roger Brown (1973), identified five stages of language acquisition based on the average length of the child's utterances. An infant enters the first stage when the average sentence length (MLU) is more than one word. The infant enters a new stage each time the MLU increases by 0.5. Infants work carefully on the correct grammatical structure of their sentences as they increase the average length of their utterances. Brown (1973) studied the speech of infants from such diverse languages as Spanish, Finnish, and Russian. He found that children from all the cultures used words with similar meanings and combined them in the same way.

Two-word utterances are more definite indicators than holophrases that the child is learning the rules for putting words together in proper order. Such utterances are almost always constructed according to basic grammatical rules, with the subject first and the verb second. Even at this early stage, infants combine words with meanings that fit together in a sensible statement. For example, you may hear a toddler say "Daddy eat!" but not "Eat Daddy!"

TELEGRAPHIC SPEECH. Brown (1973) referred to the two-word expressions of infants as **telegraphic speech** because they are similar to a telegram, which omits all but the key words. The concept of telegraphic speech focuses on the efficiency and simplicity of the child's speech, as in "See truck?" instead of "Do you see the truck?" Such sentences consist mainly of nouns and verbs occurring in the order that corresponds to adult usage (Brown & Fraser, 1963).

PIVOT-OPEN GRAMMAR. A number of theorists (Braine, 1976; McNeil, 1970) have attempted to explain the rules children use to develop two-word sentences by looking at the arrangements of the words. They have concluded that a child uses certain words in a particular position and builds sentences around them. The child uses the word order to express grammatical relationships. Two classes of words have been distinguished: pivot words and open words. Pivot words consist of a small number of words that are used frequently, such as *allgone, my,* and *more.* Open words consist of a larger number of words that are used less frequently such as *sock, dolly,* and *truck.*

In combining two words into a single statement, infants appear to operate systematically using the following rules: (1) pivot words (P) and open words (O) are used only in the following combinations: P + O, O + P, or O + O. (2) Open-class words may be used with each other (O + O), or alone in single-word utterances, but pivot words are not combined (P + P) and typically do not appear as single-word statements. (3) Once a pivot word appears in a position, either first or second, it tends to be used consistently in that position as in *more* milk, *more* soup, or doggie *fell,* me *fell* (McNeil, 1970).

The concept of pivot-open grammar has been viewed by many linguists as an oversimplification and incomplete description of the characteristics of speech at the two-word stage. While some researchers (Braine, 1976) have estimated that as many as 75 percent of children's utterances are pivotal, others (Bloom, 1970) have found that only 17 percent of the two-word utterances are based on pivot-open grammar (Clark & Clark, 1977). It appears that neither telegraphic speech nor pivot-open grammar is used by all infants.

Despite the fact that infants everywhere begin to use two-word combinations at approximately the same age, they vary considerably in the patterns they follow as they enter the world of formal grammar.

Pragmatic Aspects of Language

At the same time infants are working on phonology, semantics, and other components of language, they are becoming increasingly proficient in the pragmatic aspects of language. *Pragmatics* refers to affective language behavior or social competency in language (Bangs, 1982). The essence of pragmatics is that language is used functionally—to do things (Hopper & Naremore, 1978). Pragmatics include the following features: (1) rules governing conversations, (2) selection of appropriate verbal as well as nonverbal language to convey intended meaning, and (3) proxemics—the proximity of physical distance people maintain in their interpersonal interactions (Wood, 1976).

Early Language Functions.　Very young infants learn to use crying, cooing, and other prespeech sounds as well as body language to communicate their needs and influence the behavior of others. Halliday (1975) identified seven basic functions of language that may be practiced by infants:

1. Instrumental—getting needs met ("I want").
2. Regulatory—controlling the behavior of others ("Do as I tell you").
3. Interactional—relating to others ("Me and you").
4. Personal—expressing self-awareness ("Here I come").
5. Heuristic—exploring the environment ("Tell me why").
6. Imaginative—creating an environment ("Let's pretend").
7. Informative—communicating information ("I've got something to tell you").

Halliday concluded that infants are capable of using the first four functions by 10-1/2 months, and that functions five and six are added by 18 months of age. The seventh function appears around 22 months.

Nonverbal Communication.　Nonverbal communication includes various body movements, postures, facial expressions, and gestures such as pointing, reaching, approach-avoidance behavior, smiling, and eye contact. The acquisition of nonverbal communication apparently parallels verbal expression. As verbal abilities become more complex, the child acquires greater varieties and fluency in the use of gestures and facial expression (Hopper & Naremore, 1978).

The pointing gesture that appears around 9 months of age is the major communication device used by babies everywhere to attract the attention of another person (Bates et al., 1987). It is also a means of saying "Look at that!"

Gestures are an important
means of communication.

or "I want that!" (Bower, 1977). Soon after infants begin to point, they begin to extend or uplift their arms in the unmistakable universal gesture that says "Hold me" or "Pick me up." At approximately 1 year of age, they begin to look at objects other people point to (Lempers et al., 1977). Infants begin to point to themselves at approximately 18 months of age (Bates et al., 1987). They continue to use gestures after they begin to talk. The toddler who can say "milk" may still point to the refrigerator instead of speaking, or point at the same time a request is made.

Eye contact plays a major role in the communication rituals between caretaker and child very early in an infant's life. Smiling also is a very important early facial expression that facilitates adult-infant interactions. Eye contact and smiling are complementary behaviors that serve to instigate and maintain interaction sequences with infants. The absence of eye language and smiling presents extraordinary problems for a parent in communicating and establishing emotional intimacy. Mothers of blind infants sometimes find their babies perplexing and unresponsive and have difficulty knowing what their babies want (Fraiberg, 1974).

Conversational Turn-taking.   Infants apparently learn some of the basic rules of polite conversation such as taking turns, recognizing one's turn to speak, and not dominating the conversation even before they say their first words. Parents apparently encourage turn-taking in interactions with infants as early as 1 month of age by phrasing questions and responses in such a way that burps, yawns, and blinks may be considered as a conversational turn. (Snow, 1977). Infants reciprocate by making a sound such as a coo and waiting for a response. Turn-taking is also found in games such as peek-a-boo and build-and-bash (the parent builds and the child bashes) (de Villiers & de Villiers, 1979). These playful "dialogues" prepare the infant for more sophisticated conversations during the linguistic stage.

Proxemics.   Hall (1969) identified four zones of space people maintain in communicating under various circumstances: (1) the intimate zone (0–6 inches); (2) the personal zone (1-1/2–2-1/2 feet); (3) the social zone (4–7 feet); and (4) the public zone (12–25 feet). Children learn to use space in their communications in developmental stages. Infants typically prefer to communicate in the intimate zone. They engage in touching, hugging, and vocal interchanges in the intimate and personal zones. After 3 years of age, children gradually establish preferences for the less intimate zones, which involve less body contact and greater physical distance (Wood, 1976).

FACTORS INFLUENCING LANGUAGE DEVELOPMENT

Parent-Child Interactions

In recent years, researchers and language specialists have emphasized the importance of the interactions between infants and their caretakers, particularly the mother, in the acquisition of language (Leavitt, 1980). The special language mothers use in talking to their infants is sometimes referred to as **motherese** (Newport, Gleitman & Gleitman, 1977) or *baby talk* (Brown, 1977). Mothers from all linguistic communities tend to talk to their babies in much the same way. Kaye (1980) has summarized the following characteristics of "motherese":

1. A higher pitch, greater range of sound features, more varied tones.
2. Simplified words and special forms, such as *potty* and *mama.*
3. Shorter and simplified utterances, slower pace, and occasional whispering.
4. Immediate repetition and more repetition of the same words or phrases over a period of time.
5. Restriction of topics to the child's world.

The importance of motherese is more than the provision of sounds or words for the baby to imitate. What mothers are mainly attempting to accomplish when they use baby talk is to communicate, to understand, to be understood, and to keep two minds focused on the same topic (Brown, 1973).

Evidently the mother's efforts are not wasted. Studies of vocal interactions between young infants and their mothers have found that infants as young as 3 months of age vocalize in response to their mother's speech (Bates et al., 1977; Lewis & Freedle, 1973).

The baby appears to be trying just as hard as the mother to communicate. The process of verbal interchanges between infant and caretaker encourages turn-taking, which prepares the child for later linguistic communication (Bruner, 1978). Apparently, the baby is almost instinctively following the rules of polite conversation. As mother and child take turns vocalizing to each other, the process evolves into what has been referred to as the "fine-tuning" of the baby's language by the parent. Maternal vocalizations are thus adjusted to match the child's changing linguistic abilities according to cues from the child (Bruner, 1978).

The process of fine-tuning the baby's speech may involve the techniques of prompting, echoing, and expansion (Dale, 1976). For the preverbal child, a parent may talk and make sounds while feeding or bathing the child, such as "You are a sweet baby—Yes—Ooh—Ooh—," which prompts the child to reciprocate with sounds. For the older infant, the parent may prompt by asking, "What do you want?" as the child points to the refrigerator. In echoing, the parent imitates or repeats the child's utterances, which stimulate the child to continue to vocalize. Expansion is similar to echoing, but with something added to the child's utterance by the adult, as in: "Mommy's dress." "Yes, this is Mommy's *blue* dress." In the following interchange all three processes are used:

> Mother: (Pointing to a ball); "What's that?" (Prompting)
>
> Child: "Ball."
>
> Mother: "Ball." (Echoing)
>
> Child: "Blue ball."
>
> Mother: "Yes! It's a round, blue ball." (Expansion).

Father-Infant Speech

Does father-infant speech display the same modification and characteristics as mother-infant interchanges? Unfortunately, information on father-child verbal interactions is more limited. The available information indicates that fathers' speech to their babies is similar to that of the mother, but with some notable differences. Fathers adjust their speech to baby talk or **parentese** when talking to young infants. Like mothers, they use shorter phrases and repeat sounds more frequently when talking to an infant than when talking to an adult (Belsky & Volling, 1987).

In contrast to mothers, fathers tend to use fewer repetitions and expansions of child utterances (Giattino & Hogan, 1975), but use more imperatives and directives. An example of an imperative is "Come and get your toy truck!" Fathers appear to misunderstand childrens' utterances more often and to be less attentive and less attuned to their children's speech (Gleason, 1975). Rebelsky & Hanks (1971) found that fathers spend little time interacting with their very young infants (up to three months old). Generally, fathers spend more time interacting with male offspring than with female children.

Sex Differences

Popular beliefs and scholarly opinion have generally perpetuated the view that female infants typically learn to talk earlier than male infants by two or three weeks and tend to maintain superiority in almost every aspect of language development. However, the validity of the claim for sex differences in language development has been questioned. After a critical review of the research studies of sex differences in cognition, Fairweather (1976) concluded that "there is very little evidence of an overall sex difference in verbal ability" (p. 266). Macaulay (1978) also found the evidence of consistent sex differences to be too tenuous and self-contradictory to justify the claim that one sex is superior in language acquisition. In addition, recent research has not found sex differences in the age of beginning to talk, age of first sentences, mean length of utterances, or picture vocabulary ability (Shepherd-Look, 1982). Thus, if female superiority in language development exists, it does not emerge during the infancy period.

Twins

There is some evidence that twins and other children of multiple births have more problems in language development than children from single births. In comparison to singletons, twins tend to lag behind in language ability (McCarthy, 1954). They apparently do not receive as much individual attention from their parents and may develop a private communication system of their own that includes gestures and jargon.

Multilingualism

Under certain circumstances, being born into a family in which more than one language is spoken may be a handicap in the early stages of language acquisition. Infants from bilingual families have trouble separating phonological components of the languages until about 3 years of age unless there is a marked separation of situation or speakers (Ervin-Tripp, 1966). Infants and young children who were exposed to two languages continue to display elements of conflict between the different languages in late childhood. However, they eventually speak each language without one interfering with the other (Obler, 1985). Eventually such a child may have an intellectual advantage from the mastery of two languages which results in greater cognitive flexibility.

Social Class Differences

Infants from upper- and middle-social class environments are sometimes considered to have a linguistic advantage over infants from lower social classes. However, studies on social class differences in language development are surprisingly ambiguous, and there is much less support for this popular assumption than generally believed (Dale, 1976). The poorer performance of children from poverty backgrounds appears to be related mainly to vocabulary rather than to syntactic or other elements of grammar. In any event, social class differences do not appear before 2-1/2 to 3 years of age (Golden & Birns, 1976).

FACILITATING LANGUAGE DEVELOPMENT

Although theorists differ about the extent to which language development can be facilitated through environmental stimulation, the importance of exposure to a supportive and enriched environment is generally recognized. The following are examples of activities that can be used by parents and other caretakers to enhance communication and language development during the various stages of infancy. Keep in mind, however, that these activities should be natural, spontaneous, informal, and free from pressure on the infant to "perform."

Birth to 6 Months

1. Imitate the baby's facial expressions, gestures, and sounds. Maintain eye contact and talk to the baby during diapering, feeding, and other routines (Senter, 1983).
2. Engage in turn-taking with the infant. Initiate the cycle when the baby is quiet and alert by making a series of sounds ("ooh-ooh," "ah-ah") (Senter, 1983).
3. Play records with soothing sounds for the baby. Sing lullabies while rocking the baby.
4. When talking to an infant at this age, frequently keep your face about 12–18 inches from the baby's, so that the baby can watch your face and lips (Meier & Malone, 1979).
5. Gently bounce the baby on your knee and sing songs like "trot-a-little-horsey" (Sparling & Lewis, 1979).
6. Say the baby's name frequently (Cataldo, 1983).

6 to 12 Months

1. Continue activities suggested above (except number 4).
2. Play peek-a-boo. Vary the game by attaching a cloth to the top of a mirror. Ask "Where is (baby's name)?" and raise the cloth to let the baby see the reflected image (Sparling & Lewis, 1979).
3. Say "Hi" when you come close to the baby. Wave and say "bye-bye" when you are leaving the room (Sparling & Lewis, 1979).
4. Play pat-a-cake.
5. Toward the end of this age period, read simple short stories when baby is quiet and alert. Avoid forcing the child to be quiet or sit still (White, 1975).

6. Carry the child around the house or other places on "word walks," and point to objects of interest (Meier & Malone, 1979).

7. Use a tape recorder to record the infant's sounds and play them back (Meier & Malone, 1979).

12 to 18 Months

1. Continue activities suggested for 6–12 months.

2. Talk to the baby during bath time about soap, water, washcloth, and toys. Discuss how they feel and what they do (Sparling & Lewis, 1979).

3. Use learning exercises such as the following: Find a book with stiff pages with only one brightly colored object on each page. Place the book where the baby can see and point to the picture of an object, and say, "See the _____." Point to the _____." "Where is the _____?" If the baby makes any sounds, repeat the sounds or words vocalized (Meier & Malone, 1979).

18 to 24 Months

1. Continue reading and naming objects from books at least once a day.

2. Listen carefully to what the child is trying to say, and respond positively. If the words are not clear, venture a guess (e.g., "You want some water?")

3. Repeat and expand the child's one- or two-word utterances into complete sentences. For example, if the baby says, "Go bye-bye," respond by saying, "You want to go outside?"

4. Continue to structure games and activities to stimulate language (e.g., This little piggy).

5. Be very specific when giving instructions and directions to your child. Instead of saying, "Bring me your things," say, "Bring me your shoes and socks." Then expand further by saying, "I see you brought your blue socks." (Sparling & Lewis, 1979).

6. Raise or lower your voice from time to time to make sounds more interesting. Sing your words at times.

SUMMARY

Scientists do not fully understand why and how humans acquire language, but the accomplishments during the infancy period are remarkable. By the end of the second year of life, the typical infant has progressed from the first crying and other biologically rooted sounds to the use of short but meaningful sentences. Most of the infant's efforts are devoted to mastering the sounds of the native language and combining the sounds into words. However, considerable progress is also made in putting words together in proper sequence and in using verbal as well as nonverbal expressions in socially competent ways.

    1. Language is a complex system of mutually agreed-upon symbols used to express and understand ideas and feelings. Speech is the vocal component of language, which includes expressive and receptive functions.

2. Behaviorists maintain that language is acquired through systematic reinforcement, whereas nativists claim that infants are innately equipped to master language. Cognitive development theorists emphasize the interaction between the infant's sensorimotor intelligence and environmental influences.

3. Language consists of five components: phonology (sounds), morphology (words), syntax (structure), semantics (meaning), and pragmatics (social usage). Developing proficiency in a language involves mastering the rules governing the various components.

4. The ability to produce speech sounds is affected by the development of the vocal mechanism, which changes rapidly during infancy.

5. The prespeech sounds include crying, cooing, babbling, and echolalia. The significance of these sounds for language development has been the subject of debate and controversy. Some research studies indicate that each type of prespeech sound is an important link in the chain of language acquisition.

6. The first word represents a major milestone in morphological development and usually appears around the child's first birthday. Its appearance marks the transition from the prespeech stage to the speech stage.

7. Semantic development is based upon the infant's growing cognitive capacity to acquire new words, add new meaning to old words, and understand relationships among words. Vocabulary development accelerates during the latter part of infancy.

8. Word comprehension (receptive speech) progresses ahead of word production (expressive speech) during all stages of language development.

9. Infants begin to acquire the grammar (syntax) of their language when they can understand and produce multiple-word utterances. The first two-word combinations, sometimes called telegraphic speech, are usually produced around 18 months. However, some linguists believe that sentencelike words, called holophrases, may be the first indicators of syntactic awareness.

10. Infants demonstrate their growing competency in the pragmatic aspects of language early in life by using crying, cooing, and other prespeech sounds to interact with adults and get their needs met.

11. Parent-child interactions are an important influence on language acquisition during infancy. Mothers use their own special language, called "motherese," in talking to their babies.

12. The speech of fathers to infants is similar to "motherese," but there are some notable differences, such as fewer repetitions and expansions of the baby's utterances.

13. Current research studies do not support the belief that female infants master language skills earlier than males.

14. Twins may be at a disadvantage in language acquisition.

15. Parents and other caretakers are advised to use a variety of informal games and stimulating activities to enhance language development during infancy.

10

Personality

I am the only ME I AM
who qualifies as me;
no ME I AM has been before
and none will ever be.

—*Jack Prelutsky*

An infant is a person, even from the beginning of life. Although parents are frequently preoccupied with routine caregiving activities, they quickly recognize the uniqueness and individuality of their newborn infant. Even identical twins display their own unique behavior patterns. Jan is quiet and placid, while her sister Jean is active and exuberant. One of the most important features distinguishing one baby from another is personality.

The term **personality** has many general meanings as well as specific definitions. The following definition has been widely used: "Personality refers to more or less stable internal factors that make one person's behavior consistent from one time to another, and different from the behavior other people would manifest in comparable situations" (Child, 1968, p. 83). Personality is thus viewed as the sum total of the internal qualities and enduring patterns of behavior that establish a person's individuality.

In this chapter we examine a number of concepts and theories associated with the development of infant personality. Two important components of personality that emerge during the infancy period—temperament and the concept of self—are discussed. Finally, the practical implications of the theoretical and research literature for facilitating personality development during infancy are considered.

THEORIES OF PERSONALITY DEVELOPMENT

There are numerous theories about what makes up human personality and how it develops. A classic textbook (Hall & Lindzey, 1978) on personality includes a discussion of eighteen different theories. For our purposes, however, we consider the four most influential and prominent theories: the classical psychoanalytic theory of Sigmund Freud; Erik Erikson's contemporary psychosocial theory; the behavioristic theory of B. F. Skinner; and Maslow and Rogers' theory of self-actualization.

Freud's Psychoanalytic Theory

Freud was probably the first theorist to emphasize the importance of infancy and the first few years of life in personality development. He believed that the "child is father of the man," and that the basic personality structure is formed by the fifth year of life (Hall & Lindzey, 1978). Consequently, the experiences a person has during infancy have a profound influence on the adult personality.

Freud identified three major components of personality: the **id,** the **ego,** and the **superego.** The id is the biological part of personality that is present at birth. It includes the basic instincts and physiological urges such as hunger and libido (sexual energy). The id provides the energy that motivates the personality. According to Freud, the newborn infant has a very simple personality consisting solely of the primitive urges of the id. The infant seeks immediate gratification and has little ability to tolerate tension created in the id when needs are not met.

The irrational, pleasure-seeking, uninhibited id remains part of the personality throughout life. However, people cannot realistically always have what they want as soon as they want it. Consequently, a second part of the personality, the ego, develops during infancy to exercise control over the id's instinctual urges. The ego is the rational, planning, and organizing part of the personality. Its primary function is to help the id find ways to achieve gratification that are, in the long run, most satisfactory.

The gradual emergence of the ego during the infancy period lays the foundation for the formation of the superego during preschool years (ages 3 to 5). The superego consists of the conscience and the ego-ideal (the person you would like to be). It functions primarily to inhibit the impulses of the id that are socially unacceptable, and works to perfect moral behavior (Hall & Lindzey, 1978). The superego is often in conflict with the id, while the ego works to reconcile the differences. If the ego is not successful in resolving the conflict, personality problems may develop.

According to Freud, personality develops through a series of stages: oral, anal, phallic, latency, and genital. The personality is shaped by the quality of the experiences related to the area of the body that is dominant in each stage. The two stages that occur during the infancy period will be discussed in more detail.

The Oral Stage (Birth to 18 Months).   During the first part of infancy the oral region—the mouth, tongue, and lips—is dominant. Feeding experiences, nonnutritive sucking, and other sensations incorporated through the mouth provide the infant's first experiences of pleasure and frustration. If the baby receives too much or too little gratification through the mouth, oral fixation is likely to occur. Oral fixation through deprivation results in such personality traits as pessimism, self-depreciation, and passivity. Opposite personality characteristics develop from overindulgence in the oral stage.

The Anal Stage (18 Months to 3 Years).   Toward the end of the infancy period, the anal region of the body gradually becomes the focal point of the baby's experiences. During this stage, bowel movements become a source of pleasure and potential conflict. The toilet training that typically begins during this period is likely to have long-term consequences. If the infant is treated too harshly, a personality dominated by excessive orderliness, stinginess, stubbornness, and compulsivity is likely to develop. On the other hand, overpermissiveness in toilet training can result in the opposite personality traits.

Erikson's Psychosocial Theory

Erik Erikson was a follower of Freud, but he disagreed with some of Freud's ideas. Erikson (1963) reinterpreted Freudian theory, with more optimism about human nature and an emphasis on cultural influences. He translated Freudian theory into completely different, more contemporary terms.

Erikson's theory is usually discussed in relation to eight psychosocial stages of development, from birth through old age. The personality forms as the individual passes through this series of interrelated stages. Each stage involves a conflict, or crisis of emotional opposites. The quality of the individual's experience in each stage determines how the conflict is resolved. The emotional crisis that occurs in each stage must be resolved before personality development can proceed smoothly in succeeding stages. The first two stages occur during the infancy period.

Trust versus Mistrust (Birth to 18 Months). Erikson's first stage, trust versus mistrust, roughly parallels Freud's oral stage. The trust versus mistrust stage is considered to be the most critical because it provides the foundation for resolving crises and developing a healthy sense of identity in other stages of life. The basic psychosocial attitude the infant must develop in this stage is that the world and the people in it can be trusted. According to Erikson (1963), consistency and continuity of experience provide the foundation for the sense of trust to develop.

Infants are inclined to be uncertain and mistrusting because their knowledge about the world is very limited. Some feelings of mistrust are normal and healthy. However, if the baby is treated harshly and the basic needs are not consistently met, feelings of mistrust are reinforced and become dominant. Distrustful infants have difficulty separating from their mothers and may exhibit other emotional problems later in life.

Autonomy versus Shame and Doubt (18 Months to 3 Years). The second period coincides with Freud's anal stage. Developing a sense of autonomy begins with the feeling of being in control of one's body during infancy. With increasing mobility, infants begin to explore their environment. They want to see new places and things, undertake new activities, and generally do things for themselves. During this period they also become capable of establishing bowel and bladder control. They frequently have difficulty staying within designated boundaries and complying with adult wishes. The negativism that is characteristic of toddlerhood results from the need for autonomy.

The crisis of this period occurs when the infant's natural inclination to be self-assertive collides with adult demands and restrictions. A major area of potential conflict is toilet training. The successful resolution of the crisis involves the parents' willingness to allow reasonable freedom without being overly permissive. Problems occur when parents are too restrictive or over-protective and impose unrealistic expectations. The child may develop a dominant sense of shame and doubt. Such a child is handicapped by feelings of incompetence, insecurity, and unworthiness.

Skinner's Behaviorism

According to B. F. Skinner (1961), personality is nothing more than a collection of behavior patterns. The personality is acquired over time—response by response. In contrast to Freud, Skinner rejects the idea that there are internal personality mechanisms such as an ego, or unconscious motivational forces. He identified no personality components or developmental stages. To Skinner, we are products of our environment (Hall & Lindzey, 1978).

The main concern of Skinner and other behaviorists is how behaviors are acquired and extinguished. Skinner's system consists mainly of laws or principles that control the formation of stimulus-response relationships. To understand personality, you need only to understand an individual's conditioning history. An infant becomes passive and compliant if the responses of parents and other caregivers reinforce that particular type of behavior. The infant's personality is not as complex and fully developed as an adult's because

As he explores the environment, this toddler is attempting to develop a sense of autonomy.

the infant has had fewer experiences. Each infant develops a unique personality because of a history of unique experiences (Hjelle & Ziegler, 1976).

Self-actualization Theory of Maslow and Rogers

In contrast to behavioral theorists, Maslow (1970) and Rogers (1961) believe that individuals are free to choose what they want to be. Implicit in this theory is the idea that infants are born with the urge to grow. Under favorable conditions, individuals are always striving to develop all their capacities and inner potential. This process is referred to as **self-actualization,** which is the main motivational force of personality.

The core personality component is the *self-concept,* which begins to develop during infancy. It provides the basic mechanism through which a person interprets experiences and ultimately behaves (Lazarus & Monat, 1979). The self-concept is defined and discussed more fully in the next section.

The self-actualizing tendency is a strong force for growth that is evident even during infancy. For example, infants persist in learning to walk and performing other tasks in spite of great effort and the pain of falling down. This persistence results, not simply because the infant is genetically programmed to walk, but also because of a strong tendency for growth (Lazarus & Monat, 1979). Since personality is in a constant process of change, Maslow and Rogers did not emphasize one period of life, such as infancy, as being more important than any other period.

Evaluating Personality Theories

Personality has proven to be as difficult to study as it has been to define. Consequently, there is no overwhelming research evidence in favor of any single theory. Each theory has been praised as well as criticized. As a student of infant development, you will have to decide which theory you prefer. Many people prefer an eclectic approach, combining the best and most promising ideas from several different theories. In the remainder of this chapter, some of the attributes of infant personality that have become the focal points of current research are considered.

THE DEVELOPMENT OF SELF

Two-year-old Ginny grabs her doll from Michael and says, "Mine." Another toddler, Tanya, notices her picture on the nursery school bulletin board and tells her teacher, "That's me." As these incidents clearly indicate, 2-year-old children have developed an awareness of themselves as individuals distinct and separate from others. In all probability, a concept of self exists much earlier than this (Lewis & Brooks, 1978).

Many psychologists believe that the self-concept is the core of the personality and a primary determinant of behavior. Generally, self-concept refers to a composite, or sum total of the images, attitudes, and feelings one uses to describe or think about one's self as an individual. Other terms that are sometimes used to mean the same thing include "self-image" and "sense of self." A baby is not born with a self-concept but gradually develops one during infancy. It evolves by degrees along with an increasing level of cognitive functioning (Maccoby, 1980).

Like other concepts, the self-concept is subject to change throughout the life cycle. Although psychologists do not agree on exactly how the self-concept develops, there appear to be three important accomplishments during the infancy period—self-awareness, self-recognition, and self-definition.

Self-awareness

In the beginning, an infant has to develop an awareness of being distinct and separate from other people and objects. Margaret Mahler, a Freudian theorist, believes that infants must go through a second birth, one that is psychological in nature (Mahler, Pine, & Bergman, 1975). She refers to this process as **separation-individuation.** Separation involves the child's emerging self-consciousness, or "hatching" from a symbiotic (interdependent) union with the mother. Individuation consists of the achievements that contribute to the child's identity as an autonomous person.

The separation-individuation process takes place mainly between the fourth month and the third year of life. Prior to this time, the infant has gone through two preliminary stages—autistic and symbiotic—and developed a dim awareness of having needs met by an outside source.

Mahler (1968) divides the period of separation-individuation into the following four subphases:

1. Differentiation, or Hatching (5–10 months). The baby learns to distinguish between the mother and other people.
2. Practicing (10–15 months). An infant rapidly becomes aware that its own body is distinct from that of its mother. By physically moving away from the mother for brief intervals, an infant practices separation.
3. Reapproachment (15–24 months). The toddler experiences an increased awareness of separateness from the mother. Ironically, the mother becomes even more important to the infant. This period is thus characterized by the ambivalent feelings of wanting to be separate from the mother while wanting to hold onto her.
4. Consolidation of Individuality (24–36 months). The child develops a mental image of the mother that provides security while the mother is away. Mental images of the self as a distinct individual develop rapidly during this phase and provide the basis for identity formation.

Mahler conceptualized the development of the self as a struggle between separateness and relatedness, reflected in the baby's ability to handle separation from the mother. The infant's resolution of the oneness-separateness conflict between the ages of 5 and 18 months ultimately shapes the adult personality. Thus, successful acquisition of a favorable self-concept depends largely upon the quality of the mother-child interaction in each of the above stages.

Mahler's theory about the separation-individuation process is based upon her observations in a clinical setting and individual case reports. However, there is little support from independent researchers to support many of the crucial features of her theory, including the developmental stages (Campos et al., 1983). Consequently, Mahler's theory has not received wide acceptance among psychologists.

Daniel Stern (1985) believes that the views of psychoanalysts, such as Mahler, need to be modified in view of new discoveries about self-concept formation. Stern, who is both a psychoanalyst and a developmentalist, used information from experimental and clinical studies to form his own theory. He believes that infants never experience a period of a total lack of self-consciousness. Stern describes four different senses of self that emerge during infancy:

1. Emergent Self (birth–2 months). The process of coming into being through the integration of diverse activities such as sensorimotor perceptions, memories, and other cognitive functions.
2. Core Self (2–6 months). Infants sense that they are physically separate from the mother; they discover that they are different agents who have distinct experiences and separate histories.
3. Subjective Self (7–15 months). Infants discover that there are other minds "out there" besides their own; other people can and will share the infants' feelings.
4. Verbal Self (15 months +). Infants understand that the sense of self (and others) has a storehouse of knowledge and experience. The ability to take an objective view of the self (to be self-reflective) develops along with language ability.

The senses of self, as viewed by Stern, are not successive phases that replace one another. Rather, after each sense of self is formed it remains fully functional and active throughout life. All four continue to grow and coexist.

Stern believes that the infant's personality is shaped more by everyday interactions with parents than by dramatic events or developmental stages. Infants learn very powerful lessons from the countless small interchanges that occur with the caregiver each day. According to Stern, the response of the parent must match or be harmonious with the baby's response. For example, the infant squeals with delight and the mother, in turn, gives the baby a gentle "bounce." This is a response that matches and acknowledges the baby's level of excitement. If the parent consistently overresponds or underresponds, the baby's sense of self will be negatively affected. Stern's theory about how the sense of self develops has been controversial and remains to be proven.

Much of the research on the development of self-awareness in infants has been conducted by Lewis and Brooks-Gunn (1979). They have identified five periods in the infant's self-other differentiation (Lewis, 1986, 1987):

Period 1: 0–3 Months. This period is characterized initially by the predominance of reflexive interactions with caregivers and objects. These interactions serve as a basis for the beginnings of self-other differentiation, which begins to emerge at the end of this period.

Period 2: 3–8 Months. During this period, the infant makes additional progress in the distinction between self and others through active learning. However, self-awareness is not totally achieved yet because an infant cannot make self-other distinctions in all situations.

Period 3: 8–12 Months. At this time, complete self-other differentiation is accomplished. Awareness of the self as unique and permanent in time and space is evident.

Period 4: 12–18 Months. This period is sometimes referred to as the "coy stage" or the stage of "self-conscious emotions," such as embarrassment and separation anxiety. This period is also characterized by the infant's growing sense of self-recognition (see "Self-recognition" section below).

Period 5: 18–30 Months. The development of language capacity enables the infant to label the features of social objects (e.g., as age and gender) including themselves. This period is sometimes referred to as the "stage of self-definition" and is discussed further below.

Self-recognition

The ability of infants to correctly identify images as their own is called **self-recognition** (Fogel, 1984). The development of visual self-recognition has been explored in experiments designed to determine when infants can understand the significance of their own reflection in a mirror. Lewis and Brooks (1978) observed infants from 6 to 24 months of age with a mark of rouge on their faces. None of the 9- to 12-month-old babies responded to the mark when they looked in the mirror. One-quarter of the babies in the 15- to 18-month age range, and three-quarters of the 21- to 24-month-olds touched the mark on their own face as if to say, "That's me!"

Infants recognize their own pictures at about the same age as they identify their reflections in a mirror. By 2 years of age most infants can recognize a picture as their own and distinguish between it and a picture of another baby (Lewis & Brooks, 1974). Infants can also identify themselves in a videotape at this age (Brooks & Lewis, 1976).

Bertenthal and Fischer (1978) believe that the development of self-recognition is related to the acquisition of the object concept (Chapter 8). They identified seven stages in the development of self-recognition. These researchers presented a series of tasks designed to assess the development of the concept of object permanency in a group of infants between the ages of 6 and 24 months of age. The same infants were also given a test to determine their ability to recognize their own mirror image. The ages at which the infants achieved each of the stages closely coincided with the ages at which they progressed through a series of steps leading to the acquisition of the object concept. The concept of self apparently develops in much the same way as other concepts (Maccoby, 1980).

This toddler is probably beginning to recognize the reflection in the mirror as her own image.

In summary, research studies indicate that infants begin to recognize their own visual images by the end of the first year, but this ability is not very well developed at that age. By approximately 18 months of age, a more sophisticated level of visual self-recognition can be clearly observed in some infants. Almost all infants demonstrate the ability by the time they are 2 years old (Lewis & Brooks, 1978). However, self-recognition of visual images by mentally retarded infants does not occur until around 3 years of age (Mans, Cicchetti, & Sroufe, 1978). The emergence of self-awareness thus closely parallels the development of intelligence.

Self-definition

As infants begin to acquire expressive language ability, they progress beyond self-recognition to self-definition. That is, the self-concept is further defined and elaborated through the use of verbal labels. In Stern's stages, this is referred to as the "verbal self." Infants notice differences and make comparisons between the self and others on various dimensions such as age, size, and gender. They can define themselves categorically in terms of personal pronouns (*I, me, you*), gender identity, personal attributes, and possessions (*mine, yours*).

The appropriate use of the pronouns *I, me,* and *you* represents the acquisition of verbal labels for the self. It is also an indication that an infant has developed a self-concept that includes the perspective of others. Some infants begin to use their own name as early as 15 months (Brooks-Gunn & Lewis,

1982). Personal pronoun usage follows a few months later. Most infants use *I* (along with *me, my,* or *mine*) as their first personal pronoun around 20 to 22 months of age (Charney, 1980, Maccoby, 1980). This pronoun is frequently used interchangeably with the child's own name or the word *baby* (Maccoby, 1980). The second pronoun most children use is *you,* which appears at about 2 years of age (Charney, 1980).

Young children have difficulty using pronouns correctly because they can be used to refer to different people. For example, *I* and *my* sometimes refer to the child's mother, the father, or other people, depending on who is speaking. The pronoun *you* is even more confusing because it is frequently used to refer to the baby as well as other people. Consequently, an infant may say such things as "you go" for "I go." Surprisingly, though, most infants have little difficulty using pronouns correctly (Maccoby, 1980). The proper use of pronouns is an indication that the infant's self-concept is becoming more objective, more socialized, and slightly less egocentric.

Kagan (1981a) found that infants' self-descriptive statements such as "I play" or "I can do this" increase in frequency around 2 years of age. This research indicates that in addition to knowledge about the self's physical features (e.g., "I have red hair"), the 2-year-old is aware of the self's capabilities and actions ("I play"). Awareness of capabilities is cognitively more advanced than the awareness of physical features (Damon & Hart, 1982). An infant who demonstrates such awareness has taken a further step in the development of self-knowledge.

Age (or size) is a feature that infants use very early in the development of a self-concept. Infants are able to distinguish adults and babies between 6 and 12 months of age (Lewis & Brooks-Gunn, 1979). By the time they are 1 year old, infants exhibit more social responses to strange babies than to strange adults (Brooks-Gunn & Lewis, 1979). Presumably, infants perceive other infants as more similar to themselves than adults.

Gender is also a category that infants use in defining themselves on the basis of external characteristics. Brooks-Gunn and Lewis (1982) indicate that infants discriminate between male and female adults in the first year of life. They can tell the difference between boys and girls in the second year of life. Gesell (1940) found that one-third of the 2-year-olds and three-quarters of the 3-year-olds he questioned knew whether they were boys or girls.

Self-esteem

An infant's self-concept and self-esteem develop together. Self-esteem (self-love, self-respect, self-acceptance, self-worth) is one's self-evaluation based on the self-concept. The self-concept is the descriptive part of the self, whereas self-esteem is the evaluative component of the self. A child who has a positive self-concept will have a high level of self-esteem, whereas a negative self-concept will result in a sense of low self-esteem.

The amount of respect, acceptance, and concerned treatment infants receive from their caregivers is especially important in developing a healthy self-concept (Coopersmith, 1967). The development of self-esteem is affected by the extent to which infants perceive themselves as good or bad, pleasing or displeasing to their caregivers. The parent who usually scolds and frowns when changing a diaper is communicating that the infant is a "bad" person. On the other hand, the parent who talks pleasantly to the infant during diaper changing is, in effect, saying, "You are a good person."

The development of self-esteem is also influenced by the child's ability to cause things to happen and control the behavior of others (Coopersmith, 1967). This ability is referred to as the infant's **perceived personal effectance** (Lamb, 1981a). Infants learn very early in life the extent to which they can or cannot control their world. At approximately 12 months, they are typically capable of determining when their behavior has had an effect and when it has not (Piaget, 1952). Black and other minority infants face problems developing feelings of control as they grow up because of overt and subtle forms of racial discrimination.

Infants experience a sense of power or helplessness depending upon whether or not they can accomplish what they set out to do. Gunnar (1978, 1980) found that 12-month-olds were considerably less afraid of a scary toy when they could control it than when they could not. Before that age, infants could not determine that they were completely in control of the circumstances activating the toy.

Realistically, infants experience feelings of power at certain times and a sense of weakness at other times. For healthy self-esteem to develop, an infant needs to learn how to manage both types of feelings. When one feeling or the other—power or weakness—predominates, self-esteem suffers. "Healthy personality growth is always between the extremes" (Weiner & Elkind, 1972, p. 32).

An infant's self-esteem is influenced by the ability to solve problems and to "make things work."

TEMPERAMENT

Much of the theoretical debate as well as research on infant personality has focused on the development of temperament. The terms *personality* and *temperament* are sometimes used interchangeably. In other instances, temperament is considered to be a developmental forerunner, or the "raw material," of personality (Berger, 1982). According to prevailing opinion, however, temperament is viewed as a subdomain in the broader field of personality study. As such, it is *one* of the important components of personality (Rothbart & Derryberry, 1981; Strelau, 1985).

There are numerous definitions of temperament (Goldsmith et al., 1987). The most widely used definition has been developed by Chess, Thomas, and Birch (1965): Temperament is "the basic style which characterizes a person's behavior" (p. 32). This definition encompasses behavior such as whether responses are "fast or slow, mild or intense, sparse and unelaborated or adorned and elaborated" (Buss & Plomin, 1975, p. 9). Temperament has also been defined as individual differences in the behavioral expressions of emotionality and arousal (Campos et al., 1983). Thus, temperament is not only responsible for the style, or "how" of behavior, but the content of behavior as well.

Dimensions of Temperament

A variety of dimensions or components of temperament have been identified (e.g., Buss & Plomin, 1975; Rothbart, 1981; Thomas & Chess, 1977). The nine components developed by Thomas and Chess (1977) in a long-term research study are the ones most widely used (Campos et al., 1983):

1. Activity level. Inactive versus active motor behavior (reaching, crawling, sleep-wake cycle).
2. Rhythmicity. Regularity of schedule; predictability versus unpredictability of behavior (eating, sleeping, etc.).
3. Approach or withdrawal. Typical initial response to a new stimulus (people, food, toys, etc.).
4. Adaptability. Response to change in routine (bedtime, feeding, travel, etc.).
5. Sensory threshold. Level of stimulation needed to evoke a response (noise, pain, light, etc.).
6. Intensity of response. Energy level of response (crying, body movements, etc.).
7. Quality of mood. The degree of pleasant, happy, and friendly behavior versus unpleasant, unhappy, and unfriendly behavior.
8. Distractibility. The extent to which extraneous stimuli (noise, objects, etc.) interfere with or change ongoing behavior.
9. Persistence and attention span. Length of time an activity is pursued, and the continuation of an activity in the face of interruptions or obstacles.

Thomas and Chess (1985) found that three basic temperamental patterns of behavior could be identified soon after birth. About 65 percent of the infants in their study were classified in one of the following groups:

1. The Easy Child. Babies in this group display regularity, respond positively to new situations, adapt quickly to change, and exhibit a relatively mild and generally positive mood. These babies quickly develop regular schedules of sleeping and eating. They smile a lot, accept most frustrations with little protest, and are easily comforted. They are a joy and a delight to their caregivers. About 40 percent of the babies in the Thomas and Chess study displayed this temperament.

2. The Difficult Child. At the opposite end of temperamental extremes, these babies are irregular in body functions and are slow to develop good eating and sleeping routines. They cry longer and louder than other babies. The difficult child does not adjust easily to new foods, strangers, or changes in routine. This group comprised about 10 percent of the sample. Such an infant requires a lot of patience, stamina, and resourcefulness on the part of parents and other caregivers.

3. The Slow-to-Warm-Up Child. These babies are characterized by mild intensity of reactions (positive or negative). Although they are very active, infants in this group do not respond well initially to new situations. A mildly negative response can be observed in such a baby's first bath or encounter with a new person. However, over time and without pressure, the slow-to-warm-up infant will make appropriate adjustments and display quiet interest and enjoyment. About 15 percent of the infants studied were in this category.

Not all infants can be placed into one of these three groups on the basis of temperamental characteristics. Also, the percentage of infants identified by Thomas and Chess in each group does not necessarily represent the general population. Most children display a wide range of behavioral styles between the extremes and do not fit neatly into a particular category. "Easy" children are not always easy, and "difficult" children are not difficult in all situations (Thomas & Chess, 1985).

Some researchers (e.g., Bates, 1980) have questioned the validity of Thomas and Chess's categories. A basic problem has been the use of parental ratings to measure infant temperament. Such reports are not considered to be very objective or accurate. Parent ratings of the same child may vary from time to time and from parent to parent. Parental perceptions of infant temperament are also likely to be colored by the personality of the parents and their child-rearing values. Thus, temperament may be in the eyes of the beholder as much as in the behavior of the infant.

The concept of the "difficult child" has been especially controversial, and there are growing doubts about the usefulness of this classification (Rothbart, 1982). If an infant is labeled "difficult," parents and other caregivers may focus on the negative characteristics of the child. By expecting the child to be difficult, problem behaviors may develop as a kind of self-fulfilling prophecy in which the child behaves as expected. On the other hand, the difficult child classification has been defended as a useful way of explaining to parents how infants vary in behavioral style. Bates (1987) has concluded that there is more evidence for difficult behavior than for any other aspect of temperament. Parents need to develop special strategies to cope with the behavior of the difficult child.

Origins of Temperament

Numerous researchers have attempted to determine the extent to which an infant's temperament is inherited or environmentally controlled. Some researchers have studied twins, while others have used adopted children in attempts to answer this question. If temperament is inherited, identical twins should be more alike temperamentally than fraternal twins. Adopted children would be expected to display temperamental characteristics that more closely resemble those of their biological parents than of their adoptive parents.

On the basis of available research evidence, the genetic contribution to temperament is still uncertain. The results of an extensive study comparing adopted children with children living with their biological parents indicates that "at most, parental personality predicts less than 10 percent of the overall variance of infant temperament" (Plomin & DeFries, 1985, p. 237).

However, that study, as well as other studies using twins as subjects, suggests the possibility of a rather strong genetic influence on some specific aspects of temperament. Traits that appear to be inherited include shyness (Daniels & Plomin, 1985), emotionality, activity level, and attention span (Campos et al., 1983; Goldsmith, 1983; Goldsmith & Gottesman, 1981; Torgersen, 1982). There are indications that genetic influences on temperament become more evident as the infant grows a little older (Goldsmith & Campos, 1982; Plomin & DeFries, 1985).

Cultural and ethnic factors apparently play an important role in the development of temperament. Friedman (1981) compared the temperament of Chinese, Japanese, and Caucasian (European ancestry) newborn infants. The Oriental infants were calmer, more passive, less excitable, and more adaptable than the Caucasian infants. Chisholm (1981) found that Australian aboriginal infants were less irritable and more easily soothed than Caucasian infants. The extent to which such differences in temperament are attributable to variations in genetic backgrounds, differences in child-rearing practices, and other factors has not been determined.

Researchers are now beginning to explore how body chemistry is related to temperament. For example, the level of progesterone has been linked with the temperamental traits of intensity and approach-withdrawal. Infants who are classified as "easy babies" tend to have higher amounts of progesterone (Weissbluth & Green, 1984). Synthetic progestins administered to mothers to prevent threatened abortions may increase aggressive behavior in their infants after birth (Reimish, 1981). Our knowledge about hormones and infant temperament is limited, but the list of body chemicals that are potential sources of influence is growing.

Continuity of Temperament

Most theorists believe that, to a large extent, temperament is consistent and stable throughout the life span (Campos et al., 1983). If this assumption is correct, a baby who is highly active will continue to display a similar temperamental characteristic as an adult. The research evidence is far from conclusive, but there is a modest amount of support for the contention that at least some behaviors related to temperament are relatively enduring. The Colorado Adoption Project (Plomin & DeFries, 1985) found a fairly high level of temperament correlations (.60) from infancy to adulthood.

Temperament does not, however, always follow a consistent, predictable course over time. Thomas and Chess (1985) traced the development of temperamental traits from infancy through adolescence. Some of their subjects displayed clear-cut consistency in one or several characteristics. On the other hand, some subjects were consistent in certain aspects of temperament during one period and in other aspects during other times. They found that some of the subjects changed completely in a number of temperament traits.

Thomas and Chess (1985) found that the broad category of the "difficult infant" does not reliably predict a child's chances of developing behavior problems at a later age. Other researchers (Daniels, Plomin, & Greenhalgh, 1984; Rothbart, 1982) have also failed to find evidence that behavioral difficulties related to temperament at one age necessarily create difficulties at a later age. On the other hand, Bates (1987) believes that there is a modest amount of evidence suggesting that infant temperament might predict future behavior problems such as acting out. The most difficult and the most easy infants are the ones who are most likely to have difficulties. However, environmental factors such as parental stress and depression are likely to be involved in some way.

Temperament and Parent-Infant Interactions

An infant's temperamental characteristics obviously have an impact upon interactions with caregivers and other people. Fussy babies who cry a lot are likely to evoke more negative social responses than infants who are calmer and more easygoing. The baby who is friendly and approachable is likely to obtain more positive responses than the infant who is shy and withdrawn. Of course, the temperament and expectations of parents and other primary caregivers have to be taken into consideration.

The way the temperament of the infant matches the caregiving style of the parents greatly influences the socialization process. This is referred to as the **goodness-of-fit** between infant and caregiver (Thomas & Chess, 1977). Obviously, the more closely parental behaviors match the temperamental style of the infant, the better the social interactions will be.

Temperament and Cognitive Development

The temperamental traits expressed by an infant may be very important in the development of cognitive functioning. Scientific evidence indicates that temperamental traits such as persistence, distractibility, attention span, and activity level affect cognitive growth (Campos et al., 1983). Infants with a difficult temperament have lower scores on measures of intellectual performance (Plomin & DeFries, 1985; Thomas & Chess, 1977; Wachs & Gandour, 1983). The baby who is alert, attentive, and persistent in solving problems is likely to demonstrate superior cognitive competence.

ENHANCING PERSONALITY DEVELOPMENT

Parents and other caregivers can make a positive contribution to the personality development of infants in numerous ways. The following are examples of some recommended activities and practices.

Promoting a Positive Sense of Self

1. Parents should select a baby's name with great care. Names should not be sexually ambiguous, difficult to spell or pronounce, or the basis for undesirable nicknames, initials, or rhymes, nor should they be otherwise exceptionally odd within the context of the child's cultural heritage.

2. Hold the young baby in front of a mirror and play games such as touching and naming body parts; making faces; and "See ＿＿＿ in the mirror?" (Sparling & Lewis, 1979). Give the baby an unbreakable mirror to play with at about 2 months of age.

3. Take the baby's picture at various ages and look at them together with the baby, pointing out such characteristics as hair and eyes (McDonald, 1980).

4. Minority infants should be given dolls and toys that match their color and ethnic heritage, along with other dolls, toys, and materials. Parents should talk about characteristics of the body in ways that include skin color. In naming colors, point to the child's arm to indicate "brown," "black," "red," or "yellow" (Comer & Poussaint, 1976).

Establishing Basic Trust

1. Respond to the infant's cries and other signals promptly and consistently. Smile, talk, and relate to the infant cheerfully during caregiving routines.

2. Don't try to sneak away unnoticed when leaving the baby with a substitute caregiver. Never leave without saying goodbye.

3. "Peek-a-boo" and "hide-and-seek" are excellent games for teaching the baby that people disappear and return (Sparling & Lewis, 1979).

Promoting Autonomy

1. Encourage infants to do things for themselves as much as possible (e.g., pull a sock part of the way off and let the infant finish the task). Suggest solutions to problems without taking over.

2. Give the infant choices when possible and reasonable (e.g., what to eat or wear, things to do, materials to use, and ways to spend time).

3. Handle the infant's negativism with positive responses, firmness, and understanding. Avoid using shame as a response to undesirable behavior.

4. Allow the child to explore the environment, particularly new places, as freely as possible within the limits of safety, available supervision, and situational restraints.

5. Play games with infants that facilitate motor control (see Chapter 5).

Matching the Baby's Temperament

1. Accept and enjoy each baby's individuality.

2. Try to find caregiving strategies that match the baby's behavioral style. For example, infants who are more active and difficult to manage need more structure, more environmental control, and less stimulation. Very young infants who are sensitive to being touched sometimes respond favorably to being held on a pillow. Avoid trying to force "noncuddlers" to be held closely (see Chess, Thomas, & Birch, 1965).

SUMMARY

1. Personality is the total of the internal qualities and enduring, observable patterns of behavior that make up a person's individuality.

2. Freud emphasized the importance of experiences during infancy in shaping personality development. He identified three components of personality: id, ego, and superego. Personality development progresses through the oral and anal stages during infancy. If infants and children are treated too harshly or too permissively in each stage, personality problems are likely to arise.

3. The two stages of personality growth during infancy identified by Erikson that occur during infancy are trust versus mistrust, and autonomy versus shame and doubt. The emotional crisis that occurs during each stage must be resolved before healthy personality development can proceed.

4. Skinner believes that personality is simply a collection of behavior patterns that are acquired over time through the process of conditioning.

5. According to Maslow and Rogers, the main motivational force shaping personality is self-actualization. The basic component of personality is the self-concept. Maslow also identified a hierarchy of needs that must be met in the process of personality development.

6. One major component of personality that emerges during the infancy period is the self-concept, or the "sense of self." Three important accomplishments in the development of the self-concept occur during infancy: self-awareness, self-recognition, and self-definition.

7. Mahler believes that self-awareness involves the process of separation-individuation that takes place from the fourth month to the third year of life in four stages.

8. Stern proposes four different senses of the self that emerge during infancy: emergent self, core self, subjective self, and verbal self.

9. The infant's individuality and basic style of behavior are referred to as temperament. Many infants can be classified as temperamentally "easy," "difficult," or "slow-to-warm-up." Some temperamental characteristics are inherited and are relatively enduring throughout life. Infant temperament apparently influences social interactions and cognitive development.

10. Parents and other caregivers are advised to use child-rearing strategies that match the baby's temperament and promote a positive sense of self and establish basic trust and autonomy.

11

Social And Emotional Development

> When the first baby laughed for the first time, the laugh broke into a thousand pieces, and they all went skipping about, and that was the beginning of fairies.
>
> —J. M. Barrie

Babies are social and emotional beings from birth. The newborn's slightest expressions elicit responses from parents, siblings, and strangers. As they get just a little older, infants become partners in the give-and-take of human relationships. Their interactions with other people are punctuated with various nuances of emotional moods and expressions. These emotions play a pioneering role, not only in the infant's social experiences, but in every area of development.

In this chapter we explore social and emotional development during infancy. The domain of social development includes ways infants interact with their caregivers, peers, and people in general. The development of social competence is one of the most important tasks of infancy. Emotional development encompasses the origin and differentiation of specific emotions. It also includes developmental changes in emotional expression and the infants' understanding of emotions in themselves and others. Emotional and social development are combined in one chapter because these areas are closely interrelated during the infancy period.

SOCIAL DEVELOPMENT

Socialization is the "process by which the newborn child is molded into the culture . . . and hence becomes an acceptable person in that society" (Smelser & Smelser, 1963, pp. 102–103). Infants become socialized through interactions with parents and other people. The process of socialization involves learning that other people are necessary and becoming dependent on them. Almost as soon as this awareness develops, however, infants must begin to move in the direction of establishing independence. The crying, clinging behavior of the baby must be eventually replaced by more mature forms of social behavior such as verbal requests and independent locomotion. A timetable for the development of some of the major milestones of social development is given in Table 11-1.

The Socially Competent Infant

Social competence refers to an infant's ability "to make use of environmental and personal resources to achieve a good developmental outcome" (Waters & Sroufe, 1983, p. 81). Socially competent infants possess the skills necessary to get their needs met and to accomplish their desired social goals.

TABLE 11-1   Milestones of Social Development

BEHAVIOR	USUAL AGE (MONTHS)
Knows mother by sight	1–2
Social smile	2–3
Social laughter	3–4
Notices and begins to interact with peers	3–6
Holds out arms to be held	5–6
Plays peek-a-boo	5–8
Shy with strangers	8–10
Plays pat-a-cake	9–10
Waves bye-bye	9–10
Gives a toy when asked	11–12
Negativism begins	18–24
Plays interactive games (e.g., tag)	24–30
Dresses self with supervision	30–36

Sources: Taken from the Bayley Scales of Infant Development, Copyright © 1969 by the Psychological Corporation. Reproduced by permission. All rights reserved. Frankenburg, Dodds, & Fandal, 1973; Knobloch, Stevens, & Malone, 1980. Used by permission.

Burton White (1985) has identified some of the abilities an infant must eventually develop to become socially competent:

1. Getting and holding the attention of adults in socially acceptable ways.

2. Expressing affection and annoyance when appropriate.

3. Using adults as resources if a task is too difficult to accomplish alone.

4. Showing pride in personal accomplishments.

5. Engaging in role-play and make-believe activities.

6. Leading and following peers.

7. Competing with peers.

These social abilities gradually emerge and develop during the first two years of life. The socially competent infant makes behavior changes as needed to conform with age-appropriate expectations. For example, very young infants get the attention of adults by crying, but older infants are expected to use other means to get their needs met.

Parents of socially competent infants are accessible (but not overwhelming) and spend time interacting with their babies (White & Watts, 1973). They organize a stimulating, safe, and nonrestrictive environment in which the infants can develop a sense of autonomy. The type of discipline that is positive, affectionate, and encouraging of autonomy is also a very important ingredient in the development of social competence. Infants who are exposed to discipline that is negative, rigid, and overprotective demonstrate less social competence (Clarke-Stewart & Fein, 1983).

Smiling.   One of the earliest social behaviors is the social smile. Smiling is the "most significant aspect of social development to occur in the first half-year of life" (Bower, 1977, p. 49). The onset of a true social smile is a major milestone in social development. However, distinguishing social smiling from other types of smiling behavior is not an easy task. Infant smiles have been classified in two categories—**endogenous** and **exogenous** (Spitz, Emde, & Metcalf, 1970).

Newborn infants can sometimes be observed smiling while they are asleep. These smiles are called endogenous, or spontaneous, smiles because they are passive and internally controlled. They appear to be triggered by changes in the level of arousal affecting central nervous system activity (Wolff, 1963). Contrary to what parents are sometimes led to believe, the newborn is not smiling because of "gas" or hunger sensations. Endogenous smiles cannot be thought of as indicating any conscious awareness of happiness (Sroufe, 1977).

Within a week or two after birth, another type of smile can sometimes be elicited by gentle stimulation such as high-pitched baby talk or blowing on the baby's stomach. Such stimulation apparently increases the level of nervous-system excitation or arousal. A tiny smile follows within 6 to 8 seconds as the baby relaxes (Sroufe, 1977). These smiles are labeled as exogenous because they are triggered by sources of stimuli that are outside the infant (Wolff, 1963). The first elicited smiles, like the spontaneous smiles, are only partial smiles limited to the corners of the mouth.

During the second week of life, infants begin to smile when their eyes are open. Such smiles usually occur only when an infant is sated with food, drowsy, and "glassy-eyed" (Wolff, 1963). The smiles may occur spontaneously or can be elicited by the caregiver's voice. By the third week of life, babies begin to smile when they are fully awake and attentive. These smiles are fuller and more expressive. A nodding head accompanied by a high-pitched voice is a more potent stimulus for eliciting smiling at this age than a voice alone (Sroufe & Waters, 1976).

As they get older (4 to 5 weeks), infants smile in response to silent moving faces, sudden appearance of objects, and pat-a-cake games. At this point, sights are more effective than sounds in evoking smiles. As Bower (1977) points out, "the first complete smile appears to be elicited by the human voice; later the controlling stimulus shifts to the human face" (p. 38).

The age at which a true social smile appears is a matter of debate. Wolff (1963) considers the infant's first smile in response to a human voice, which occurs around 3 or 4 weeks of age, to be the beginning of social smiling. The prevailing opinion, though, is that the social smile appears at approximately 6 to 8 weeks. At this point, the stimulus is clearly social, because the infant smiles in response to human faces (Emde, Gaensfauer, & Harmon, 1976).

Between 3 and 6 months of age, infants become more discriminating in their smiling behavior. Adults have to work harder to elicit smiles from them. They are less likely to smile at familiar stimuli unless a new feature is intro-

The social smile displayed by this infant is a major milestone of development.

duced. At the same time, however, infants smile at a wider range of stimuli and smile more often over the first two years of life. The frequency of smiling increases during the third and fourth month at about the same rate in infants from many cultures around the world (Super & Harkness, 1982). Mothers from all cultures and races appear to be equally capable of eliciting smiles from their infants, although their techniques vary from culture to culture (Super, 1981). Apparently the development of smiling is related to the infant's growing cognitive awareness and sophistication (Lewis & Michalson, 1983).

Laughter. Infants typically begin to laugh between 6 weeks and 3 months of age (Frankenburg, Dodds, & Fandal, 1973). At first, infants laugh only in response to physical stimulation such as tickling or to intense sounds such as "boom boom boom." During the second six months of life, infants laugh more at visual and social stimuli. Interactions such as peek-a-boo games or the mother shaking her hair or crawling on the floor elicit laughter (Sroufe & Wunsch, 1972).

During the second year of life, infants begin to laugh at things they can participate in, such as reaching for a protruding tongue (Sroufe & Waters, 1976). Babies thus progress developmentally from laughter produced from physical stimulation to laughter based on cognitive interpretations (Sroufe, 1977). The developmental progression of laughter may be seen when the same stimuli that make younger babies cry (e.g., mother wearing a mask), make older babies laugh.

Crying. Crying has been defined as the highest "state of arousal produced by nervous system excitation triggered by some form of biological
threat . . . such as hunger, pain, sickness or insult, or individual differences in
threshold for stimulation" (Lester, 1985, p. 12). Crying begins as a reflex
response that has survival value. It is designed to elicit nurturing and protective responses from the baby's caregivers.

The amount of crying typically increases until about 6 weeks of age,
followed by a gradual decline as the infant gets older (Hunziker & Barr, 1986).
Although the evidence is not conclusive, it appears that babies cry less often
when their caregivers respond promptly and consistently (Bell & Ainsworth,
1972). Decreased crying and fussiness at night have been associated with
increased holding and carrying throughout the day (Hunziker & Barr, 1986).
Cross-cultural studies have found less prolonged crying in societies in which
infants remain close to the caretaker and in which extended carrying and
rocking are practiced (Hunziker & Barr, 1986). However, infant caregivers
should not get the impression that they need to extinguish all crying. A certain
amount of crying is necessary for the infants' behavioral organization and
normal physiological functioning.

Socially, the functional significance of crying changes with age. For the
first six months of life, infants cry to attract attention so that their physical and
psychological needs will be met. Crying is also one way an infant tells a caregiver that it wants to be let alone. In other cases, crying may be used as a means
of releasing energy or tension. However, there are periods when infants cry
for no apparent reason. Some of the young infant's unexplained crying may
be due to maturational changes in the brain that occur between 3 and 12 weeks
of age (Emde et al., 1976).

Crying, like smiling, progresses from internal to external sources of
stimulation and control (Hodapp & Mueller, 1982). During the newborn
period, infants cry primarily because they are hungry, too hot or cold, or
otherwise physically uncomfortable. As they get older, infant cries can be
traced to external stimuli such as loud noises, "looming objects," frustration
with play objects, fear of strangers, and the disappearance of the mother.
Crying thus gradually becomes more related to cognitive and emotional functions than to strictly physical demands (Lester, 1985).

Social Behavior with Peers

The socialization process involves interactions with the child's age mates,
or peers. Infants in our society begin to interact with each other very early in
life. Their interactions become increasingly social and more complex as their
skills in other areas (e.g., language) become more fully developed (Campos et
al., 1983). When infants master a particular skill, such as babbling, they begin
to use it to relate to a peer (Mueller & Vandell, 1979).

The earliest infant-infant interactions take the form of exploratory
behaviors. At about 2 months of age, infants begin to look at other infants.

Around 3 or 4 months of age, an infant will reach out and touch another infant. Smiles and vocalizations may be observed between infants by 6 months of age. As soon as they become mobile, infants follow and attempt to make physical contact with one another, exploring each other's eyes, mouths, and ears (Vandell & Mueller, 1980).

Early infant behavior directed toward a peer is relatively infrequent, brief, and simple. One study (Finkelstein et al., 1978) conducted in a day care center found that infants made contact with adults about seven times more often than they did with other babies. Most interactions of infants who are younger than 9 months old consist of a single overture and a response. In many instances (38 to 50 percent), social overtures of one infant to another do not elicit a response (Hartup, 1983).

During the last quarter of the first year of life, infant behaviors become more clearly social. Babies play peek-a-boo, run-and-chase, play ball, and they offer and accept toys (Campos et al., 1983). A month or two later, infants imitate each other and take turns in vocal interchanges. Negative and aggressive behaviors, such as biting and hair pulling, increase during the second year (Mueller & Vandell, 1979) along with positive social behaviors. However, as infants get older, the proportion of negative interchanges relative to positive ones decreases.

The frequency and complexity of peer interactions increase rapidly with age. There are some indications that toddlers are capable of forming genuine friendships with each other. An infant *peer friendship* has been defined as a relationship characterized by "proximity seeking, sharing, positive affect, and play, . . . with the two friends specifically preferring each other as interaction partners" (Vandell & Mueller, 1980, p. 190).

Press and Greenspan (1985a) followed the development of a friendship between two children in a toddler play group over a year's time. During that year their friendship progressed through several stages, from attraction and exploration to including other children in their friendship circle. They shared such activities as looking at books, working puzzles, and loading and unloading trucks and containers together. The following incident illustrates how their friendship included the discovery and sharing of humor:

> Dan and Ned's first shared joke happened like this: One day at snack time, when the children were 21 and 23 months old, respectively, Dan slapped his hand on a small blob of applesauce that had fallen from his spoon onto the table. He then looked across the table at Ned and wriggled with pleasure. Ned stared, caught his breath in surprise, and then laughed the most infectious belly laugh ever heard in that room. Dan was delighted and responded by repeating his act, after which Ned again dissolved in laughter (Press & Greenspan, 1985a, p. 28).

Influences on Peer Interactions.   Peer interactions are affected by a variety of factors. Prior experience with peers, siblings, and older children tends to contribute to the ability of an infant to engage in peer interactions (Campos et

An infant will reach out and touch another infant at an early age.

al., 1983; Shirley, 1931). These interactions are more frequent and complex among infants who are acquainted with each other and who play in dyads (twos) rather than in a larger group. (Campos et al, 1983). Infants from disadvantaged backgrounds tend to be less willing to interact with peers than infants from middle-class families (Press & Greenspan, 1985b).

Infants interact more with peers when they are in a familiar setting than an unfamiliar place. The availability of toys and the type of toys available affect peer interactions. Although toys are not essential for interaction, they are important, especially during the second year of life (Hodapp & Mueller, 1982). In some instances, infants interact more with each other under "toy absent" conditions than they do under "toy present" conditions (Vandell, Wilson, & Buchanan, 1980). However, toys appear to be necessary for infants to sustain interactions with each other over a period of time.

The influence of parents appears to be critical in determining the quantity and quality of peer interactions. Toddlers who are not securely attached to their mothers have been observed initiating the greatest number of social overtures to unfamiliar peers. However, toddlers who are securely attached to their mothers are more effective in peer interactions (Jacobson et al., 1986). Socially competent infants typically have socially competent parents. Researchers (Vandell & Wilson, 1987) found that 6- and 9-month-old infants who had extensive turn-taking experiences with their mothers engaged in extensive turn-taking interactions with a peer.

EMOTIONAL DEVELOPMENT

The term **emotion** comes from a Latin word meaning to "excite," "stir up," or "agitate." In common usage, emotions are defined simply as "feelings." Greenspan and Greenspan (1985) provide a more specific definition: "We view emotions as complex, subjective experiences that have many components, including physical, expressive, cognitive, and organizing, as well as highly personalized, subjective meanings" (p. 7). The term **affect** is sometimes used to mean the same thing as emotion or feeling.

Theories of Emotional Development

The varying definitions of emotions are the result of many divergent theories about their nature, function, and development. The various theories can be summarized in terms of biological, socialization (learning), and interactionist positions. The biological model emphasizes that an infant is innately equipped, or prewired, with emotions. The infant's emotions are viewed as comparable to sneezes and knee jerks. They are "unlearned, biologically controlled and subject to relatively little socialization influence" (Lewis & Saarni, 1985, p. 2).

According to socialization, or learning, theories, emotional development is shaped chiefly by social influences. This approach does not deny the existence of biological foundations but places more emphasis on environmental experiences. In recent years, theorists have tended to adopt an interactionist position whereby emotions are seen as a synthesis of biological and socialization processes. The innate potential for emotional expression is realized in different ways, depending on the infant's experiences with caregivers and other socialization circumstances (Murphy, 1983).

Studying Emotions

Researchers have used a variety of techniques to measure emotional expression in infants. Heart-rate monitoring, electrogalvanic skin responses, parental reports, and rating scales are some of the procedures that have been used through the years (Yarrow, 1979). In recent years, Izard (1979) has developed an elaborate system of identifying emotions through facial expressions. This system is based on the belief that the neurological foundation of the emotions results in organized facial movements in response to stimulation. Infant cries and gestural expressions have also been used as measures of emotional expression.

Influences on Emotional Development

Emotional expressiveness varies considerably from one infant to another. Numerous factors are potential sources of individual differences in the emotional responses of infants. The infant's temperamental characteristics probably exercise a major influence on emotional expression. Researchers (Derryberry & Rothbart, 1984) have found temperamental characteristics, such as activity level and soothability, to be related to the expression of both positive and negative emotions. Temperament may also affect the environmental stimuli that elicit emotional responses in infants (Yarrow, 1979).

Social class and cultural influences play an important role in emotional development. For example, in a cross-cultural study (Caudill & Schooler, 1973), American infants made more happy vocalizations than Japanese infants. At 30 months of age, American infants were more emotionally expressive and independent. Social class differences in maternal interpretations of infant emotions have also been found. Lower-class mothers who were separated from their infants labeled their infant's reactions as anger more frequently than middle-class mothers (Lewis & Michalson, 1983). Thus, adults from various cultural and subcultural backgrounds are likely to socialize the emotional displays of their infants in different ways (Zahn-Waxler, Cummings, & Cooperman, 1984).

The sex of an infant is likely to influence the socialization of emotional behavior. In face-to-face play, mothers tend to respond differently to the same emotional expressions of male and female infants. Mothers tend to smile more at boys than at girls (Malatesta & Haviland, 1985). Mothers also give a greater variety of emotional responses to a female's emotional expressions than to a male infant's. Malatesta and Haviland (1985) believe that male infants are more excitable, so mothers soon learn to limit their range of emotional response to avoid overstimulation. The exposure to more diverse emotional stimuli may partially explain why girls are better than boys at understanding emotional expression. However, few sex differences in the expression of emotions emerge during the infancy period (Zahn-Waxler et al., 1984).

Developmental Changes

Scientists who study emotional development have been interested in determining when the basic emotions first appear. The first question they ask is: "What emotions are present at birth?" For many years, it was believed that newborns display only an undifferentiated emotional state of general excitement (Bridges, 1932) and that other discrete emotions gradually appear with age and experience. New research evidence indicates that many of the basic emotions, if not all, are present at birth. Studies by Izard (1978) indicate that newborns show signs of interest, disgust, and sadness. By the time an infant is 4 months old, anger, surprise, and joy have emerged (see Table 11-2). During the second six months of life, the emotions of fear and shyness are displayed.

Other researchers (e.g., Emde, 1980) have developed a timetable of emotional development that differs from Izard's. In any case, scientists generally agree that by the end of the first year of life, infants are well equipped with basic emotional expressions. Some of the more complex emotions and emo-

TABLE 11-2   Infant Emotions: Age First Expressed

EMOTION	AGE (MONTHS)
Interest (excitement)	Birth
Sadness	Birth
Disgust	Birth
Rage, anger	2–3
Surprise	3–4
Shyness	4–5
Fear	6–8
Guilt	12–15
Shame	18–24
Contempt	24–36

Source: C. Izard, & S. Buechler, (1979). Emotion expression and personality integration in infancy. In C. Izard (Ed.), *Emotions in personality and psychopathology.* New York: Plenum Press, p. 454. Adapted by permission. C. Izard, and C. Malatesta (1987). "Perspectives on Emotional Developments I: Differential Theory of Emotional Development." In J. Osofsky (ed.), *Handbook of Infant Development* (rev. ed.). Copyright © 1987 by John Wiley and Sons, Inc. Reprinted by permission of John Wiley and Sons, Inc.

tional blends, such as guilt, sympathy, empathy, and jealousy are not expressed until the second year of life (Zahn-Waxler et al., 1984).

Infants' Understanding of Emotions

There is no general agreement about when infants recognize their own emotions (Yarrow, 1979). Due to the neurological immaturity of the newborn and very young infant, it seems likely that external indicators (e.g., crying, facial expressions) of emotional expressions are not reliable indicators of the underlying emotional experience (Campos et al., 1983). For example, when a baby first smiles, it is not necessarily an expression of joy, as it is in an adult. After the first few weeks of life, the baby's emotional expressions more closely match the underlying emotional experiences.

When do infants begin to recognize the feelings of caregivers and other people? This question is important because it involves the infant's capacity to receive emotional signals. Newborn infants sometimes begin to cry in an apparent empathic gesture when they hear other newborns crying (Martin & Clarke, 1982). Current evidence, however, indicates that infants do not understand emotional expressions of others to any meaningful degree until about 5 or 6 months of age (Michalson & Lewis, 1985). At this point, they begin to respond positively or negatively on the basis of emotions exhibited by other people (Campos et al., 1983). For example, infants smile while looking at happy faces, frown at angry faces, or cry in response to angry voices.

The ability to interpret the emotions of others improves with age. Around 9 months of age, infants begin to look for emotional indicators in the faces, voices, and gestures of their caregivers to decide what to do in uncertain situations. The term **social referencing** is used to describe this tendency

(Campos & Stenberg, 1981). For example, infants are more willing to explore a strange toy when the mother smiles than when her facial expressions show fear (Zarbatany & Lamb, 1985).

At about 18 months to 2 years of age, babies begin to comprehend verbal labels that adults use to describe emotional expressions. Michalson and Lewis (1985) found that most 2-year-olds they studied (80 percent) could point to pictures of happy and sad faces. Some of the infants (40 percent) correctly selected surprised and angry faces. The ability to produce these verbal labels ("What kind of face is this?") began to develop around 3 years. The first words infants use to correctly label corresponding facial expressions are "happy," and "sad," and "angry" (Michalson & Lewis, 1985). The following incident illustrates the infant's growing recognition of emotions:

> Today, my husband Jack came home . . . in a really good mood. He came in, dancing around and he kept picking me up and hugging me. Our daughter Jennie (18 months) came running out of the bedroom to see her daddy. When she saw us, she stopped dead in her tracks and started giggling and laughing and started saying, "Kiss, kiss." Then Jack put me down and she came up to us and said, "Me, me, kiss, kiss, love, love" and we gave her a hug (Zahn-Waxler et al., 1984, p. 45).

Two- and 3-year-old children also begin to associate emotional expressions with the situations that produced them (Michalson & Lewis, 1985). Bretherton and her colleagues (1980) found that the 28-month-old infants they studied made such cause-effect statements as "I cry (so) lady pick me up and hold me," and "Grandma angry (because) I write on wall." At this stage, infants have begun to understand that others have the same feelings as they do (Zahn-Waxler et al., 1984).

Specific Emotions

Up to this point we have been considering emotional development from a global perspective. However, it is important to keep in mind that each of the discrete emotions has its own unique pattern of evolution. Consequently, we need to consider in more detail some of the basic emotions that emerge during the infancy period.

Attachment.   Attachment is defined as "a relatively enduring emotional tie to a specific other person" (Maccoby, 1980, p. 53). Infants display attachment by behaviors such as maintaining close physical contact with the other person, crying when that person leaves, and expressing joy when the person returns (Ainsworth, 1967). The quality of parent-infant attachment has a lasting influence on socioemotional development. The formation of attachment is a two-way process in which the parent becomes attached to the child (bonding) and the child becomes attached to the parent.

INFANT-MOTHER ATTACHMENT.   The most widely used method of assessing infant-mother attachment is the Ainsworth Strange Situation

(Ainsworth et al., 1978). Infants are observed during a series of eight episodes in an unfamiliar room with a stranger. The mother is present part of the time and absent part of the time. The episodes provide an opportunity for researchers to observe the infant's reunion with the mother after being under the stress that results from being alone with a strange person in a strange situation.

Using this procedure, Ainsworth and her associates (1978) identified three basic patterns of attachment in 12-month-old infants. The largest number of infants (66 percent) were classified as *securely attached* (group B). These babies were able to use the mother as a secure base to explore the environment. They were interested in the objects in the room, did not cling to the mother, and interacted positively with the stranger. Although they were distressed when the mother left the room, they were easily comforted when the mother returned and they soon resumed their play.

A second group of infants were rated as *insecurely attached*. Two patterns of this type of attachment were observed. A few of the infants (12 percent) were labeled *anxiously attached* or *avoidant* (group A). They did not protest when separated from their mothers. When the mothers returned, they were avoided or completely ignored. Another group (22 percent) of the infants (group C) displayed an *ambivalently attached* or *resistant* pattern of attachment. These infants were very upset when their mothers left the room. Although they ran to their mothers when they were reunited, they demonstrated insecurity by a mixture of clinging and resistant (kicking and pushing away) behavior.

Much of the research on infant-mother attachment has been based on the theory of John Bowlby (1969), who identified four stages in the formation of attachment:

1. *Preattachment: Undiscriminating social responsiveness (birth to 8–12 weeks)*. During this phase, infants do not typically differentiate one person from another and can be comforted by anyone.

2. *Beginnings of attachment: Discriminating social responsiveness (3 to 6–8 months)*. The infant begins to recognize the primary caregiver and a few other familiar people. These preferred adults are usually able to soothe the baby and elicit social responses more quickly than strangers.

3. *Clear-cut attachment: Maintaining proximity (6–8 months to about 3 years)*. Around the middle of the first year, infants are typically attached to one specific person. This person is usually the mother, although some infants prefer the father or other caregivers.

4. *Formation of a goal-corrected partnership (third or fourth year on)*. This phase begins when children recognize that other people have needs and desires of their own and that the mother has to give priority to other activities at times.

INFANT-FATHER ATTACHMENT. Bowlby believed that, at first, infants do not have the capacity to form more than one attachment bond. Research studies have shown, however, that most babies become attached to both

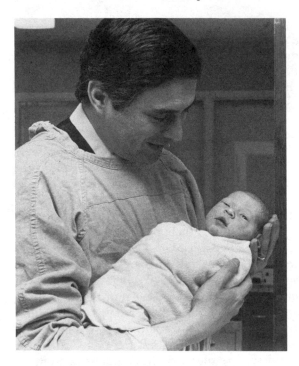

A father becomes as attached to
an infant as a mother does.

mother and father at about the same time—7 months (Lamb & Bornstein, 1987). Although infants spend less time interacting with their fathers than their mothers, they seek physical contact and comfort from both parents in about equal proportions (Lamb, 1982c). Infants apparently go through a period, between 12 and 18 months, when they turn to their mothers more than their fathers in stressful situations. The preference for the mother under stress disappears around 24 months of age (Lamb, 1982c).

INFLUENCES ON INFANT-PARENT ATTACHMENT.   The characteristics of the primary caregiver (usually the mother) are probably the most important factor in the attachment process. Caregiver behaviors associated with secure attachment include acceptance, warmth and affection, accessibility, and cooperation with the infant (Maccoby, 1980). Mothers of securely attached infants have been found to be more accepting, sensitive, and emotionally expressive than mothers of insecurely attached infants (Main et al., 1979).

Harlow's studies of infant monkeys reared in isolation from their mothers may offer some clues about the formation of attachment bonds (Harlow & Zimmerman, 1959). The monkeys were reared in a cage with two artificial mothers. One of the mothers was made of wire mesh, and the other consisted of wire mesh covered with terry cloth. The monkeys invariably became attached only to the terry cloth mother, even when the plain mother held the nursing bottle. Harlow concluded that contact comfort is an important variable in the formation of attachment.

The temperament of the infant may be an important source of influence on the way attachment develops. Theoretically, the infant's temperament affects the quality of the parent-infant interaction, which subsequently determines the quality of attachment. Infants who are "ambivalently attached" tend to have characteristics of temperament (e.g., irritability, crying) that fit the "difficult child" classification. (Miyake, Chen, & Campos, 1985). However, researchers have not been able to confirm a strong relationship between all aspects of temperament and attachment behavior (Bretherton & Waters, 1985).

MULTIPLE CAREGIVING. In many societies, infants are exposed to a variety of caregivers. Does an infant suffer emotional harm as the result of having to develop emotional ties with several different people? Evidence from infants reared in the Israeli kibbutzim is relevant to this question. A kibbutz is an agricultural settlement where infants are, to a large extent, reared outside the home. Their time is spent largely in "infant houses" under the care of professional caregivers called *metaplot* (singular—*metapelet*). The parents, however, are accessible and frequently spend time with their infants. Researchers have found that kibbutz infants demonstrate normal patterns of attachment and emotional development (Super, 1981). In comparison to American infants cared for at home, kibbutz infants demonstrate no significant differences in attachment to their mothers (Maccoby & Feldman, 1972).

MOTHER-INFANT ATTACHMENT: BONDING. The process by which a parent becomes attached to an infant is sometimes called **bonding** (Klaus & Kennell, 1982). In some cases, however, bonding is used more specifically to refer to the establishment of an enduring affectionate attachment of a mother to her infant as the result of skin-to-skin contact during the first few hours after birth (Campos et al., 1983).

The belief that the first few hours after birth represent a "sensitive period" for maternal-infant attachment originated in the study of animals. In some species, such as sheep and goats, the mother will reject her offspring if they are separated from her for a short period of time as soon as they are born. In recent years, researchers have attempted to determine whether or not the sensitive period hypothesis applies to human infants.

A number of studies have reported increased frequencies of affectionate behaviors by mothers who were given extended early contact with their infants (Klaus & Kennell, 1976; Svejda, Pannabecker, & Emde, 1982). These studies, however, have been criticized for serious methodological problems as well as their failure to find any long-term effects (Lamb, 1982a). More carefully controlled studies (e.g., Svejda, Campos, & Emde, 1980) have failed to find evidence that early contact experiences are necessary for bonding to occur. Furthermore, in 80 percent of the world's cultures, mother and infants do not have immediate skin-to-skin contact, and nursing is not started until three days after birth (Super, 1981). Consequently, the belief that mothers will not love their infants adequately if extended skin-to-skin contact does not occur soon after birth seems to be unfounded.

FATHER-INFANT BONDING.   The importance of father-infant bonding has been recognized in recent years. Researchers have not been successful in identifying a critical or sensitive period for establishing father-infant attachment (Jones, 1985). In one study (Svejda et al., 1982), fathers were given extra contact with their infants during the first two days after delivery. When the interactions of these fathers with their infants were compared with those of another group of fathers who were not given extra contact, no differences were found.

In any case, though, fathers apparently become just as attached to infants as mothers. Studies (Parke & O'Leary, 1976; Parke & Sawin, 1977) have found fathers to be just as interested as mothers in their infants during the newborn period. Fathers tend to be just as nurturing and stimulating with their infant as mothers. Like mothers, fathers touch, talk to, look at, and kiss their newborns. They are competent caregivers and are responsive to infant distress such as spitting up (Belsky & Volling, 1987).

Anxiety-Fear.   Infants typically begin to show signs of fear and anxiety around 6 months of age (Izard, 1977). At about this time, infants react negatively or warily to strangers, heights (visual cliffs), approaching (looming) objects, separation from their attachment figures, and stimuli associated with pain (doctors' offices). Fear responses in infants include the startle reflex, crying, clinging to the caregiver, and a fearful facial expression. The stimuli that elicit fear in infants generally increase in number over the first eighteen months of life (Lewis & Michalson, 1983). During the third year of life, the sources of fear change and begin to include imaginary stimuli such as wild animals. The development of two types of fear—stranger anxiety and separation anxiety—parallel the development of attachment.

STRANGER ANXIETY.   A 9-month-old infant is sitting on the living room floor playing with a ball. A new neighbor who is visiting walks over, kneels down close to the infant, and says, "She is a beautiful baby!" The baby takes one look at the stranger and begins to cry. Fear of strangers emerges during the last half of the first year of life and reaches a peak frequency around 12 months. Girls tend to display negative reactions to strangers a little earlier than boys (Lewis & Michalson, 1983). The incidence declines slightly at the beginning of the second year and rises once again between 18 and 24 months (Scarr & Salapatek, 1970; Lewis & Michalson, 1983). After that time, stranger fear gradually declines.

Infants are less likely to show a fear of strangers if they are being held by a primary caregiver (Mussen, Conger, & Kagan, 1974), and if the strangers are children, especially of the same sex (Brooks & Lewis, 1976). Infants react more negatively to strangers who intrude in familiar, predictable settings (Brookhart

& Hock, 1976). Babies who are free to move away are less likely to cry in response to a strange person than babies who are restrained (Bronson, 1972). They also are more likely to be afraid of male than female strangers (Lewis & Brooks, 1974). The extent to which a stranger's behavior is predictable or contingent upon the infant's own responses (e.g., a smile for a smile) is likely to affect the amount of anxiety exhibited (Bronson, 1972).

The infant's responsiveness to strangers is affected by the security of attachment to the mother and experiences within the family. Infants who are securely attached to the mother are much more sociable with strangers than less securely attached infants (Thompson & Lamb, 1984). The quality of the baby's attachment to other family members is also an important influence in stranger sociability. No consistent relationship has been found between the infant's previous experiences with other people outside the family and stranger anxiety (Thompson & Lamb, 1984). However, cross-cultural studies suggest that stranger anxiety is more intense and lasts longer in societies in which infants have more limited contact with strangers than they typically do in America (Super & Harkness, 1982).

SEPARATION ANXIETY. An 11-month-old boy is playing in the living room of a neighbor. He looks up and sees his mother disappear into the kitchen with the neighbor. He begins to follow as quickly as possible, crying loudly. This is an example of separation anxiety that is typically seen in infants around 8 or 9 months of age. It reaches a peak around 12 months and begins to disappear toward the end of the second year (Lewis & Michalson, 1983).

A case of separation anxiety: This infant is very reluctant to leave the mother.

However, displays of separation anxiety continue longer in some cultures than in others. Separation distress remains longer in infants who are cared for exclusively by the mother than in infants who are also cared for by siblings and other persons (Super & Harkness, 1982).

Both separation and stranger anxiety are emotions that typically are not learned through unpleasant experiences, although that is possible. Some theorists believe that these are among a group of innate emotions that have survival value by keeping the infant close to the parent. The emergence of stranger fear and separation anxiety have also been attributed to cognitive growth, including changes in recall memory, and the object concept (Bronson, 1972). With growing cognitive maturity, infants learn more about the environment and develop a set of expectations. Unfamiliar persons are perceived by infants as discrepant or contradictory stimuli that do not match familiar mental images. The infant thus responds with expressions of anxiety.

Pleasure-Joy.   The development of pleasurable feelings in young infants is expressed mainly in smiling and laughter. The exact age at which the infant's smiles and laughter actually reflect an underlying state of pleasure and happiness is not known. The argument has been made (Emde et al., 1976) that the neonatal smile represents a positive or pleasurable emotional tone, since smiling has not been observed when infants are distressed. However, the signs of pleasure and joy are more definite about the time the infant begins to smile in response to the human face (Izard, 1978).

Anger.   Mothers and scientists alike have reported expressions of anger in the cries and facial expressions of infants as early as the neonatal period. Sroufe (1979) believes that these early "mad" expressions are more correctly identified as primitive responses to extreme distress. Anger is more differentiated and readily identified in infants around the third month of life (Izard, 1978). Expressions of anger become more frequent during the latter half of the first year (Sroufe, 1977; Emde et al., 1976) and gradually increase with age throughout infancy (Lewis & Michalson, 1983).

Young infants usually express anger through crying, angry, flushed facial expressions, and increased motor activity. By 1 year of age an infant's angry reactions are likely to include foot stomping, kicking, throwing, or knocking away objects (Sroufe, 1979). Two-year-olds also use defiant verbal expressions ("No!") and aggressive acts such as pushing, biting, and hitting. Their responses are more directly targeted toward the source of anger. Parents begin to socialize infants very early in acceptable ways to express anger (e.g., no biting).

The earliest sources of anger are physical restraints that inhibit an infant's movements. Barriers that prevent a baby from reaching a goal, such as a toy, also cause anger. The developing sense of self-awareness and the need for independence result in new sources of anger as the infant's goals come into conflict with parental demands and expectations. The "terrible twos" are characterized by increased resistance to adult demands as temper tantrums reach a peak.

Autistic Infants

In some cases infants fail to develop normal socioemotional relationships with their parents and other people. A small percentage of these infants (about 2 to 4 per 10,000) are affected by a syndrome known as **autism** (Rutter & Garmezy, 1983). In some infants, the symptoms of this disorder become evident during the first few weeks of life. In other cases, infants display normal development for the first year or two of life before any signs of autism appear (Freeman & Ritvo, 1984).

A major characteristic of autistic infants is their lack of responsiveness to other people. These infants usually do not make normal eye-to-eye contact or hold out their arms to be picked up the way normal infants do. They are typically "noncuddlers," although at times they may cling to a caregiver. Autistic infants apparently do not give or receive pleasure in their relationships with others. Caregivers find them unaffectionate and difficult to engage in games such as peek-a-boo. They tend to be easily upset by changes in their environment and caregiving routines (Freeman & Ritvo, 1984; Rutter & Garmezy, 1983).

Autistic infants also have problems in acquiring normal speech and nonverbal communication skills. Many do not speak at all, whereas others only echo what another person says. Another group of symptoms involves abnormal and uneven patterns of sensorimotor development. Autistic infants tend to either underrespond or overrespond to stimuli. They may engage in repetitive activities and motor movements such as rocking, hand flapping, or staring (Ritvo & Freeman, 1977). Some autistic infants may bang their heads, bite themselves, and engage in other self-destructive behaviors.

Autism occurs at about the same rate all over the world. It affects all races, social classes, and types of families in equal proportions. However, boys are more frequently affected by autism than girls by a ratio of about three or four to one (Freeman & Ritvo, 1983; Rutter & Garmezy, 1984). The problems associated with autism are frequently combined with other syndromes, diseases and developmental disabilities such as mental retardation and epilepsy (Freeman & Ritvo, 1984).

A few years ago, it was widely believed that autism was caused by disturbances in normal mothering and family functioning. However, there is no scientific evidence to support the assumption that autism results from bad parenting. At present, scientists believe that autism is the result of some type of defect in the central nervous system caused by genetic or environmental problems. (Ritvo & Freeman, 1984).

Autistic infants have a normal life expectancy, but the outlook for their life's quality is not good. Currently there is no cure for autism. Approximately

75 percent of all autistic infants remain mentally retarded throughout life. Even infants with the mildest form and fewest symptoms continue to have problems in personality, emotional, social, and mental functions. Current methods of treating autism include structured education programs based on behavior-modification technology, along with medications to control some of the symptoms (Ritvo & Freeman, 1984).

FACILITATING SOCIAL/EMOTIONAL DEVELOPMENT

Parents cannot control all the factors that influence an infant's social and emotional development. However, there are numerous practices and activities that parents as well as other caregivers can use to promote healthy development in those areas. In general, the most important thing to give the infant is a feeling of being cared for and loved. The same caregivers should be consistently available to play and interact with the baby. The following are some recommended principles and practices.

1. "Woo" the baby. Fall in love with the baby and allow it to fall in love with you. Set aside time for loving and pleasant interchanges, including rocking, hugging, cuddling, smiling, touching, eye contact, talking, and singing.

2. Allow babies to have moments of peace. It is important to respect an infant's desire not to interact with people or other outside stimuli from time to time. (Provence, 1967).

3. Accept an infant's feelings as real and valid even if the behavior is not acceptable ("I can't allow you to hit me, but I understand that you are angry with me right now.") (Gonzalez-Mena & Eyer, 1980).

4. Express your own emotions honestly but appropriately. Infants benefit from being exposed to a wide range of emotions (Greenspan & Greenspan, 1985).

5. Help infants identify and label their feelings through reflective listening. ("You feel sad because Mommy has gone to work." "Look at your brother smile. He looks happy!").

6. Help babies find appropriate and alternative ways to express emotional intentions. ("Show me what you want without crying.") (Greenspan & Greenspan, 1985).

7. Some infants need to have a stuffed animal, blanket, and other "security" object to help make the transition from parental dependency to personal independence easier. This is normal as long as it does not represent a deficit in parental attention.

8. Insofar as possible and appropriate, control the stimuli that evoke negative feelings such as anger and fear (e.g., a night light can be provided for the infant who is afraid of the dark). However, infants should not be overprotected.

9. Never use fear and guilt to control an infant's behavior. Avoid statements such as "There is a ghost in that closet that will come out and get you if you don't stop crying!"

10. Encourage independency and self-sufficiency. In general, avoid doing things for infants that they can do for themselves.

11. Child care facilities should arrange for each caregiver to have responsibility for the same infants each day.

12. There should be opportunities for the baby to be part of the adult world. An infant should have opportunities to interact with adults of both sexes and of various ages.

Additional suggestions may be found in sources such as Bromwich (1980); Grasselli and Hegner, 1980; Karnes, 1982; Sparling and Lewis, 1979; Weiser, 1982; and White, 1985.

SUMMARY

1. Socialization is the process by which infants learn to behave in accordance with cultural expectations through interactions with parents and other people.

2. Socially competent infants possess the ability to relate to other people effectively and to get their needs met. Mothers of socially competent babies are accessible, create a safe, stimulating environment, and provide appropriate discipline.

3. Social smiling, laughing, and crying are the first indicators of the infant's social awareness. The age at which the first true social smile typically appears is debatable and depends on the criteria that are used to define smiling. The earliest age at which social smiling is considered to appear is 3 or 4 weeks. Babies begin to laugh at 3 or 4 months of age. Crying is a reflexive activity that is present at birth but becomes more socially responsive with age.

4. The earliest infant-peer social interactions begin at approximately 2 months of age, when infants look at each other. Their interactions become more complex and frequent with age as they begin to combine smiling and laughter with playing games. Peer interactions during infancy are influenced by social class, the social setting, availability of toys, and parent-infant attachment.

5. Emotions are generally viewed as complex, subjective experiences that are influenced by a combination of biological and social forces. The infant's temperament, social class, sex, and cognitive sophistication are included among the factors that affect emotional responses.

6. Infants begin to exhibit many of the basic emotions at birth or soon thereafter (e.g., disgust, distress, anger). Most of the additional basic emotions appear during the second six months of life (e.g., fear). The more complex emotions and emotional blends emerge during the second year (e.g., guilt, sympathy).

7. Infants begin to understand the emotional expressions of others at approximately 5 or 6 months of age. The ability to interpret, label, and comprehend emotions improves with age.

8. Basic patterns of infant-mother attachment include securely attached, anxiously attached, and ambivalently attached. Bowlby identified four stages in the formation of infant-parent attachment. Infants become equally attached to both fathers and mothers when given appropriate opportunities. In stressful situations, however, 12- to 18-month-old infants prefer their mothers.

9. Recent research studies have not supported the theory that the first few hours after birth are a critical period for bonding, or parent-infant attachment.

10. Stranger anxiety and separation anxiety are closely related emotions that appear during the second six months of life, after infants have become attached to their parents. After reaching a peak around 12 months of age, the strength of these emotions declines.

11. Infants may exhibit expressions of anger during the newborn period, although this emotion is more clearly observable after 3 or 4 months of age. Physical restraints or other barriers and the infant's need to develop autonomy are major sources of anger during infancy.

12. Autism is a major socioemotional disorder that affects a small percentage of infants. The symptoms of autism, which begin before 30 months of age, include lack of responsiveness to other people, failure to acquire normal speech, repetitive motor activities, and self-destructive behaviors. Boys are more likely to be affected by this disorder than girls. Autism is apparently caused by a defect in the central nervous system.

13. To facilitate healthy socioemotional development, caregivers need to consistently engage in practices that give infants the feeling that they are cared for and loved.

12

Infant Caregiving And Education

Your children are not your children
They are the son's and daughters of Life's longing for itself.
They come through you but not from you,
And though they are with you yet they belong not to you . . .
You are the bows from which your children as living arrows are sent forth . . .
Let your bending in the archer's hand be for gladness.

—*Kahil Gibran*

Most infants experience the world and the people in it within the setting of a family. Society assigns primary responsibility for the care of the young to the family. The infant must receive a certain amount of personal care and nurturing for healthy growth and development to occur. The crucial nature of those family experiences for every aspect of infant development cannot be overstated. But the influence is mutual. Infants interact with their caregivers from the beginning. In those interactions, infants influence parents and others just as they are influenced. Infants give as they receive.

In this chapter we consider some of the changes occurring in the American family that have implications for infant development, such as single parenting, maternal employment, and father absence. A major portion of the chapter is devoted to the experiences infants have in nonparental care outside the home. We also look at various types of early-intervention programs designed to enhance the development of infants from impoverished families. In addition, we consider the characteristics of a favorable home environment, including the processes of parent-infant interaction, discipline, and the provision of appropriate toys and play materials.

CURRENT TRENDS IN THE AMERICAN FAMILY

The traditional American family with the breadwinner father and the homemaker mother is rapidly disappearing. A diversity of family forms is emerging to replace the traditional family, including dual-worker families, single-parent families, and blended or stepfamilies (Strong & DeVault, 1986). Increasing divorce rates, the movement of women into the labor force, increased rates of teen-age pregnancy, decreasing family size, and numerous other social changes have contributed to the transformation. Changes that have significant implications for infant development are the increases in the number of single-parent families and the number of working mothers.

Single-Parent Families

The numbers of single-parent families have grown more rapidly than the numbers of married couple families in recent years. Between 1970 and 1985 the number of children living with only one parent rose by 6 million. This represents more than a 50 percent increase in the one-parent population. During the same time period, the number of children living with both parents actually declined by 13 million. In 1985, one out of four children in the United

States (23.4 percent) lived with only one parent (U.S. Bureau of the Census, 1987a). That number is expected to double, to two out of four, by the year 2000. The rise in the number of single-parent households can be attributed mainly to increases in rates of divorce and separation.

Researchers have been interested in determining the extent to which the presence or absence of children contributes to the decision to divorce. Although marriage counselors do not advise couples to have a baby to save a shaky marriage, divorce and separation appear to be moderately lower for couples who have children than for the childless (Cherlin, 1977). Also, couples with children who eventually divorce stay together longer than childless couples (Wallerstein & Kelly, 1980; Rankin and Maneker, 1985). However, when the age of the child is taken into consideration, a slightly different conclusion emerges. Rankin & Maneker (1985) found that the presence of one or more children under 2 years of age resulted in an earlier divorce.

The majority of children in single-parent families are being reared by their mothers. In 1985, 88.1 percent of the one-parent families were being maintained by mothers, in comparison to the 11.9 percent maintained by fathers. There are indications, however, that more men are assuming the responsibility for maintaining single-parent families. Between 1980 and 1985, the families headed by men alone increased at a greater rate than families maintained by women alone as well as married-couple families (U.S. Bureau of the Census, 1986). The single-parent home headed by the father is more likely to contain older children than infants and toddlers.

Impact of Single-Parent Families.   Does it make any difference whether an infant grows up in a single-parent family or a two-parent family? Eidusun

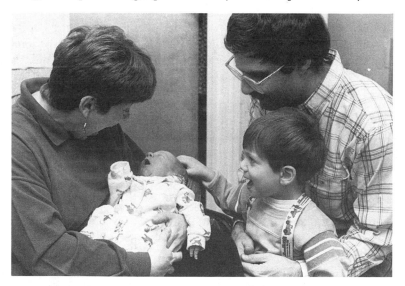

The number of infants who are reared in two parent families is declining.

and colleagues (1982) compared infants who were reared from birth in single-mother families with infants reared in traditional two-parent families and alternative families (communal and unmarried social-contract families). A variety of psychological variables, including attachment, cognitive functioning, and social adjustment, were assessed repeatedly during the infant's first three years. No significant differences between the single-mother infants and infants reared in the other families were discovered. There is little additional research that addresses the impact of the single-parent family on infants. Consequently, studies dealing with the effects of divorce, stress, and father absence on children must be examined for additional information on this issue.

Effects of Divorce.   Because of their cognitive immaturity, very young infants are expected to be less affected by some of the trauma caused by divorce. However, their immaturity and greater dependency needs may actually make them developmentally more vulnerable to the effects of divorce in some ways. Santrock (1970, 1972) assessed the effects of divorce on children who were under age 2 at the time. These children displayed less basic trust, more guilt and shame, less industry, and more feelings of inferiority as they grew older. When divorce occurs during infancy, there may also be negative effects upon intellectual development and achievements later in life.

Effects of Stress.   Single parents experience far greater levels of tension, stress, and conflict in coping with the practical problems of living than parents in intact families. This is particularly true when infants are involved. Some of the most prevalent stresses include economic problems, finding adequate child care, and simply having time and energy to devote to children (Hetherington, 1979).

Wallerstein and Kelly (1980) found that the stress and conflict that accompany divorce result in a "diminished parenting" effect whereby the parents' ability to maintain interaction and communication with their children is lessened. These findings are consistent with the results of other studies. In a laboratory setting, parents were more critical and irritable with their toddlers when they were mildly stressed while performing a task than when the parents were not preoccupied (Zussman, 1980). Hetherington, Cox, and Cox (1982) found that during the first year after divorce, mothers tend to decrease their responsiveness and affection to their children.

The most important factor in the ability of single parent families to cope with stress appears to be the support system available in the extended family network and in society. When adequate economic resources, assistance with child care, housing, and the emotional support of a kinship and social network are available, the potential stresses and problems faced by single-parent families are dramatically reduced (Hetherington, 1979).

Effects of Father Absence.   The quality and the degree of the father's involvement, even in the first year of life, are important factors in the child's sex role, personality, and mental development (Biller, 1981). In one study, black male infants from low socioeconomic single-mother families scored lower on measures of mental development and social responsiveness than their peers from two-parent families (Pedersen, Rubenstein, & Yarrow, 1979). Wachs and Gruen (1982) concluded that boys raised without fathers may have problems establishing appropriate sex role behavior, such as a tendency to be less masculine or to display exaggerated masculinity. The effects are particularly noticeable if the separation occurred before 5 years of age. Sex role development of girls is also negatively affected by father absence, but the effects are not usually observed until adolescence.

Apparently father absence does more damage when it occurs during infancy than at later ages (Lamb, 1976). Santrock (1970) found that fifth-grade boys who experienced father absence before the age of 2 had more personality problems than boys who lost their fathers at a later age. The boys who experienced father absence during infancy were less trusting, less industrious, and exhibited more feelings of inferiority than boys who were without fathers between 3 and 5 years of age. A study conducted on the Caribbean island of Barbados revealed that school-age males had same-sex identification problems if their father had been absent during the first two years of life (Burton, 1972). Other studies have found early father absence to be associated with increased susceptibility to a variety of behavioral and psychological problems (Biller, 1981).

Working Mothers

Each year more and more women enter the labor force. The majority of these women are mothers. The fastest-growing segment of working women is the group of mothers who have children under 1 year of age. Between 1982 and 1983, this group of working women increased by 45 percent (Belsky, 1987). In 1985, approximately one out of every two mothers of infants under 12 months of age were employed (Belsky, 1987; Kamerman, 1986).

Effects of Maternal Employment. Questions and concerns about the effects of maternal employment on family living have generated considerable interest by social scientists. In general, research on maternal employment indicates that employment affects the mother's emotional state in both positive and negative ways (Hoffman, 1974). Sometimes the mother is happier working than staying home. On the other hand, the role overload and conflict as well as a sense of guilt, which often occurs, may create a negative emotional mood at home. One of the most important factors is the mother's satisfaction with her job.

Whether or not the quality of parent-infant relations is affected by maternal employment is uncertain. Two studies (Cohen, 1978; Hock, 1980) reviewed by Hoffman (1979) found no difference in the quality of mother-child interactions between working and nonworking mothers during the infant's first year of life. One of the studies (Cohen, 1978) found differences during the infant's second year that favored infant relationships with non-working mothers. The results of the study (Hoffman, 1979) are questionable, though, because of inadequate controls for the possible effects of father absence and prematurity.

Additional studies reviewed by Lamb (1982b) suggest that insecure infant-mother attachments are more likely to develop in infants of working mothers as compared to nonworking mothers. Chase-Lansdale and Owen (1987) found that infant boys in employed-mother families were more likely to be insecurely attached to both parents than infant boys in nonemployed-mother homes. Apparently male babies are perceived as tougher and less in need of nurturing than female babies. The mother's attitude appears to be a crucial factor. When working mothers value both parenthood and their job, their infants tend to have no problems in forming secure attachment relationships (Lamb, 1982b). Most researchers have studied the effects of maternal employment indirectly by assessing the impact of day care on infants.

Infant Day Care

Day Care Arrangements. Working parents are presented with a variety of options when shopping for a child care arrangement. The choices are usually categorized according to three basic types of care: center day care; family day care in the home of a relative, friend or professional caregiver; and care in the infant's own home by a relative or "sitter." Approximately 27 percent of children under 3 years of age participating in day care are cared for by a relative in the parent's home, and 18 percent are cared for in the relative's

Group day care is a common experience for infants from many contemporary families.

home (U.S. Bureau of the Census, 1987b). An additional 24 percent of infants in day care are placed in a family day care home, and 10 percent are cared for in day care centers (Kamerman, 1986; Belsky, 1987). Although only a small proportion of infants are enrolled in day care centers, this is the fastest-growing type of day care offered to the general public.

Effects of Day Care. Questions and concerns about possible negative effects of nonmaternal care on infants have generated a substantial amount of research in the past two decades. The earliest studies on the effects of day care were conducted in the 1970s and were limited mostly to high-quality day care centers designed specifically for research purposes. During the 1980s additional studies that are more representative of the quality of care available to the general public have emerged. In spite of some of the problems and limitations of the studies, there are a number of consistent findings on how day care affects various aspects of infant development.

PHYSICAL DEVELOPMENT.   In general, day care has not been perceived as a threat to normal physical growth, so very little research has been done in this area. The limited research available indicates that infants from poor families who participate in good-quality day care experience positive gains in height, weight, and motor performance. The physical growth of infants from middle-class families apparently is not affected by day care (Clarke-Stewart & Fein, 1983).

HEALTH.   Infants who attend any type of day care with more than three other infants can be expected to be sick more frequently than infants who do not participate in day care. They have more incidents of colds, flu, and other respiratory illnesses than infants who stay at home (Strangert, 1976; Kendall, 1983). In addition, type B influenzae, hepatitis A, and diarrhea are some of the most common and persistent health problems that are associated with day care. The transmission of diarrhea and hepatitis is usually the result of the breakdown of proper sanitation practices, such as hand washing after diaper changes (Trump & Karasic, 1983; Snow, 1983).

INTELLECTUAL DEVELOPMENT.   Good-quality day care has no obvious harmful or beneficial effects on the intellectual development of middle-class infants. However, the stimulation provided in a high-quality day care program prevents the decline in scores of intelligence typically observed in infants from the lower socioeconomic class after 2 years of age. Clarke-Stewart and Fein (1983) believe that some programs actually contribute to an increase in the IQ score.

SOCIAL DEVELOPMENT.   The results of studies that have assessed the effects of day care on social development have produced a mixed picture. While some studies have found no differences between home-reared and day care subjects, others suggest that day care can have both positive and negative effects on social behavior. Children who begin day care as infants have a tendency to display more aggression and other negative interactions with peers and are less obedient than children who were not enrolled in day care (Belsky, in press). On the positive side, day care children have been found to exhibit more social competence in interacting with peers and adults (Snow, 1983).

EMOTIONAL DEVELOPMENT.   Research on the effects of day care on emotional development has been limited mostly to studies on the infant's attachment to the mother. The reviewers of these studies generally agree that infants who participate in good day care do not suffer loss of attachment or become overtly anxious or insecure. However, Belsky (1988) asserts that recent studies (e.g., Belsky & Rovine, 1988; Barglow, Vaughan, & Molitor, 1987) indicate that full-day nonmaternal care for infants *under 1 year of age* may be risky. Infants who are enrolled in day care at that age for more than 20 hours per week may have problems in forming secure attachments with their parents. When combined with the studies that show negative effects on social development, Belsky believes that the evidence favors an overall conclusion that day care is harmful for very young infants.

Belsky's conclusion has evoked considerable controversy and debate about infant day care. There is general agreement, however, that this is a very important issue that merits further exploration. Additional studies that reveal consistent findings will be necessary before this issue can be settled. In the meantime, the overall weight of the evidence and professional opinion does not merit advising parents to avoid day care for young infants, as long as the quality is good.

Day Care Quality.   The most critical factor in considering the effects of day care on infants is the quality of the care that is used. The quality of day care varies widely among facilities. Rating day care quality on a scale ranging from poor to excellent, Endsley and Bradbard (1981) estimate that approximately 22 percent of all day care centers fall within the poor range. Only about 7 percent of the centers are expected to obtain an excellent rating. Most of the "center" type of day care available to the general public thus falls somewhere in the middle range of the quality scale. Generally, nonprofit facilities (e.g., community agencies, churches) are rated as superior in quality to profit-making centers (Hall & Weiner, 1977). Unfortunately, the availability of nonprofit facilities is very limited.

Much less is known about the quality of family day care in which care is provided in a home other than the child's residence. These facilities are difficult to identify and study because many states do not have laws regulating this type of care. A government-sponsored national day care home study (Fosberg, 1981) found that the quality of family day care varies considerably among facilities. Generally, homes that were sponsored by a government or nonprofit agency provided better care than homes that were simply registered or licensed or not regulated at all. Other reports (Emlen, cited in Belsky et al., 1982; Hall & Weiner, 1977) indicate that licensed and supervised homes have more favorable adult-child staff ratios than unlicensed homes.

Components of Day Care Quality. Researchers and caregivers have identified many of the critical factors that are associated with good-quality day care. There is general agreement that the staff-child ratio, group size, caregiver training and other qualifications, continuity of care, and parent involvement are the most important factors in assessing day care for infants.

The maximum number of infants that can be adequately cared for by one caregiver is generally considered to be three or four. (Kagan, Kearsley, & Zelazo, 1978; Ruopp et al., 1979). The maximum group size is eight infants or toddlers. Unfortunately, most licensing laws do not require day care facilities to meet ideal standards. In some states, one adult may be allowed to care for as many as eight babies. The caregiver-infant ratio is the major factor affecting the cost of care. Staff salaries are the most expensive part of day care, so when more staff are employed, the cost of care increases. Thus, most day care facilities do not maintain higher standards than those required by law.

The second most important factor in assessing the quality of infant day care appears to be the qualifications of the provider. Researchers have found that day care providers who have education related to understanding and meeting the needs of infants provide better care with superior results than caregivers without appropriate training (Fosberg, 1981; Ruopp et al., 1979). Effective interpersonal skills along with commitment and concern for infants and their families are also important caregiver qualifications (Clarke-Stewart, 1982). Unfortunately, many states do not require day care providers to have any training or preparation in the care of infants and young children.

Continuity and stability of caregivers and caregiving arrangements appear to be very important considerations for infants, especially when they are in the peak period for stranger anxiety. Although not all of the research studies (e.g., Schiller, 1980) have found negative consequences associated with frequent changes in care givers, conventional wisdom and much of the research (e.g., Cummings, 1980) support this conclusion. The child's family situation is an important variable that affects the outcome of care in any event. Continuity of care is apparently more important for children from broken families than it is for infants who live with both parents (Belsky, 1984; Belsky, Steinberg & Walker, 1982).

High-quality day care programs include parent involvement and participation as a major component. The more parents are involved in the day care program, the more children benefit (Zigler & Turner, 1982). Parents can become involved in an infant-toddler day care program in numerous ways, including serving on an advisory board, as a program observer, or helping with special projects. Regular communication between parent and caregiver is viewed as an essential feature of good day care. Unfortunately, parents average only about seven minutes per day in their child's day care center (Zigler & Turner, 1982). Most of the parent-caregiver contacts occur at "transition points" when children arrive and depart (Powell, 1978).

EARLY-INTERVENTION PROGRAMS

As a part of the War on Poverty initiated by the federal government in the 1960s, a variety of early intervention programs were developed for infants and their parents. These programs were designed primarily to prevent the decline in intelligence scores that often results from environmental deprivation. Many of these efforts were designed as experimental programs to test the effectiveness of intervention in general as well as specific educational models (Beller, 1979). Some of the programs were designed to teach parents how to teach their infants. Other programs focused directly on providing stimulation for the infants. The programs also varied on whether the activities were conducted on an individual basis in the home or in groups at a center. A few model programs were developed in the form of centers designed to work both with parents and their infants.

The first intervention programs were directed primarily at infants considered to be developmentally "at risk" because of the effects of poverty. More recent programs have been developed to serve infants affected by handicapping conditions such as genetic disorders, hearing impairments, and visual handicaps (Trohanis, Cox, & Meyer, 1982).

Lasting Effects of Early Intervention

The results of early-intervention programs are consistent in demonstrating positive short-range effects on the development of lower-class disadvantaged infants (Beller, 1979). To determine whether or not these benefits last, investigators from twelve early-intervention programs pooled their information and conducted a joint follow-up study. Their participants were aged 9 to 19 at the time. The findings clearly show that the early-intervention programs had long-lasting beneficial effects (Lazar & Darlington, 1979; Lazar & Darlington, 1982). The children who participated in the early-intervention programs were more likely than the control children to perform better in their schools in the following ways:

1.   The number of children assigned to special-education classes was reduced by approximately 50 percent.
2.   The number of children failing a grade in school was reduced.
3.   The program participants achieved superior scores on fourth-grade math tests. There was also a trend toward increased scores on fourth-grade reading tests.
4.   The children who received the intervention surpassed their controls on IQ tests for up to three years after the programs ended. The participants of the three

programs, which involved infants and toddlers, maintained superior IQ scores approximately ten to fifteen years after the programs ended.

In addition, mothers' attitudes toward school performance and their vocational hopes for their children were affected in positive ways.

THE HOME ENVIRONMENT

The quality of the environment within the home is a critical factor affecting the infant's development. The home environment is directly related to the developmental status of the infant (Gottfried, 1985). What are the characteristics of a favorable home environment for infant development? Betty Caldwell, a nationally recognized expert in infant development and child care, has developed a list of the six environmental characteristics of homes that are most likely to foster early development (Caldwell & Bradley, 1979):

1. Emotional and verbal responsivity of the mother.
2. Avoidance of restriction and punishment.
3. Organization of the physical and temporal (day-to-day) environment.
4. Provisions of appropriate play materials.
5. Maternal (parental) involvement with the child.
6. Opportunities for variety in daily stimulation.

These characteristics have been developed into an inventory (Caldwell & Bradley, 1979) that has been used widely in infant research and developmental screening programs to measure the quality of home environments. The two most important home environment characteristics that are related to intellectual development during infancy are the quantity and quality of parent-infant relations and the availability of play materials (Gottfried, 1985). Homes that rate highly on those qualities tend to produce infants who score highest on measures of cognitive performance.

Characteristics of Parent-Infant Relations

We have long recognized that "the parent-child relationship is unique among human ties" (Maccoby & Martin, 1983, p. 1). More recently, we have begun to appreciate and try to understand the complexity of that relationship. Much of the early research simply dealt with how parents influence children. Currently, though, the emphasis is being placed upon a reciprocal or circular process in which infants and parents influence each other, both directly and indirectly. As a part of this process, Belsky (1981) notes that "the infant may both influence and be influenced by the reciprocal impact of marital relations on parenting and parenting on marital relations" (p. 16).

Fathers tend to engage in "rough and tumble" play with their infants.

Parent-Infant Interactions.   In spite of the changes that have occurred in the American family structure, the mother continues to serve as the primary caregiver. Even when the mother is employed, the father spends less time caring for the baby than the mother (Belsky & Volling, 1987). However, this does not mean that fathers are less competent caregivers than mothers. Studies have shown that fathers are as successful as mothers in interpreting a baby's signals and in responding to its needs (Parke & Tinsley, 1987).

Fathers and mothers differ not only in the amount of time which they spend with their infants, but in their styles of interaction. A greater proportion of father-infant interactions are spent in play activities, whereas mothers are more involved in routine caregiving activities (Kottlecheck, 1976). Fathers tend to play with infants in different ways than mothers. They are more likely to engage in physical play by bouncing their infants, moving the infant's limbs, and engaging in rough-and-tumble games. In contrast, mothers are more likely to engage in quieter, more conventional playful interactions with toys, and games such as peek-a-boo (Parke & Tinsley, 1987).

The sex of the parent and the sex of the baby make a difference in parent-infant interaction patterns. Fathers are more directly involved in the rearing of sons than they are daughters (Lamb, 1981b). Boys are handled more roughly and receive more physical punishment from both parents than girls (Huston, 1983). When given a choice, infants tend to prefer the same-sex parent as a playmate (Parke & Tinsley, 1987).

Studies on father-infant interactions have been limited mostly to white, nonminority, middle-class practices. However, differences are likely to exist according to the parent's race, ethnic group, social class, education, and other factors. Unfortunately, information is not available on the nature of the differences (Berman & Pederson, 1987).

How Infants Influence Parents.   Infants initiate many of the parent-child interactions and are highly effective in gaining parental attention (Maccoby & Martin, 1983). The young infant's sighs, cries, smiles, gaze, state of alertness, helplessness, and "baby face" are some of the characteristics to which parents respond. Yet not all of their responses are positive. Parents typically do not respond as positively to infants with physical impairments, to preterm infants, to noncuddlers, or to "difficult infants" as they do to infants perceived as more normal (Maccoby & Martin, 1983; Osofsky & Connors, 1979). Research suggests that low-income mothers of minority families demonstrate a tendency not to interact with an irritable infant (Ramey & Brownlee, 1981). Infants are very adaptive, however, and tend to alter many of their responses to match parental behaviors.

How Infants Influence Marital Relations.   With the birth of children, the husband-wife relationship changes. For many couples, the birth of the first child constitutes a crisis that disrupts the marital relationship. For others the "blessed event" requires only minor adjustments (Dyer, 1963; Hobbs, 1968). In most marriages, though, the quality of the husband-wife relationship is apparently affected. In a study of 250 couples, Belsky (cited in Schneck, 1986) found that between the last trimester of pregnancy and the third month after the baby is born, marital satisfaction slightly declined. After the initial change, however, the marital quality leveled off.

A number of factors determine the extent to which infants affect the marriage relationship. Couples who are older and who have been married for longer periods of time tend to have fewer problems adjusting to parenthood (Belsky, 1981). The quality of the marriage before the baby is born is another major factor. Couples who report the highest levels of marital satisfaction before pregnancy, tend to remain the happiest after the baby is born (Schneck, 1986). The number of children and the years between their birthdays also make a difference. Finally, the individual characteristics of an infant are probably the most important factor in determining how the marriage is affected. Parents of babies who cry more frequently and who are more active tend to be more stressed than parents of less demanding, quieter babies (Russell, 1974).

Marital Relationships and Parenting.   The quality of the marriage has important implications for the quality of parenting the infant receives. Belsky (cited in Schneck, 1986) found that "in marriages where marital quality declines the most, the bond between mother and child is weakest" (p. 12). Studies have also shown that marital tension and conflict have a negative impact on the mother's ability to enjoy her baby, to regard it with affection, to be competent as a parent, and to achieve a high quality of infant-mother attachment (Belsky, 1981; Parke & Tinsley, 1987).

Fathers can be as competent
as mothers in meeting the
needs of an infant.

The father's involvement in caregiving, playfulness, satisfaction with fatherhood, and competence in caregiving are also linked to the quality of the marriage (Belsky, 1979; Dickie & Matheson, 1984; Feldman, Nash, & Aschenbrenner, 1983). A happy and supportive marital relationship is apparently even more important for the father's competence as a parent than it is for the mother's. The father may depend more on the mother's support because of uncertainties about how to care for an infant and reluctance to intrude into what is traditionally perceived as the mother's territory. (Parke & Tinsley, 1987).

Cultural Differences.   Parents in all cultures share a common set of goals in their concern for the physical health and survival of their infants and efforts to maximize their future social adjustment and future economic welfare (Levine, 1980). However, the specific child-rearing attitudes and strategies parents use in implementing these goals vary widely around the world. In many parts of the world, such as Kenya and South America, infants are held and carried most of the time. Parenting styles are relaxed and casual. Attention is devoted to meeting the baby's physical needs, but efforts are not made to stimulate precocious social or intellectual development (Levine, 1980). In contrast, many American parents are less involved physically with their infants but are more concerned about social and intellectual stimulation. However, child-rearing practices vary widely within, as well as between, ethnic and cultural groups.

Managing Infant Behavior: Discipline

Discipline is an essential part of child rearing. In its broadest meaning, **discipline** refers to the process of teaching and learning that fosters human growth and development (Dodson, 1970; DuBois, 1952). According to Hurlock (1972), discipline gives young children a sense of security by letting them know what they can and cannot do. Children gain approval from others by learning to behave according to socially accepted standards. Discipline thus facilitates the development of self-esteem. Appropriate discipline also fosters achievement motivation and the development of a conscience. The ultimate goal of discipline, though, is the development of self-discipline. Infants begin life with little ability to control their own behavior. They depend upon their caregivers to guide them through the process of establishing impulse control and self-regulation.

Discipline and behavior control are usually not a major concern of parents during the early months of life. Excessive crying and fussing are the behaviors that present the most problems for caregivers before infants begin to move around. As they learn to creep and walk, infants begin to explore the environment and begin to "get out of bounds." Biting, hitting, temper tantrums, failure to comply with requests, clinging, and other types of negative behavior are problem behaviors that develop during the toddler stage. Parents and other caregivers are then faced with decisions about how much freedom to allow, what limits to set, and what methods of discipline and guidance to use.

Setting Limits.   Parental expectations of infant behavior and limits must be reasonable to be most effective. Arbitrary and unnecessary limits contribute to negativism, noncompliance, and parent-child conflict. Generally, limits should be designed to (1) ensure the child's health and safety, (2) protect the health, safety, and rights of others, (3) prevent the destruction of property, and (4) teach the moral and social values of the family and society.

Realistic behavioral expectations can be established only if adults keep in mind the age-level characteristics, needs, and limited abilities of infants and toddlers. Cognitive immaturity and limited language ability prevent infants from understanding and complying with adults' wishes, as well as from communicating their own desires. Their struggle to establish autonomy frequently results in negative responses to adult requests. Toddlers need physical activity and freedom of movement. Thus, they have difficulty sitting still and keeping quiet. Infants and toddlers are very egocentric, which means that they view things only from their own point of view. For example, to the parent bath water is used for bathing, but to an infant bath water is something used for playing.

Children need to be informed of the limits that are set and the expectations their caregivers hold. They react to ambiguity with confusion and should not be expected to conform to unclear limits. Toward the end of the first year, infants can begin to understand simple restrictions, such as the meaning of "no." As language development proceeds, verbal explanations can become a little more complex. For young children, it is more important to explain *what* they should do rather than *why* (Greenfield & Tronick, 1980). When possible, directions should be stated in a positive form that tells an infant what to do instead of what *not* to do ("Keep the sand in the sandbox!").

Strategies for Guiding Behavior. Once limits have been clearly established, they need to be consistently enforced. However, this should be done in positive ways that "preserve the self-respect of the parent as well as the child" (Ginott, 1965, p. 96). The restrictions are applied firmly and kindly without excessive anger or force and without attacking the personality of the child. Children need to be given the right to have feelings, just as adults. Their feelings can be accepted even though the behavior is objectionable. Name-calling and personality attacks, such as "you stupid brat," should never be used.

Adults have numerous options for enforcing limits and guiding the behavior of their children. The following are included among the strategies usually recommended for positive guidance of infants and toddlers. Keep in mind, however, that no single technique is equally effective with all children. A child's compliance will vary with the person making the request, the situation, and other factors such as how tired the child is at the time. The temperament of the infant is also an important factor in how resourceful an adult has to be.

DISTRACTION AND REDIRECTION. Infants who are crying or engaged in unacceptable activities can be distracted or diverted to another activity. For example, young infants can sometimes be distracted by being held in front of mirror or a window. They can be moved to a new, more appropriate location. Alternative activities and toys can be provided as substitutes for those that are prohibited. When Tanya was 18 months old, she was found playing in the toilet bowl. Her mother's response was "You need to play somewhere else." She then took Tanya to her room and found some toys for her to play with. Whenever possible, children should be given choices. "Do you want to play here or go outside?" However, a choice should not be given if it is not really available or acceptable.

ENVIRONMENTAL CONTROL. Many problem behaviors can be avoided if the environment is properly structured. An infant needs a place to play that is "child-proof." Breakable objects and other valuables should be placed where infants cannot reach them. Safety hazards should be eliminated. An adequate supply of age-appropriate toys and interesting activities should be provided to keep the child busy. Nine-month-old Jamal opened a kitchen cabinet and pulled out the pots and pans from the bottom shelves. Jamal's mother put fasteners on the cabinet doors to keep him away from her cooking utensils. She also put some old pots and pans in a cabinet which she left open for Jamal to play with.

MODELING.   It is important for adults to model the behaviors they want to teach. For example, the best way to teach children to use good manners is to practice them in caregiving interactions. When adults say "Please" and "Thank you" when making requests, the child will eventually reciprocate. Young children are more likely to imitate a model that is warm and nurturing than someone cold and aloof.

POSITIVE REINFORCEMENT.   Children tend to repeat behaviors that are reinforced with a social reinforcer such as praise, a hug, or a smile. Parents and caregivers are generally encouraged to praise desirable behavior and ignore, as much as possible, behaviors they don't want to encourage. However, praise or other social reinforcers should be sincere and nonmanipulative. It should be perceived as a means of fostering the infant's self-esteem rather than simply as a means to achieve behavior control (Seefeldt, 1987).

To be most effective, praise must be given immediately after the behavior. Praise is also most effective when it is a recognition of the child's specific behavior (Ginott, 1965) ("Thank you for sharing your toy! That was a nice thing to do!"). General praise that addresses the child's personality is less helpful ("You're the best child!").

TIME-OUT.   The use of time-outs to discipline toddlers is another option available to parents and caregivers. In this procedure, a child who is being disruptive is removed from the situation and given a chance to calm down. In some cases, the child is taken to another room and isolated for a while. After a brief interval, the child may return to the situation or resume another activity. This gives the child who is out of control a chance to regain equilibrium and self-control. It is unrealistic, however, to expect an infant or a toddler to sit in a specified place for more than a few seconds. Time-out should be viewed as a teaching act rather than as a punishment.

PUNISHMENT.   The use of punishment in controlling the behavior of infants and toddlers is controversial. Scolding, spanking, withdrawal of love, isolation, and other negative responses to a child's behavior are types of punishment commonly used. Punishment is the least desirable means of behavior control. Holden (1983) observed the strategies mothers used in controlling the behavior of 2-year-old infants. Some of the mothers used scolding or reprimands when the infant misbehaved. Other mothers used "preventive" measures such as engaging the child in conversation to control behavior. The mothers who used preventive measures had fewer problems and less conflict with their infants.

Most parents feel that there are times when punishment is necessary, but it should be brief and clearly linked to what the child has done (Laishley, 1983). Punishment is effective in suppressing some behavior, but that does not mean that the behavior is eliminated. Punishment may produce undesirable side effects, such as associating the punishment with the parent. Punishment does not foster the development of internal control and can lead to excessive reliance on external authority for behavioral inhibition (Maccoby, 1980). Punishment is most effective when it immediately follows the problem behavior and when it is consistent. It is also more effective when administered by someone who has a warm and caring relationship with the child (Hetherington & Parke, 1979).

Spanking is the type of punishment that is most vigorously debated by child-rearing specialists. For example, Yussen and Santrock (1982) believe that "mild forms of physical punishment may be the most effective method of disciplining infants and toddlers in some situations. The two-year-old child does not understand complex reasoning and has difficulty following verbal instructions; a light tap on his bottom may be more effective in efforts to keep him from touching a hot stove, wandering into the street, or playing on the stairs" (p. 385).

On the other hand, Ginott (1965) argues that spanking is ineffective and should be avoided: "If spanking is so effective, why do we have such uneasy feelings about it. . . . What is wrong with spanking is the lessons it demonstrates. It teaches children undesirable methods of dealing with frustration. It dramatically tells them: when you are angry—hit!" (p. 107).

Ginott's argument is illustrated by the cartoon that shows a father vigorously spanking his son. The caption reads: "That will teach you to hit your younger sister!" The father is right. It will.

In actual practice, the large majority (95 percent) of parents use spanking as a method of discipline, out of a sense of frustration if for no other reason. However, if parents are resourceful, they can find a more positive means of behavior control.

LOVE WITHDRAWAL. One of the most common methods used by parents to control a child's behavior is withdrawal of love. The parent expresses anger and disappointment when the child misbehaves: "I don't like you when you cry like that!" The parent follows up by isolating the child emotionally. The child's efforts to communicate are ignored as the parent turns away from the child, refusing to speak or listen. The parent may even threaten to leave (Maccoby, 1980). Love withdrawal is punitive and implicitly says to the child, "If you don't please me, I won't love you!" The results of love withdrawal are mostly negative. It produces a high level of arousal and anxiety in children and does not lead to the establishment of internal control (Hoffman, 1970). Discipline begins with the loving care that a baby receives (Keister, 1973), so the very foundation of discipline is threatened by the use of love withdrawal.

DEALING WITH AGGRESSION. Soon after they are old enough to interact with their peers, infants begin to express aggression in the form of biting, hitting, grabbing, and pushing. These early forms of aggression usually result from frustration and attempts at being self-assertive. Young children do not think about or fully understand the consequences of their behavior. Their aggressive acts at this stage are not deliberate, premeditated efforts to hurt another person. However, caregivers have to control this type of behavior and teach children other ways to get their needs met.

Hitting.   When one child hits or pushes another, the caregiver quickly assesses the situation to see what happened. For older toddlers it may not be necessary to intervene because they often work things out on their own. For younger toddlers and in cases when a child is being a bully, the caregiver needs to respond. Next, the caregiver makes eye contact with the aggressor and states firmly: "Hitting is not allowed because it hurts!" At the same time, an alternative response is suggested: "I know that Seth made you angry when he took your hat, but you need to *ask* him to give it back, or come to me for help" (Leavitt & Eheart, 1985). The child who continues to be aggressive can be removed from the situation briefly but should be given praise and reinforcement for solving conflicts at other times in nonaggressive ways.

Biting.   Day care providers who work with toddlers typically report biting to be one of the most common and difficult behavior problems. Biting can be handled in much the same way as other aggressive acts, with firmness and suggestions for alternative ways to respond to frustration. Most of the attention should be focused on the child who has been bitten. It is not advisable to bite the child in return or to tell the victim to bite back. This response is generally not effective and may only reinforce biting behavior. In group situations, biting behavior can be prevented or minimized by providing plenty of toys, interesting activities, and close supervision, while avoiding too many adult restrictions.

Temper Tantrums.   During the second year of life, temper tantrums are a common occurrence. If adults respond appropriately, most toddlers grow out of this behavior. Adults need to ignore tantrums insofar as possible. In some cases it may be necessary to prevent the child from attacking someone or destroying property. In a group situation the child needs to be removed until the tantrum subsides. However, the child should not receive special attention in the process. Above all, this behavior should not be reinforced. A child should not be allowed to use a tantrum to obtain a desired goal or to gain any benefit. Adults need to remain as calm as possible and avoid angry, violent responses.

Noncompliance.   Infants and toddlers engage in a wide range of behaviors that adults label as defiant or noncompliant. They may refuse to eat, take a bath, or go to bed. Adults can encourage compliance by telling the child in advance when a change of activity is necessary. "As soon as the cartoon is over, we will be going home." Adults should not insist on instant obedience.

Parents and other adults should also avoid nagging and repeating demands over and over. The adult should be sure that the child hears and understands the instructions (Laishley, 1983). The toddler's "no" should not be interpreted literally (Weiser, 1982), because it may be an experimental response to see what will happen. Children usually comply willingly if the adult is firm and positive, as in the following example:

> Two-year-old Karen was busily engaged in caring for her baby doll right before lunch time. The teacher approached, saying "Let's go to the sink, Karen, and I'll help you wash your face and hands." "No!" replied Karen. The teacher smiled, took Karen by the hand, and said "Come on, Karen, it will only take a minute, and then it's time to eat. Let's go." Karen smiled and teasingly pretended a reluctant walk over to the sink (Weiser, 1982, p. 197).

If adults are reasonable, firm, and kind in their demands, children tend to respond favorably.

Parental Attitudes. The effectiveness of any disciplinary technique depends largely upon the nature of the parent-child relationship. Discipline is administered in the context of parental attitudes. The message and meaning of the disciplinary action, especially punishment, are determined to a large extent by the attitude of the disciplinarian. Parental attitudes can be placed on a continuum ranging from love and acceptance to hostility and rejection. The most competent children are reared by parents who use positive methods to control behavior within the context of a warm and loving attitude (Baumrind, 1973; Hoffman, 1981). This combination of authority and positive attitudes tends to result in children who are self-reliant, self-confident, curious, and happy (Becker, 1964).

Selecting Toys and Materials

Choosing a baby's toys and play materials is as important as choosing the baby's clothing. However, the task is not easy because of the almost endless variety of toys available. Some general criteria should be considered by parents and caregivers in selecting toys and materials for infants and toddlers:

1. Toys and materials should be appropriate for the child's age and developmental level. Fortunately, infants are adaptable and play with toys in their own way. Information about recommended toys for infants according to age is readily available in numerous publications (e.g., Aston, 1984; Greenfield & Tronick, 1980; White, 1985). Many toy manufacturers label their toys according to a general age range.

2. Toys and materials should provide a challenge to the child without being impossible to master. Adults cannot always predict which toys will present an optimum challenge. However, given a reasonable variety of toys, an infant will select the ones that are most appealing.

3. All toys and play materials should be free from safety hazards (see Chapter 7).

4. The infant's toy collection should be balanced and comprehensive. There should be a variety of toys to cover each area of development, including small

and large muscle, sensorimotor, eye-hand coordination, social, emotional, language, and cognitive as well as imagination and creativity.

5. The infant's toy collection should be built around the "basics." It should include play things that can be used in a variety of ways and which are universal and timeless favorites, such as balls, blocks, puzzles, books, records, dolls, and stuffed animals.

6. Toys should be cost effective. A toy should be durable, sturdy, and worth the investment. In some cases this may mean paying a little more for a better-quality toy, and perhaps buying fewer toys. For example, although a wooden puzzle costs more than a cardboard puzzle, the wooden puzzle is a better buy because it lasts longer and "works" better. Parents do not need to purchase a lot of expensive educational toys and materials. Old pots and pans, spools, cans, and other common household items make excellent play materials.

7. Toys should match the available storage and be easily accessible to the infant. Shelves are better than a toy box for organizing and storing toys. Toys should be rotated from time to time. When an infant has grown tired of a toy, it should be stored away and reintroduced at a later time.

SUMMARY

1. Dramatic increases in the number of single-parent families and the number of employed mothers represent changes in the structure of the American family that have affected the ways infants are reared.

2. High rates of divorce and illegitimacy are the main causes of the increased number of single-parent families. Most single-parent families with infants are headed by divorced mothers.

3. Infants are especially vulnerable to the effects of divorce.

4. The extra stress and conflict experienced by single-parent families is frequently accompanied by a "diminished-parenting" effect.

5. Father absence during infancy has been associated with difficulty in sex role development and various psychological problems. Males appear to be more adversely affected by father absence than females.

6. Apparently maternal employment does not ordinarily have negative effects on infant development, provided the mother likes her work and is happy being a parent. However, there is a possibility that maternal employment may place male infants at risk for socioemotional difficulties.

7. Good-quality day care for infants has no harmful effects on most aspects of infant development. It has been found to be beneficial to infants from economically deprived families. However, infants who participate in group day care are sick more frequently than infants who stay at home. Day care may also increase aggressiveness as infants get older. There are growing concerns about the possibility of negative effects of day care on infant-parent attachment for infants under 1 year of age.

8. The components of good-quality day care include (a) an adequate caregiver-infant ratio, (b) well-qualified caregivers, (c) small group size, (d)

continuity of caregivers, (e) a well-planned curriculum, and (f) parental involvement.

9. Various types of early-intervention programs were established in the 1960s to facilitate the development of infants from low-income families. The long-term results of those programs show that infant intervention can be effective in alleviating the effects of an impoverished environment.

10. Two important characteristics of the home environment that are related to infant development are parent-infant interactions and the provision of adequate play materials.

11. Parent-infant interactions are complex and multidimensional. Parents and infants influence each other. In addition, the quality of marital relationships is influenced by the presence of an infant, just as the marital relationship influences parent-infant interactions.

12. In most American families, the mother continues to be the primary caregiver. However, fathers can be just as capable as mothers in taking care of an infant. Fathers and mothers use different styles in playing and interacting with their infants.

13. The quality of a marital relationship tends to decline slightly and level off after the birth of a baby. Couples who have been married longer, couples who were older when they married, and couples who have a relatively high level of marital satisfaction before pregnancy have the least trouble adjusting to parenthood.

14. The decline in the quality of marital relationships is accompanied by a decline in the quality of parenting.

15. Positive discipline is an essential part of effective parent-infant relationships. Useful strategies for guiding the behavior of infants include distraction and redirection, controlling the environment, modeling, positive reinforcement, and the use of time-outs. The use of spanking and love withdrawal as means of behavior control should be avoided.

16. Toys and play materials for infants should be (a) appropriate to the child's age and development, (b) challenging but not too difficult, (c) free from safety hazards, (d) available in sufficient types and quantity to cover each area of development, (e) cost effective, and (f) easily stored and accessible.

Glossary

Accommodation. The process of changing existing patterns of thought or behavior to conform to new information or experiences.

Adaptation. The processes by which an individual adjusts and changes to get along in the environment; includes assimilation and accommodation.

Affect. Feelings, emotions.

Amniocentesis. The procedure in which a sample of amniotic fluid is withdrawn through a hollow needle for laboratory analysis.

Amnion; Amniotic Sac. The inner fluid-filled membrane, resembling a plastic bag, that encloses the developing embryo or fetus; the "bag of waters."

Analgesic. Any type of medicine used to relieve pain without affecting consciousness.

Anesthesia. Any type of medicine used to relieve pain by inducing unconsciousness or blocking the transmission of pain signals to the brain.

Anoxia. A condition in which the tissues of the body are not receiving an adequate supply of oxygen.

Apgar Scale. A test administered one minute and again five minutes after birth to check the physiological condition of the infant.

Apnea. A pause in breathing for 20 seconds or longer.

Assimilation. The process of incorporating new information into existing patterns of thought or action.

Autism. An extreme psychological disorder characterized by a lack of responsiveness to other people, failure to communicate, and other abnormal behaviors.

Babbling. Sound play consisting of the repetition of consonants and vowels in alternating sequences; thought to be the forerunner of the first meaningful utterances.

Beikost. Semisolid, strained baby food.

Blastocyst. A fertilized ovum about the time it enters the uterus and a central cavity is formed inside.

Bonding. The process by which a parent forms an emotional attachment to an infant.

Braxton Hicks Contractions. Mild contractions of the uterus that occur before true labor begins; sometimes referred to as false labor.

Brazelton Neonatal Behavior Assessment Scale. An instrument used to assess the basic functioning of the newborn infant's nervous system and behavioral response capacities.

Breech Birth. The birth of an infant with the buttocks, feet or knees as the part that emerges first.

Caesarean Section. Childbirth by means of a surgical incision through the abdomen and uterus.

Caregiver. A person who provides care for an infant, such as a parent, nurse, or day care worker.

Cartilage. A rubbery, gristlelike tissue found in the human body and from which the skeleton is formed.

Catchup Growth. The ability of the individual to achieve normal growth potential after a period of malnutrition, intrauterine crowding, illness, or other adversity.

Cephalocaudal Principle. The principle which holds that growth and development proceeds from the upper part of the body to the lower extremities.

Cervical Pregnancy. A pregnancy in which the fertilized ovum is implanted in or close to the cervix.

Cervix.   The mouth, or opening, of the uterus (womb).

Chorion.   The outer prenatal membrane that encloses the developing baby. One side of the chorion becomes attached to the uterus as the placenta.

Chorionic Villus Sampling.   The procedure whereby a sample of tissue from the chorion is removed and tested for genetic defects.

Circular Reaction.   The term Piaget used to describe a continuous response that stimulates its own repetition.

Classical Conditioning.   A procedure in which a neutral stimulus and a stimulus that automatically evokes a response are presented at approximately the same time. Eventually, the presentation of the neutral stimulus alone evokes the response.

Cognition.   All the mental processes such as thinking, remembering, perceiving, learning and concept formation.

Cooing.   Early vowel-like, rhythmic sounds made by infants during the early part of the prespeech stage.

Competence Motivation.   The tendency to seek out and master the most challenging aspects of the environment; a human characteristic considered by some theorists to be innate.

Congenital Malformation.   A defect present at birth.

Critical Period.   The span of time when a developing organism is most likely to be permanently influenced by environmental factors.

Crowning.   The point during childbirth when the top of the baby's head becomes visible at the vaginal opening.

Deciduous Teeth.   The first set of twenty teeth developed by an infant, which are replaced by thirty-two permanent teeth; also called temporary, primary, or milk teeth.

Dental Caries.   Tooth decay.

Dilation; Dilatation.   The process by which the cervix opens to its widest capacity to allow a baby to be born.

Discipline.   Procedures used by parents and other adults to guide, correct, punish, and control the behavior of children.

Dishabituation.   The renewal of interest in a stimulus arising from a noticeable change in the stimulus characteristics.

Dominant Gene.   A gene carrying a trait that is always expressed.

Double Substitution Play.   The most advanced form of pretend play whereby the infant uses two imaginary objects or materials in a play sequence.

Echolalia.   The tendency of an infant to repeat the same sounds over and over.

Ectopic Pregnancy.   A pregnancy in which the fertilized ovum becomes implanted outside the uterus.

Effacement.   The process during labor through which the cervix becomes thinner and shorter.

Ego.   The term used by Freud to label the rational, or thinking, component of personality.

Egocentrism.   The inability to see things from another person's point of view.

Embryo.   The developing infant from the seventh or eighth day after conception until the end of the eighth week of pregnancy.

Emotion.   Feelings; complex internal states consisting of perceptions, thoughts, body responses, and impulses.

Endogenous Smile.   Spontaneous smile, usually observed when an infant is sleeping, that is triggered by internal body processes.

Epiphyses.   Ossification centers which form near the end of the long bones.

Episiotomy.   A surgical incision made in the tissue between the vagina and the rectum to facilitate childbirth and prevent tearing of the tissue.

Equilibrium.   The term Piaget used to describe a state of balance between assimilation and accommodation.

Exogenous Smile.   Smiling behavior elicited by stimuli outside the infant's body.

Expressive Speech.   The meaningful vocal utterances and sounds composed and expressed by an individual in communication with others.

Fetal Alcohol Syndrome.   Congenital abnormalities resulting from maternal alcohol consumption during pregnancy.

Fetoscope.   A surgical instrument used in combination with other special equipment to view the inside of the uterus, and to obtain samples of tissue and amniotic fluid for testing.

Fetus.   An unborn infant from the eighth prenatal week to birth.

Fontanels.   The soft spots in the young infant's skull that harden and disappear as the separate pieces of the skull grow together.

Forceps. An instrument, shaped like tongs, sometimes used in difficult deliveries to help the baby emerge from the birth canal.

Frank Breech. The position of a fetus in which the feet and legs are extended straight up beside the ears, the buttocks are the first part to enter the birth canal.

Full (Complete) Breech. The position of a fetus in which the knees are pulled tightly against the stomach with the feet extended downward and the buttocks are the first part to enter the birth canal.

Functional-relational Play. The second stage of sensorimotor play; the stage is characterized by the infant's ability to use play with two or more objects at the same time in ways that are increasingly appropriate to the relationships of the objects.

Gestational Age. The age of the infant calculated from the estimated date of fertilization of the ovum until birth.

Goodness-of-fit. The extent to which the caregiving style of the parents appropriately matches the temperament of the infant.

Habituation. The weakening or decline of responsiveness to a stimulus over a period of time.

Holophrase. A single word considered to be equivalent to a whole phrase or a complete sentence.

Human Growth Hormone (HGH). A substance produced by the thyroid gland that is necessary for normal body growth.

Hyaline Membrane Disease. See respiratory distress syndrome.

Hypertension. A blood pressure level that is abnormally high.

Id. The term Freud used to represent the personality component consisting of the basic instincts and physiological urges, such as hunger, thirst, and sex.

Infanticide. Murder of unwanted infants.

Infant State. The baby's level of alertness and availability for contact with the outside world.

Intelligence. The ability to think, learn, remember, and solve problems.

Intelligence Quotient (IQ). The score derived from an intelligence test that is typically calculated as:

Mental age (Test Score) divided by Chronological Age $\times$ 100.

Interactionist. A theorist who believes that growth and development are the result of the interaction of hereditary and environmental forces.

Intrauterine. Inside the uterus.

Iron-Deficiency Anemia. A low supply of red blood cells caused by an inadequate amount of iron in the diet.

Jaundice. A yellowish appearance of the skin caused by excessive bilirubin, a pigment formed when the red blood cells are destroyed by disease or by the aging of the blood cells.

Language. Vocal utterances, nonverbal behavior, written expressions, and other behaviors used in the process of communication.

Lanugo. The fine hair that covers the fetus from approximately the twentieth week until the seventh month of pregnancy.

Learning. The process of acquiring knowledge or skills through experience.

Lightening. The point prior to the onset of labor when the baby's head "drops," or moves into the mother's pelvic opening, thereby reducing pressure on the mother's diaphragm.

Long-term Memory. Information that is stored in the mind indefinitely.

Low-birthweight Infant. A baby who weighs less than 5½ pounds at birth.

Maturationist. A theorist who believes growth and development result from the aging process that is largely controlled by a genetic timetable.

Meconium. The greenish black material eliminated in the baby's first bowel movement.

Meiosis. The process through which the body forms reproductive cells (sperm and ovum) by reducing the number of chromosomes from forty-six to twenty-three.

Mitosis. The formation of body cells containing forty-six chromosomes for tissue growth and replacement.

Monotrophy. The term used by Bowlby to express his belief that infants are capable of becoming attached to only one person at a time.

Morpheme. The smallest unit of meaning in a language.

Morula. The fertilized ovum, or zygote, after a mulberry-shaped cluster of sixteen cells has formed at approximately the third day after fertilization.

Motherese. The vocal expressions characteristically used by mothers in talking to their infants.

Motor Biases. The tendency of infants to practice the newest body movements they have learned.

Myelination; Myelinization. The formation of a fatty tissue covering, called myelin, over the nerve cells.

Nativist.   A theorist who believes infants are genetically endowed with some basic ideas, feelings, personality, and other characteristics that provide the foundation for future growth and development.

Neonate.   The newborn baby from birth through the first two weeks of life.

Neuroglial Cells.   Central nervous systems cells that serve as connecting links between the neurons and the blood supply.

Neurons.   Basic nerve cells that transmit impulses and control central nervous system functions.

Nutrition.   The process by which the body takes in and uses food and other digestible substances.

Object Permanence.   The concept of an object as being present somewhere even if it cannot always be seen, touched, or heard.

Operant Conditioning.   The process by which behavior is repeated or changed as the result of a reward or punishment given as a consequence for a particular response.

Ossification.   The process by which cartilage hardens into bone.

Ovum.   The reproductive cell produced by the female.

Parentese.   The characteristic vocal expressions used by parents, including fathers, in talking to their infants.

Peers.   Individuals of about the same age or developmental level who interact with each other in some way; equals.

Perceived Personal Effectance.   The extent to which infants perceive that they control what happens in their environment.

Personality.   The relatively enduring patterns of behavior and personal qualities that establish one's individuality.

Pica.   The eating of nonfood substances that have no nutritional value.

Phonemes.   The basic units of sounds in a language that are combined to form words.

Placenta.   The organ or membrane attached to the unborn baby's umbilical cord on one side and the mother's uterine lining on the other. The baby receives nutrients and oxygen and gets rid of waste products through the placenta.

Placental Previa.   A condition in which the placenta is attached too close to the cervix, resulting in a risk of early placental separation and maternal bleeding.

Postterm; Postmature.   An infant born after 42 weeks of gestational age.

Prehension.   The ability to grasp with the fingers and thumb.

Prereaching.   The first stage of reaching during which infants reflexively reach for or swat at objects with little or no motor coordination or control.

Preterm; Premature.   An infant born before 37 weeks of gestational age.

Prostaglandins.   A variety of chemical substances found in most tissues of the human body which influence blood pressure, muscle contractions, and numerous other body functions.

Proximodistal Principle.   The principle which holds that growth and development proceed from the internal parts of the body to the outer extremities.

Quickening.   The first movements of the fetus that are felt by the mother.

Recall Memory.   The ability to retrieve information from the memory in the absence of direct sensory perceptions of the stimulus in question.

Receptive Speech.   The meanings and understandings that are attached to the vocal expressions of others.

Recessive Gene.   A gene which carries traits that are expressed only if the gene is paired with the identical recessive gene.

Reciprocal Interactions.   The process whereby infants and caregivers influence one another's responses.

Recognition Memory.   The ability to determine whether a stimulus has been previously encountered; the ability to recognize the correct stimulus (answer) when given a choice.

Reflex.   An automatic, involuntary response to a stimulus.

Respiratory Distress Syndrome.   A disease of preterm infants caused by a deficiency of surfactant, a substance necessary for efficient breathing.

Retrolental Fibroplasia.   A disease of preterm and low-birthweight-infants caused by exposure to too much oxygen, causing scarring of the eye tissue and possibly blindness.

Rhythmical Stereotypies.   Repetitive, rythmical movements sometimes used by infants to prepare for more advanced and better coordinated motor activities.

Rooming-in.   The practice of allowing the newborn baby to stay in the mother's room rather than in the hospital nursery.

Scheme.   The term Piaget used to label a pattern or unit of thought or action.

Sedative. Medications that have a calming effect and, when taken in sufficient doses, induce drowsiness and sleep.

Self-actualization. A term used by Maslow and Rogers to refer to the need or motivation of humans to achieve their full potential.

Self-awareness. The perception or awareness of oneself as a distinct individual with an existence and identity separate from other people and objects.

Self-concept. The sum total, or composite picture, of how you perceive yourself as an individual.

Self-esteem. The evaluation you make of your self-concept, including positive and negative thoughts and feelings.

Self-recognition. The ability of infants to recognize their own images in mirrors, pictures, videotapes and other forms.

Sensory Memory. Information from immediate sensory impressions that is stored in the mind for an instant.

Separation Anxiety. Emotional distress resulting from an infant's separation from a parent or other attachment figure.

Separation-individuation. The process by which an infant achieves a sense of separateness from the mother.

Short-term Memory. The ability to recall information that is stored for a brief period of time, usually about a minute.

Social Competence. The ability to use environmental and personal resources to get one's needs met and to achieve a satisfactory developmental outcome.

Socialization. The process through which a person acquires the attitudes, behaviors, and skills needed to get along in a given society.

Social Referencing. The use of behavioral cues or indicators displayed by others in deciding how to respond in a situation in which the decision is not clear.

Somites. The budlike segments in the developing embryo from which the skeleton is formed.

Speech. The vocal or spoken component of language.

Sperm. The reproductive cell produced by the male.

Stranger Anxiety. A negative emotional response to a stranger characterized by withdrawal, avoidance, crying, or other signs of distress.

Strawberry Nevi. Large red patches of skin that are sometimes present at birth on caucasian infants; these marks disappear with age.

Sudden Infant Death Syndrome (SIDS). The sudden, unexpected death of an infant for which no adequate medical explanation can be found.

Superego. The term Freud used to label the personality component which consists of the moral principles and social standards; includes the conscience and the ideal self.

Surfactant. A chemical manufactured by the lungs to facilitate breathing.

Sutures. The narrow seams of cartilage that connect the separate sections of the newborn infant's skull.

Syntax. Rules that govern the ways words can be combined to form sentences or meaningful phrases.

Telegraphic Speech. Linguistic utterances or sentences of limited length that use word order to convey meaning; conjunctions and other nonessential parts of speech are omitted as in a telegram.

Temperament. The basic patterns and style of behavior that are characteristic of an individual.

Teratogen. Any substance that can produce a developmental abnormality in an embryo or a fetus.

Thyroxine. A hormone produced by the thyroid gland that is necessary for normal physical growth.

Toddler. An infant who is in the early stage of walking; covers the period of time from approximately one year to two years of age.

Tranquilizer. A type of drug used to reduce tension and anxiety.

Tryphoblasts. The outer layer of cells on the fertilized ovum that bury into the lining of the uterus by secreting enzymes.

Umbilical Cord. The ropelike cord containing two arteries and one vein, and connecting the unborn infant to the placenta.

Vernix Caseosa. The whitish, oily substance that covers the fetus to protect the skin from the amniotic fluid.

Zygote. A fertilized ovum.

References

Abel, E. (1983). *Marijuana, tobacco, alcohol and reproduction*. Boca Rata, FL: CRC Press.

Adams, M. (1985). The descriptive epidemiology of sudden infant deaths among natives and whites in Alaska. *American Journal of Epidemiology, 122*, 637–643.

Adams, R., & Maurer, D. (1983, April). *A demonstration of color perception in the newborn*. Paper presented at the Society for Research in Child Development, Detroit, MI.

Adams, R., & Maurer, D. (1984, April). The use of habituation to study newborns' color vision. Paper presented at the 4th International Conference on Infant Studies, New York, NY.

Addy, D. P. (1976). Infant feeding: A current view. *British Medical Journal, 1*, 1268–1271.

Adelson, E., & Fraiberg, S. (1974). Gross motor development in infants blind from birth. *Child Development, 45*, 114–126.

Ainsworth, M. (1967). *Infancy in Uganda: Infant care and the growth of attachment*. Baltimore: Johns Hopkins Press.

Ainsworth, M., Blehar, M., Waters, E., & Wall, S. (1978). *Patterns of Attachment*. Hillsdale, NJ: Erlbaum.

Alan Guttmacher Institute. (1981). *Teenage pregnancy: The problem that hasn't gone away*. New York: Author.

Aldrich, R., & Hewitt, E. (1947). Self-regulating feeding program for infants. *Journal of the American Medical Association, 135*, 915–917.

Allergy Foundation of America. (1971). *Why are allergies a national health problem?* (Fact Sheet). New York: Author.

American Academy of Pediatrics. (1978). Breast-feeding. *Pediatrics, 62*, 591–601.

American Academy of Pediatrics. (1987). Neonatal anesthesia. *Pediatrics, 80*, 446.

American Academy of Pediatrics. (1982). Task force report. The promotion of breast-feeding. *Pediatrics, 69*, 654–661.

American Academy of Pediatrics. (1985). Prolonged infantile apnea. *Pediatrics, 76*, 129–130.

American Medical Association. Report of the council on scientific affairs. (1985). AMA diagnostic and treatment guidelines concerning child abuse and neglect. *Journal of the American Medical Association, 254*, 796–800.

Anderson, S., Chinn, H., & Fisher, K. (1982). History and current status of infant formulas. *American Journal of Clinical Nutrition, 35*, 381–397.

Annis, L. (1978). *The child before birth*. Ithaca, NY: Cornell University Press.

Appleton, T., Clifton, R., & Goldberg, S. (1975). The development of behavioral competence in infancy. In F. Horowitz, (Ed.), *Review of child development research* (Vol. 4, pp. 101–186). Chicago: University of Chicago Press.

Ashmead, D., & Perlmutter, M. (1980). Infant memory in everyday life. In M. Perlmutter (Ed.), *New directions for child development: Children's memory* (Vol. 10, pp. 1–16). San Francisco: Josey-Bass.

Aslin, R., & Dumais, S. (1980). Binocular vision in infants: A review and theoretical framework. In H. Reese & L. Lipsitt (Eds.), *Advances in child development and behavior* (Vol. 15, pp. 54–99). New York: Academic Press.

Aslin, R., Pisoni, D., & Jusczyk, P. (1983). Auditory development and speech perception in infancy. In P. H. Mussen (Ed.), *Handbook of child psychology: Vol. 2. Infancy and developmental psychobiology* (4th ed., pp. 573–688). New York: Wiley.

Aston, A. (1984). *Toys that teach your child.* Charlotte, NC: East Woods Press.

Austin, G. (1978). *The parents' medical manual.* Englewood Cliffs, NJ: Prentice Hall.

Bachman, J. (1983). Prenatal care and the normal pregnant woman. *Primary care, 10* (2), 145–160.

Bandura, A. (1977). *Social learning theory.* Englewood Cliffs, NJ: Prentice Hall.

Baldwin, A. (1967). *Theories of child development.* New York: Wiley.

Bangs, T. (1982). *Language and learning disorders of the preacademic child* (2d ed.). Englewood Cliffs, NJ: Prentice Hall.

Banks, M., & Salapatek, P. (1983). Infant visual perception. In P. Mussen (Ed.), *Handbook of child psychology: Vol. 2. Infancy and developmental psychobiology* (4th ed., pp. 435–571). New York: Wiley.

Barclay, L. (1985). *Infant development.* New York: Holt, Rinehart, Winston.

Barglow, P., Vaughn, B., & Moliter, N. (1987). Effects of maternal absence due to employment on the quality of infant-mother attachment in a low risk sample. *Child Development, 58,* 945–954.

Barnes, G., Lethin, A., Jackson, E., & Shea, N. (1953). Management of breast-feeding. *Journal of the American Medical Association, 151,* 192–199.

Barr, H., Streissguth, A., Martin, D., & Herman, C. (1984). Infant size at 8 months of age: Relationship to maternal use of alcohol, nicotine, and caffeine during pregnancy. *Pediatrics, 74,* 336–341.

Baruffi, G., Dellinger, W., Stobino, D., Rudolph, A., Timmons, R., & Ross, A. (1984). A study of pregnancy outcomes in a maternity center and a tertiary care hospital. *American Journal of Public Health, 74,* 973–978.

Bates, E., Benigni, L., Bretherton, I., Camaioni, L., & Volterra, V. (1977). From gesture to the first word: On cognitive and social prerequisites. In M. Lewis & L. Rosenblum (Eds.), *Interaction, conversation and the development of language* (pp. 247–317). New York: Wiley.

Bates, E., O'Connell, B., & Shore, C. (1987). Language and communication in infancy. In J. Osofsky (Ed.), *Handbook of infant development* (2d ed., pp. 149–203). New York: Wiley.

Bates, J. (1980). The concept of difficult temperament. *Merrill-Palmer Quarterly, 25,* 299–319.

Bates, J. (1987). Temperament in infancy. In J. Osofsky (Ed.), *Handbook on infant development* (2d ed., pp. 1101–1149). New York: Wiley.

Batshaw, M., & Perret, Y. (1981). *Children with handicaps A medical primer.* Baltimore: Brooks.

Baumrind, D. (1973). The development of instrumental competence through socialization. In A. Picke (Ed.), *Minnesota symposia on child psychology* (Vol. 7, pp. 3–46). Minneapolis: University of Minnesota Press.

Baxter, A. (1985). *Techniques for dealing with child abuse.* Springfield, IL: Charles C. Thomas.

Bayley, N. (1935). The development of motor abilities during the first three years. *Monographs of the Society of Research in Child Development, 1* (Serial No. 1).

Bayley, N. (1969). *Bayley scales of infant development.* New York: Psychological Corp.

Bayley, N., & Schaefer, E. (1964). Corelations of maternal and child behaviors with the development of mental abilities; Data from the Berkeley Growth Study. *Monographs of the Society for Research in Child Development, 29* (6, Serial No. 97).

Beal, V. (1980). *Nutrition in the life span.* New York: Wiley.

Beauchamp, G. (1981). The development of taste in infancy. In J. Bond, L. Filer, G. Lavielle, A. Thomson, & W. Weil (Eds.), *Infant and child feeding* (pp. 413–426). New York: Academic Press.

Beauchamp, G., & Cowart, B. (1986, March). When tots taste salt. *Science, 86,* 10.

Beauchamp, G., & Moran, M. (1984). Acceptance of sweet and salty tastes in 2 year old children. *Appetite, 5,* 291–305.

Beck, S. (1979). *Baby talk: How your child learns to speak.* New York: New American Library.

Becker, W. (1964). Consequences of different kinds of parental discipline. In M. Hoffman, & L. Hoffman (Eds.), *Review of child development research* (Vol. 1, pp. 169–208). New York: Russell Sage Foundation.

Bee, W., Barnard, K., Eyeres, S., Gray, C., Hammond, M., Spietz, A., Snyder, C., & Clark., B. (1982). Prediction of IQ and language skill from perinatal status, child performance, family circumstances and mother-infant interaction. *Child Development, 53,* 1134–1156.

Beedle, G. (1984). Teeth. In C. Kempe, H. Silver, & D. O'Brien. *Current pediatric diagnosis and treatment.* (8th ed., pp. 290–293). Los Altos, CA: Lange.

Behrman, R., & Vaughan, V. (1983). *Nelson textbook of pediatrics* (12th ed). Philadelphia: Saunders.

Bell, S., & Ainsworth, D. (1972). Infant crying and maternal responsiveness. *Child Development, 43,* 1171–1190.

Beller, E. (1979). Early intervention programs. In J. Osofsky (Ed.), *Handbook of infant development.* (pp. 852–894). New York: Wiley.

Belsky, J. (1979). The interrelation of parental and spousal behavior during infancy in transitional nuclear families: An exploratory analysis. *Journal of Marriage and the Family, 41,* 62–68.

Belsky, J. (1981). Early human experience: A family perspective, *Developmental Psychology, 17,* 3–23.

Belsky, J. (1984). Two waves of day care research: Developmental effects and conditions of quality. In R. Ainslie (Ed.), *The child in the day care setting* (pp. 1–34). New York: Praeger.

Belsky, J. (1988). The "effects" of infant day care reconsidered. *Early Childhood Research Quarterly. 3,* 235–272.

Belsky, J., & Most, R. (1981). From exploration to play: A cross-sectional study of infant free play behavior. *Developmental Psychology, 17,* 630–639.

Belsky, H., & Rovine, M. (1988). Nonmaternal care in the first year of life and the security of infant-parent attachment security. *Child Development, 59,* 157–167.

Belsky, J., & Steinberg, L. (1978). The effects of day care: A critical review. *Child Development, 49,* 929–949.

Belsky, J., Steinberg, L., & Walker, H. (1982). The ecology of daycare. In M. Lamb (Ed.), *Nontraditional families: Parenting and child development* (pp. 71–116). Hillsdale, NJ: Erlbaum.

Belsky, J., & Volling, B. (1987). Mothering, fathering, and marital interaction in the family triad: Exploring family systems processes. In P. Berman & F. Pedersen (Eds.), *Men's transition to parenthood: Longitudinal studies of early family experience* (pp. 37–63). Hillsdale, NJ: Erlbaum.

Bench, J., Collyer, Y., Langford, C., & Toms R. (1972). A comparison between the neonatal sound-evoked startle response and the head-drop (Moro) reflex. *Developmental Medicine and Child Neurology, 14,* 308–314.

Berg, W., Adkinson, C., & Strock, B. (1973). Duration and frequency of periods of alertness in neonates. *Developmental Psychology, 15,* 760–769.

Berger, M. (1982). Personality development and temperament. In R. Porter & G. Collins (Eds.), *Temperamental differences in infants and young children.* Ciba Foundation Symposium, 89 (pp. 176–190). London: Pittman.

Berman, P., & Pederson, F. (1987). Research on men's transition to parenthood. In P. Berman & F. Pederson (Eds.), *Men's transition to parenthood: Longitudinal studies of family experience* (pp. 217–242). Hillsdale, NJ: Erlbaum.

Bernhardt, J. (1987). Sensory capabilities of the fetus. *Maternal Child Nursing Journal, 12,* 44–46.

Berry, K. (1975). Developmental study of recognition of antecedents of infant vocalizations. *Perceptual and Motor Skills, 41,* 400–402.

Bertenthal, B., & Fischer, K. (1978). Development of self-recognition in the infant. *Developmental Psychology, 14,* 44–50.

Bettleheim, B. (1970). Food to nurture the mind. *Washington, DC: The Children's Foundation.*

Biller, H. (1981). Father absence, divorce and personality development. In M. Lamb (Ed.), *The role of the father in child development* (2d ed., pp. 489–552). New York: Wiley.

Birnholz, J., & Benacerraf, B. (1983). The development of fetal hearing. *Science, 222,* 516–518.

Blass, E., Ganchrow, J., & Stiener, J. (1984). Clinical conditioning in newborn humans 2–48 hours of age. *Infant Behavior and Development, 7,* 223–235.

Bloom, B. (1964). *Stability and change in human characteristics.* New York: Wiley.

Bloom, L. (1970). *Language development: Form and function in emerging grammars.* Cambridge, MA: MIT Press.

Bloom, L. (1973). *One word at a time: The use of single word utterances before syntax.* The Hague: Mouton.

Bloom, L. (1975). Language development. In F. Horowitz (Ed.), *Review of child development research* (Vol. 4, pp. 245–303). Chicago: University of Chicago Press.

Boklage, C. (1980). The sinisitral blastocyst: An embryonic perspective on the development of brain-function asymetries. In J. Herron (Ed.), *Neuropsychology of left-handedness* (pp. 115–137). New York: Academic Press.

Boring, E. (1923, June). Intelligence as the tests test it. *New Republic, 35,* 35–37.

Bornstein, M. (1985). Human infant color vision and color perception. *Infant Behavior and Development, 8,* 109–113.

Bower, T. (1977). *A primer of infant development.* San Francisco: Freeman.

Bower, T. (1982). *Development in infancy* (2d ed). San Francisco: Freeman.

Bower, T., Broughton, J., & Moore, M. (1970). Demonstration of intention in the reaching behavior of neonate humans. *Nature, 228,* 679–681.

Bowlby, J. (1969). *Attachment and loss. Vol. 1: Attachment.* New York: Basic.

Brackbill, Y. (1979). Obstetrical medication and infant behavior. In J. Osofsoky, (Ed.), *Handbook of infant development* (pp. 76–125). New York: Wiley.

Brackbill, Y., McManus, K., & Woodard, L. (1985). *Medication in maternity: Infant exposure and maternal information.* Ann Arbor, MI: The University of Michigan Press.

Bradley, R. (1974). *Husband coached childbirth.* New York: Harper & Row.

Braine, M. (1976). Children's first word combinations. *Monographs of the Society for Research in Child Development, 41* (Serial No. 164).

Brambati, B., & Oldrini, A. (1986). Methods of chorionic villus sampling. In B. Brambati, G. Simoni, & S. Fabro (Eds.), *Chorionic villus sampling* (pp. 73–97). New York: Dekker.

Brazelton, T. (1973). *Neonatal behavioral assessment scale.* Clinics in Developmental Medicine, No. 50. Philadelphia: Lippincott.

Bredberg, G. (1985). The anatomy of the developing ear. In S. Trehub & B. Schmeiter (Eds.), *Auditory development in infancy* (pp. 3–20). New York: Plenum Press.

Brengman, S., & Burns, M. (1983). Vaginal delivery after C-section. *American Journal of Nursing, 83,* 1544–1547.

Brennan, W., Ames, E., & Moore, R. (1983). Age differences in infants' attention to patterns of different complexity. *Science, 151,* 354–356.

Bretherton, I., Beeghly-Smith, M., Williamson, C., & McNew, S. (1980, April). *"I hurt your feelings 'cause I was mean to you." Toddlers' person knowledge as expressed in their language.* Paper presented at the meeting of the International Conference on Infant Studies. New Haven, CT.

Bretherton, I., & Waters, E. (Eds.). (1985). Growing points of attachment theory and research. *Monographs of the Society of Research in Child Development, 50* (1–2, Serial No. 209).

Bridges, K. (1932). Emotional development in early infancy. *Child Development, 3,* 324–341.

Brody, S. (1951). *Patterns of mothering.* New York: International University Press.

Bromwich, R. (1980). *Working with parents and infants: An interactional approach.* Baltimore: University Park Press.

Bronson, G. (1972). Infants' reactions to unfamiliar persons and novel objects. *Monographs of the Society of Research in Child Development, 37* (3, Serial No. 148).

Brookhart, J., & Hock, E. (1976). The effects of experimental context and experimental background on infants' behavior toward their mothers and strangers. *Child Development, 47,* 333–340.

Brooks, J., & Lewis, M. (1976). Infants' response to strangers: Midget, adult and child. *Child Development, 47,* 323–332.

Brooks, J., & Lewis, M. (1976, July). *Visual self-recognition in infancy: Contingency and the self-other distinction.* Paper presented at the Southeastern Conference 21st International Congress, Paris.

Brooks-Gunn, J., & Lewis, M. (1979). The effects of age and sex on infants' playroom behavior. *Journal of Genetic Psychology, 134,* 99–105.

Brooks-Gunn, J., & Lewis, M. (1982). The development of self-knowledge. In C. Kropp & J. Krakow (Eds.), *The child: Development in a social context* (pp. 333–387). Reading, MA: Addison-Wesley.

Broome, C., and Frazer, D. (1981). Pertussis in the United States, 1979: A look at vaccine efficacy. *Journal of Infectious Diseases, 144,* 187–190.

Brooten, D., & Jordan, C. (1983). Caffeine and pregnancy: A research review and recommendations for clinical practice. *JOGN Nursing, 12*(2), 190–195.

Brown, R. (1973). *A first language: The early stages.* Cambridge, MA: Harvard University Press.

Brown, R. (1977). Introduction. In C. Snow & C. Ferguson (Eds.), *Talking to children* (pp. 1–27). London: Cambridge University Press.

Brown, R., & Fraser, C. (1963). The acquisition of syntax. In C. Cofer & B. Musgrave (Eds.), *Verbal behavior and learning: Problems and processes* (pp. 158–197). New York: McGraw-Hill.

Bruck, K. (1961). Temperature regulation in the newborn infant. *Biologic Neonatorum, 3,* 65–119.

Bruner, J. (1978). Learning the mother tongue. *Human Nature, 1,* 42–49.

Bryen, D. (1982). *Inquiries into child language.* Boston: Allyn & Bacon.

Burnett, C., & Johnson, E. (1971). Development of gait in childhood: Part 2. *Developmental Medicine and Child Neurology, 13,* 207.

Burroughs, A. (1986). *Bleier's maternity nursing* (5th ed.). Philadelphia: Saunders.

Burton, R. (1972). Cross-sex identity in Barbados. *Developmental Psychology, 6,* 365–374.

Bushnell, E. (1985). The decline of visually guided reaching during infancy. *Infant Behavior and Development, 8,* 139–155.

Buss, A., & Plomin, R. (1975). *A temperament theory of personality.* New York: Wiley.

Butler, N., & Goldstein, H. (1973). Smoking in pregnancy and subsequent child development. *British Medical Journal, 4,* 573.

Butterfield, E., & Siperstein, N. (1974). Influence of contingent auditory stimulation upon non-nutritional suckle. In J. Bosma (Ed.), *Third symposium on oral sensation and perception: The mouth of the infant* (pp. 313–334). Springfield, IL: Charles C. Thomas.

Byers, T., Graham, S., Rzepka, T., & Marshall, J. (1985). Lactation and breast cancer. *American Journal of Epidemiology, 121,* 644–674.

Bzoch, K., & League, R. (1971). *Assessing language skills in infancy.* Tallahassee, FL. Anhinga Press.

Caldwell, B. (1964). The effects of infant care. In M. Hoffman & L. Hoffman (Eds.), *Review of child development research* (Vol. 1, pp. 9–87). New York: Russell Sage Foundation.

Caldwell, B., & Bradley, R. (1979). *Home observation for measurement of the environment.* Little Rock, AR: University of Arkansas.

Campos, J., Barrett, K., Lamb, M., Goldsmith, H., & Stenberg, C. (1983). Socioemotional development. In P. Mussen (Ed.), *Handbook of child psychology: Vol. 2. Infancy and developmental psychobiology* (4th ed., pp. 784–915). New York: Wiley.

Campos, J., Langer, A., & Krowitz, A. (1970). Cardiac responses on the visual difference in prelocomotor human infants. *Science, 170,* 196–197.

Campos, J., & Stenberg, C. (1981). Perception, appraisal, and emotion: The onset of social referencing. In M. Lamb & L. Sherrod (Eds.), *Infant social cognition: Empirical and theoretical considerations* (pp. 273–314). Hillsdale, NJ: Erlbaum.

Canadian Paediatric Society Nutrition Committee. (1979). Infant feeding. *Canadian Journal of Public Health, 70,* 376–385.

Capalbo-Moore, L., & Jacobellis, J. (1983). *Maternal postural selections during the active phase of first stage labor.* Unpublished master's thesis. The University of Utah, St. Lake City.

Carr, D. (1971). Chromosome studies on selected spontaneous abortions: Polyploidy in man. *Journal of Medical Genetics, 8,* 164.

Cataldo, C. (1983). *Infants and toddler programs: A guide to very early education programs.* Reading, MA: Addison-Wesley.

Cattell, P. (1940). *The measurement of intelligence of infants and young children.* New York: Psychological Corp.

Caudill, W., & Schooler, C. (1973). Child behavior and child rearing in Japan and the United States: An interim report. *Journal of Nervous and Mental Disease, 157,* 323–338.

Charney, R. (1980). Speech roles and the development of personal pronouns. *Journal of Child Language, 7,* 509–528.

Chase-Lansdale, P., & Owen, M. (1987). Maternal employment in a family context: Effects of infant-mother and infant-father attachment. *Child Development, 58,* 1505–1512.

Cherlin, A. (1977). The effect of children on marital disruption. *Demography, 14,* 265–272.

Chess, S., Thomas, A., & Birch, H. (1965). *Your child is a person.* New York: Viking.

Child, I. (1968). Personality in culture. In E. Borgatta & W. Lambert (Eds.), *Handbook of personality theory and research* (pp. 82–145). Chicago: Rand McNally.

Chisholm, J. (1981). Prenatal influences on aboriginal-white Australian differences in neonatal irritability. *Ethology and Sociobiology, 2,* 67–73.

Chomsky, N. (1968). *Language and mind.* New York: Harcourt, Brace, Jovanovich.

Chomsky, N. (1975). *Reflections on language*. New York: Pantheon.

Clark, E. (1973). What's in a word: On the child's acquisition of semantics in his first language. In T. Moore (Ed.), *Cognitive development and the acquisition of language* (pp. 65–110). New York: Academic Press.

Clark, H., & Clark, E. (1977). *Psychology and language*. New York: Harcourt, Brace, Jovanovich.

Clarke-Stewart, A. (1982). *Daycare*. Cambridge, MA: Harvard University Press.

Clarke-Stewart, A., & Fein, G. (1983). Early childhood programs. In P. Mussen (Ed.), *Handbook of child psychology: Vol. 2. Infancy and developmental psychobiology* (4th ed., pp. 917–999). New York: Wiley.

Cockburn, F. (1984). The newborn. In J. Forfar & G. Arneil (Eds.), *Textbook of pediatrics* (3d ed.) (Vol. 1, pp. 117–258). New York: Churchill Livingstone.

Cogan, R. (1980). Effects of childbirth preparation. *Clinical Obstetrics and Gynecology, 23*, 1–14.

Cohen, L., DeLoache, J., & Strauss, M. (1979). Infant visual perception. In J. Osofsky (Ed.), *Handbook of infant development* (pp. 393–438). New York: Wiley.

Cohen, S. (1978). Maternal employment and mother-child interaction. *Merrill-Palmer Quarterly, 24*, 189–197.

Colburn, D. (1986, June 19). Children still perish for lack of vaccine. *Greenville Daily Reflector*, p. 22.

Collins, E., & Turner, G. (1975). Maternal effects of regular salicylate in gestation in pregnancy. *Lancet, 2*, 335–337.

Comer, J., & Poussaint, A. (1976). *Black child care*. New York: Pocket Books.

Committee on Infectious Diseases. American Academy of Pediatrics. (1986). *Report of the Committee on Infectious Diseases* (20th ed.). Elk Grove Village, IL: American Academy of Pediatrics.

Committee on Nutrition. American Academy of Pediatrics. (1974). Salt intake and eating patterns of infants and children in relation to blood pressure. *Pediatrics, 53*, 115–121.

Committee on Nutrition. American Academy of Pediatrics. (1976a). Commentary on breast-feeding and infant formulas, including proposed standards for formulas. *Pediatrics, 57*, 287–285.

Committee on Nutrition. American Academy of Pediatrics. (1976b). Iron supplementation for infants. *Pediatrics, 58*, 765–768.

Committee on Nutrition. American Academy of Pediatrics. (1979). Fluoride supplementation: Revised dosage schedule. *Pediatrics, 63*, 150–152.

Committee on Nutrition. American Academy of Pediatrics. (1980). On the feeding of supplemental foods to infants. *Pediatrics, 65*, 1178–1181.

Committee on Nutrition. American Academy of Pediatrics. (1985). *Pediatric nutrition handbook* (2d ed.). Elk Grove Village, IL: American Academy of Pediatrics.

Committee to Study the Prevention of Low Birthweight. (1985). *Preventing Low Birth Weight*. Washington, DC: National Academy Press.

Condon, W., & Sander, L. (1974). Synchrony demonstrated between movements of the neonate and adult speech. *Child Development, 45*, 456–462.

Connolly, K., & Stratton, P., (1969). An exploration of some parameters affecting classical conditioning in the neonate. *Child Development, 40*, 431–441.

Connor, F., Williamson, G., & Siepp, J. (Eds.). (1978). *Program guide for infants and toddlers with neruomotor and other developmental disabilities*. New York: Teachers College Press.

Conway, D., Prediville, W., Morris, A., & Stirrat, C. (1984). Management of spontaneous rupture of the membranes in the absence of labor in primigravid women at term. *American Journal of Obstetrics and Gynecology, 150*, 947–951.

Coopersmith, S. (1967). *The antecedents of self-esteem*. San Francisco: Freeman.

Cox, J., & Gallagher-Allred, C. (1980). *Normal diet: Age of dependency*. Columbus, OH: The Ohio State University.

Cratty, B. (1979). *Perceptual and motor development in infants and young children* (2d ed.). Englewood Cliffs, NJ: Prentice Hall.

Cravioto, J., & Robles, B. (1965). Evolution of adaptive and motor behavior during rehabilitation from kwashiorkor. *American Journal of Orthopsychiatry, 35*, 449–464.

Crittenden, P. (1985). Maltreated infants: Vulnerability and resilience. *Journal for Child Psychology and Psychiatry, 26*, 85–96.

Crook, C. (1977). Taste and the temporal organization of neonatal sucking. In J. Weiffenbach (Ed.), *Taste and development: The genesis of sweet preference* (pp. 146–158). Bethesda, MD: National Institutes of Health. (DHEW Pub No. NIH 771068).

Crook, W. (1975). *Your allergic child.* Jackson, TN: Professional Books.

Cruttenden, A. (1970). A phonetic study of babbling. *British Journal of Disorders in Communication, 5,* 110–118.

Cummings, F. (1980). Caregiver stability and day care. *Developmental Psychology, 16,* 31–37.

Daehler, M., & Greco, C, (1985). Memory in very young children, In M. Pressley & C. Brainerd (Eds.), *Cognitive learning and memory in children* (pp. 49–79). New York: Springer-Verlag.

Dahl, L. (1972). Salt and hypertension. *American Journal of Clinical Nutrition, 25,* 231.

Dale, P. (1976). *Language and development* (2d ed.). New York: Holt, Rinehart and Winston.

Damon, W., & Hart, D. (1982). The development of self-understanding from infancy through adolescence. *Child Development, 53,* 841–864.

Daniels, D., & Plomin, R. (1985). Differential experience of siblings in the same family. *Developmental Psychology, 21,* 747–760.

Daniels, D., Plomin, R., & Greenhalgh, J. (1984). Correlates of difficult temperament in infancy. *Child Development, 55,* 1184–1194.

Darley, F., & Winitz, H. (1961). Age of the first word: Review of research. *Journal of Speech and Hearing Disorders, 26,* 272–290.

Darwin, C. (1877). A biographical sketch of an infant. *Mind, 2,* 285–294.

Davis, D. (1985). Infant car safety: The role of perinatal caregivers. *Birth, 12* (Supplement), 21–27.

Davis, H., Gartner, J., Galvis, A., Michaels, R., & Mestad, P. (1981). Acute upper airway obstruction: Croup and epiglottis. *Pediatric Clinics of North America, 28,* 859–880.

Davis, J., & Rovee-Collier, C. (1983). Alleviated forgetting of a learned contingency in 8-week-old infants. *Developmental Psychology, 19,* 353–365.

Day, R. (1967). Factors influencing offspring. *American Journal of Diseases of Children, 142,* 6.

Decarie, T. (1969). A study of the mental and emotional development of the thalidomide child. In B. Foss (Ed.), *Determinants of infant behavior* (Vol. 4, pp. 110–114) London: Methuen.

DeCasper, A., & Fifer, W. (1980). Of human bonding: Newborns prefer their mothers' voices. *Science, 208,* 1174–1176.

DeCasper, A., & Prescott, P. (1984). Human newborns' perception of male voices: Preference, discrimination and reinforcing value. *Developmental Psychobiology, 17,* 481–491.

DeCasper, A., & Spence, M. (1986). Prenatal maternal speech influences newborns' perception of speech sounds. *Infant Behavior and Development, 9,* 133–150.

DeKaban, A. (1970). *Neurology of early childhood.* Baltimore: Williams and Wilkins.

de Mause, L. (1974). The evolution of childhood. In L. de Mause (Ed.), *The history of childhood* (pp. 1–73). New York: Psychohistory Press.

Dennis, W. (1941). Infant development under conditions of restricted practice and of minimal social stimulation. *Genetic Psychology Monographs, 23,* 143–191.

Derryberry, D., & Rothbart, M. (1984). Emotions, attention and temperment. In C. Izard, J. Kagan, & R. Zajonc (Eds.), *Emotions, cognition, and behavior* (pp. 132–166). London: Cambridge University Press.

Desmond, M., Wilson, G., Alt, E., & Fisher, E. (1980). The very low birth weight infant after discharge from intensive care: Anticipatory health care and developmental course. *Current Problems in Pediatrics, 10,* 1–59.

Desor, J., Maller, O., & Andrews, K. (1975). Ingestive responses of human newborns to salty, sour and bitter stimuli. *Journal of Comparative and Physiological Psychology, 89,* 966–970.

Desor, J., Maller, O., & Greene, L. (1977). Preference for sweet in humans: Infant children and adults. In J. Wiffenbach (Ed.), *Taste and development: The genesis of sweet preference* (pp. 161–172). Bethesda, MD: National Institutes of Health. (DHEW Pub. No. NIH 77-1068).

de Villiers, J., & de Villiers, P. (1978). *Language acquisition.* Cambridge, MA: Harvard University Press.

de Villiers, J., & de Villiers, P. (1979). *Early language.* Cambridge, MA: Harvard University Press.

Devitt, N. (1979b). How doctors conspired to eliminate the midwife even though scientific data supports midwifery. In D. Stewart and L. Stewart (Eds.), *Compulsory hospitalization: Freedom of choice in childbirth* (Vol. 2, pp. 345–370). Marble Hill: MO: National Association of Parents and Professionals for Safe Alternatives in Childbirth.

Dickie, J., & Matheson, P. (1984, August). *Mother-father-infant: Who needs support.* Paper presented at the meeting of the American Psychological Association, Toronto, Ontario, Canada.

Dick-Read, Grantley. (1972). *The practice of natural childbirth.* New York: Harper & Row.

Dobbing, J. (1976). Vulnerable periods in brain growth and somatic growth. In D. Roberts & A. Thomson (Eds.), *The biology of human fetal growth* (pp. 137–147). New York: Halsted Press.

Dodson, F. (1970). *How to parent.* New York: Signet.

Doering, P., & Stewart, R. (1978). The extent and character of drug consumption during pregnancy. *Journal of the American Medical Association, 239,* 843–846.

Doman, G. (1982). *Teach your baby math.* New York: Pocket Books.

Doman, G. (1984). *How to multiply your baby's intelligence.* New York: Doubleday.

Dreikurs, R. (1958). *The challenge of parenthood* (rev. ed.). New York: Hawthorn.

Dryden, R. (1978). *Before birth.* London: Heinemann.

DuBois, F. (1952). The security of discipline. *Mental Hygiene, 36,* 353–372.

Dubowitz, V. (1980). *The floppy infant* (2d ed.). Philadelphia: Lippincott.

Dubowitz, L., Dubowitz, V., & Goldberg, C. (1970). Clinical assessment of gestational age in the newborn infant. *Journal of Pediatrics, 77,* 1–10.

Dyer, E. (1963). Parenthood as crisis: A restudy. *Marriage and Family Living, 25,* 488–496.

Eagan, B., Whelan-Williams, S., and Brooks, W. (1985). The abuse of infants by manual shaking: Medical, social and legal issues. *Florida Medical Association Journal, 72,* 503–507.

Eastham, E., & Walker, W. (1977). Effect of cow's milk on the gastrointestinal tract: A persistant dilemma for the pediatrician. *Pediatrics, 60,* 477.

Eddy, T. (1973). Past and present malnutrition and its effect on health today. *Childhood and society.* New York: Norton.

Eichorn, D. (1979). Physical development: current foci of research. In J. Osofsky (Ed.), *Handbook of infant development* (pp. 283–282). New York: Wiley.

Eiduson, B., Kornfein, M., Zimmerman, I., & Weisner, T. (1982). Comparative socialization practices in traditional and alternative families. In M. Lamb (Ed.), *Nontraditional families: Parenting and child development* (pp. 315–346). Hillsdale, NJ: Erlbaum.

Eilers, R., & Minifie, F. (1975). Fricative discrimination in early infancy. *Journal of Speech and Hearing Research, 18,* 158–167.

Eimas, P. (1975). Speech perception in early infancy. In L. Cohen & P. Salapatek (Eds.), *Infant perception: From sensation to cognition* (Vol. 2, pp. 193–231). New York: Academic Press.

Eimas, P., Siqueland, E., Juzcyk, P., & Vigorito, J. (1971). Speech perception in early infancy. *Science, 1971, 171,* 303–306.

Eisenberg, R. (1976). *Auditory competence in early life.* Baltimore: University Park Press.

Elkind, D. (1981). *The hurried child: Growing up too fast too soon.* Reading, MA: Addison-Wesley.

Emde, R. (1980). Levels of meaning for infant emotions: A biosocial view. In W. Collins (Ed.), *Minnesota symposia of child psychology: Vol. 13. Development of cognition, affect and social relations* (pp. 1–38). Hillsdale, NJ: Erlbaum.

Emde, R., Gaensbauer, T., & Harmon, R. (1976). Emotional expression in infancy: A biobehavioral study. *Psychological Issues* (Vol. 10, No. 1) (Monograph 37) New York: International Universities Press.

Endsley, R., & Bradbard, M. (1981). *Quality day care: A handbook for parents and caregivers.* Englewood Cliffs, NJ: Prentice Hall.

Epstein, H. (1978). Growth spurts during brain development: Implications for educational policy and posture. In J. Chall & A. Mirsky (Eds.), *Education and the brain: The seventy-seventh yearbook of the National Society for the Study of Education* (pp. 343–370). Chicago: University of Chicago Press.

Erikson, E. (1963). *Childhood and society* (2d ed.) New York: Wiley.

Ervin-Tripp, S. (1966). Language development. In L. Hoffman & M. Hoffman (Eds.), *Review of child development research* (Vol. 2, pp. 55–105). New York: Russell Sage Foundation.

Espenschade, A., & Eckert, H. (1967). *Motor development.* Columbus, OH: Merrill.

Evans, G., & Hall, J. (1976). The older sperm. *Ms., 4* (7), 48–50.

Ewy, D., & Ewy, R. (1982). *Preparation for childbirth: A Lamaze guide.* Boulder, CO: Pruett.

Fabry, P., & Tepperman, J. (1970). Meal frequency: A possible factor in human pathology. *American Journal of Clinical Nutrition, 23,* 1059.

Fagan, J. (1971). Infants' recognition memory for a series of visual stimuli. *Journal of Experimental Child Psychology, 11,* 244–250.

Fairweather, H. (1976). Sex differences in cognition. *Cognition, 4,* 231–280.

Family Life Council of Greater Greensboro, North Carolina's battered children. (1973). Leaflet.

Fan, L. (1984). Apnea of infancy and childhood. *Primary Care, 11,* 443–452.

Fantz, R. (1958). Pattern vision in young infants. *Psychological Review, 8,* 43–49.

Fantz, R. (1961). The origin of form perception. *Scientific American, 204,* 66–72.

Fantz, R. (1963). Pattern vision in newborn infants. *Science, 140,* 296–297.

Fantz, R., & Nevis, S. (1967). Pattern preferences and perceptual-cognitive development in early infancy. *Merrill-Palmer Quarterly, 13,* 77–108.

Feldman, S. (1978). *Choices in childbirth.* New York: Grosset and Dunlop.

Feldman, S., Nash, S., & Aschenbrenner, B. (1983). Antecedents of fathering. *Child Development, 54,* 1628–1636.

Fenson, L., Kagan, J., Kearsley, R., & Zelazo, P. (1976). The developmental progression of manipulative play in the first two years. *Child Development, 47,* 232–236.

Finberg, L., Kiley, J., & Luttrell, C. (1963). Mass accidental salt poisoning in infancy. *Journal of the American Medical Association, 184,* 121–124.

Finkelstein, N., Dent, C., Gallagher, J., & Ramey, C. (1978). Social behavior of infants and toddlers in a daycare environment. *Developmental Psychology, 14,* 257–262.

Fleischer, K. (1955). Unterschugen zur entuicklung der inneohrfunktion (intrauterine kindsbewegungen nach schallreizen). *Laryngologie, Rhinologie, Otologie, 34,* 733–740.

Fogel, A. (1984). *Infancy: Infant in family and society.* St. Paul: West.

Foman, S. J. (1974). *Infant nutrition* (2d ed.). Philadelphia: Saunders.

Foman, S., Lloyd, J., Thomas, A., & Ziegler, E., (1979). Recommendations for feeding normal infants. *Pediatrics, 63,* 52–58.

Foman, S., Thomas, L., & Filer, L., (1970). Acceptance of unsalted strained foods by normal infants. *Journal of Pediatrics, 76,* 242.

Food and Nutrition Board. (1980). *Recommended dietary allowances* (9th ed.). Washington, DC: National Research Council, National Academy of Sciences.

Ford, C. (1945). *A comparative study of human reproduction.* Yale University Publications in Anthropology No. 32. New Haven, CO: Yale University Press, 84–85.

Fosberg, S. (1981). *Family day care in the United States: Summary of findings: Vol. 1. Final report of the national day care home study.* Cambridge, MA: ABT Associates.

Foundation for the Study of Infant Death and the British Paediatric Respiratory Group. (1985). Apnoea monitors and sudden infant death. *Archives of Disease of Children, 60,* 76–80.

Fowler, W. (1980). *Infant and child care: A guide to education in group settings.* Boston: Allyn & Bacon.

Fraiberg, S. (1971). Interaction in infancy: A program for blind infants. *Journal of the American Academy of Child Psychiatry, 10,* 381–405.

Fraiberg, S. (1974). Blind infants and their mothers: An examination of the sign system. In M. Lewis & L. Rosenblum (Eds.), *The effect of the infant on its caregivers* (pp. 215–232). New York: Wiley.

Fraiberg, S., Smith, M., & Adelson, E. (1969). An educational program for blind infants. *Journal of Special Education, 3,* 121–139.

Frank, L. (1968). Play is valid. *Childhood Education, 44,* 433–440.

Frankenburg, W., Dodds, J., & Fandal, A. (1973). *Denver Developmental Screening Test.* Denver, CO: Denver Developmental Materials, Inc.

Freedman, D., & Keller, B. (1948). Inheritance of behavior in infants. *Science, 140,* 196.

Freedman, E., Sachtleben, M., Dahrouge, D., & Neff, R. (1984). Long term effects of labor and delivery on offspring: A matched pair analysis. *American Journal of Obstetrics and Gynecology, 150,* 941–945.

Freeman, B., & Ritvo, E. (1984). The syndrome of autism: Establishing the diagnosis and principles of management. *Pediatric Annals, 13,* 284–296.

Freud, S. (1940). *An outline of psychoanalysis.* New York: Norton.

Freud, S. (1917). *Psychopathology of everyday life.* New York: Macmillan.

Fried, P., Watkinson, B., & Willan, A. (1984). Marijuana use during pregnancy and decreased length of gestation. *American Journal of Obstetrics and Gynecology, 150,* 23–27.

Friedman, D. (1981). Ethnic differences in babies. In E. Hetherington & R. Parke (Eds.), *Contemporary readings in child psychology* (pp. 6–12). New York: McGraw-Hill.

Frietas, B. (1984). The development of taste acceptance in human infants. *Dissertation Abstracts International, 44*(7–5), 2272. (University Microfilms No. DA83226288).

Fuhrmann, W., & Vogel, F. (1983). *Genetic counseling* (3d ed.). New York: Springer-Verlag.

Fulginiti, V. (1984). Immunization. In C. Kempe, H. Silver, & D. O'Brien. *Current pediatric diagnosis and treatment* (8th ed., pp. 129–148). Los Altos: CA: Lange.

Gallahue, D. (1982). *Understanding motor development in children.* New York: Wiley.

Gamble, T., & Zigler, E. (1986). Effects of infant day care: Another look at the evidence. *American Journal of Orthopsychiatry, 56,* 26–41.

Garn, S. (1966). Body size and its implication. In L. Hoffman & M. Hoffman (Eds.), *Review of child development research* (Vol. 2, pp. 529–566). New York: Russell Sage Foundation.

Garrow, J. (1967). The long-term prognosis of severe infantile nutrition. *Lancet, 1,* 1.

Gasser, R. (1975). *Atlas of human embryos.* New York: Harper & Row.

Gellis, S., & Kagan, B. (1986). *Current pediatric therapy.* Philadelphia: Saunders.

Gerber, M. (1981). What is appropriate curriculum for infants and toddlers? In B. Weissbound & J. Musick (Eds.), *Infants: Their social environments* (pp. 77–85). Washington, DC: National Association for the Education of Young Children.

Gerrard, J., Mackenzie, J., Goluboff, N., Garson, J., & Maningas, C. (1973). Cow's milk allergy: Prevalence and manifestations in an unselected series of newborns. *Acta Paediatrica Scandinavica,* (Suppl. 234), 1–21.

Gesell, A. (1925). *The mental growth of the preschool child.* New York: MacMillan.

Gesell, A. (1940). *The first five years of life: A guide to the study of preschool child.* New York: Harper & Brothers.

Gesell, A. (1945). *The embryology of behavior.* New York: Harper.

Gesell, A. (1954). The ontogenesis of infant behavior. In L. Carmichael, *Manual of child psychology* (2d ed., pp. 335–373). New York: Wiley.

Gesell, A., & Ames, L. (1947). The development of handedness. *Journal of Genetic Psychology, 70,* 155–175.

Gesell, A., & Ilg, F. (1937). *Feeding behavior of infants.* Philadelphia: J. B. Lippincott.

Gesell, A., & Thompson, H. (1934). *Infant behavior: Its genesis and growth.* New York: McGraw-Hill.

Ghent, W., DaSylva, N., & Farren, M. (1985). Family violence: Guidelines for recognition and management. *Canadian Medical Association Journal, 132,* 541–549.

Giattino, J., & Hogan, J. (1975). Analysis of father's speech to his language learning child. *Journal of Speech and Hearing Disorders, 40,* 524–537.

Gibson, E., & Walk, R. (1960). The "visual cliff." *Scientific American, 202,* 64–71.

Ginott, H. (1965). *Between parent and child.* New York: Macmillan.

Gleason, J. (1975). Fathers and other strangers: Men's speech to young children. *Georgetown University 26th Round Table on Language and Linguistics.* Washington, DC: Georgetown University.

Gleason, J. (1985). Studying language development. In J. Gleason (Ed.), *The development of language* (pp. 1–35). Columbus, OH: Merrill.

Golden, M., & Birns, B. (1976). Social class and infant intelligence. In M. Lewis (Ed.), *Origins of intelligence: Infancy and early childhood* (pp. 299–352). New York: Plenum.

Golding, J., Limerick, S., & Macfarlane, A. (1985). *Sudden infant death syndrome: Patterns, puzzles and problems.* Seattle: University of Washington Press.

Goldman, A. (1984). Drugs and the mechanism of the drug induced teratogenesis. In L. Stern (Ed.), *Drug use in pregnancy* (pp. 68–98). Balgowlah, Australia: ADIS Health Science.

Goldsmith, H. (1983). Emotionality in infant twins: Longitudinal results. *Abstracts of the Fourth International Congress on Twin Studies.* London.

Goldsmith, H., Buss, A., Plomin, R., Rothbart, M., Thomas, A., Chess, S., Hinde, R., & McCall, R. (1987). Roundtable: What is temperament?: Four approaches. *Child Development, 58,* 505–529.

Goldsmith, H., & Gottesman, I. (1981). Origin of variation in behavioral style: A longitudinal study of temperament in young twins. *Child Development, 52,* 91–103.

Goldstein, G., & Heiner, D. (1970). Clinical and immunological perspectives in food sensitivity. *Journal of Allergy, 46,* 270–291.

Gonzalez-Mena, J., & Eyer, D. (1980). *Infancy and caregiving.* Palo Alto, CA: Mayfield.

Gordon, I., Guinagh, B., & Tester, R. (1977). The Florida parent education infant and toddler programs. In M. Day & R. Parker (Eds.), *The preschool in action* (2d ed., pp. 95–127). Boston: Allyn & Bacon.

Gordon, J., & Haire, D. (1981). Alternatives in childbirth. In P. Ahmed (Ed.), *Pregnancy, childbirth, and parenthood* (pp. 287–313). New York: Elsevier.

Goren, C. (1975). *Form perception, innate form preferences and visually-mediated head turning in human newborns.* Paper presented at the Society for Research in Child Development, Denver, CO.

Gormican, A., Valentine, J., & Sutter, E. (1980). Relationships of maternal weight gain and infant birthweight. *Journal of the American Dietetic Association, 77,* 662–668.

Gottfried, A. (1984). Touch as an organizer of human development. In C. Brown (Ed.), *The many facets of touch* (pp. 114–120). Skillman, NJ: Johnson & Johnson.

Gottfried, A. (1985). The relationship of play materials and parental involvement to young children's development. In C. Brown & A. Gottfried (Eds.), *Play interactions: The role of toys and parental involvement in children's development* (pp. 181–185). Somerville, NJ: Johnson & Johnson.

Graham, G. C., & Adrianzen, T. B. (1972). Late "catch-up growth" after severe infantile malnutrition. *Johns Hopkins Medical Journal, 131,* 204.

Grasselli, R., & Hegner, P. (1980). *Playful parenting.* New York: Putman.

Gravett, M. (1984). Causes of preterm delivery. *Seminars in Perinatology, 8,* 246–257.

Greco, C., Rovee-Collier, C., Hayne, H., Greisler, P., & Earley, L. (1986). Ontogeny of early event memory: I. Forgetting and retrieval by 2- and 3-month-olds. *Infant Behavior and Development, 9,* 441–461.

Greenfield, P., & Tronick, E. (1980). *Infant curriculum: The Bromley-Heath Guide to the care of infants in groups* (rev. ed.). Santa Monica, CA: Goodyear.

Greenspan, S., & Greenspan, N. (1985). *First feelings: Milestones in the emotional development of your baby and child.* New York: Viking.

Guerrero, V., & Rojas, O. (1975). Spontaneous abortion and aging of human ova and spermatozoa. *New England Journal of Medicine, 293,* 573–575.

Guillory, A., Self, P., & Paden, L. (1980, April). *Odor sensitivity in one month infants.* Paper presented at the International Conference on Infant Studies, New Haven, CT.

Gunnar, M. (1978). Changing a frightening toy into a pleasant toy by allowing the infant to control its actions. *Developmental Psychology, 14,* 157–162.

Gunnar, M. (1980). Control, warning signals and distress in infancy. *Developmental Psychology, 16,* 281–289.

Gurney, J. (1979). The young child: Protein-energy malnutrition. In D. Jelliffe & E. Jelliffe (Eds.), *Nutrition and growth* (pp. 185–216). New York: Plenum.

Hainline, L., & Lemerise, E. (1982). Infants' scanning of geometric forms varying in size. *Journal of Experimental Child Psychology, 33,* 235–256.

Haith, M. (1979). Visual competence in early infancy. In R. Held, H. Leibowitz and H. Teuber (Eds.), *Handbook of sensory physiology: Vol. 8. Perception* (pp. 311–356). Berlin: Springer-Verlag.

Hall, A., & Weiner, S. (1977). *The supply of day care services in Denver and Seattle.* Meade Park, CA: Stanford Research Institute, Center for the Study of Welfare Policy.

Hall, C., & Lindzey, G. (1978). *Theories of personality* (3d ed.). New York: Wiley.

Hall, D. (1985). The outlook for low birth weight babies: *The Practitioner, 229,* 779–783.

Hall, E. (1969). *The hidden dimension.* New York: Doubleday.

Hall, G. (1891). Notes on the study of infants. *The Pedagogical Seminary, 1,* 127–138.

Halliday, M. (1975). *Learning how to speak: Explorations in the development of language.* New York: Elsevier.

Halverson, H. (1931). An experimental study of the prehension in infants by means of systematic cinema records. *Genetic Psychology Monographs, 10,* 107–286.

Hamill, P., Johnston, F., & Lemeshaw, S. (1972). *Height and weight of children: Socio-economic status: United States.* Rockville, MD: U.S. Department of Health, Education and Welfare. Pub. No. HRA 73-1601.

Hamilton, M. (1984). *Basic maternity nursing* (5th ed.). St. Louis: Mosby.

Hanawalt, B. (1977). Childrearing among the lower classes of late medieval England. *Journal of Interdisciplinary History, 8,* 1–22.

Hanson, R., & Reynolds, R. (1980). *Child development: Concepts, issues, and readings.* St. Paul: West.

Harley, R. (1983). *Pediatric opthalmology.* Philadelphia: Saunders.

Harlow, H., & Zimmerman, R. (1959). Affectional responses in the infant monkey. *Science, 130,* 431–432.

Harrigan-Hamamoto, K. (1983). *Pain in infants.* Unpublished master's thesis, California State University, Long Beach.

Hartup, W. (1983). Peer relations. In P. Mussen (Ed.), *Handbook of child psychology: Vol. 4. Socialization, personality and development* (4th ed., pp. 103–196). New York: Wiley.

Harvey, E., Boife, J., Honeyman, M., & Flannery, J. (1985). Prenatal x-ray exposure and childhood cancer in twins. *New England Journal of Medicine, 312,* 541–545.

Hassid, P. (1984). *Textbook for childbirth educators* (2d ed.). Philadelphia: Lippincott.

Hawkins, J., & Higgins, L. (1981). *Maternal and gynecological nursing.* Philadelphia: Lippincott.

Haynes, H., White, B., & Held, R. (1965). Visual accommodation in human infants. *Science, 148,* 528–530.

Hecaen, H., & Ajuriagurra, J. (1964). *Left-handedness: Manual superiority and cerebral dominance.* New York: Grune & Stratton.

Heidelise, A., Tronick, E., Lester, B., & Brazelton, T. (1979). Specific neonatal measures: The Brazelton Neonatal Behavioral assessment scale. In J. Osofsky (Ed.), *Handbook of infant development* (pp. 185–215). New York: Wiley.

Heins, M. (1984). The battered child revisited. *Journal of the American Medical Association, 251,* 3295–3300.

Held, R., & Hein, A. (1963). A movement-produced stimulation in the development of visually guided behavior. *Journal of Comparative Physiological Psychology, 56,* 872–876.

Helms, D., & Turner, J. (1976). *Exploring child behavior: Basic principles.* Philadelphia: Saunders.

Henig, R. (1982, April 5). Tiny babies living; future uncertain. *The News and Observer, 1,* 18.

Henig, R., & Fletcher, A. (1983). *Your premature baby.* New York: Rawson Associates.

Herron, M., Katz, M., & Creasy, R. (1982). Evaluation of a birth prevention program: Preliminary report. *Obstetrics and Gynecology, 59,* 452–456.

Hershenson, M. (1964). Visual discrimination in the human newborn. *Journal of Comparative and Physiological Psychology, 58,* 270–276.

Hershenson, M., Munsinger, H., & Kessen, W. (1965). Preferences for shapes of intermediate variability in the human newborn. *Science, 147,* 630–631.

Hetherington, E. (1979). Divorce: A child's perspective. *American Psychologist, 34,* 851–858.

Hetherington, E., Cox, M., & Cox, R. (1982). Effects of divorce on parents and children. In M. Lamb (Ed.), *Nontraditional families* (pp. 233–288). Hillsdale, NJ: Erlbaum.

Hetherington, E., & Parke, R. (1979). *Child Psychology: A contemporary viewpoint* (2d ed.). New York: McGraw-Hill.

Hill, L., & Breckle, R. (1983). Current uses of ultrasound in obstetrics. *Primary Care, 10*(2), 205–223.

Hill, L., & Kleinberg, F. (1984a). Effects of drugs and chemicals on the fetus and newborn (First of two parts). *Mayo Clinic Proceedings, 59,* 707–716.

Hill, L., & Kleinberg, F. (1984b). Effects of drugs and chemicals on the fetus and newborn (Second of two parts). *Mayo Clinic Proceedings, 59,* 755–765.

Himmelberger, D., Brown, B., & Cohen, E. (1978). Cigarette smoking during pregnancy and the occurrence of spontaneous abortion and congenital abnormality. *Journal of Epidemiology, 108,* 470.

Hinton, S., & Kerwin, D. (1981). *Maternal, infant and child nutrition.* Chapel Hill, NC: Health Services Consortium.

Hjelle, L., & Ziegler, D. (1976). *Personality theories: Basic assumptions and research applications.* New York: McGraw-Hill.

Hobbs, D. (1968). Transition to parenthood: A replication and extension. *Journal of Marriage and the Family, 30,* 413–417.

Hock, E. (1980). Working and nonworking mothers and their infants: A comparative study of maternal caregiving characteristics and infant social behavior. *Merrill-Palmer Quarterly, 26,* 79–101.

Hodapp, R., & Mueller, E. (1982). Early social development. In B. Wolman (Ed.), *Handbook of developmental psychology* (pp. 284–300). Englewood Cliffs, NJ: Prentice Hall.

Hoffman, L. (1974). Effects of maternal employment on the child: A review of the research. *Developmental Psychology, 10,* 204–228.

Hoffman, L. (1979). Maternal employment: 1979. *American Psychologist, 34,* 859–865.

Hoffman, M. (1970). Moral development. In P. Mussen (Ed.), *Carmichael's handbook of child psychology* (Vol. 2, pp. 261–359). New York: Wiley.

Hoffman, M. (1981). Development of moral thought, feeling and behavior. In E. Hetherington & R. Parke (Eds.), *Contemporary readings in child psychology* (2d ed., pp. 366–373). New York: McGraw-Hill.

Holden, G. (1983). Avoiding conflict: Mothers as tacticians in the supermarket. *Child Development, 50,* 1020–1035.

Holmes, D., Reich, J., & Pasternak, J. (1984). *The development of infants born at risk.* Hillsdale, NJ: Erlbaum.

Homan, W. E. (1973). Mother's milk or other milk? In *Annual editions: Readings in human development '73–'74* (pp. 72–76). Guilford, CO: Dushkin.

Hook, E., & Lindsjo, A. (1978). Down's syndrome in live births by single year maternal age interval in a Swedish study: Comparison with results from a New York study. *American Journal of Human Genetics, 30,* 19–27.

Hooker, D. (1952). *The prenatal origin of behavior.* Lawrence, KS: The University of Kansas Press.

Hopper, H., & Naremore, R. (1978). *Children's speech: A practical introduction to communication development* (2d ed.). New York: Harper & Row.

Horowitz, F. (1982). Methods of assessment for high-risk and handicapped infants. In C. Ramey & P. Trohanis (Eds.), *Finding and educating high-risk and handicapped infants* (pp. 101–118). Baltimore: University Park Press.

Hottinger, W. (1977). Motor development: Conception to age five. In C. Corbin (Ed.), *A textbook of motor development* (pp. 1–28). Dubuque, IA: Brown.

Hoving, K., Spencer, T., Robb, K., & Schulte, D. (1978). Developmental changes in visual information processing. In P. Ornstein (Ed.), *Memory development in children* (pp. 21–67). Hillsdale, NJ: Erlbaum.

Hubel, D. (1979). The brain. *Scientific American, 241,* 44–53.

Hunziker, U., & Barr, R. (1986). Increased carrying reduces infant crying: A randomized control trial. *Pediatrics, 43,* 641–648.

Hurlock, E. (1972). *Child development* (5th ed.). New York: McGraw-Hill.

Huston, A. (1983). Sex-typing. In P. Mussen (Ed.), *Handbook of child psychology: Vol. 4. Socialization, personality and development* (4th ed., pp. 387–367). New York: Wiley.

Illingworth, R. (1983). *The development of the infant and young child* (8th ed). London: Churchill Livingstone.

Immunization Practices Advisory Committee. Public Health Service. (1983). General recommendations on immunization. *Morbidity and Mortality Weekly Report, 32,* 1–17.

Immunization Practices Advisory Committee. Public Health Service. (1986). Update: Prevention of haemophilus Type b disease. *Morbidity and Mortality Weekly Report, 35,* 170–173.

Irwin, O. C. (1948). Infant speech: Development of vowel sounds. *Journal of Speech and Hearing Disorders, 13,* 31–34.

Izard, C. (1977). *Human emotions.* New York: Plenum.

Izard, C. (1978). On the ontogenesis of emotions: Cognition relationships in infancy. In M. Lewis & L. Rosenblum (Eds.), *The development of affect* (pp. 389–413). New York: Plenum.

Izard, C. (1979). *The maximally discriminative facial movement coding system (Max).* Newark, DE: University of Delaware, Instructional Resources Center.

Jacobson, J., Tianen, R., Wille, D., & Aytck, D. (1986). Infant-mother attachments and early peer relations: The assessment of behavior in an interactive context. In E. Mueller & C. Cooper (Eds.), *Process and outcome in peer relations* (pp. 57–78). New York: Academic Press.

Jakobson, R. (1968). *Child language, aphasia, and phonological universals.* The Hague: Mouton.

Jakobsson, I., & Lindberg, T. (1978). Cow's milk as a cause of infantile colic in breast-fed infants. *Lancet, 2,* 237–239.

James, T. (1985). Editorial comment: Crib death. *Journal of the American College of Cardiology, 5,* 1185–1187.

James, W. (1890). *The principles of psychology.* New York: Henry Holt.

Jarrell, M., Ashmead, G., & Mann, L. (1985). Vaginal delivery after Caesarean section: A five-year study. *Obstetrics and Gynecology, 65,* 628–632.

Jelliffe, D., & Jelliffe, E. (1972). Lactation, conception and nutrition of the nursing mother and child. *Journal of Pediatrics, 81,* 829.

Jelliffe, D., & Jelliffe, E. (1977). Breast fed is best: Modern meanings. *New England Journal of Medicine, 297,* 912–915.

Jenista, J., Powell, K., and Menegus, M. (1984). Epidemiology of neonatal enterovirus infection. *Journal of Pediatrics, 104,* 685–694.

Jenkins, J. (1969). Language and thought. In J. Voss (Ed.), *Approaches to thought* (pp. 211–237). Columbus, OH: Merrill.

Jensen, A. (1969). How much can we boost IQ and scholastic achievement? *Harvard Educational Review, 39,* 1–123.

Jirasek, J. (1983). *Atlas of human prenatal morphogenesis.* Boston: Martinus Nijhoff.

Johnson, G., Purvis, G., & Wallace, R. (1981). What nutrients do our infants really get? *Nutrition Today, 16*(4), 4–10.

Johnson, J., & Ershler, J. (1982). Curricular effects on the play of preschoolers. In D. Pepler & K. Rubin (Eds.), *Contributions to human development: Vol. 5. The play of children: Current theory and research* (pp. 130–143). Basel, Switzerland: S. Karger.

Jones, L. (1985). Father-infant relations in the first year of life. In M. Hanson & F. Bozett (Eds.), *Dimensions of fatherhood* (pp. 93–114). Beverly Hills, CA: Sage.

Kagan, J. (1979). Overview: Perspectives on human infancy. In J. Osofsky (Ed.), *Handbook of infant development* (pp. 1–25). New York: Wiley.

Kagan, J. (1981a). *The second year: The emergence of self awareness.* Cambridge, MA: Harvard University Press.

Kagan, J. (1981b). Universals in human development. In R. H. Munroe, R. L. Munroe, & B. Whiting (Eds.), *Handbook of cross-cultural human development* (pp. 53–62). New York: Garland.

Kagan, J., Kearsley, R., & Zelazo, P. (1978). *Infancy: Its place in human development.* Cambridge, MA: Harvard University Press.

Kagan, J., & Klein, R. (1973). Cross-cultural perspectives on early development. *American Psychologist, 28,* 947–961.

Kagan, J., & Lewis, M. (1965). Studies in the attention of the human infant. *Merrill-Palmer Quarterly, 11,* 95–127.

Kaiser, I. (1982). Amniocentesis. *Women and Health, 7* (3/4), 29–38.

Kamerman, S. (1986, February). *Infant care usage in the United States.* Report presented to the National Academy of Sciences Ad Hoc Committee on Policy Issues in Child Care for Infants and Toddlers, Washington, DC.

Kaminer, R., & Jedrysek, E. (1983). Age of walking and mental retardation. *American Journal of Public Health, 73,* 1094–1096.

Kane, D. (1985). *Environmental hazards to young children.* Phoenix: Onyx Press.

Karnes, M. (1982). *You and your small wonder: Book II.* Circle Pines, MN: American Guidance Service.

Kaufman, J., & Zigler, E. (1987). Do abused children become abusive parents? *American Journal of Orthopsychiatry, 57,* 186–192.

Kaye, K. (1980). Why we don't talk 'baby talk' to babies. *Journal of Child Language, 7,* 489–507.

Keister, M. (1973). *Discipline: The secret heart of child care.* Greensboro, NC: The University of North Carolina at Greensboro.

Kelly, D., & Shannon, D. (1982). Sudden infant death syndrome and near sudden infant death syndrome: A review of the literature, 1964–1982. *Pediatric Clinics of North America, 29,* 1241–1261.

Kempe, C., & Helfer, R. (1972). *Helping the battered child and his family.* Philadelphia: Lippincott.

Kendall, E. (1983). Child care and disease: What's the risk. *Young Children, 38*(5), 68–77.

Kent, R. (1980). Articulatory and acoustic perspectives on speech development. In A. Reilly (Ed.), *The communication game: Perspectives on the development of speech, language and nonverbal communication skills* (pp. 38–48). Skillman, NJ: Johnson & Johnson.

King, W., & Seegmiller, B. (1973). Performance of 14- to 22-month-old black firstborn male infants on two tests of cognitive development. *Developmental Psychology, 8,* 317–326.

Kinsbourne, M. (1978). *Asymmetrical function of the brain.* London: Cambridge University.

Klaus, M., & Kennell, J. (1976). *Maternal-infant bonding.* St. Louis: Mosby.

Klaus, M., & Kennell, J. (1982). *Parent-infant bonding.* (2d ed.). St. Louis: Mosby.

Klein, H., Papageorgiou, A., Westreich, R., Spector-Dunsky, L., Elkins, V., Kramer, M., & Gelfand, M. (1984). Care in a birth room versus a conventional setting: A controlled trial. *Canadian Medical Association Journal, 131,* 1461–1466.

Knittle, J. (1972). Obesity in childhood: A problem in adipose tissue cellular development. *Journal of Pediatrics, 81,* 1048–1059.

Knobloch, H., Stevens, F., & Malone, A. (1980). *Manual of developmental diagnosis.* New York: Harper & Row.

Kopelman, A. (1982, November). *Intraventricular hemorrhage in prematures: An update.* Program presented at the Continuing Medical Education Seminar. East Carolina University School of Medicine, Greenville, NC.

Kopp, C. (1983). Risk factors in development. In P. Mussen (Ed.), *Handbook of child psychology: Vol. 2. Infancy and developmental psychobiology.* (4th ed., pp. 1081–1188). New York: Wiley.

Kopp, C., & Parmelee, A. (1979). Prenatal and perinatal influences on infant development. In J. Osofsky (Ed.), *Handbook of infant development* (pp. 29–75). New York: Wiley.

Korner, A. (1984). The many facets of touch. In C. Brown (Ed.), *The many facets of touch* (pp. 107–113). Skillman, NJ: Johnson & Johnson.

Kottlecheck, M. (1976). The infant's relationship to the father: Experimental evidence. In M. Lamb (Ed.), *The role of the father in child development* (pp. 329–344). New York: Wiley.

Krashen, S. (1973). Lateralization, language learning, and the critical period: Some new evidence. *Language Learning, 23*(1), 63–74.

Krugman, R. (1984). Child abuse and neglect. *Primary Care, 11,* 527–534.

Krugman, S., Katz, S., Gershon, A., and Wilfert, C. (1986). *Infectious diseases of children* (8th ed.). St. Louis: Mosby.

Kuhl, P. (1981). Auditory category formation and developmental speech perception. In R. Stark (Ed.). *Language behavior in infancy and early childhood* (pp. 165–183). New York: Elsevier.

Kulka, A., Walter, R., & Fry, C. (1966). Mother infant interaction as measured by simultaneous recording of physiological processes. *Journal of American Academy of Child Psychiatry, 5,* 496.

Kullander, S., & Kaellen, B. (1971). A prospective study of smoking and pregnancy. *Acta Obstetrics and Gynecology of Scandanavia, 50,* 83.

Kunz, J. (Ed.). (1982). *American Medical Association family medical guide.* New York: Random House.

Kurokawa, J., & Zilkoski, J. (1985). Adapting hospital obstetrics to birth in a squatting position. *Birth, 12*(2), 87–90.

Lagerspetz, K., Nygard, M., & Strandwick, C. (1971). The effects of training in crawling on the motor and mental development of infants. *Scandanavian Journal of Psychology, 12,* 192–197.

Laishley, J. (1983). *Working with young children.* London: Edward Arnold.

Lamaze, F. (1970). *Painless childbirth: The Lamaze method.* Chicago: Henry Regency.

Lamb, M. (1976). *The role of the father in child development.* New York: Wiley.

Lamb, M. (1981a). Developing trust and perceived effectance in infancy. In L. Lipsitt (Ed.), *Advances in infancy research* (Vol. 1, pp. 101–127). Norwood, NJ: Ablex.

Lamb, M. (1981b). Fathers and child development: An integrative review. In M. Lamb (Ed.), *The role of the father in child development* (2d ed.) (pp. 1–73). New York: Wiley.

Lamb, M. (1982a). Early context and maternal-infant bonding: One decade later. *Pediatrics, 70,* 763–768.

Lamb, M. (1982b). Maternal employment and child development: A review. In M. Lamb (Ed.), *Nontraditional families: Parenting and child development* (pp. 45–69). Hillsdale, NJ: Erlbaum.

Lamb, M. (1982c). Parent-infant interaction, attachment and socioemotional development in infancy. In R. Emde & R. Harmon (Eds.), *The development of attachment and affiliative systems* (pp. 195–214). New York: Plenum.

Lamb, M., & Bornstein, M. (1987). *Development in infancy: An introduction* (2d ed.). New York: Random House.

Lamb, M., & Campos, J. (1982). *Development in infancy.* New York: Random House.

Langer, W. (1975). Infanticide: A historical survey. In L. deMause (Ed.), *The new psychohistory* (pp. 55–67). New York: Psychohistory Press.

Lazar, I., & Darlington, R. (1979). *Lasting effects after preschool: Summary report.* (DHEW Publication No. OHDS 79-30179). Washington, DC: U.S. Department of Health, Education and Welfare.

Lazar, I., & Darlington, R. (1982). Lasting effects of an early education. *Monographs of the Society for Research in Child Development, 47* (2–3, Serial No. 195).

Lazarus, R., & Monat, A. (1979). *Personality* (3d ed.). Englewood Cliffs, NJ: Prentice Hall.

Leach, P. (1976). *Babyhood.* New York: Knopf.

Leach, P. (1984). *The child care encyclopedia.* New York: Knopf.

Leavitt, L. (1980). The development of speech comprehension and speech production. In A. Reilly (Ed.), *The communication game: Perspectives on the development of speech, language and non-verbal communication skills* (pp. 21–30). Skillman, NJ: Johnson & Johnson.

Leavitt, R., & Eheart, B. (1985). *Toddler day care: A guide to responsive caregiving.* Lexington, MA: Heath.

Leboyer, F. (1975). *Birth without violence.* New York: Knopf.

Lechat, M., Borlee, I., Bouckaert, A., & Mission, C. (1980). Caffeine study (letter to the editor). *Science, 207,* 1296–1297.

Lehane, S. (1976). *Help your baby learn.* Englewood Cliffs, NJ: Prentice Hall.

Lempers, J., Flavell, E., & Flavell, J. (1977). The development in very young children of tacit knowledge concerning visual perception. *Genetic Psychology Monographs, 95,* 3–53.

Lenneberg, E. (1967). *Biological foundations of language.* New York: Wiley.

Lenneberg, E., Rebelsky, G., & Nichols, I. (1965). The vocalizations of infants born to deaf and hearing parents. *Human Development, 8,* 23–27.

Lester, B. (1985). There's more to crying than meets the ear. In B. Lester & C. Boukydis (Eds.), *Infant crying: Theoretical and research perspectives* (pp. 1–27). New York: Plenum.

Leventhal, J., Edgerter, S., & Murphy, J. (1984). Reassessment of the relationship of perinatal factors and child abuse. *American Journal of Diseases of Children, 138,* 1034–1039.

Leventhal, A., & Lipsitt, L. (1964). Adaptation, pitch discrimination, and sound localization in the neonate. *Child Development, 35,* 759–767.

Levin, G. (1983). *Child Psychology.* Monterey, CA: Brooks/Cole.

Levine, R. (1980). A cross-cultural perspective on parenting. In M. Fantini & R. Cardenas (Eds.), *Parenting in a multicultural society* (pp. 17–40). New York: Longman.

Levy, J. (1973). *The baby exercise book.* New York: Random House.

Lewis, C. (1979). *The infant nutrition trip.* Chapel Hill, NC: University of North Carolina School of Nursing, (Filmstrip).

Lewis, M. (1986). Origins of self-knowledge and individual differences in early self-recognition. In J. Suls & A. Greenwood (Eds.), *Psychological perspectives on the self* (Vol. 3, pp. 55–78). Hillsdale, NJ: Erlbaum.

Lewis, M. (1987). Social development in infancy and early childhood. In J. Osofsky (Ed.), *Handbook of infant development* (2d ed., pp. 419–494). New York: Wiley.

Lewis, M., & Brooks, J. (1974). Self, others and fear: Infants reactions to people. In M. Lewis & L. Rosenblum (Eds.), *The origins of fear* (pp. 195–227). New York: Wiley.

Lewis, M., & Brooks, J. (1978). Self-knowledge in emotional development. In M. Lewis & L. Rosenblum (Eds.). *The development of affect* (pp. 205–226). New York: Plenum.

Lewis, M., & Brooks-Gunn, J. (1979). *Social cognition and the acquisition of self.* New York: Plenum.

Lewis, M., & Freedle, R. (1973). Mother-infant dyad: The cradle of meaning. In P. Pliner, L. Krames, & T. Alloway (Eds.), *Communication and affect: Language and thought* (pp. 127–155). New York: Academic Press.

Lewis, M., & Michalson, L. (1983). *Children's emotions and moods: Developmental theory and measurement.* New York: Plenum.

Lewis, M., & Saarni, C. (1985). Culture and emotions. In M. Lewis & C. Saarni (Eds.), *The socialization of emotions* (pp. 1–17), New York: Plenum.

Liggins, G. (1979). What factors initiate human labor? *Contemporary Obstetrics and Gynecology, 13,* 147–149.

Lindfors, J. (1980). *Children's language and learning.* Englewood Cliffs, NJ: Prentice Hall.

Linn, L., Schoenbaum, S., Monson, R., Rosner, B., Subblefield, P., & Ryan, K. (1982). No association between coffee consumption and adverse outcomes of pregnancy. *New England Journal of Medicine, 306,* 141–145.

Linn, S., Schoenbaum, S., Monson, R., Rosner, R., Stubblefield, P., & Ryan, K. (1983). The association of marijuana use with outcome of pregnancy. *American Journal of Public Health, 73,* 1161–1164.

Lipsitt, L. (1977). Taste in human neonates: Its effect on sucking and heart rate. In J. Weiffenbach (Ed.), *Taste and development: the genesis of sweet preference* (pp. 125–141). Bethesda: MD: National Institutes of Health. (DHEW Pub. No. NIH 77–1068).

Lipsitt, L., Engen, T., & Kaye, H. (1963). Developmental changes in the olfactory threshold of the neonate. *Child Development, 34,* 371–376.

Lipsitt, L., & Levy, N. (1959). Electrotactual threshold in the neonate. *Child Development, 30,* 547–554.

Little, A., Lipsitt, L., & Rovee-Collier, C. (1984). Classical conditioning and retention of the infant's eyelid response: Effects of age and interstimulus interval. *Journal of Experimental Child Psychology, 37,* 512–524.

Locke, J. (1961). *An essay concerning human understanding.* London: Dent. (Originally published in 1690).

Lowrey, C. (1978). *Growth and development of children* (7th ed.). Chicago: Medical Yearbook.

Lowrey, C. (1986). *Growth and development of children* (8th ed.). Chicago: Medical Yearbook.

Lorenz, K. (1965). *Evolution and modification of behavior.* Chicago: University of Chicago Press.

Lubchenco, L., Hansman, C., Dressler, M., & Boyd, E. (1963). Intrauterine growth as estimated from liveborn birth-weight data at 24 to 42 weeks of gestation. *Pediatrics, 32,* 793–796.

Lunt, R., & Law, D. (1974). A review of the chronology of eruption of deciduous teeth. *Journal of the American Dental Association, 89,* 872–879.

Lumley, J., & Astbury, J. (1980). *Birth rites, birth rights.* Melbourne, Australia: Sphere Books.

Macauley, R. (1978). The myth of female superiority in language. *Journal of Child Language, 5,* 353–363.

McCall, R. (1974). Exploratory manipulation and play in the human infant. *Monographs of the Society of Research in Child Development, 39* (2, Serial No. 155).

McCandless, B. (1967). *Children: Behavior and development* (2d ed.). New York: Holt, Rinehart, & Winston.

McCarthy, D. (1954). Language development in children. In L. Carmichael (Ed.), *Manual of child psychology* (pp. 492–630). New York: Wiley.

McCarthy, P. (1979). Controversies in pediatrics: What tests are indicated for the child under 2 with fever? *Pediatric Review, 1,* 51–56.

McClenaghan, B., & Gallahue, D. (1978). *Fundamental movement: A developmental and remedial approach.* Philadelphia: Saunders.

Maccoby, E. (Ed.). (1966). *Development of sex differences.* Stanford, CA: Stanford University Press.

Maccoby, E. (1980). *Social development: Psychological growth and the parent-child relationship.* New York: Harcourt, Brace, Jovanovich.

Maccoby, E., & Feldman, S. (1972). Mother-attachment and stranger-reaction patterns in the third year of life. *Monographs of the Society for Research in Child Development, 37*(1, Serial No. 146).

Maccoby, E., & Martin, J. (1983). Socialization in the context of the family. In P. Mussen (Ed.), *Handbook of child psychology: Vol. 4. Socialization, personality and social development* (4th ed., pp. 1–101). New York: Wiley.

McDonald, K. (1980). Enhancing a child's positive self concept. In T. Yawkey (Ed.), *The self-concept of the young child* (pp. 51–61). Provo, UT: Brigham Young University Press.

McDonald, R., & Avery, D. (1983). *Dentistry for the child and adolescent* (4th ed.). St. Louis: Mosby.

MacFarlane, J. (1975). Olfaction in the development of social preferences in the human neonate. In *Parent-infant interaction: Ciba Foundation Symposium 33 (new series)* (pp. 103–117). Amsterdam: Elsevier.

McGraw, M. (1966). *The neuromuscular maturation of the human infant.* New York: Hafner, 1966.

Mckusick, V. (1981). The genetics of birth defects: A map of chromosomes in relation to diagnosis and management. In A. Bloom & L. James (Eds.), *Birth defects: Original article series, 17* (1), 229–248.

McLaren, D., & Burman, D. (1982). *Textbook of paediatric nutrition* (2d ed.). London: Churchill Livingstone.

MacMahon, B., Lin, T., Lowe, C., Mirra, A., Roynihor, B., Salber, E., Trichopoulos, D., & Valaloras, V. (1970). Lactation and cancer of the breast: Summary of an international study. *Bulletin WHO, 42,* 185.

McManus, T., & Calder, A. (1978). Upright posture and efficiency of labour. *Lancet, 1,* 72–74.

McNeil, D. (1970). The development of language. In P. Mussen (Ed.), *Carmichael's manual of child psychology* (Vol. 1, pp. 1061–1161). New York: Wiley.

Mahler, M. (1968). *On human symbiosis and the vicissitudes of individuation.* New York: International Universities Press.

Mahler, M., Pine, F., & Bergman, A. (1975). *The psychological birth of the human infant.* New York: Basic Books.

Main, M., Tomasini, L., & Tolan, W. (1979). Differences among mothers of infants judged to differ in security. *Developmental Psychology, 15,* 72–73.

Malatesta, C., & Haviland, J. (1985). Signals, symbols and socialization: The modification of emotional expression in human development. In M. Lewis & C. Saarni (Eds.), *The socialization of emotions* (pp. 89–116). New York: Plenum.

Malina, R. (1973a). Environmental factors in motor development. In C. Corbin (Ed.), *A textbook of motor development* (pp. 46–58). Dubuque, IA: Brown.

Malina, R. (1973b). Physical development factors in motor performance. In C. Corbin (Ed.), *A textbook of motor development* (pp. 36–46). Dubuque, IA: Brown.

Mandler, J. (1984). Representation and recall in infancy. In M. Moscovitch (Ed.), *Advances in the study of communication and affect: Vol. 9. Infant memory* (pp. 75–101). New York: Plenum.

Manion, J. (1977). A study of fathers and infant caretaking. *Birth and the Family Journal, 4,* 174–178.

Mans, L., Cicchetti, D., & Sroufe, L. (1978). Mirror reactions of Down's syndrome infants and toddlers: Cognitive underpinnings of self-recognition. *Child Development, 49,* 1247–1250.

Marks, M. (1985). *Pediatric infectious diseases for the practitioner.* New York: Springer-Verlag.

Martin, B. (1975). Parent-child relations. In F. Hetherington (Ed.), *Review of research in child development* (Vol. 4, pp. 463–540). Chicago: University of Chicago Press.

Martin, E., & Beal, V. (1978). *Robert's nutrition work with children* (4th ed.). Chicago: University of Chicago Press.

Martin, G., & Clarke, R. (1982). Distress crying in neonates: Species and peer specificity. *Developmental Psychology, 18,* 3–10.

Martin, H. P. (1973). Nutrition: Its relation to physical, mental and emotional development. *American Journal of Clinical Nutrition, 26,* 766–775.

Martinez, G., & Dodd, D. (1983). 1981 milk feeding patterns in the United States during the first 12 months of life. *Pediatrics, 71,* 166–170.

Marzollo, J. (1977). *Super tot: Creative activities for children from one to three.* New York: Harper & Row.

Maslansky, E., Cowell, C., Carol, R., Berman, S., & Grossi, M. (1974). Survey of infant feeding practices. *American Journal of Public Health, 64,* 780–785.

Maslow, A. (1970). *Motivation and personality* (2d ed.). New York: Harper & Row.

Mata, L., & Wyatt, R. (1971). Host resistance to infection. *American Journal of Clinical Nutrition, 24,* 976.

Matsungaga, E., Tonomura, A., Oishi, H., & Kikuchi, Y. (1978). Re-examination of paternal age effect in Down syndrome. *Human Genetics, 40,* 259–268.

Mayer, J. (1965). Genetic factors in human obesity. *Annals of the New York Academy of Science, 131,* 412–421.

Mayhall, P., & Norgard, K. (1983). *Child abuse and neglect.* New York: Wiley.

Maziade, M., Boudreault, M., Côté, R., & Thivierge, J. (1986). Influence of gentle birth delivery procedures and other perinatal circumstances on infant temperament: Developmental and social implications. *The Journal of Pediatrics, 108,* 134–136.

Mehl, M., & Peterson, G. (1981). Home birth versus hospital birth: Comparisons of outcomes of matched populations. In P. Ahmed (Ed.), *Pregnancy, childbirth, and parenthood* (pp. 315–334). New York: Elseiver.

Meier, J., & Malone, P. (1979). *Facilitating children's development* (Vol. 1). Baltimore: University Park Press.

Meltzoff, A., & Borton, R. (1979). Intermodal matching by human neonates, *Nature, 282,* 403–404.

Meltzoff, A., & Moore, M. (1977). Imitation of facial and normal gestures of human neonates. *Science, 198,* 75–78.

Melzack, R. (1984). The myth of painless childbirth. *Pain, 19,* 321–337.

Melzack, R., Kinch, R., Dobkin, P., LeBrun, M., & Taenzer, P. (1984). Severity of labour pain: Influence of physical as well as psychologic variables. *Canadian Medical Association Journal, 130,* 579–584.

Menyuk, P. (1982). Language development. In C. Kopp & J. Krakow (Eds.), *The child: Development in a social context* (pp. 282–331). Reading, MA: Addison-Wesley.

Merritt, T., & Valdes-Dapena, M. (1984). *Pediatric Annals, 13,* 193–207.

Metropolitan Life Insurance Co. (1985). The risky first year of life. *Statistical Bulletin, 66*(1), 2–8.

Meyer, M. (1982). Smoking and pregnancy. In J. Niebyl (Ed.), *Drug use in pregnancy* (pp. 133–153). Philadelphia: Lea & Febiger.

Michalson, L., & Lewis, M. (1985). What do children know about emotions and when do they know it? In M. Lewis & C. Saarni (Eds.), *The socialization of emotions* (pp. 117–139). New York: Plenum.

Miles, R., Rutherford, G., & Coonley, R. (1983). *Structural entrapment hazards to infants and children.* Washington, DC: U.S. Consumer Product Safety Commission.

Miller, H., Hassanein, K., & Hensleigh, P. (1976). Fetal and growth retardation in relation to maternal smoking and weight gain in pregnancy. *American Journal of Obstetrics Gynecology, 125,* 55–61.

Miller, S. (1987). *Developmental research methods.* Englewood Cliffs, NJ: Prentice Hall.

Mills, J., Graubard, B., Harley, E., Rhoads, G., & Berendes, H. (1984). Maternal alcohol consumption and birth weight. *JAMA, 14,* 1875–1879.

Milner, A. (1985). Apnoea monitors and sudden infant death. *Archives of Disease in Childhood, 60,* 76–80.

Mistretta, C., & Bradley, R. (1977). Taste in utero: Theoretical considerations. In J. Weiffenbach (Ed.), *Taste and development: The genesis of sweet preference* (pp. 51–64). Bethesda: MD: National Institute of Health, (DHEW Pub. No. NIH 77-1068).

Miyake, K., Chen, S., & Campos, J. (1985). Infant temperament, mothers mode of interaction, and attachment in Japan: An interim report. In I. Bretherton & E. Waters (Eds.), Growing points of attachment theory and research (pp. 276–297). *Monographs of the Society for Research in Child Development, 50,* (1–2, Serial No. 209).

Moffitt, A. (1971). Consonant cue perception by 20–24 week old infants. *Child Development, 42,* 717–731.

Montagu, A. (1964). *Life before birth.* New York: American Library.

Montagu, A. (1971). *Touching: The human significance of skin.* New York: Columbia University Press.

Moore, K. (1977). *The developing human* (2d ed.). Philadelphia: Saunders.

Moore, K. (1983). *Before we are born* (2d ed.). Philadelphia: Saunders.

Moore, M. (1978). *Realities in childbearing.* Philadelphia: Saunders.

Morse, P. (1972). The discrimination of speech and nonspeech stimuli in early infancy. *Journal of Child Language, 6,* 199–204.

Mueller, E., & Vandell, D. (1979). Infant-infant interaction. In J. Osofsky (Ed.). *Handbook of infant development* (pp. 591–622). New York: Wiley.

Muir, D. (1985). The development of infants' auditory spatial sensitivity. In S. Trehub & B. Schneider (Eds.), *Auditory development in infancy* (pp. 51–84). New York: Plenum.

Muir, D., & Field, J. (1979). Newborn infants orient to sound. *Child Development, 50,* 431–436.

Murphy, K., & Smyth, C. (1962). Response of fetus to auditory stimulation. *Lancet, 1,* 972–973.

Murphy, L. (1983). Issues in the development of emotion in infancy. In R. Plutchik & H. Kellerman (Eds.), *Emotion: theory, research and experience: (Vol. 2). Emotions in early development* (pp. 1–34). New York: Academic Press.

Mussen, P., Conger, J., & Kagan, J. (1974). *Child development and personality* (4th ed.). New York: Harper & Row.

Naeye, R. (1979). Weight gain and the outcome of pregnancy. *American Journal of Obstetrics and Gynecology, 135,* 3–9.

Naeye, R. (1983). Maternal age, obstetric complications and the outcome of pregnancy. *Obstetrics and Gynecology, 61,* 210–216.

National Center for Health Statistics. (1976, June). NCHS Growth Charts, 1976. *Monthly Vital Statistics Report,* (Vol. 25, No. 3, Supplement, HRA 76-1120). Rockville, MD: U.S. Department of Health, Education and Welfare.

National Safety Council. (1987). *Accident facts.* Chicago: Author.

Nelms, B., & Mullins, R. (1982). *Growth and development: A primary care approach.* Englewood Cliffs, NJ: Prentice Hall.

Nelson, N., Enkin, M., Saigel, S., Bennet, K., Milner, R., & Sackett, D. (1980). A randomized clinical trial of the Leboyer approach to childbirth. *New England Journal of Medicine, 202,* 655–660.

Newell, K. (1984). Physical constraints to motor development. In J. Thomas (Ed.), *Motor development during childhood and adolescence* (pp. 105–122). Minneapolis: Burgess.

Newport, E., Gleitman, H., & Gleitman, L. (1977). Mother I'd rather do it myself: Some effects and non-effects of maternal speech style. In C. Snow & C. Ferguson (Eds.), *Talking to children* (pp. 109–149). London: Cambridge University Press.

News and Observer, Raleigh, NC, Burlington wife has miracle baby. (1979, July 17, p. 6).

Newton, N. (1971). Psychologic differences between breast and bottle feeding. *American Journal of Clinical Nutrition, 24,* 993–1004.

Niebyl, J. (1982). *Drug use in pregnancy.* Philadelphia: Lea & Febiger.

Nilsson, L., Furuhjelm, M., Ingelman-Sundberg, A., & Wirsen, C. (1977). *A child is born.* New York: Delacorte.

Obler, K. (1985). Language through the life-span. In J. Gleason (Ed.), *The development of language* (pp. 277–305). Columbus, OH: Merrill.

Oller, D., & Eilers, R. (1982). Similarity in Spanish and English learning babies. *Journal of Child Language, 9,* 565–577.

Oller, D., Willmar, L., Doyle, W., & Ross, C. (1976). Infant babbling and speech. *Journal of Child Language, 3,* 1–12.

Olney, R., & Scholnick, E. (1976). Adult judgements of age and linguistic differences in infant vocalizations. *Journal of Child Language, 3,* 145–156.

Olson, G., & Strauss, M. (1984). The development of infant memory. In M. Moscovitch (Ed.), *Advances in the study of communication and affect: Vol. 9. Infant memory* (pp. 29–48). New York: Plenum.

Orr, B., Hall, W., Woodword, A., Marchetti, L., Scuttles, D., & Council, F. (1984). *Progress report on increasing child restraint usuage through local education and distribution efforts.* Chapel Hill, NC: University of North Carolina Highway Safety Research Center.

Osofsky, J., & Connors, K. (1979). Mother-infant interaction: An integrative review. In J. Osofsky (Ed.), *Handbook of infant development* (pp. 519–548). New York: Wiley.

Oxorn, H. (1980). *Oxorn-Foote human labor and birth* (4th ed.). New York: Appleton-Century-Crofts.

Painter, G. (1971). *Teach your baby.* New York: Simon & Schuster.

Painti, D. (1982). Mid-cavity forceps delivery. *British Journal of Obstetrics and Gynecology, 89,* 495–500.

Panneton, R., & DeCasper, A. (1982, March). *Newborns are sensitive to temporal and behavioral contingencies.* Paper presented at the meeting of the International Conference on Infant Studies, Austin, TX.

Pansky, B. (1982). *Review of medical embryology.* New York: Macmillan.

Parfitt, R. (1977). *The birth primer.* Philadelphia: Running Press.

Parke, R. (1978). The father's role in infancy: A re-evaluation. *Birth and the Family Journal, 5,* 211–213.

Parke, R., & O'Leary, S. (1976). Family interaction in the newborn period. In K. Riegal & J. Meacham (Eds.), *The developing individual in a changing world. Vol. 2: Social and environmental issues* (pp. 49–62). The Hague: Mouton.

Parke, R., & Sawin, D. (1977, March). *The family in early infancy: Social interactional and attitudinal analysis.* Paper presented at the Society for Research in Child Development, New Orleans.

Parke, R., & Tinsley, B. (1987). Family interaction in infancy. In J. Osofsky (Ed.), *Handbook of infant development* (2d ed., pp. 579–641). New York: Wiley.

Parmelee, A., & Sigmon, M. (1983). Perinatal brain development and behaviors. In P. Mussen (Ed.), *Handbook of child psychology: Vol. 2. Infancy and developmental biology* (4th ed., pp. 95–155). New York: Wiley.

Parmelee, A., Wenner, W., & Schulz, H. (1964). Infant sleep patterns from birth to 16 weeks of age. *Journal of Pediatrics, 65,* 576–582.

Pedersen, F., Rubenstein, J., & Yarrow, L. (1979). Infant development in father-absent families. *The Journal of Genetic Psychology, 135,* 51–61.

Peeples, D. & Teller, D. (1975). Color vision in two month old human infants. *Science, 189,* 1102–1103.

Peterson, C. (1974). *A child grows up.* New York: Alfred.

Peterson, G., Mehl, L., & Leiderman, P. (1979). The role of some birth-related variables in father attachment. *American Journal of Orthopsychiatry, 49,* 330–338.

Phillips, C., & Anzalone, J. (1982). *Fathering: Participation in labor and birth* (2d ed.). St. Louis: Mosby.

Phillips, J. (1975). *The origins of intellect: Piaget's theory.* San Francisco: Freeman.

Piaget, J. (1929). *The child's conception of the world.* New York: Harcourt & Brace.

Piaget, J. (1951). *Play, dreams and imitation in childhood.* New York: Norton.

Piaget, J. (1952). *The origins of intelligence in children* (M. Cook, Translator). New York: International Universities Press.

Piaget, J. (1954). *The construction of reality in the child.* New York: Basic Books.

Piaget, J. (1962). *Play, dreams and imitation in childhood.* New York: Norton.

Piaget, J. (1971). *Biology and knowledge.* Chicago: University of Chicago Press.

Pikler, E. (1968). Some contributions to the study of gross motor development of children. *Journal of Genetic Psychology, 113,* 27–39.

Pipes, P. (1982). Nutrition in infancy and childhood. *Primary Care, 9,* 497–516.

Pipes, P. (1985). *Nutrition in infancy and childhood,* (2d ed.). St. Louis: Mosby.

Plomin, R., & DeFries, J. (1980). Genetics and intelligence: Recent data. *Intelligence, 4,* 15–24.

Plomin, R., & DeFries, J. (1985). *Origins of individual differences in infancy: The Colorado Adoption Project.* New York: Academic Press.

Pollock, L. (1983). *Forgotten children: Parent-child relations from 1500 to 1900.* Cambridge, London: Cambridge University Press.

Powell, D. (1978). Correlates of parent-teacher communication frequency and diversity. *Journal of Educational Research, 71,* 331–341.

Powledge, T. (1983). Windows on the womb. *Psychology Today, 17*(5), 37–42.

Press, B., & Greenspan, S. (1985a). Ned and Dan: The development of a toddler friendship. *Children Today, 14,* 24–29.

Press, B., & Greenspan, S. (1985b). The toddler group: A setting for adaptive social-emotional development of disadvantaged one- and two-year-olds in a peer group. *Zero to Three, 5*(4), 6–11.

Preyer, W. (1888). *The mind of the child: Part 1. The senses and the will.* New York: Appleton-Century-Crofts.

Price, J. (1984). Allergy in infancy and childhood. In M. Lessof (Ed.), *Allergy: Immunological and clinical aspects* (pp. 127–173). New York: Wiley.

Pritchard, J., MacDonald, P., & Gant, N. (1985). *Williams obstetrics* (17th ed.). Norwalk, CO: Appleton-Century-Crofts.

Provence, S. (1967). *Guide for the care of infants in groups.* New York: Child Welfare League of America.

Prudden, B. (1964). *How to keep your child fit from birth to six.* New York: Harper & Row.

Prudden, S., & Sussman, J. (1972). *Suzy Prudden's creative fitness for baby and child.* New York: Morrow.

Public Health Service. U.S. Department of Health and Human Services. (1980). *Immunizations against disease: 1980.* Atlanta, GA: Author.

Public Health Service. (1986). Premature mortality due to sudden infant death syndrome. *Mortality and Morbidity Weekly Report, 35,* 169–170.

Pulaski, M. (1978). *Your baby's mind and how it grows.* New York: Harper and Row.

Pulaski, M. (1980) *Understanding Piaget* (rev. ed.). New York: Harper & Row.

Quigley, M., Sheehan, K., Wilkes, M., & Yen, S. (1979). Effects of maternal smoking on circulating catecholamine levels and fetal heart rates. *American Journal of Obstetrics and Gynecology, 133,* 685–690.

Radetsky, M. (1984). The clinical evaluation of a febrile infant. *Primary Care, 11*(3), 395–404.

Ramey, C., & Brownlee, J. (1981). Improving the identification of high-risk infants. *American Journal of Mental Deficiency, 85,* 504–511.

Rankin, R., & Maneker, J. (1985). The duration of marriage in a divorcing population: The impact of children. *Journal of Marriage and the Family, 47,* 43–52.

Ranly, D. (1980). *A synopsis of craniofacial growth.* New York: Appleton-Century-Crofts.

Rappoport, D. (1976). Pour une naissance sans violence: Resultats d'une premiere enquete. *Bulletin Psychologie, 29,* 552–560.

Rebelsky, F., & Hanks, C. (1971). Fathers' verbal interactions with infants in the first three months of life. *Child Development, 42,* 63–69.

Redshaw, M., Rivers, R., & Rosenblatt, B. (1985). *Born too early: Special care for your preterm infant.* Oxford, NY: Oxford University Press.

Reimish, J. (1981). Prenatal exposure to synthetic progestins increases potential for aggression in humans. *Science, 211,* 1171–1173.

Reinisch, E., and Minear, M. (1978). *Health of the preschool child.* New York: Wiley.

Remington, J., and Klein, J. (Eds.). (1983). *Infections of the fetus and newborn infant* (2d ed.). Philadelphia: Saunders.

Ricciuti, H. (1973). Malnutrition and psychological development. In J. Nurnberger (Ed.), *Biological and environmental determinants of early development.* Baltimore: Williams and Wilkins.

Ridenour, M. (1978). Programs to optimize infant motor development. In M. Ridenour (Ed.), *Motor development: Issues and implications* (pp. 39–61). Princeton, NJ: Princeton Book Co.

Ritvo, E., & Freeman, B. (1977). National Society for Autistic Children. Definition of the syndrome of autism. *Journal of Pediatric Psychology, 4,* 146–148.

Ritvo, E., & Freeman, B. (1984). A medical model of autism: Etiology, pathology and treatment. *Pediatric Annals, 13* (4), 298–305.

Robertson, M. (1984). Changing motor patterns during childhood. In J. Thomas (Ed.), *Motor development during childhood and adolescence* (pp. 48–90). Minneapolis: Burgess.

Robinson, R. (1981). The whooping-cough immunization controversy. *Archives of Disease in Childhood, 56,* 577–580.

Robinson, H., and Robinson, N. (1965). *The mentally retarded child.* New York: McGraw-Hill.

Rogers, C. (1961). *On becoming a person.* Boston: Houghton Mifflin.

Rosenblith, J., & Sims-Knight, J. (1985). *In the beginning: Development in the first two years of life.* Monterey, CA: Brooks/Cole.

Rose, S. (1984). Preterm responses to passive, active, and social touch. In C. Brown (Ed.), *The many facets of touch* (pp. 91–106). Skillman, NJ: Johnson & Johnson.

Rose, S., & Ruff, H. (1987). Cross modal abilities in human infants. In J. Osofsky (Ed.), *Handbook of infant development* (2d ed., pp. 318–362). New York: Wiley

Ross, H. (1974). Forms of exploratory behavior in young children. In B. Foss (Ed.), *New perspectives in child development* (pp. 138–163). Harmondsworth, England: Penguin.

Rosser, A. (1983). Position is everything. *Nursing Times, 79,* 42–43.

Rothbart, M. (1973). Laughter in young children. *Psychological Bulletin, 80,* 247–256.

Rothbart, M. (1981). Measurement of temperament in infancy. *Child Development, 52,* 569–578.

Rothbart, M. (1982). The concept of difficult temperament. *Merrill-Palmer Quarterly, 28,* 35–39.

Rothbart, M., & Derryberry, D. (1981). Development of individual differences in temperament. In M. Lamb & A. Brown (Eds.), *Advances in developmental psychology* (Vol. 1, pp. 37–86). Hillsdale, NJ: Erlbaum.

Rugh, R. and Shettles, L. 1971. *From Conception to Birth.* New York: Harper and Row.

Ruopp, R., Travers, J., Glantz, F. & Coelen, C. (1979). *Children at the center: Final report of the national day care study* (Vol. 1). Cambridge, MA: ABT Associates.

Russell, C. (1974). Transition to parenthood: Problems and gratifications. *Journal of Marriage and the Family, 36,* 294–301.

Russell, M. (1976). Human olfactory communication. *Nature, 260,* 520–522.

Russell-Jones, D. (1985). Sudden infant death in history and literature. *Archives of Disease in Childhood, 85,* 278–281.

Rutherford, G., & Kelly, S. (1981). *Accidental strangulations (ligature) of children less than 5 years of age.* Washington, DC: U.S. Consumer Product Safety Commission.

Rutter, M. (1985). Family and school influences on cognitive development. *Journal of Child Psychology and Psychiatry, 26,* 683–704.

Rutter, M. (1987). Continuities and discontinuities from infancy. In J. Osofsky (Ed.), *Handbook of infant development* (2d ed., pp. 1256–1296). New York: Wiley.

Rutter, M., & Garmezy, N. (1983). Developmental psychopathology. In P. Musen (Ed.), *Handbook of child psychology: Vol. 4. Socialization, personality and social development* (4th ed., pp. 775–911). New York: Wiley.

Sachs, J., & Truswell, L. (1978). Comprehension of two-word instructions by children in the one-word stage. *Journal of Child Language, 5,* 17–24.

Sagi, A. (1981). Mothers' and non-mothers' identification of infant cries. *Infant Behavior and Development, 4,* 37–40.

Sagor, S., Feinbloom, R., Spindel, P., & Brodsky, A. (1983). *Home birth: A practitioner's guide to birth outside the hospital.* Rockville, MD: Aspen.

Salapatek, P., Bechtold, A., & Bushnell, E. (1976). Infant visual acuity as a function of viewing distance. *Child Development, 47,* 860–863.

Salisbury, G., & Hart, R. (1970). Gamete aging and its consequences. *Biology of Reproduction, 2* (Supplement), 1.

Sameroff, A. (1968). The Components of sucking in the human newborn. *Journal of Experimental Psychology, 6,* 607–623.

Sameroff, A., & Cavanagh, P. (1979). Learning in infancy: A developmental perspective. In J Osofsky (Ed.) *Handbook of infant development* (pp. 344–392). New York: Wiley.

Sammons, W., & Lewis, J. (1985). *Premature babies: A different beginning.* St. Louis: Mosby.

Santos, J. I., Arrendo, J. L., & Vitale, J. J. (1983). Nutrition, infection and immunity. *Pediatric Annals, 12*(3), 182–194.

Santrock, J. (1970). Influence of onset and type of parental absence on the first Ericksonian crisis. *Developmental Psychology, 3,* 272–274.

Santrock, J. (1972). Relation of type and onset of father absence to cognitive development. *Child Development, 42,* 1721–1734.

Satter, E. (1983). *Child of mine: Feeding with love and good sense.* Palo Alto, CA: Bull.

Scarr, S., & Salapatek, P. (1970). Patterns of fear development during infancy. *Merrill-Palmer Quarterly, 16,* 53–90.

Scarr-Salapatek, S. (1983). An evolutionary perspective on infant intelligence species patterns and individual variation. In M. Lewis (Ed.), *Origins of intelligence* (2d ed., pp. 191–223). New York: Plenum.

Scarr, S., & Weinberg, R. (1978, April). Attitudes, interests and IQ. *Human Nature, 1,* 29–36.

Schiller, J. (1980). *Child care alternatives and emotional well being.* New York: Pregena.

Scherz, R. (1981). Fatal motor vehicle accidents of child passengers from birth to four years of age in Washington state. *Pediatrics, 68,* 572–575.

Schmitt, B., and Berman, S. (1984). Ear, nose and throat. In H. Kempe, H. Silver, and D. O'Brien (Eds.), *Current Pediatric Diagnosis and Treatment* (8th ed., pp. 297–328). Los Altos, CA: Lange.

Schneck, M. (1986, April). And baby makes three. *Human Development Research at Penn State, 3,* 10–12.

Scott, E., Jan, J., & Freeman, R. (1977). *Can't your child see?* Baltimore: University Park Press.

Scrutton, D. (1969). Footprint sequences of normal children under five years old. *Developmental Medicine and Child Neurology, 115,* 44–51.

Seefeldt, C. (1987). Praise—good or bad? *Dimensions, 15* (4), 18–20.

Senter, S. (1983). *Infant communication: Learning to understand your baby.* Irvine, CA: National Pediatric Support Services.

Sheperd-Look, D. (1982). Sex differentiation and the development of sex roles. In B. Wolman (Ed.), *Handbook of developmental psychology* (pp. 403–433). Englewood Cliffs, NJ: Prentice Hall.

Sherrod, K., Vietze, P., & Friedman, C. (1978). *Infancy.* Monterey, CA: Brooks/Cole.

Shirley, M. (1931). *The first two years: A study of twenty-five babies: Vol. 1. Postural and locomotor development.* Minneapolis: University of Minnesota Press.

Shoemaker, W., & Tower, W. (1970). Out of the oven and into the winner's circle. *Sports Illustrated, 32,* 20–25.

Silver, H. (1984). Growth and development. In C. Kempe, H. Silver, & D. O'Brien (Eds.). *Current pediatric diagnosis and treatment.* (8th ed., pp. 9–25). Los Altos, CA: Lange.

Sinclair, D. (1978). *Human growth after birth* (3d ed.). New York: Oxford University Press.

Siqueland, E. (1968). Reinforcement and extinction in human newborns, *Journal of Experimental Child Psychology, 6,* 431–442.

Skinner, B. (1957). *Verbal behavior.* New York: Appleton-Century-Crofts.

Skinner, B. (1961). *Cummulative record.* New York: Appleton-Century.

Skinner, B. (1972). *The shaping of a behaviorist.* New York: Knopf.

Slater, W. (1983, April 20). A short and tragic life for Michael M. *Greenville Daily Reflector,* p. 26.

Sleigh, G., & Ounsted, M. (1975). Present-day practice in infant feeding. *Lancet, 1,* 7909.

Slocum, D., & James, S. (1968). Biomechanics of running. *Journal of the American Medical Association, 97,* 205.

Smelser, N., & Smelser, W. (1963). *Personality and social systems.* New York: Wiley.

Smith, M. (1926). An investigation of the development of vocabulary in young children. *University of Iowa Studies in Child Welfare, 3,* No. 5.

Smith, N. (1973). *The acquisition of phonology: A case study.* Cambridge: Cambridge University Press.

Smoll, F. (1982). Developmental kinesiology. In J. Kelso & J. Clark (Eds.), The development of movement control and co-ordination. New York: Wiley.

Snow, C. E. (1977). The development of conversation between mothers and babies. *Journal of Child Language, 4,* 1–22.

Snow, C. W. (1982). *Pediatrician's advice to parents on infant feeding practices.* Paper presented at the meeting of the North Carolina Home Economics Association, Raleigh, NC.

Snow, C. W. (1983, November). *As the twig is bent: A review of research on the consequences of day care with implications for caregiving.* Paper presented at the annual meeting of the National Association for the Education of Young Children, Atlanta, GA. (Eric Document Reproduction Service No. Ed 238-590).

Solomons, G. (1984). Child abuse and neglect. In J. Blackman (Ed.), *Medical aspects of developmental disabilities* (pp. 39–41). Rockville, MD: Aspen.

Sparling, J., & Lewis, I. (1979). *Learninggames for the first three years.* New York: Berkley Books.

Speer, F. (1973). Management of food allergy. In F. Speer & R. Dockhorn (Eds.), *Allergy and immunology in children.* Springfield, IL: Charles C. Thomas.

Spelt, D. (1948). The conditioning of the human fetus in utero. *Journal of Experimental Psychology, 38,* 375–376.

Spitz, R. (1945). Hospitalism. *Psychoanalytic Study of the Child, 1,* 45–74.

Spitz, R., Emde, R., & Metcalf, D. (1970). Further prototypes of ego formation: A working paper from a research project on early development. *The Psychoanalytic Study of the Child, 25,* 417–441.

Spock, B., & Rothenberg, M. (1985). *Dr. Spock's baby and child care* (rev. ed.). New York: Pocket Books.

Sroufe, L., and Wunsch, J. (1972). The development of laughter in the first year of life. *Child Development, 43,* 1326–1344.

Sroufe, L. (1977). *Knowing and enjoying your baby.* Englewood Cliffs, NJ: Prentice Hall.

Sroufe, L. (1979). Socioemotional development. In J. Osofsky (Ed.), *Handbook of infant development* (pp. 462–516). New York: Wiley.

Sroufe, L., & Waters, E. (1976). The ontogenesis of smiling and laughing: A perspective on the organization of development in infancy. *Psychological Review, 83,* 173–189.

Stangler, S., Huber, C., & Routh, D. (1980). *Screening growth and development of preschool children.* New York: McGraw-Hill.

Stark, A., & Frantz, I. (1986). Respiratory distress syndrome. *The Pediatric Clinics of North America, 33,* 533–542.

Stark, R. (1978). Features of infant sounds: The emergence of cooing. *Journal of Child Language, 5,* 379–390.

Stark, R. (1979). Prespeech segmental feature development. In P. Fletcher & M. Garman (Eds.), *Language acquisition* (pp. 15–32). Cambridge, England: Cambridge University Press.

Starr, R. (1979). Child abuse. *American Psychologist, 34,* 872–878.

Stechler, G., & Halton, A. (1982). Prenatal influences on human development. In B. Wolman (Ed.), *Handbook of developmental psychology* (pp. 175–189). Englewood Cliffs, NJ: Prentice Hall.

Stein, Z., & Kline, J. (1983). Smoking, alcohol and reproduction. *American Journal of Public Health, 73,* 1154–1156.

Stein, Z., Susser, M., Saenger, G., & Morolla, F. (1974). *Famine and human development: The Dutch hunger winter of 1944–1945.* New York: Oxford University Press.

Steiner, J. (1977). Facial expressions of the neonate indicating the hedonics of food related chemical stimuli. In J. Wiffenbach, (Ed.), *Taste and development: The genesis of sweet preference* (pp. 173–204). Bethesda, MD: National Institute of Health. (DHEW Pub. No. NIH 77–1068).

Stene, J., Fischer, G., Stene, E., Mikkelesen, M., & Petersen, E. (1977). Paternal age effect in Down's syndrome. *American Human Genetics, 40,* 299–306.

Stern, D. (1985). *The interpersonal world of the infant.* New York: Basic Books.

Strangert, K. (1976). Respiratory illness in preschool children with different forms of day care. *Pediatrics, 57,* 219–229.

Stratmeyer, M., & Christman, C. (1982). Biological effects of ultrasound. *Women and Health, 7(3/4),* 65–84.

Straus, M., Gelles, R., & Steinmetz, S. (1979). *Behind closed doors: Violence in the American family.* Garden City, NY: Doubleday/Anchor.

Strelau, J. (1985). Temperament and personality. In J. Strelau, F. Farley, & A. Gale (Eds.), *The biological basis of personality and behavior: Vol. 1. Theories, measurement, techniques and development* (pp. 25–43). Washington, DC: Hemisphere.

Strong, B., & DeVault, C. (1986). *The marriage and family experience* (3d ed.). St. Paul: West.

Stunkard, A., Foch, T., & Krubec, Z. (1986). A twin study of human obesity. *JAMA, 256,* 51–54.

Super, C. (1981). Behavioral development in infancy. In R. H. Munroe, R. L. Munroe, & B. Whiting (Eds.), *Handbook of cross-cultural human development* (pp. 181–270). New York: Garland.

Super, C., & Harkness, S. (1982). The development of affect in infancy and early childhood. In D. Wagner & H. Stevenson (Eds.), *Cultural perspectives in child development* (pp. 1–19). San Francisco: Freeman.

Svejda, M., Campos, J., & Emde, R. (1980). Mother-infant "bonding": Failure to generalize. *Child Development, 51,* 775–779.

Svejda, M., Pannabecker, B., & Emde, R. (1982). Parent-to-infant attachment: A critique of the early "bonding model." In R. Emde & R. Harmon (Eds.), *The development of attachment and affiliative systems* (pp. 83–93). New York: Plenum.

Tanner, J. (1978). *Fetus into man.* Cambridge, MA: Harvard University Press.

Tatzer, E., Schubert, M., Timisch, W., & Simbruner, G. (1985). Discrimination of taste preference for sweet in premature babies. *Early Human Development, 12,* 23–30.

Tesh, J., & Glover, T. (1969). Aging of rabbit spermatozoa in the male and its effect on fertility. *Journal of Reproductive Fertility, 20,* 573.

Thacker, S., & Banta, H. (1983). Benefits and risks of episiotomy: An interpretative review of the English language literature 1860–1980. *Obstetrical and Gynecological Survey, 38,* 232–250.

Thelen, E. (1981). Rythmnical behavior in infancy: An ethological perspective. *Developmental Psychology, 17,* 237–257.

Thomas, A., & Chess, S. (1977). *Temperament and development.* New York: Brunner/Mazel.

Thomas, A., & Chess, S. (1985). The behavioral study of temperament. In J. Strelau, F. Farley, & A. Gale, *The biological bases of personality and behavior: Vol. 1. Theories, measurement, techniques and development* (pp. 213–225). Washington, DC: Hemisphere.

Thompson, R., & Lamb, M. (1984). Infants mothers, families and strangers. In M. Lewis (Ed.), *Beyond the dyad* (pp. 195–221). New York: Plenum.

Torgersen, A. (1982). Influence of genetic factors on temperament development in early childhood. In R. Porter & G. Collins (Eds.), *Temperamental differences in infants and young children.* Ciba Foundation Symposium 89 (pp. 141–154). London: Pittman Books.

Traub, A., Morrow, R., Ritchie, J., & Dornan, K. (1984). A continuing use of Kielland's forceps? *British Journal of Obstetrics and Gynecology, 91,* 894–898.

Trevarthen, C. (1978). The psychobiology of speech development. *Neurosciences Research Program Bulletin, 12* (4), 570–585.

Trohanis, P., Cox, J., & Meyer, R. (1982). A report on selected demonstration programs for infant intervention. In C. Ramey & P. Trohanis (Eds.), *Finding and educating high-risk and handicapped infants* (pp. 137–191). Baltimore: University Park Press.

Trotter, R. (1987). You've come a long way baby. *Psychology Today, 21*(5), 34–45.

Trump, C., & Karasic, R. (1983). Management of communicable diseases in day care centers. *Pediatric Annals, 12,* 219–229.

Turner, G., & Collins, E. (1975). Fetal effects of regular salicylate ingestion in pregnancy. *Lancet, 2,* 338–339.

Ungerer, J., Brody, L., & Zelazo, P. (1978). Long term memory for speech in 2–4-week-old infants. *Infant Behavior and Development, 1,* 177–186.

U.S. Bureau of the Census. (1980). *Statistical Abstract of the United States* (100th ed.). Washington, DC: U.S. Government Printing Office.

U.S. Bureau of the Census. (1986). *Current population reports: Household and family characteristics: March 1985* (Series P-20, No. 411). Washington, DC: U.S. Government Printing Office.

U.S. Bureau of the Census. (1987b). *Statistical abstracts of the United States* (107th ed.). Washington, DC: U.S. Government Printing Office.

USDHEW. (1972). *Tips for tots.* DHEW Publication No. (FDA) 73-7012. Washington, DC: U.S. Government Printing Office.

Uzgiris, I. (1967). Ordinality in the development of schemes for relating to objects. In J. Hellmuth (Ed.), *Exceptional infant: Vol. 1. The normal infant* (pp. 315–334). New York: Bruner/Mazel.

Uzgiris, I., & Hunt, I. (1975). *Assessment in infancy.* Urbana, IL: University of Illinois Press.

Valadian, I., & Porter, D. (1977). *Physical growth and development from conception to maturity.* Boston: Little, Brown & Co.

Vandell, D., & Mueller, E. (1980). Peer play and friendships during the first two years. In H. Foot, A. Chapman, & J. Smith (Eds.), *Friendship and social relations in children* (pp. 181–208). New York: Wiley.

Vandell, D., & Wilson, K. (1987). Infants' interactions with mother, sibling, and peer contacts: Contrasts and relations between interaction systems. *Child Development, 58,* 176–186.

Vandell, D., Wilson, K., & Buchanan, N. (1980). Peer interaction in the first year of life: An examination of its structure, content and sensitivity to toys. *Child Development, 51,* 481–488.

Vander Vliet, W., & Hafez, E. (1974). Surviving and aging of spermatozoa: A review. *American Journal of Obstetrics and Gynecology, 118,* 1006.

Von Hofsten, C. (1982). Eye-hand coordination in the newborn. *Development Psychology, 18,* 450–461.

Von Hofsten, C. (1984). Developmental changes in the organization of prereaching movements. *Developmental Psychology, 20,* 378–388.

Vulliamy, D. (1982). *The newborn child* (5th ed.). Edenburgh, London: Churchill Livingstone.

Vygotsky, L. (1962). *Thought and language.* Cambridge, Mass: MIT Press.

Wachs, T. (1982). *Relation of home noise-confusion to infant cognitive development.* Paper presented at the meeting of the American Psychological Association, Washington, DC.

Wachs, T., & Gruen, G. (1982). *Early experiences and human development.* New York: Plenum.

Wachs, T., & Gandour, M. (1983). Temperament, environment, and six-month cognitive-intellectual development: A test of organism specificity hypothesis. *International Journal of Behavioral Development, 6,* 135–152.

Wadsworth, B. (1979). *Piaget's theory of cognitive development* (2d ed.). New York: Longren.

Waletzky, L. (1979). Breast-feeding and weaning: Some Psychological considerations. *Primary Care, 6*(2), 341–364.

Wallerstein, J., & Kelly, J. (1980). *Surviving the break-up: How children and parents cope with divorce.* New York: Basic Books.

Wasz-Hocket, O., Lind, J., Vucrenkoski, V., Partenen, T., & Valanne, E. (1968). The infant cry: A spectrographic and auditory analysis. *Clinics in Developmental Medicine, 29.* London: Heinemann.

Waters, E., & Sroufe, L. (1983). Social competence as a developmental construct. *Developmental Review, 3,* 79–97.

Weiffenbach, J., Daniel, P., & Cowart, B. (1979). Saltiness in developmental perspective. In M. Kare, M. Fregly, & R. Bernard, *Biological and behavioral aspects of salt intake* (pp. 13–30). New York: Academic Press.

Weiner, I., & Elkind, D. (1972). *Child development: A core approach.* New York: Wiley.

Weir, R. (1970). *Language in the crib.* The Hague: Mouton.

Weiser, M. (1982). *Group care and education of infants and toddlers.* St. Louis: Mosby.

Weissbluth, M., & Green, O. (1984). Plasma progesterone concentrations and infant temperament. *Developmental and Behavioral Pediatrics, 5,* 251–253.

Wellman, B. (1937). Motor achievements of preschool children. *Childhood Education, 13,* 311–316.

Werner, E. (1979). *Cross-cultural child development.* Montery, CA: Brooks/Cole.

Werner, J., & Wooten, B. (1985). Unsettled issues in infant color vision. *Infant Behavior and Development, 8,* 99–107.

Weston, W., Lane, A., & Weston, J. (1980). Diaper dermatitis: Current concepts. *Pediatrics, 66,* 532–536.

Whetnall, E., & Fry, D. (1964). *The deaf child.* London: Heinemann.

White, B. (1975). *The first three years of life.* Englewood Cliffs, NJ: Prentice Hall.

White, B. (1985). *The first three years of life* (rev. ed.). Englewood Cliffs, NJ: Prentice Hall.

White, B., & Watts, J. (1973). *Experience and environment* (Vol. 1). Englewood Cliffs, NJ: Prentice Hall.

White, R. (1959). Motivation reconsidered: The concept of competence. *Psychological Review, 66,* 297–333.

Whitehurst, G. (1982). Language development. In B. Wolman (Ed.), *Handbook of developmental psychology* (pp. 367–386). Englewood Cliffs, NJ: Prentice Hall.

Whitten, C., & Stewart, R. (1980). The effect of dietary sodium in infancy on blood pressure and related factors. *ACTA Paediatrica Scandinavica,* (Suppl. 279), 1–17.

Whorf, B. (1956). *Language, thought and reality.* Cambridge, MA: MIT Press.

WHO/UNICEF. (1981). *Infant and young child feeding: Current issues.* Geneva: World Health Organization.

Wickstrom, R. (1983). *Fundamental motor patterns* (3d ed.). Philadelphia: Lee & Febiger.

Wiesenfeld, A., Malatesta, C., & Deloache, L. (1981). Differential parental response to familiar and unfamiliar infant distress signals. *Infant Behavior and Development, 4,* 281–295.

Williams, H. (1977). Gross motor behavior patterns in children. In C. Corbin (Ed.), *A textbook of motor development* (pp. 117–129). Dubuque, IA: Brown.

Williams, H. (1983). *Perceptual and motor development.* Englewood Cliffs, NJ: Prentice Hall.

Williams, R., Thom, M., & Studd, J. (1980). A study of the benefits and acceptability of ambulation in spontaneous labour. *British Journal of Obstetrics and Gynaecology, 87,* 122–126.

Winick, M. (1976). *Malnutrition and brain development.* New York: Oxford University Press.

Winick, M. (1979). Nutrition and brain development. In F. Balli (Ed.), *Nutritional problems in childhood.* Padova, Italy: Piccin Medical Books.

Winick, M., Meyer, K., & Harris, R. (1975). Malnutrition and environmental enrichment by early adoption. *Science, 190,* 1173–1175.

Woelfel, J. (1984). *Dental Anatomy* (3d ed.). Philadelphia: Lea & Febiger.

Wolff, P. (1963). Observations on the early development of smiling. In B. Foss (Ed.), *Determinants of infant behavior* (Vol. 2, pp. 113–138). London: Methuen.

Wolff, P. (1966). The causes, controls, and organization of behavior in the neonate *Psychological Issues, 5* (1, Whole No. 17), 7–11.

Wolff, P. (1969). The natural history of crying and other vocalizations in early infancy. In B. Foss (Ed.), *Determinants of infant behavior* (Vol. 4, pp. 81–109). London: Methuen.

Wollman, L. (1981). A case of galoctopoiesis in a male. *Journal of the American Society of Psychosomatic Dentistry and Medicine. 28,* 2.

Wood, B. (1976). *Children and communication: Verbal and nonverbal language development.* Englewood Cliffs, NJ: Prentice Hall.

Wood, B., & Walker-Smith, J. (1981). *Mackeith's infant feeding and feeding difficulties* (6th ed.). London: Churchill Livingstone.

Woodruff, C. (1978). The science of infant nutrition and the art of infant feeding. *JAMA, 240,* 657–661.

Word, M. (1985). Child abuse and neglect. *Journal of the Medical Association of Georgia, 74,* 224–225.

World Health Organization. (1985). *Treatment and prevention of acute diarrhoea.* Geneva: Author.

Yarrow, L. (1979). Emotional development. *American Psychologist, 34,* 951–957.

Ymada, H. (1983). *Pediatric cranial computed tomography.* New York: Medical Publishers.

Yonas, A., & Granrud, C. (1985). Development of visual space perception in young infants. In J. Mehler & R. Fox (Eds.), *Neonate cognition: beyond the blooming buzzing confusion* (pp. 45–67). Hillsdale, NJ: Erlbaum.

Young, H., Buckley, A., Bechir, H., & Mandarano, C. (1982). Milk and lactation: Some social and developmental correlates among 1,000 infants. *Pediatrics, 69,* 169–175.

Yussen, S., & Santrock, J. (1982). *Child Development* (2d ed.). Dubuque, IA: Brown.

Zahn-Waxler, C., Cummings, E., & Cooperman, G. (1984). Emotional development in childhood. In G. Whitehurst (Ed.), *Annuals of child development* (Vol. 1, pp. 45–106). Greenwich, CO: JAI Press.

Zarbatany, L., & Lamb, M. (1985). Social referencing as a function of information source: Mothers versus strangers. *Infant Behavior and Development, 8,* 25–33.

Zelazo, P., Zelazo, N., & Kolb, S. (1972). Walking in the newborn. *Science, 176,* 314–315.

Zeskind, P. (1983). Cross-cultural differences in maternal perceptions of cries of low and high-risk infants. *Child Development, 54,* 1119–1128.

Zeskind, P., Sale, J., Maio, M., Huntington, M., & Wiseman, J. (1984, April). *Adult perceptions of pain and hunger cries: A synchrony arousal.* Paper presented at the International Conference on Infant Studies, New York, NY.

Zigler, E., & Turner, P. (1982). Parents and day care workers: A failed partnership? In E. Zigler & A. Gordon (Eds.), *Day care: Scientific and social policy issues* (pp. 174–182). Boston: Auburn House.

Zussman, J. (1980). Situational determinants of parental behavior; Effects of competing cognitive activity. *Child Development, 51,* 792–800.

Appendixes

GIRLS: BIRTH TO 36 MONTHS
PHYSICAL GROWTH
NCHS PERCENTILES*

NAME_____ RECORD #_____

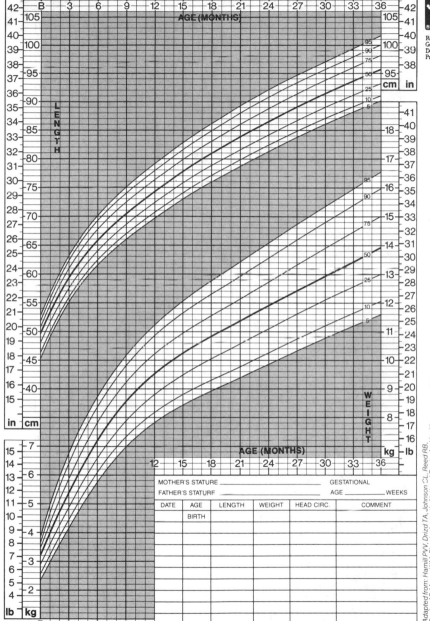

*Adapted from: Hamill PVV, Drizd TA, Johnson CL, Reed RB, Roche AF, Moore WM: Physical growth: National Center for Health Statistics percentiles. AM J CLIN NUTR 32:607–629, 1979 Data from the Fels Research Institute, Wright State University School of Medicine, Yellow Springs, Ohio.

© 1982 Ross Laboratories

Ross Growth & Development Program

APPENDIX 1 Growth Curves for Girls: Birth to 36 Months
Length by Age and Weight By Age

Source: National Center for Health Statistics, *NCHS Growth Charts* (1976). Adapted by Ross Laboratories. Reprinted by permission.

BOYS: BIRTH TO 36 MONTHS
PHYSICAL GROWTH
NCHS PERCENTILES*

NAME_____ RECORD #_____

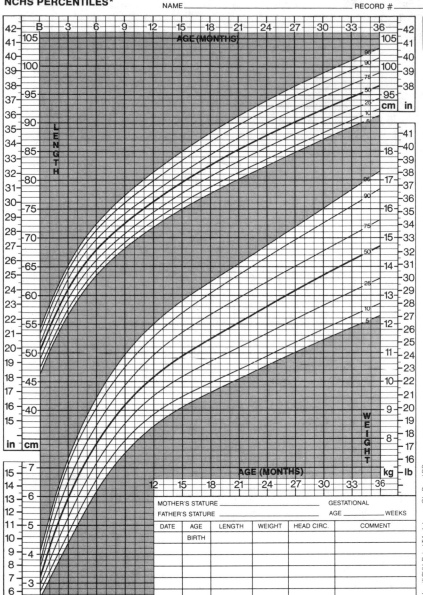

*Adapted from: Hamill PVV, Drizd TA, Johnson CL, Reed RB, Roche AF, Moore WM: Physical growth: National Center for Health Statistics percentiles. AM J CLIN NUTR 32:607–629, 1979. Data from the Fels Research Institute, Wright State University School of Medicine, Yellow Springs, Ohio.

© 1982 Ross Laboratories

Ross
Growth &
Development
Program

MOTHER'S STATURE _____   GESTATIONAL
FATHER'S STATURE _____   AGE _____ WEEKS

DATE	AGE	LENGTH	WEIGHT	HEAD CIRC.	COMMENT
	BIRTH				

APPENDIX 2 Growth Curves for Boys: Birth to 36 Months
Length by Age and Weight by Age

Source: National Center for Health Statistics, *NCHS Growth Charts,* (1976). Adapted by Ross Laboratories.
Reprinted by permission.

Appendix #2

GIRLS: BIRTH TO 36 MONTHS
PHYSICAL GROWTH
NCHS PERCENTILES*

NAME_____ RECORD #_____

AGE (MONTHS)

B 3 6 9 12 15 18 21 24 27 30 33 36

HEAD CIRCUMFERENCE

WEIGHT

LENGTH

cm 50 55 60 65 70 75 80 85 90 95 100
in 19 20 21 22 23 24 25 26 27 28 29 30 31 32 33 34 35 36 37 38 39 40

*Adapted from: Hamill PVV, Drizd TA, Johnson CL, Reed RB, Roche AF, Moore WM: Physical growth: National Center for Health Statistics percentiles. AM J CLIN NUTR 32:607-629, 1979. Data from the Fels Research Institute, Wright State University School of Medicine, Yellow Springs, Ohio.

© 1982 Ross Laboratories

DATE	AGE	LENGTH	WEIGHT	HEAD CIRC.	COMMENT

APPENDIX 3   Growth Curves for Girls: Birth to 36 Months
Head Circumference and Length by Weight

Source: National Center for Health Statistics, *NCHS Growth Charts,* (1976). Adapted by Ross Laboratories.
Reprinted by permission.

NAME_____ RECORD #_____

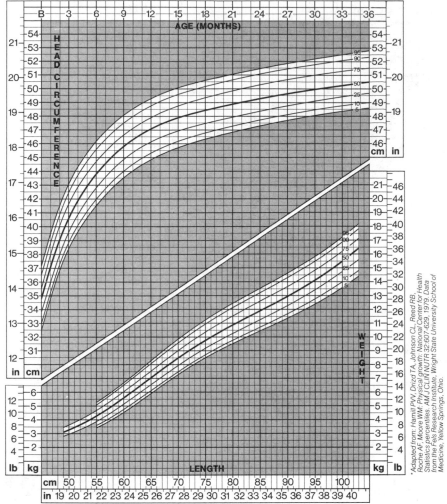

DATE	AGE	LENGTH	WEIGHT	HEAD CIRC.	COMMENT

in vivo performance...

SIMILAC® Infant Formulas
in vivo performance...
closest to mother's milk

ISOMIL® Soy Protein Formulas
When the baby can't take milk.

ADVANCE® Nutritional Beverage
Instead of 2% milk.

ROSS LABORATORIES
COLUMBUS, OHIO 43216
DIVISION OF ABBOTT LABORATORIES, USA

G105(0.05)/DECEMBER 1985   LITHO IN USA

Adapted from: Hamill PVV, Drizd TA, Johnson CL, Reed RB, Roche AF, Moore WM: Physical growth: National Center for Health Statistics percentiles. AM J CLIN NUTR 32:607-629, 1979. Data from the Fels Research Institute, Wright State University School of Medicine, Yellow Springs, Ohio.

© 1982 Ross Laboratories

APPENDIX 4   Growth Curves for Boys: Birth to 36 Months
                 Head Circumference and Length by Weight
Source: National Center for Health Statistics, *NCHS Growth Charts* (1976). Adapted by Ross Laboratories.
Reprinted by permission.

Appendix #4

Chapter Opening Quotations

Introduc-
tion
— Shakespeare, W. S. (1623/1952). "As you like it." In G. Harrison (ed.), *Shakespeare: The complete works*. New York: Harcourt, Brace, p. 789.

Chapter 1 — MacDonald, G. (1924). *At the back of the north wind*. New York: Macmillan, p. 321. Reprinted by permission.

Chapter 2 — "Animula" from *Collected poems 1909-1962* by T. S. Eliot, copyright 1936 by Harcourt Brace Jovanovich, Inc., copyright © 1963, 1964 by T. S. Eliot. Reprinted by permission of the publisher and Faber and Faber Ltd.

Chapter 3 — From an American Greeting card. Used by permission of American Greetings Corp., Cleveland, OH.

Chapter 4 — An English proverb. In W. Mieler. (1986). *The Prentice Hall encyclopedia of world proverbs*. Englewood Cliffs, NJ: Prentice-Hall, p. 71.

Chapter 5 — Kierkegaard, S. (1948). *Purity of heart is to will one thing*. Trans. D. Steere. New York: Harper & Row, p. 85. Reprinted by permission.

Chapter 6 — Anthony, E. (1947). "Advice to small children" in *Every dog has his say*. New York: Watson-Guptill. Reprinted by permission.

Chapter 7 — Lamb, M. (1903). "The first tooth." In E. Lucas (ed.), *The works of Charles and Mary Lamb* (Vol. 3, p. 362). London: Methuen. (Reprinted by AMS Press, New York, 1968). Reprinted by permission of Methuen & Co.

Chapter 8 — Holland, J. (1879). "Bitter-sweet" from *The complete poetical writings of J. G. Holland* (New York: Charles Scribner's Sons, 1879). Reprinted by permission.

Chapter 9 — Psalm 8:2; Matthew 21:16. *The Holy Bible*. King James Version.

Chapter 10 — Prelutsky, J. (1983). *The Random House book of poetry for children*. New York: Random House, p. 117. Reprinted by permission of the author.

Chapter 11 — Barrie, J. (1949). *Peter Pan*. New York: Charles Scribner's Sons, p. 36. Reprinted by permission.

Chapter 12 — Gibran, K. (1972). *The prophet*. New York: Alfred A. Knopf, p. 17. Reprinted by permission.

Photo Credits

Photo on page	17	Carnegie Institute
Photo on page	26	From the *Journal of the American Medical Association*, 1976, Vol. 235, 1458-1460. Courtesy, James W. Hanson, M.D.
Photo on page	38	WHO phto by E. Mandelmann
Photo on page	45	WHO photo by E. Mandelmann
Photo on page	56	Shirley Zeiberg
Photo on page	66	Teri Stratford
Photo on page	69	Laima Druskis
Photo on page	86	Teri Stratford
Photo on page	99	Eugene Gordon
Photo on page	103	Ken Karp
Photo on page	106	Teri Stratford
Photo on page	122	Paul Conklin
Photo on page	137	Page Poore
Photo on page	148	WHO photo by J. Abcede
Photo on page	157	Major Morris
Photo on page	163	WHO photo by H. Oomen
Photo on page	173	Photoquest, Inc.
Photo on page	200	Ken Karp
Photo on page	205	Teri Stratford
Photo on page	209	Ken Karp
Photo on page	220	Teri Stratford
Photo on page	225	Courtesy Gerber Products Company
Photo on page	227	Teri Stratford
Photo on page	239	Photoquest, Inc.
Photo on page	242	Shirley Zeiberg
Photo on page	248	Shirley Zeiberg
Photo on page	251	Ken Karp
Photo on page	259	Shirley Zeiberg
Photo on page	262	Teri Stratford
Photo on page	268	Page Poore
Photo on page	270	Ken Karp

SUBJECT INDEX

AUTHOR INDEX